INTRODUCTION TO
SOCIAL
RESEARCH
QUANTITATIVE & QUALITATIVE APPROACHES

KEITH F PUNCH

Los Angeles | London | New Delhi
Singapore | Washington DC

Los Angeles | London | New Delhi
Singapore | Washington DC

SAGE Publications Ltd
1 Oliver's Yard
55 City Road
London EC1Y 1SP

SAGE Publications Inc.
2455 Teller Road
Thousand Oaks, California 91320

SAGE Publications India Pvt Ltd
B 1/I 1 Mohan Cooperative Industrial Area
Mathura Road
New Delhi 110 044

SAGE Publications Asia-Pacific Pte Ltd
3 Church Street
#10-04 Samsung Hub
Singapore 049483

Editor: Katie Metzler
Development editor: Amy Jarrold
Production editor: Nicola Marshall
Copyeditor: Jennifer Hinchliffe
Proofreader: Sharon Cawood
Indexer: Silvia Benvenuto
Marketing manager: Ben Griffin-Sherwood
Cover designer: Francis Kenney
Typeset by: C&M Digitals (P) Ltd, Chennai, India
Printed and bound in Great Britain by
CPI Group (UK) Ltd, Croydon, CR0 4YY

First edition published 1998. Reprinted 1999, 2000, 2001, 2003, 2004.
Second edition published 2005. Reprinted 2007, 2008, 2009, 2010, 2011 (twice), 2012.
Third edition published 2014.

Library of Congress Control Number: 2013935252

British Library Cataloguing in Publication data

A catalogue record for this book is available from the British Library

ISBN 978-1-4462-4092-2
ISBN 978-1-4462-4093-9 (pbk)

INTRODUCTION TO

SOCIAL

RESEARCH

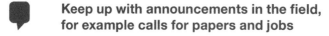
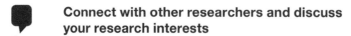

BRIEF CONTENTS

CONTENTS

LIST OF TABLES

LIST OF FIGURES

PREFACE

This third edition of *Introduction to Social Research* contains substantial new content, and a number of new features.

The new content is:

- A chapter on theory and method in social science research
- A chapter on searching and reviewing the relevant literature
- A chapter on ethics
- A chapter on research and the Internet

The new features, which focus on pedagogical aspects of this material, are:

- Learning objectives, added at the start of each chapter
- New chapter summaries, key terms, and exercises and study questions, added at the end of each chapter

At the same time, the basic structure and rationale for this new edition remain the same as for the two earlier editions. Thus, with respect to structure, the book begins with a view of research and a simple but robust model of research, and then uses the model to guide the planning of quantitative, qualitative and mixed method empirical research in the social sciences. In the process of doing that, it stresses the need for the development of genuine empirical questions, and describes the connections between concepts and their empirical indicators. It then proceeds to show the implementation of this model in both qualitative and quantitative research.

With respect to rationale, the intention is to lay bare the logic of all stages of the empirical research process (whatever the nature of the data), and to give a basis for students to proceed immediately with planning and developing research. As before, therefore, I have tried to stress the logic behind research and its techniques, rather than technical issues per se. One of my aims in doing this is to 'demystify' the research process, and where necessary to simplify it, in an effort to demonstrate clearly the logic behind it, and thus to show that good quality research is within the reach of very many people.

For their assistance in preparing this new edition, I want to thank Alis Oancea, for her contributions on searching and reviewing literature, and Wayne McGowan, for his contribution on research and the Internet.

As with all my previous publications with SAGE, I also want to thank the SAGE editorial team in London who have helped me in many different ways. I particularly want to thank Katie Metzler and, especially, Amy Jarrold for their encouragement, support and assistance, especially in updating readings, and in preparing material for the website attached to this book.

COMPANION WEBSITE

The website contains key material on qualitative and quantitative research, as well as all the figures and tables from the book and my own guide to lecturing on social research. You can visit it at: www.sagepub.co.uk/punch3e

SAGE

Home | Contact Us | Help

INTRODUCTION TO SOCIAL RESEARCH
QUANTITATIVE & QUALITATIVE APPROACHES

Book Home | Instructor Resources | Student Resources

Author: Keith F Punch
Pub Date: November 2013
Pages: 392
Learn more about this book

About the Book

Welcome to the companion website for the third edition of *Introduction to Social Research*.

In the new edition of *Introduction to Social Research*, Keith Punch takes a fresh look at the entire research process, from formulating a research question to writing up your research. Covering qualitative, quantitative and mixed methods, the book focuses on matching research questions to appropriate methods. Offering concise, balanced coverage, this book clearly explains the underlying principles of social research and shows you how to put this understanding into practice.

The third edition has been fully updated and now includes:

- A new chapter on literature searching and reviewing
- Expanded coverage of ethics
- A new section on using the internet in research
- A range of additional student learning features

Using a range of examples from student research and published work, the book is an ideal introduction for any social science student taking a research methods course or embarking on their own undergraduate or postgraduate research project.

On this companion website, you will find...

Instructor Resources

This site is password protected 🔒

Please read the information to your right. To access the site, click on the sign in button on the right hand side below.

This site is designed to help create a significant learning opportunity for your students by encouraging active participation, experience and reflection.

Student Resources

This section contains a wealth of resources for use as you carry out your research, including:

- **Free chapters:** access to free content to help you develop your understanding of the research process.
- **Web links:** links to resources that are helpful to all those carrying out research.
- **Further reading:** expand your learning with selected titles.
- **Video tutorials:** get to grips with SPSS for free.

First-time Users

Many of the materials on the instructor site, are only available to Faculty and Administrative Staff at Higher Education Institutions who have been approved to request Review Copies by SAGE.

To create an account, please click here. In order to be approved, you must provide your institution and the course that you are or will be teaching. Once you have created an account and you have been validated as a faculty member, you will be able to access the instructor site.

Please note: Validation usually takes approximately 24-48 hours to be completed.

If you have any questions, please contact SAGE Customer Service at +44 (0) 20 7 324 8500 from 8:30 am to 5:00 pm.

Returning Users

If you already have an account with SAGE, log in using the email address and password created when registering with SAGE.

Sign In ▶

SAGE Publications, Ltd. | © 2013

ABOUT THE AUTHOR

Keith Punch began his working life as a teacher of French, German and mathematics in Western Australian secondary schools, before moving to the university sphere. He completed his PhD at the Ontario Institute for Studies in Education in the University of Toronto in 1967. He has since worked in universities in several countries, and is now Emeritus Professor in the Graduate School of Education at the University of Western Australia, and Adjunct Professor at several other universities. For the last 20 years of his career, he concentrated on research supervision and research training, and on developing and managing transnational graduate programs in education in several countries in South East Asia, on behalf of the University of Western Australia.

one

INTRODUCTION

Contents

After studying this chapter you should be able to:

- Explain the word 'empirical' and say what is meant by an empirical research question
- Describe main differences between qualitative and quantitative data and research
- Show the relationship between research questions and research methods
- Reproduce and explain the model of research shown in Section 1.7
- Describe the central characteristics of the scientific method
- Explain what is meant by social science

This book is about methods for doing empirical research in social science. It covers both quantitative and qualitative approaches, and focuses on the essential elements of each. It places both approaches within the same framework for organising research, and it deals with them under the same three main headings – design, data collection, data analysis. It includes mixed methods, where qualitative and quantitative data and methods are combined. The stress is on the logic of what is done in research, rather than its technical aspects. Therefore it is not a 'how to do it' book, but aims instead to develop a basic understanding of the issues involved and of the ideas behind the main techniques.

In selecting material for the book, I have been guided by two central questions:

- What should be the content of an introductory course in social research methods, before any methodological specialisation?
- How can that content be presented in a way which shows how research works, and which gives enough tangible and practical understanding of issues, methods and techniques to get a project under way?

The book is written primarily for upper-level undergraduate and beginning graduate students in different areas of social science, but I hope it will also be suitable for other researchers who want to overview the logic of social research and the main ideas behind its methods.

This first chapter sets a context for the material to be covered, and describes the book's approach and its rationale. The chapter outline of the remainder of the book is in Section 1.8.

Empirical research

1.1 Our subject is empirical social science research. *Empiricism* is a philosophical term to describe the theory that regards experience as the foundation or source of knowledge (Aspin, 1995: 21). Since experience refers here to what is received through the senses, to sense-data or to what can be observed, I will use the general term 'observation' alongside and interchangeably with the term 'experience'. Thus 'empirical' means based on direct experience or observation of the world. To say that a question is an empirical question is to say that we will answer it – or try to answer it – by obtaining direct, observable information from the world, rather than, for example, by theorising, or by reasoning, or by arguing from first principles. The key concept is 'observable information about (some aspect of) the world'. The term used in research for this 'observable information about the world', or 'direct experience of the world', is *data*. The essential idea in empirical research is to use data as the way of answering questions, and of developing and testing ideas.

Empirical research is the main type of research in present day social science, but it is not the only type. Examples of other types of research are theoretical research, analytical research, conceptual–philosophical research and historical research. This book concentrates on empirical research. At the same time, I believe many of the points it makes have applicability to other types of research.

Quantitative and qualitative data

1.2 Data is obviously a very broad term, so we subdivide data for empirical research into two main types:

- quantitative data – which are data in the form of numbers (or measurements), and
- qualitative data – which are data not in the form of numbers (most of the time, though not always, this means words).

This leads to two simplifying definitions:

- Quantitative research is empirical research where the data are in the form of numbers.
- Qualitative research is empirical research where the data are not in the form of numbers.

These simplified definitions are useful for getting started in research, but they do not give the full picture of the quantitative–qualitative distinction. The term 'quantitative research' means more than just research which uses quantitative or numerical data. It refers to a whole way of thinking, or an approach, which involves a collection or cluster of methods, as well as data in numerical form. Similarly, qualitative research is much more than just research which uses non-numerical data. It too is a way of thinking, or an approach, which similarly involves a collection or cluster of methods, as well as data in non-numerical or qualitative form.

Thus full definitions of the terms 'quantitative research' and 'qualitative research' would include:

- the way of thinking about the social reality being studied, the way of approaching it and conceptualising it (this is part of what is meant by the term 'paradigm' – see Section 2.1);
- the designs and methods used to represent this way of thinking, and to collect data;
- the data themselves – numbers for quantitative research, not-numbers (mostly words) for qualitative research.

In teaching about research, I find it useful to approach the quantitative–qualitative distinction primarily through the third of these points – the nature of the data. Later, the distinction can be broadened to include the first two points – ways of conceptualising the reality being studied, and methods. Also, I find that in the practical business of planning and doing research, students very often focus on such questions as: Will the data be numerical or not? Am I going to measure variables in this research, or not? Or, in other words, will my research be quantitative or qualitative?

For these reasons, I think that the nature of the data is at the heart of the distinction between quantitative and qualitative research, and that is why I start with the simplified definitions shown above. But we need also to remember that there is more to the distinction than this, as shown in the other two points above, and that qualitative research is much more diverse than quantitative research, in its ways of thinking, in its methods and in its data. We also need to recognise that, while the quantitative–qualitative distinction has been of major significance in social science research, there has been a marked recent increase in the development and growth of mixed methods research, where quantitative and qualitative data and methods are combined in some way.

The importance of research

1.3 The central importance of research in today's world is something we take so much for granted that we seldom step back and focus on it explicitly. But an outstanding feature of our culture is that research is seen as <u>the</u> way of answering questions, solving problems and developing knowledge. This is true across all areas of life, including social areas.

Three things are worth noting about this centrality of research in our culture:

1. First, research in this context means empirical research, the type of research we deal with in this book.
2. Second, while research as <u>the</u> way to answer questions, solve problems and develop knowledge saturates our culture and thinking today, it was not always so. Indeed, despite how widespread it is today, it is surprising to realise how relatively recent this way of thinking is in human history. As Kerlinger and Lee (2000) have pointed out, different 'ways of knowing' have long been used by humans, and our modern research-based way of knowing and building knowledge is relatively recent.
3. Third, an implication of the central importance of research is that it is desirable for people today to understand the basic logic behind research. This is true for everybody, but particularly for those in the professions. Even if the professionals of the future do not become doers of research, they will inevitably be consumers of research, working in a world where research is central to professional practice and development. Knowledge of the logic and methods of research can help them become more critical and intelligent consumers.

A view of research

1.4 Faced with the many definitions, descriptions and conceptions of research in the methodological literature, I think it is sufficient for present purposes

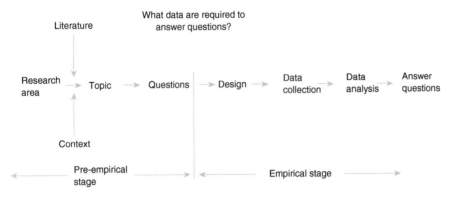

FIGURE 1.1 Simplified model of research

to see research as an organised, systematic and logical process of inquiry, using empirical information – that is, data – to answer questions (or test hypotheses). Seen this way, it has much in common with how we find things out in everyday life – thus, the description of scientific research as 'organised common sense' is useful. Perhaps the main difference is the emphasis in research on being organised, systematic and logical.

This view of research is shown in diagram form as Figure 1.1. It stresses the central role of research questions, and of using empirical data to answer those questions. It has four main features:

- framing the research in terms of research questions;
- determining what data are necessary to answer these questions;
- designing research to collect and analyse these data;
- using the data to answer the questions.

A modification of this model, to include hypothesis-testing research, is shown as Figure 4.1 in Chapter 4.

As well as capturing essential elements of the research process, this view also takes much of the mystery out of research, and enables students immediately to get started in planning research. It focuses on research questions, whereas some other writers focus on research problems. Whether to define the research in terms of questions or problems is a matter of choice for the researcher.

Research questions or research problems?

1.5 I focus on the concept of research questions, as a useful way of helping students to get their research planning and proposal under way. When a student is having trouble getting started or making progress with the proposal, or is confused, overloaded or just stuck in developing it, one of the most helpful questions I can raise is 'What are we trying to find out here?' It is a short step from this to 'What questions is this research trying to answer?' or 'What are the research questions?' This approach makes *research questions* central.

By contrast, some writers tend to focus more on the 'problem behind the research', or on research problems, rather than on research questions. Thus, Coley and Scheinberg (1990: 13) write this about proposal development in the human services context: 'Proposal writing includes the entire process of assessing the nature of the problem, developing solutions or programs to solve or contribute to solving the problem, and translating those into proposal format.' This approach makes the *research problem* central.

Other writers draw a sharp distinction between question and problem. Locke, Spirduso and Silverman (2010: 44–49), for example, arguing for 'semantic and conceptual hygiene', distinguish sharply between problem and question, and recommend a logical sequence of problem, question, purpose and hypothesis as the way forward in research planning and proposal development. Similarly, some writers see proposal development as constructing the research problem, and see research question(s) as one central component of that. I think both of these frameworks are useful for preplanned research, and especially for intervention studies, but are less useful for more unfolding studies (see Section 2.6). In these cases, the distinction between problem and question is not so sharp.

Sometimes social science research is concerned with interventions, and assessing their outcomes. Some areas of nursing research are a good example, especially those concerned with nursing in the clinical setting. Behind this focus on interventions lies the idea of a problem which needs a solution, and it is the intervention which is proposed as a solution. Similarly, programs and interventions in education or management might be driven by the same logic – a problem requiring a solution, which takes the form of an intervention. The research then becomes an evaluation or assessment of the effects of the intervention.

This line of thinking concentrates on the identification of a problem – something requiring a solution – followed by an intervention or activity designed to solve it, and the research becomes the evaluation of that intervention. This is intervention research. Another, more general, line of thinking concentrates on the identification of question(s) – something requiring an answer – followed by an investigation designed to collect the data to answer the question(s). This is naturalistic research, where the social world is studied in its natural state, rather than contrived for research purposes.

In intervention research, the intervention is designed to solve or change some unsatisfactory situation. This unsatisfactory situation is the problem. On the other hand, thinking about research in terms of research questions is a more general approach, which can be used in naturalistic research as well as in intervention research (the effects of an intervention can always be assessed through a series of research questions). I focus on research questions as a way both of getting started in research, and of organising the subsequent project. This focus also has the benefits of reinforcing the 'questions first–methods later' approach of this book, and of flexibility, in the sense that students often find it easier to generate research questions than to focus on a problem. But if it helps to think in terms of identifying a research problem, rather than identifying research questions, there is no reason at all not to do so. Nor is there any reason not to use both concepts – problems and questions – and to switch between them as appropriate, in developing and presenting a proposal for research. In any case, there is interchangeability between the two concepts. Thus, a problem – as something requiring a solution – can always be phrased as questions. Likewise, a question – as something requiring an answer – can always be phrased as a problem.

In this book, research questions are strongly highlighted, and the model of research used here stresses their central role. Developing the research questions is the goal of the pre-empirical stage of the research. The questions provide the foundation for the empirical procedures, and they are the organising principle for the report. This model is stressed in order to clarify and illustrate the research planning process, and it is set up as a useful goal for this process. Actual research situations may require this model to be modified, in two ways. Firstly, research questions worked out in advance may change as the empirical work proceeds: there is no requirement that they be 'set in concrete'. Secondly, it may not be desirable or possible to plan certain types of studies in terms of prespecified research questions. Rather, the strategy in these cases is to identify and clarify the research questions as the study proceeds. When this happens, research questions retain a central role, but emerge at a different stage of the study. This points ahead to the contrast between prespecified and emerging research questions, designs and methods – an important distinction and a theme which is discussed in Chapter 2.

Questions before methods

1.6 This book stresses that methods should follow from questions. How we do something in research depends on what we are trying to find out. This point is stressed because, too often in the past teaching of research methods, we have put the methodological cart before the substantive (or content) horse. This has been called 'methodolatry', the idolatry of method, and has been particularly characteristic of (though not exclusive to) the quantitative approach. Many earlier research methods books have taught methods 'in the abstract'. They are only about methods, and there is little connection between methods, on the one hand, and identifying research questions, on the other. I think research methods texts at the introductory level now need to be both eclectic, and stronger in connecting methods to problem and question identification, definition and analysis. This book aims to do both of these things. Therefore, before it covers quantitative and qualitative methods, it deals with identifying, defining and analysing research questions, with the phrasing of research questions, and with connections between questions, data, and techniques for their collection and analysis.

In other words, the book, especially in the early chapters, stresses the influence of research questions on research methods as a useful teaching/learning device. In actually doing research, methods can constrain and influence the questions that can be asked. These influences are recognised in later chapters, and the reciprocal interaction between question and method is discussed. But the question–to–method influence is deliberately stressed, because of its value in ensuring a close fit between the research questions and the methods. In the end, a main objective of the planning is to maximise the fit between questions on the one hand, and design and procedures on the other. This point is also an important theme, and is discussed in Chapter 2.

A sharp distinction is made in the early part of this book between the pre-empirical and empirical stages of research. It is stressed in Chapters 4 and 5 that empirical research has an important pre-empirical stage, where careful analysis of the questions clarifies the empirical, technical and methodological considerations. Question development is a good term to describe this pre-empirical work, which is important in setting up the research. It essentially comes down to clarifying and disentangling the different issues, and to restating the original problem as a series of empirical research questions. This question development work is often underemphasised, but the pre-empirical stage is important, since the issues involved in doing empirical research are as likely to be conceptual and analytical as they are to be technical and methodological. While this distinction is made sharply, in order to stress the importance of conceptual and analytical issues, these issues do not always precede the methodological issues. Sometimes the two are intertwined.

As noted, the description of research as 'organised common sense' is useful. It supports the idea that good research is within the reach of many people. It is also consistent with the view that we can simplify the more technical aspects of research methods, and enhance understanding, by showing the logic behind them. This book therefore concentrates on the logic behind techniques, in an effort to avoid obscuring that logic behind technical considerations. I do not advocate a formula approach to doing research, since I do not believe that research can be reduced to a set of mechanical steps. On the contrary, I try to stress understanding rather than 'how to do it'. I like the idea that method should be seen not as a codification of procedures, but rather as information about actual ways of working (Mills, 1959). This means that principles and guidelines are stressed throughout the book, rather than sets of mechanical rules. It also means that common sense is needed at all stages of the research process, a point which comes up many times in the different chapters.

Science, the social sciences and social research

1.7 Already, the terms 'science' and 'social science' have been used several times. What is science, and what are the social sciences? What does it mean to study something scientifically? Much has been written on the topic of the scientific method, and today, especially, there are different definitions and points of view. As a starting point in learning about research, however, I suggest a simple and traditional conception of the method of science.

In this conception, the essence of science as a method is in two parts. The first part concerns the vital role of real-world data. Science accepts the authority of empirical data and questions have to be answered and ideas tested against data. The second part is the role of theory, particularly theory which explains. The ultimate aim is to explain the data, not just to collect the data and not just to use the data to describe things. Explanatory theory has a central role in science. The two essential parts to science are therefore data and theory. Put simply, it is scientific to collect data about the world, to build theories to explain the data, and then to test these theories against further data. Whether data come before theory, or theory comes before data, is irrelevant. It only matters that both are present. This point about the irrelevance of the order of theory and data has implications later in this book. There is nothing in this definition of science about the nature of the empirical data, and certainly nothing about whether the data are quantitative or qualitative. In other words, it is not a requirement of science that it involves numerical data, or measurements. It may well do so, but it is not necessary that it does so. This point is also relevant to later chapters of this book.

The general term 'social science' refers to the scientific study of human behaviour. 'Social' refers to people and their behaviour, and to the fact that so much of human behaviour occurs in a social context. 'Science' refers to the way that people and their behaviour are studied. If the aim of (all) science is to build explanatory theory about its data, the aim of social science is to build explanatory theory about people and their behaviour. This theory about human behaviour is to be based on, and is to be tested against, real-world data.

Human behaviour can be studied from many different perspectives. The basic social sciences can be distinguished from each other according to the perspective they take on the study of human behaviour. Many would agree that there are five basic social sciences: psychology, sociology, anthropology, economics and political science. These mainly differ from each other in the perspective they take: thus, psychology typically focuses on the individual person, whereas sociology is more concerned with groups and the social context of behaviour, and so on. We should not try to take these distinctions too far, because of the variety of perspectives that exists within the basic areas, and because some would want to include other areas as basic social sciences. Also, there are fields at the intersections between these basic social sciences (for example, there is social psychology, social anthropology, and so on), but it is useful to keep these basic areas in mind. They can be thought of as disciplines, which can be applied to a variety of different areas.

The applied social sciences can now be distinguished from the basic social sciences by the setting or area of behaviour they focus on. There are many of these areas: some of the main ones are education, organisation studies, government studies, administration and management, social work, nursing studies and health research, certain areas of medicine and public health, family studies, child development, marketing and market research, recreation and leisure studies, communication studies, justice, legal and clinical studies, policy analysis, programme evaluation, and research for social and economic development.

Within these areas, there are also specialised approaches. One way to see this is to think of disciplines applied to areas. For example, with education as the area, and psychology, sociology, anthropology, economics and political science as the basic disciplines, we have five specialised areas within education: the psychology of education, the sociology of education, and so on. Thus, to see education as an applied social science means to apply one or other of the basic social sciences to the study of behaviour in the educational setting. The same applies to other areas. We do not need to worry greatly about precise classifications, and the exact borders between these areas. Rather, the point of this sketch is to indicate the reach of the applied social sciences.

Together the social sciences, basic and applied, cover a very wide domain. What unifies them is their focus on human behaviour, and the central role of empirical research in the way they are studied. Because of this central role of empirical research, a premise of this book is that there is a great deal of similarity in research methods across the various social science areas shown above. Of course, there are also differences in methodological emphasis in different social sciences, and there are affinities for (and hostilities towards) some methods in some disciplines. But the similarities in the general logic of inquiry, and in the basics of designs and empirical procedures, are very strong. This means that we can apply this logic, and these designs and procedures, in many different areas.

Organisation of the book

1.8 Including this introductory chapter, the book is presented in 15 chapters, as follows.

Chapter 2 ('Theory and Method in Social Science Research') deals with the role of both methodological and substantive theory in research, and discusses three themes that occur frequently throughout the book. They are brought together in Chapter 2 for reference purposes. Some readers may want to skim this chapter on a first reading, and to return to it for reference as the themes come up in relation to different topics.

Chapter 3 deals with ethics in social science research.

Chapters 4 and 5 deal with the pre-empirical stage of research, focusing on research questions. Chapter 4 ('Research Questions') deals with identifying and developing research questions, and with the role of hypotheses and the literature in doing this. Chapter 5 ('From Research Questions to Data') continues the consideration of research questions, but concentrates on linking the questions to data.

Chapter 6 ('Literature Searching and Reviewing') then discusses literature searching and reviewing, an important task in dissertation preparation.

Chapters 7, 8 and 9 together give an overview of qualitative research methods. Chapter 7 ('Qualitative Research Design') describes a framework for thinking about research design, linking design with strategy, discusses some main strategies used in qualitative research, and notes the complexity and diversity of contemporary qualitative research. Chapter 8 ('Collecting Qualitative Data') deals with important methods of data collection in qualitative research.

Chapter 9 ('Analysing Qualitative Data') discusses issues involved in analysing qualitative data, focuses on two of the main approaches that have been developed, and overviews several recent and more specialised approaches. These three chapters would be suitable, as a unit, for the reader who wants an overview of qualitative methods.

Chapters 10, 11 and 12 together give a similar overview of quantitative research methods, using the same general headings. Thus Chapter 10 ('Quantitative Research Design') describes the main ideas behind the design of quantitative studies. Chapter 11 ('Collecting Quantitative Data') considers what is involved in collecting quantitative data, and the central role of measurement in this process. Chapter 12 ('Analysing Quantitative Data') describes the logic behind the main statistical techniques used in quantitative social science. Again, these three chapters would be suitable, as a unit, for the reader who only wants an overview of quantitative methods.

Chapter 13 ('The Internet and Research') discusses the role of the Internet in research, and some of the issues involved. Chapter 14 ('Mixed Methods and Evaluation') deals with mixed methods, which is now a popular and increasingly used design for empirical studies in social science, and with general evaluative criteria for assessing the quality of empirical research.

Chapter 15 ('Research Writing') deals with the general topic of research writing, and discusses research proposals in some detail.

In each of these chapters, an introduction lists the main learning objectives, and final sections summarise the main content and list key terms. Exercises and study questions are then provided, and in most chapters, suggestions for further reading are given. At the end of the book, there is a glossary of key terms as well as an appendix containing additional material. Appendix 1 deals with Miles and Huberman's (1994) tactics for drawing and verifying conclusions in qualitative analysis.

Chapter summary

- This book focuses on methods for doing empirical research in the social sciences. Empiricism is the philosophy which underlies the scientific method.
- Empirical research relies on data:

  - Quantitative data are data in the form of numbers
  - Qualitative data are data not in the form of numbers (and are mostly words).

- Research is centrally important in the modern world. It can be defined as an organised, systematic and logical process of inquiry, using empirical data to answer questions.
- Research questions are central in the model of research used here; they are closely associated with research problems.
- Research questions come logically before research methods, and need to be carefully developed.
- The scientific method collects data about the world, builds theories to explain the data, and then tests those theories against further data.
- The social sciences use the scientific method to study human behaviour; different social sciences take different perspectives on human behaviour.

Empiricism: the philosophy that regards experience and observation as the foundation of knowledge

Data: observable information about the world; direct experience of the world

Quantitative data: data which are in the form of numbers

Qualitative data: data which are not in the form of numbers

Paradigm: the assumptions and way of thinking about the reality being studied

Research questions: the questions developed to guide research; empirical research questions are needed for empirical research

Intervention research: an intervention is designed and implemented to solve a problem, and the research evaluates the intervention

Naturalistic research: the world is studied in its natural state, rather than contrived for research purposes

Scientific method: building theories to explain data, and testing these theories against further data

The social sciences: using the scientific method to study human behaviour, from one perspective or another

Exercises and study questions

1. Define and discuss these key concepts:

   - empirical research
   - quantitative research
   - qualitative research
   - mixed methods research
   - the scientific method
   - the social sciences

2. Study the table of contents of this book. Then consider these questions:

   - Which parts of the book do you think you will find easiest to understand? Why?
   - Which parts do you think you will find the most difficult to understand? Why?
   - Do you think you are more of a 'numbers' person, a 'words' person, or both? Why?

two
THEORY AND METHOD IN SOCIAL SCIENCE RESEARCH

Contents

After studying this chapter you should be able to:

- Describe what is meant by methodological theory and by substantive theory
- Define paradigms, and describe the difference between paradigm-driven research and pragmatic research
- Understand the difference between description and explanation
- Describe the difference between theory verification and theory generation research
- Explain the logical priority of research questions over research methods
- Describe the essential differences between prespecified and unfolding research

The term 'theory' is used in many different ways in the literature, which can create difficulties. In this chapter, I focus on two main uses of theory – methodological theory and substantive theory. Both are important. Methodological theory concerns the theory or philosophy behind research methods, and is discussed in Section 2.1. It leads on to the topic of question–method connections (Section 2.5). Substantive theory concerns the content area of research, and is discussed in Section 2.2. It leads on to the topics of description and explanation (Section 2.3), and to theory verification and theory generation (Section 2.4). The final section of the chapter deals with the issue of structure in planning a piece of research.

2.1 Methodological theory

Methodological theory, as used here, means theory about method. Whereas substantive theory is about substance or content, methodological theory is about method – about what lies behind the approaches and methods of inquiry used in a piece of research.

Methods of inquiry are based on assumptions – assumptions about the nature of the reality being studied, assumptions about what constitutes knowledge of this reality, and assumptions about what therefore are appropriate methods of building knowledge of this reality. Very often these assumptions are implicit. A point of contention in research methods training has often been whether or not it should be required that such assumptions are made explicit in a piece of postgraduate research.

These assumptions constitute the essential idea of what is meant by the term 'paradigm' in the research methodology and philosophy of science literature. Paradigm issues are necessarily philosophical in nature. In general, paradigm means a set of assumptions about the world, and about what constitute proper topics and techniques for inquiring into that world. Put simply, it is a way of looking at the world. It means a view of how inquiry should be done (hence the term 'inquiry paradigm' which is sometimes used), and is a broad term encompassing elements of epistemology, theory and philosophy, along with methods.

Denzin and Lincoln (1994: 107–9) describe a paradigm as:

a set of basic beliefs (or metaphysics) that deals with ultimates or first principles. It represents a worldview that defines, for its holder, the nature of 'the world,' the individual's place in it, and the range of possible relationships to that world and its parts.

They point out that inquiry paradigms define what they are concerned with, and what falls within and outside the limits of legitimate inquiry, and that inquiry paradigms address three fundamental questions, which reflect the assumptions noted above:

1. The ontological question: What is the form and nature of reality and, therefore, what is there that can be known about it?
2. The epistemological question: What is the relationship between the knower and what can be known?
3. The methodological question: How can the inquirer go about finding out what can be known?

In simpler language, paradigms tell us:

- what the reality is like (ontology);
- what the relationship is between the researcher and that reality (epistemology); and
- what methods can be used for studying the reality (methodology).

These three interrelated questions illustrate the connections between methods and the deeper underlying philosophical issues. Methods are ultimately based on, and derive from, paradigms. Conversely, paradigms have implications for methods. This point became clear during methodological developments of the past 40–50 years. At this point, therefore, a brief sketch of some historical background on methods and paradigms in social science research is appropriate.

Beginning in the 1960s, the traditional dominance of quantitative methods, as the way of doing empirical social science research, was challenged. This challenge accompanied a major growth of interest in using qualitative methods, and this in turn produced a split in the field, between quantitative and qualitative researchers. A prolonged quantitative–qualitative debate ensued, sometimes described as the 'paradigm wars'.[1]

Much of that debate was characterised by either/or thinking. Some thought that only quantitative approaches should be used in research. Others were just as emphatic that only qualitative approaches are appropriate. More recently, however, there have been moves towards a detente, and an increased interest in the combination of the two approaches (Bryman, 1988, 1992; Hammersley, 1992; Tashakkori and Teddlie, 2003a). This has led to mixed methods, the topic of Chapter 14, and a major growth area in the recent research methodology literature. These methodological changes have occurred across most areas of empirical social science research, though in some areas the changes have been more pronounced than in others.

The full story of these developments and debates is more complex than this. I have focused only on one main dimension of it, the quantitative–qualitative distinction, because these remain two of the central methodological approaches in social science research today, and because this distinction is a central organising principle for this book. A major consequence of these developments is that qualitative research methods have moved much more into the mainstream of social science research, compared with their marginalised position of 40 or so years ago. As noted, a further development has been the combination of the two approaches in what is now called 'mixed methods research' (see Chapter 14). As a result, the field of research methodology in social science is now bigger and more complex than it used to be.

Because of the connections between methods and paradigms, the history briefly outlined above also has a deeper level, a level that is not just about the quantitative–qualitative debate, or about research methods, but about paradigms themselves. On this deeper level, a major rethinking began some time ago, and is ongoing. It has brought a questioning of all aspects of research (its purposes, its place and role, its context and conceptualisations of research itself) as well as the methods it uses. It has also brought the development of new perspectives, and of new approaches to data and to the analysis of data, within qualitative research especially. Prominent features of this rethinking are the detailed critique of positivism, and the emergence and articulation of several different paradigms, as alternatives to positivism. As a result, paradigm issues are in a state of change and development, and many matters are still contested.

It is the development of qualitative methods which has exposed the many different paradigm possibilities, and the situation has now become very complicated. Thus Denzin and Lincoln (1994: 109) identify four main alternative inquiry paradigms underlying qualitative research (positivism, post-positivism, critical theory, constructivism), but more detailed examples and classifications of paradigms are given by Guba and Lincoln (1994). Morse (1994: 224–5) has this classification of paradigms with associated qualitative research strategies: philosophy–phenomenology; anthropology–ethnography; sociology–symbolic interactionism–grounded theory; semiotics–ethnomethodology and discourse analysis. Janesick (1994: 212) has a more detailed list of paradigm-related qualitative research strategies, noting that it is not meant to include all possibilities: ethnography, life history, oral history, ethnomethodology, case study, participant observation, field research or field study, naturalistic study, phenomenological study, ecological descriptive study, descriptive study, symbolic interactionist study, microethnography, interpretive research, action research, narrative research, historiography and literary criticism. And examples of paradigms considered by writers in the philosophy of education are logical empiricism and post-empiricism, critical rationalism, critical theory, phenomenology, hermeneutics and systems theory.

This can be confusing and daunting territory for the beginning researcher, partly because of philosophy and partly because of terminology. Fortunately, in the light of these complications, some of the literature now seems to be converging and simplifying. In one version of this convergence, the main paradigm positions are positivism and interpretivism; in another they are positivism and constructivism. Thus we have:

- positivism (associated mostly with quantitative methods), and
- either interpretivism or constructivism (associated with qualitative methods).

These associations – positivism with quantitative methods and interpretivism–constructivism with qualitative methods – are generally true, but they are not necessary associations. It is more accurate to say that positivism is likely to be associated with quantitative methods, and interpretivism and constructivism are likely to be associated with qualitative methods.

These terms are defined slightly differently by different writers, but their main nature-of-reality ideas are as follows:

- Positivism – the belief that objective accounts of the world can be given, and that the function of science is to develop descriptions and explanations in the form of universal laws – that is, to develop nomothetic knowledge.
- Interpretivism – concentrates on the meanings people bring to situations and behaviour, and which they use to make sense of their world (O'Donoghue, 2007: 16–17); these meanings are essential to understanding behaviour.
- Constructivism – realities are local, specific and constructed; they are socially and experientially based, and depend on the individuals or groups holding them (Guba and Lincoln, 1994: 109–11).

In Section 2.5, question–method connections are discussed, and I stress that there needs to be compatibility and integrity in the way the research questions and research methods fit together in a study. This is shown in the top line in the diagram below. Paradigms expand that, because paradigms have implications both for the sorts of research questions asked and the methods used to answer them. This is shown in the bottom line in the diagram.

What does all this methodological theory mean for planning and executing a piece of research? Broadly, there are two main ways in which planning a research project can proceed:

1. Paradigm-driven approach – one way is to begin with a paradigm, articulate it and develop research questions and methods from it;
2. Pragmatic approach – the other way is to begin with research questions that need answers and then choose methods for answering them.

In the pragmatic approach, the questions may come from any source – the literature, existing substantive theory, the media, personal experience, and so on. But very often, especially in professional fields such as education, management or nursing, they will come from practical and professional issues and problems associated with the workplace. The starting point here is not a paradigm. Instead, the starting point is a problem that needs a solution or a question that needs answers. This is a pragmatic approach.

This has sometimes been a contentious issue in higher-degree research programmes. Some university departments have taken the view that paradigm issues are paramount, and insist that research should not be allowed to proceed until it has articulated its paradigm position. I believe this insistence is not well placed, because paradigm-driven research is not the only way to proceed, and because I see a big role for a more pragmatic, applied and professional approach to social science research. I have no objection to paradigm-driven research. My objection is only to the view that all research must be paradigm-driven. I take a similar view with respect to the philosophical issues involved in paradigm debates. I think we should be aware of the issues involved, and of the areas of debate. These are indicated in several places throughout the book. But we can proceed to do research, and to train researchers, mindful of those debates yet not engulfed by them, and without necessarily yet being able to see their resolution. In other words, we can acknowledge the connections of methods to these deeper issues, and discuss them from time to time as they arise, without making them the major focus of our research. This is to take the pragmatic approach noted, consistent with the view that not all questions for social research are driven by paradigm considerations, and that different sorts of questions require different methods for answering them. Both of these points are elaborated upon in later chapters.

To choose the pragmatic approach is to start by focusing on what we are trying to find out in research, and then to fit methods in with this. The important topic of question–method connections is discussed in Section 2.5.

Substantive theory

By substantive theory I mean theory about a substantive issue or phenomenon, some examples of which are shown below. Substantive theory is content-based theory, and is not concerned with methods. Its purpose is to explain some phenomenon or issue of interest – it is explanatory theory. But because explanation requires description (see Section 2.3), substantive theory both describes and explains. An explanatory theory both describes and explains the phenomenon of substantive interest. Theory, in this sense, is a set of propositions that together describe and explain the phenomenon being studied. These propositions are at a higher level of abstraction than the specific facts and empirical generalisations (the data) about the phenomenon. They explain the data by deduction, in the if–then sense. This is the model of scientific knowledge shown in Figure 2.1.

Some examples of substantive theories from different areas of social research are attribution theory, reinforcement theory, various learning theories and personal construct theory (from psychology); reference group theory and social stratification theory (from sociology); the theory of vocational personalities and career anchors (from occupational sociology); various leadership theories (from management and

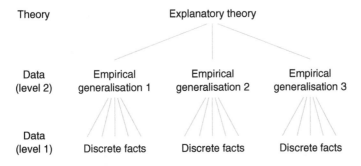

FIGURE 2.1   The structure of scientific knowledge (nomothetic view)

administration), and theories of children's moral development and of teacher career cycles (from education).

Thus an important question in planning research is 'What is the role of (substantive) theory in this study?' This question is sometimes considered more appropriate for doctoral-level research than for masters-level research. This seems to be because a common criterion among universities for the award of the doctorate centres on the 'substantial and original contribution to knowledge' a study makes, and the 'substantial' part of that criterion is often interpreted in terms of its contribution to substantive theory.

Description versus explanation

2.3   In Chapter 1 a brief description of the scientific method was given, stressing that it has the two central parts of data and theory, and that the objective of scientific inquiry is to build explanatory theory about its data. In this view, the aim is to explain the data, not just to use the data for description. This distinction between description and explanation is particularly relevant to the purposes of a piece of research.

The description–explanation distinction is easy to understand on one level, and difficult to understand on another.[2] Fortunately, it is on the easier level where the practical value of the distinction lies. Description and explanation represent two different levels of understanding. To describe is to somehow draw a picture of what happened, or of how things are proceeding, or of what a situation or person or event is like. To explain, on the other hand, is to account for what happened, or for how things are proceeding, or for what something or someone is like. It involves finding the reasons for things (or events or situations), showing why and how they have come to be what they are. Description is a more restricted purpose than explanation. We can describe without explaining, but we cannot really explain without describing. Therefore explanation goes further than description. It is more than just description – it is description plus something else.

Description focuses on what is the case, whereas explanation focuses on why (and sometimes how) something is the case. Science as a method of building knowledge has, in general, pursued the objective of explanation, not just of description. There is a good reason for this. When we know why something happens, we know much more than just what happens. It puts us in a position to predict what will happen, and perhaps to be able to control what will happen.

Thus explanatory knowledge is more powerful than descriptive knowledge. But descriptive knowledge is still important, since explanation requires description. To put it around the other way, description is a first step towards explanation. If we want to know why something happens, it is important to have a good description of exactly what happens. There are often clues to explanation in a full description, and it is hard to explain something satisfactorily until you understand just what the something is (Miles, Huberman and Saldana, 2013).

This distinction comes up mainly when the purpose of a piece of research is being considered. Is the purpose to describe, to explain or both? Descriptive studies are sometimes given a lower status than studies that aim to explain. That is why we sometimes hear the expression 'it is only a descriptive study'. But while this judgement may sometimes have merit, it has to be made carefully. There are situations where a thorough descriptive study will be very valuable. Two examples of such situations are:

- when a new area for research is being developed, and initial and exploratory studies are planned – it is very sensible then to focus on systematic description as the objective of the research;
- careful description of complex social processes can help us to understand what factors to concentrate on for later explanatory studies.

Whether description or explanation is the appropriate purpose for a piece of research depends on the particular situation. Here, as elsewhere, blanket rules are not appropriate. Rather, each research situation needs to be analysed and understood in its own context. It is useful to raise this question of whether the objective of a study is description and/or explanation, especially during the planning stages of research. A good way to do it is to ask 'why' about the things being studied, as well as 'what'.

Thus explanation is the central focus of substantive theory. The essential idea is to explain what is being studied, with the explanation being couched in more abstract terms than the terms used to describe it.[3] We will return to this idea of theory in two places later in the book. The first is in Chapter 4 (Section 4.7), where we consider the role of hypotheses in relation to research questions. There we will see that theory stands behind the hypothesis, in an inductive–deductive relationship with it (Brodbeck, 1968; Nagel, 1979). Studies that use this approach are theory verification studies. The second is in Chapter 9, where we discuss grounded theory analysis in studies that aim to develop theory. These are theory generation studies.

2.4

This distinction between theory verification and theory generation research is important. A project that has explanation as its objective can set out to test theory, or to build theory – to verify theory, or to generate it. For Wolcott (1992), this is the distinction between 'theory first' and 'theory after'. In theory-first research, we start with a theory, deduce hypotheses from it and design a study to test these hypotheses. This is theory verification. In theory-after research, we do not start with a theory. Instead, the aim is to end up with a theory, developed systematically from the data we have collected. This is theory generation.

Quantitative research has typically been more directed at theory verification, while qualitative research has typically been more concerned with theory generation. While this correlation is historically valid, there is no necessary connection between purpose and approach. That is, quantitative research can be used for theory generation (as well as for verification) and qualitative research can be used for theory verification (as well as for generation), as pointed out by various writers (for example, Hammersley, 1992; Brewer and Hunter, 2005). However, while the connection is not necessary, it is nonetheless likely that theory generation research will more often be qualitative. Research directed at theory generation is more likely when a new area is being studied, and exploration of this new area is more likely to use the less structured fieldwork techniques of qualitative research.

Is theory verification research better than theory generation research? This book does not favour one research purpose over the other, since both are needed and both have their place. Either purpose can be appropriate in a research project, and sometimes both will be appropriate. It depends on the topic, the context and practical circumstances of the research, and especially on how much prior theorising and knowledge exists in the area. As with other aspects of a project, the researcher needs to consider the alternatives, select among them according to consistent and logical criteria, and then articulate that position.

Theory generation research was given new legitimacy in social science by the development of grounded theory. As is described in Chapter 7, grounded theory is an explicit theory generation research strategy, developed in reaction against the overemphasis on theory verification research in the American sociology of the 1940s and 1950s. Glaser and Strauss stated this clearly in their original grounded theory publication:

> Verification is the keynote of current sociology. Some three decades ago, it was felt that we had plenty of theories but few confirmations of them – a position made very feasible by the greatly increased sophistication of quantitative methods. As this shift in emphasis took hold, the discovery of new theories became slighted and, at some universities, virtually neglected. (Glaser and Strauss, 1967: 10)

Glaser and Strauss argued that the emphasis on verification of existing theories kept researchers from investigating new problem areas, prevented them from acknowledging the necessarily exploratory nature of much of their work, encouraged instead the inappropriate use of verificational logic and rhetoric, and discouraged the development and use of systematic empirical procedures for generating as well as testing theories (Brewer and Hunter, 2005).

This gives us a useful general guideline for when each purpose might be appropriate. When an area has lots of unverified theories, an emphasis on theory verification research seems a good thing. On the other hand, when an area is lacking in appropriate theories, it is time for the emphasis to shift to theory generation. Also, when research is directed mostly at the verification of existing theories, looking at new problem areas is discouraged, and the logic and techniques (usually quantitative) of verification research are seen as more important. When it is important to look at new areas in research, theory generation appeals as the appropriate purpose. This aspect of grounded theory research is taken up again in Chapter 7 (Section 7.5).

The description–explanation distinction fits in with the structure of scientific knowledge shown in Figure 2.1. In line with the conception of science given in Chapter 1, we can distinguish three levels of knowledge. At the lowest level, there are discrete facts. At the next level are empirical generalisations which group those facts together. At the highest level are theories, whose function is to explain the generalisations. This structure is summarised in the diagram shown. The first two levels (facts and empirical generalisations) focus on description, while the third level focuses on explanation.

This model of the structure of scientific knowledge comes primarily from a positivistic perspective, and stresses a nomothetic view of knowledge. It can be contrasted with an ideographic view of knowledge, a more appropriate aspiration for research in the eyes of many qualitative researchers.[4] But while acknowledging its nomothetic bias, this model is very useful as a starting point in learning about social science research. Much research is based on this model, and it can often help in organising an individual project. It is clear and easy to understand, so the researcher who wishes to diverge from this model can see where and why the divergence occurs. In other words, when researchers argue about how research should proceed and contribute to knowledge, this model helps to see what the argument is about.

There is another reason for stressing this model here. It shows the hierarchical structure of knowledge, with higher levels of abstraction and generality at the top and lower levels at the bottom. This is similar to the hierarchical structure that links data indicators to variables and concepts, and which is central both to the concept–indicator model behind grounded theory coding in qualitative research, and to latent trait measurement theory in quantitative research. These topics are described in Chapters 9 and 11 respectively. This hierarchical structure of increasing levels of abstraction and generality, shown here with respect to scientific knowledge in general, and shown in later chapters with respect to concept–data links in both quantitative and qualitative research, is thus fundamental to much empirical research. An illustration of it is given in Example 2.1.

EXAMPLE 2.1

The Hierarchical Structure of Knowledge

A classic example of this way of structuring knowledge is Durkheim's work on the social aetiology of suicide, described in Durkheim (1951) and summarised in Greenwood (1968). Durkheim theorises 'upwards' from a series of empirical generalisations to a law of suicide.[5]

Question-method connections

2.5 The principle here is that the matching or fit between the research questions and research methods should be as close as possible. A very good way to do that is for methods to follow from questions.

Different questions require different methods to answer them. The way a question is asked has implications for what needs to be done, in research, in order to answer it. Quantitative questions require quantitative methods to answer them, and qualitative questions require qualitative methods to answer them. In today's research environment, with quantitative and qualitative methods often used alongside each other, the matching of questions and methods is even more important. Since this book deals directly with both approaches, it is inevitable that this issue should be a recurrent concern.

The wording of questions is also important, since some wordings carry methodological implications. Thus research questions that include such terms as 'variables', 'factors that affect' and 'the determinants or correlates of', for example, imply a quantitative approach, while questions that include such terms as 'discover', 'seek to understand', 'explore a process' and 'describe the experiences' imply a qualitative approach. (Creswell, 2013 links these last four terms to grounded theory, ethnography, case study and phenomenology respectively).

An example of different research questions and their implications for methods is given by Shulman, in education research (1988: 6–9). He takes the study of reading, suggests four different types of questions, and shows the methods that would be required to answer each.

1. A first question might be: What makes some people successful readers and others unsuccessful? (Or, how can we predict what sorts of people will have difficulty learning to read?) Such questions would be answered using a quantitative correlational study that examined relationships between variables.
2. A second question might be: What are the best possible methods for teaching reading to youngsters, irrespective of their backgrounds or attitudes? This question would involve a quantitative experimental study comparing different teaching methods.
3. A third question might be: What is the general level of reading performance across different age, sex, social or ethnic groups in the population? This would require a quantitative survey of reading performance and reading practices.

4. A fourth set of questions might be quite different from the previous ones: How is reading instruction carried on? What are the experiences and perceptions of teachers and students as they engage in the teaching and learning of reading? How is this complex activity accomplished? Here, a qualitative case study involving observation and interview might be used, perhaps using the perspective of ethnomethodology.

Shulman goes on to suggest philosophical and historical questions as well. Other illustrations of question–method connections are given in Example 2.2.

EXAMPLE 2.2

Question–Method Connections

- Shulman (1988: 6–9) shows connections between questions and methods with the topic of reading research in education; similar examples are noted by Seidman (2013).
- Marshall and Rossman (2010) show, in a table, the links between research purposes, research questions, research strategy and data collection techniques.
- Maxwell (2012) adapts a table from LeCompte and Preissle (1993) to show the links between 'What do I need to know?' and 'What kind of data will answer the questions?' and illustrates these links with actual research questions.
- Maxwell (2012) gives the example of a mismatch between questions and method, whereby, in a study of how historians work, the 'right answer' is found to be to the 'wrong question'.

A good way to achieve a fit between questions and methods is to ensure that the methods we use follow from the questions we seek to answer. In other words, the content of the research (the research questions) has a logical priority over the method of the research. To say that content precedes method is simply to say that we first need to establish what we are trying to find out, and then consider how we are going to do it. On a practical level, this is often a good way to get a research project off the ground. Sometimes it is difficult to know where and how to start, in planning research. If so, asking 'What are we trying to find out?' usually gets our thinking going, and ensures that we start with the content, not with the method. Putting questions before methods is also a good defence against overload when developing a research proposal. To delay consideration of methods until it is clear what the questions are helps in managing the inevitable complications that accompany a full examination of the possibilities for research in any area. It helps in keeping the question development stage systematic, and under control. It also helps achieve good question–method fit, a central criterion in the validity of research.

I am stressing this point here to counter a previous unfortunate tendency in social science research. In Chapter 1, the term 'methodolatry' was used:

> I use the term *methodolatry*, a combination of *method* and *idolatry*, to describe a pre-occupation with selecting and defending methods to the exclusion of the actual substance of the story being told. Methodolatry is the slavish attachment and devotion to method that so often overtakes the discourse in the education and human service fields. (Janesick, 1994: 215)

Methodolatry means putting method before content. It is first learning the research method, then finding research questions that can fit into the method. It is looking for research questions guided by methods.

This is a danger when we place too much stress on the teaching of research methods, for their own sake. Because of this danger, this book concentrates on the logic and rationale behind empirical research and its methods. Once this logic is mastered, we can focus on research questions, and then fit the techniques and methods to the questions. In my opinion, the best sequence of learning activities for research is to start by learning the logic of research, then to focus on identifying and developing the research questions, and then to fit methods and techniques to the questions.

I am using the concept of methodolatry to argue for minimising the direct influence of methods on research questions, which we can do by first getting the research questions clear, and then focusing on the methods required to answer them. But methods can also indirectly influence research questions, by constraining what can be studied. There are limits as to what can be designed in research, and to what data can be obtained and analysed. While taking this into account, the advice is nonetheless to focus on questions first, as much as possible. In the above example, after showing how different methodological approaches fit different questions, Shulman emphasises the same point: 'we are advised to focus first on our problem and its characteristics before we rush to select the appropriate method' (1988: 15). Thus, when misfit between the parts becomes apparent during the planning of the research, it is a matter of adapting the parts to each other.

Question–method fit is an aspect of conceptual clarity in a piece of research. Conceptual clarity involves the precise and consistent use of terms, internal consistency within an argument and logical links between concepts, especially across different levels of abstraction. The pre-empirical question development work described in Chapter 4 is directed at this conceptual clarity. Developing specific research questions is a good way of achieving clarity and matching questions and methods.

The different paradigms and strategies within qualitative research open up many new and different types of research questions. For example, ethnographic questions might focus on cultural and symbolic aspects of behaviour; grounded theory questions might focus on understanding social processes, and how people manage different types of situations; a conversation analysis study might focus on conversational structure and on the role of conversation in taken-for-granted everyday activities; discourse analysis questions might focus on the way an institution presents itself to the world, the symbols and language it uses, and the connection of those with its ideology, knowledge, power, and so on. Paradigms can thus be important in generating research questions. Within qualitative research especially, the range of questions of interest is now very broad. But it remains important, even with this broader range of questions, that the methods we use should follow from and fit in with the questions we seek to answer.

Prespecified versus unfolding: structure in research questions, design and data

2.6 How much should the research questions, design and data be preplanned in a piece of research, and how much should they emerge (or unfold) as the research develops?

There is a continuum we can set up for thinking about this question, with the dimension of interest being the amount of prespecified structure in the research strategy that is used. The central comparison is between research that is prespecified (or preplanned, or prefigured, or predetermined) on the one hand, and research that is unfolding (or emerging, or open-ended) on the other. Prespecified here refers to how much structure is introduced ahead of the empirical work, as opposed to during the empirical work. This continuum applies to three main areas – to research questions, to research design and to data.

Miles, Huberman and Saldana (2013) discuss this idea in the context of qualitative research under the heading of 'tight versus loose'. Those terms are equivalent to the terms used here – tight means prespecified and loose means unfolding. The key questions are: To what extent are the research questions, the design and the data focused, specified and structured ahead of the actual empirical work? To what extent does the focus in the research questions, and the structure in the design and the data, unfold and emerge as the empirical work proceeds? The continuum of possibilities is shown in Figure 2.2. This diagram shows that quantitative research typically falls towards the left-hand end of the continuum, whereas qualitative research can occupy a much greater range along the continuum.

'Structure', as used here, means showing what the different parts of the research are, how they connect with each other, what will be done in the research, and in what sequence. It means knowing what we are looking for, and how we are going to

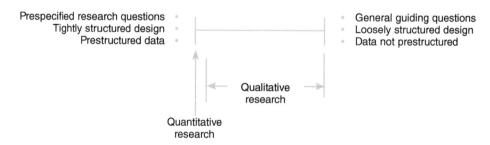

FIGURE 2.2   Prespecified versus unfolding: the timing of structure

get it – knowing what data we will want, and how they will be collected. It also means knowing what structure the data will have and how they will be analysed.

At the extreme left-hand end of the continuum, everything is prespecified – the research questions, the design and the data. It is all worked out in advance, a set of steps is laid down, and the researcher proceeds through those steps. At the other end, we can envisage a project where very little structure is determined in advance, with an open-ended and unstructured approach to the research questions, the design and the data. The strategy is that these will unfold as the study is carried out. Let us see what this contrast means for each of the three areas.

1. *Research questions:* at the left-hand end of the continuum, specific research questions are set up in advance to guide the study. It is quite clear, in advance, exactly what questions the study is trying to answer. At the right-hand end, only general questions are set up in advance. The argument there is that, until some empirical work is carried out, it is not possible (or, if possible, not sensible) to identify the specific research questions. They will only become clear as the research unfolds, and as a specific focus for the work is developed. Wolcott (1982) describes this contrast as 'looking for answers' versus 'looking for questions'. As we will see in Chapter 5, there is often a close connection between the research questions and the conceptual framework in a study. The issue described here in terms of research questions applies to conceptual frameworks as well – they can be developed and specified in advance of the research, or they can emerge as the research proceeds. The more tightly developed and pre-specified the research questions are, the more likely it is that there will be a well-developed conceptual framework as well.

2. *Design:* at the left-hand end, the design is tightly structured. The clearest examples come from quantitative research – experimental studies and non-experimental quantitative studies with carefully developed conceptual frameworks. Research questions, design and conceptual framework come together here, since a tightly structured design requires that variables be identified, and that their conceptual status in the research be made clear. At the right-hand end, the design is indicated in general terms only (for example, as in an unfolding case study, or an ethnography). Like the research questions, it will take detailed shape as the research progresses, and as the specific focus for the study is developed.

3. *Data:* at the left-hand end, data are structured in advance. A very clear example is quantitative data, where measurement is used to give the data numerical structure. Using numbers is the most common way of structuring data in advance, but there are other ways as well. Whether it is numerical or other categories, the point is that those categories are pre-established, or set up *a priori*. At the right-hand end, the data are unstructured at the point of collection. No pre-established categories or codes are used. The structure of the data, the categories and codes, emerge from the data, during the analysis – they are developed *a posteriori*. Thus the comparison is between starting with categories for the data, versus getting to them during the analysis of the data – between pre-coding the data and post-coding the data. This point about data has implications for instrumentation in data collection, not only in quantitative research, but in qualitative research as well.

The continuum shown in Figure 2.2 can now be described more accurately. It is really about when in the research process the structure is introduced. The structure can be introduced in the planning or pre-empirical stage, when the research is being set up, before data are collected; or, it can be introduced in the execution stage of the research, as the study is being carried out, as data are being collected. Either way, structure is needed. A research project will be difficult both to report and to understand, and will lack credibility as a piece of research, without structure in its research questions, its design, especially in its data, and also in its report. So this contrast is not about having structure or not having structure, but about when in the research process the structure occurs. In other words, this continuum is about the timing of structure in the research – whether that structure is introduced ahead of the empirical research, or is introduced during and as a result of the empirical research.

The possibilities along this continuum represent different possible research styles. As the diagram shows, there is a correlation between these styles, on the one hand, and the typical quantitative and qualitative research approaches on the other. The typical quantitative study is much more likely to have specific research questions, a clear conceptual framework and design for its variables, and to use measurement as its way of structuring the data. It is harder to talk about typical qualitative studies, and they may cover a wider range along the continuum. Many of them fall towards the right-hand end, with general rather than specific questions set up in advance, with only a general design and with data not coded at the point of collection. This is well captured by Miles and Huberman (1994: 17), in discussing field research as a central part of the qualitative approach:

> The conventional image of field research is one that keeps prestructured designs to a minimum. Many social anthropologists and social phenomenologists consider social processes to be too complex, too relative, too elusive, or too exotic to be approached with explicit conceptual frames or standard instruments. They prefer a more loosely structured, emergent, inductively 'grounded' approach to gathering data: The conceptual framework should emerge from the field in the course of the study; the important research questions will become clear only gradually; meaningful settings and actors cannot be selected prior to fieldwork; instruments, if any, should be derived from the properties of the setting and its actors' views of them.

This general correlation between style and approach also extends to theory verification versus theory generation research, the distinction discussed in Section 2.4. Theory verification research, by definition, is more likely to have clear-cut research questions leading to hypotheses, a tightly structured design and pre-established categories for data. Theory generation research, by contrast, will more likely use an approach where specific research questions unfold as the study develops, and where codes and categories for the data are empirically derived.

It is not a question of which strategy is best, since a large part of the answer to this question is 'it depends'. The question interacts with the overall approach to the research. Is it a quantitative study, a qualitative study or one that combines the two approaches? If quantitative, it is more likely to be towards the left-hand end of the continuum in Figure 2.2. If qualitative, there is likely to be a greater range of possibilities. Nor is it a dichotomous choice between two extreme positions – it is a continuum. For clarity, the description in this section has been given in terms of the ends of the continuum. In reality, there are many points along the continuum, and any study may combine elements of either strategy – the prespecified one or the unfolding one.

How much predetermined structure is desirable in a project is a matter for analysis in each particular research situation. Structure is necessary. But the timing of the structure – when is the appropriate point to introduce this structure – depends on such factors as the topics and goals of the research, the availability of relevant knowledge and theory about the topic, and the researcher's familiarity with the situation being studied (Miles, Huberman and Saldana, 2013). Other factors to be considered are the preferred style of the research, the resources (including time) available to the researcher, and to what extent the researcher is interested in explanation versus interpretation. Depending on these factors, there can be merit in either approach. As Miles, Huberman and Saldana (2013) point out, what is required is a careful analysis of each situation where research is proposed. The research strategy should then be custom-built, as far as is possible, on the basis of this analysis.

The discussion in this section has treated research questions, design and data together. Subsequent chapters deal with questions, design and data separately, before bringing them back together in Chapters 14 and 15. Without wishing to advise against exploratory unfolding studies, it is worth noting some of the benefits in having at least a reasonable level of specificity in the research questions. For example, they give guidance during initial data collection, thereby saving time and resources and helping to avoid confusion and overload, an especially valuable benefit for the beginning researcher. In addition, research questions that are at least reasonably focused make it easier to communicate about the research, which can be important in the presentation (and approval) of a research proposal. Brewer and Hunter (2005) point out that, once a study is completed, it is irrelevant whether the research questions initiated the study or emerged from it – but it can matter at the proposal stage. Finally, it is very often the case that the researcher does have knowledge about the proposed research problems, even in a relatively unexplored area ('experiential data' and 'experiential knowledge' – see Strauss, 1987 and Maxwell, 2012). There is great benefit in getting that knowledge out onto the table, and working carefully to develop research questions in advance of the empirical work is a good way to do that.

Developing specific research questions to a point where they are stable, and connecting them to the design, data collection and data analysis parts of the research, requires careful work. The question being considered here is whether that work is done in advance of the research or during it. That brings us back to fitting the various parts of a project together, as discussed in Section 2.5. This fitting together can be done ahead of the research, or during the research, but either way it needs to be done. Just as Section 2.1 of this chapter stressed the pragmatic benefits of 'questions first – methods later' in maximising that fit, so this section stresses the pragmatic benefits of beginning with research questions that are at least reasonably well developed.

To summarise: There is a continuum of possibilities, which is about prespecifying versus unfolding structure in the research. It applies to research questions, design and data. The issue is structure and its timing – when in the research is structure introduced? Prespecified research does it ahead of the empirical procedures. Unfolding research does it during them. As a general rule, at least a reasonable level of specificity in the initial research questions is desirable, though various factors need to be taken into account in particular situations. Chapter 4 will describe a model of research where considerable effort is invested in developing research questions ahead of the empirical work. But this is not the only model, and when research questions come later, they still require both the analytical development described in Chapters 4 and 5, and the matching with methods, design and data described in Section 2.5 of this chapter.

Chapter summary

- Methodological theory is theory about methods, and involves philosophy. This is because methods are based on paradigms. A paradigm is a set of assumptions about the world.
- The questioning of paradigms led to a prolonged quantitative–qualitative debate, characterised by either/or thinking. This was a very prominent feature of the paradigm wars among philosophers and methodologists, which took place in the 1960s, 70s and 80s.
- Paradigm issues have more recently converged into positivism (mainly associated with quantitative methods) on the one hand, and interpretivism or constructivism (mainly associated with qualitative methods) on the other.
- A research project can be paradigm-driven, where it begins with a paradigm, and develops research questions and methods from it, or pragmatic, where it begins with research questions which need answers, and chooses methods for answering them.
- The purpose of substantive theory is to explain some substantive phenomenon of interest.
- Description and explanation are two different levels of understanding of empirical data. Both are important, but the overall purpose of scientific research is explanation, not just description. This shows the importance of explanatory theory.
- Theory verification research begins with a theory, develops hypotheses from this theory, and then tests the hypotheses against empirical data. By contrast, theory generation research starts with research questions and data, and aims to end with a theory which explains the data.
- Good research has a close fit between the questions it asks and the methods it uses. A very good way to achieve this fit is for methods to follow from questions.
- In prespecified research, the research questions and methods are preplanned, and the empirical part of the research implements these methods. In unfolding research, the questions and the methods are, to some extent at least, developed as the research proceeds. The difference is in the timing of the structure of the research. Which approach is 'better' needs to be determined in each particular research situation.

Methodological theory: theory about methods, and the philosophical assumptions which (necessarily) underlie any set of research methods

Paradigm: a set of assumptions about the world, and about what constitute proper topics and techniques for inquiring into that world. Paradigms have an ontological dimension (concerned with the nature of reality), an epistemological dimension (concerned with knowledge about that reality) and a methodological dimension (concerned with methods for building knowledge of the reality)

Positivism: the philosophical position that objective accounts of the world can be given, and that the function of science is to develop descriptions and explanations in the form of universal laws – that is, to develop nomothetic knowledge

Interpretivism: the philosophical position that people bring meanings to situations, and use these meanings to understand their world and influence their behaviour

Constructivism: the philosophical position that realities are local, specific and constructed, and are socially and experientially based, depending on the people holding them

Paradigm-driven research: research which begins with a paradigm, and develops research questions and methods from it

Pragmatic research: research which begins with research questions, and then chooses methods for answering them

Substantive theory: content-based theory, which aims to develop a set of internally consistent propositions to explain a substantive phenomenon of interest; substantive theory is explanatory

Description: using data to draw a picture of a situation, event, person (people) or something similar; focuses on what is the case

Explanation: accounting for a description, showing why and how events or situations have come to be what they are; focuses on why (or how) something is the case

Theory verification research: research which sets out to test a theory, by testing hypotheses derived from the theory; begins with theory

Theory generation research: research which starts with research questions and data, and aims to build a theory to explain the data; finishes with theory

Question-method fit: the need for internal consistency between the research questions asked, and the methods used for answering them; an important aspect of the validity of a piece of research

Pre-specified research: research which has a high degree of structure before the empirical work is done; research questions, methods and data are specified in advance

Unfolding research: research which does not have a high structure before empirical work begins; initial research questions may be loose and general, and more specific questions, methods and data are developed during empirical work

Exercises and study questions

1. What is a paradigm? What are the three main dimensions of paradigms?
2. What were the 'paradigm wars'?
3. How are paradigms and methods connected?
4. What is a paradigm-driven approach to research? What is a pragmatic approach to research? How do they differ?
5. What would a *description* of the climate of (say) a London winter look like? What would an *explanation* of that climate look like? How are they different?
6. For what sorts of topics and research questions would prestructured research be appropriate?
7. For what sorts of topics and research questions would unfolding research be appropriate?

Further reading

Anfara, V.A. and Mertz, N.T. (2006) *Theoretical Frameworks in Qualitative Research.* Thousand Oaks, CA: SAGE.

Babbie, E. (2012) *The Practice of Social Research.* 13th edn. Belmont, CA: Wadsworth.

Bailey, K.D. (2008) *Methods of Social Research.* 4th edn. New York: Simon & Schuster.

Creswell, J.W. (2013) *Research Design: Qualitative and Quantitative Approaches.* 4th edn. Thousand Oaks, CA: SAGE.

Lewins, F. (1992) *Social Science Methodology.* Melbourne: Macmillan.

Little, D. (1991) *Varieties of Social Explanation: An Introduction to the Philosophy of Social Science.* Boulder, CO: Westview.

Marshall, C. and Rossman, G.B. (2010) *Designing Qualitative Research.* 5th edn. Thousand Oaks, CA: SAGE.

Maxwell, J.A. (2012) *Qualitative Research Design: An Interactive Approach.* 3rd edn. Thousand Oaks, CA: SAGE.

Miles, M.B., Huberman, A.M. and Saldana, J. (2013) *Qualitative Data Analysis.* 3rd edn. Thousand Oaks, CA: SAGE.

Neuman, W.L. (2010) *Social Research Methods: Qualitative and Quantitative Approaches.* 7th edn. Harlow: Pearson.

Wolcott, H.F. (1994) *Transforming Qualitative Data: Description, Analysis, and Interpretation.* Thousand Oaks, CA: SAGE.

Notes

1. The 'paradigm wars' were especially vigorous in the field of education research. A good record of those 'wars', including the moves towards reconciliation and detente, can be found in a series of articles in *The Educational Researcher*, beginning in the 1970s.
2. The 'difficult' level is about precise definitions of the two terms, and about philosophical investigations into the concept of explanation – see, for example, Little (1991) and Lewins (1992).
3. Explanation itself is a complex philosophical concept. Another form of it is the 'missing links' form. Here, an event, or empirical generalisation, is explained by showing the links

that bring it about. Thus the relationship between social class and scholastic achievement might be explained by using cultural capital (Bourdieu, 1973) as the link between them. Or the relationship between social class and self-esteem might be explained by using the parent–child relationship as the link between them (Rosenberg, 1968: 54–82).

4. A nomothetic view sees generalised knowledge, universal laws and deductive explanations, based mainly on probabilities derived from large samples, and standing outside the constraints of everyday life. An ideographic view sees nomothetic knowledge as insensitive to local, case-based meanings, and directs attention rather to the specifics of particular cases. It prefers to see knowledge as local and situated (Denzin and Lincoln, 2011). The ideographic view thus points towards understanding and interpretation as important goals of research, alongside description and explanation.

5. Note also Atkinson's (1978) critique of that work, focusing on how suicide rates are constructed and what they mean.

three

ETHICS IN SOCIAL SCIENCE RESEARCH

ALIS OANCEA

Contents

Introduction

3.1 Ethics is the study of what are good, right, or virtuous courses of action; applied ethics focuses this study on particular and complex issues and contexts. Research ethics is a branch of applied ethics focused on the specific contexts of planning, conducting, communicating, and following up research. The study of these contexts and of the ethical aspects of the complex judgements that they require has produced a vast literature that sets out a range of values, general principles and specific rules to guide research practice, and explores the ways in which particular contexts shape ethical decision making in research.

Some of these principles have been formalised into codes of ethical practice, which signal developing areas of consensus within communities of research about what is acceptable to do, in what conditions. For example, the codes may prompt researchers to consider issues of access and consent, of confidentiality and anonymity, or of risks and benefits in research, in light of recommendations based on moral principles, experience in the field, and insights from historical and ongoing debates around research ethics. Some of these areas of agreement have been further institutionalised to produce ethical regulations consisting of sets of procedural requirements for researchers (for example, for obtaining the approval of an ethics committee) deemed important by organisations involved in the scrutiny of research practice, including higher education institutions and funders of research.

Ethical challenges in research arise in all designs and approaches and at all stages of a project, from the choice of research topic, which raises questions about the worthwhileness of the research, through to the reporting and publication stage, and beyond it, to further uses and outcomes. The standard approach to research ethics involves a deductive move from principles and rules towards application. For example, in the context of the scrutiny of research proposals by institutional ethical committees, reviewers may identify a relevant rule (such as 'harm ought to be avoided') and use the relevant descriptive information about the proposed conduct of research to decide whether in the particular project under scrutiny the rule is likely to be infringed or not. This approach has been criticised by scholars who noted that principles and rules underdetermine practice, which is open-ended and situated (see McNamee and Bridges, 2002). Further, beyond ethical principles there can be many other constraints on ethical decision making, such as legal, methodological, political and economic considerations, which may shape research ethics procedures.

Social science researchers need to be alert to the various constraints around their research and to the ethical implications of any decisions they make. They engage in principled deliberation about morally salient issues and acceptable courses of action in particular research situations. In doing so, they can draw on their understanding of the particulars of each situation and of the personal and professional values infusing it, as well as on their critical interpretation of the regulation and various guidelines available to them.

Ethical principles and research situations

3.2 Let us take a hypothetical example of an ethically rich research situation:

> A student wishes to study effective teaching practices in higher education. Having reviewed the literature, the student is concerned about two aspects of previous research: the potential for researcher-introduced bias and, linked to this, what she sees as an insufficient focus on power relations in the classroom. In an attempt to reduce bias and to uncover power relations in the classroom, the student is considering doing covert observational research in her own higher education institution. She hopes not only to produce a trustworthy account of naturally-occurring situations, but also an authentic account that can help empower participants who may be disadvantaged by the balance of power in such situations, including women and minority ethnic participants. Would covert research in this scenario be ethically acceptable?

Regardless of how accurate the hypothetical student's assessment of the literature seems, and of how realistic her expectations might be, this example invites the reader to engage in a form of 'normative' reasoning that involves statements about what ought to be done, and why. This form of reasoning draws on factual statements about what is the case in a particular situation, and connects them with belief statements concerning aims, rules and principles about how things ought to be. The basic difference between thinking about (for example) how to achieve technically precise data collection and analysis, and deliberating about acting responsibly in ethically complex research situations is crucial in understanding the ethical context for research, researchers' responsibilities within it, and the resources available to help them navigate their way through it. What this distinction suggests is that, although factual statements about research, codes and guidelines, and rules of thumb are of help, ethical research practice is ultimately a matter of responsible, situated judgement.

So how might the student who is considering doing covert research in her own institution reason? There is no absolutely straightforward answer. Institutional guidelines may simply state that unjustified deception should be avoided, and leave it more or less to the researcher to construct a case for what may count as justified or reasonable deception. In philosophical ethics there are many traditions that may assist in this process, each of which may help illuminate a slightly different set of ethically salient aspects of research situations.

For example, the student could argue that her decision will have to be based on a trade-off in the application of different moral rules and principles. She could argue that 'do not deceive' is a lower-priority rule in a situation of perceived discrimination than 'maximise benefits for those who most need them'. Nonetheless, she could also, equally, argue that morally right aims do not justify morally wrong means, and therefore that there are no reasonable grounds for the decision to deceive.

To settle this dilemma, she may appeal to higher-order principles, such as the imperative to treat others with respect, or to exemplars of past moral behaviour, on which to model her own. The decision is ultimately hers, although it may draw on professional consensus crystallised in professional ethical codes and it may have been sanctioned by relevant committees and informed by debates within research communities. She also bears the moral – though perhaps not always, or not solely, the legal – responsibility for the consequences of her choice.

The example above looked at deception. We can interrogate other hypothetical situations in similar ways. For instance, is it acceptable to withhold benefits from participants in experimental research, if the control group is not offered a comparable alternative to the potentially beneficial treatment received by the intervention group? Also, in a different model of research, what should the researcher do when evidence of dangerous behaviour transpires from confidential interviews during the course of research?

In order to reach a decision about whether a particular way of conducting research would be acceptable in a concrete situation, the researcher needs to find ways to interrogate the situation and deliberate about her aims and the means by which they will be achieved, in the light of empirical information, ethical principles and rules of thumb, exemplars of action, and individual and collective moral and professional aspirations.

Box 3.1 illustrates three ways in which we could start to interrogate an ethically complex research scenario, each pointing to somewhat different ethical aspects and drawing on particular traditions in philosophical ethics. These show that there can be a range of focal points for thinking about ethics in research (but note that there are also many hybrid approaches that cut across particular traditions).

BOX 3.1

Interrogating Research Practice from a Range of Ethical Perspectives

1. Duties: What is my/my colleagues' duty to do in this situation? What is the right thing to do in this case? Have errors been made deliberately or due to negligence? How can these be reversed or corrected?

(Continued)

(Continued)

2. Consequences: What are the likely consequences of the courses of action available to me (including not doing anything)? How will each potential course of action affect the relevant individuals and communities (including myself) in this situation? What potential harms may result from each of these courses of action? What would be the benefits of different courses of action I might take? How do these different risks and benefits compare with each other? On balance, what is the best course of action to take now?

3. Virtues: How would a virtuous person act in this situation? Which values do I want to express in my action? How would my moral exemplars act in this situation? How should I live – what kind of person do I strive to be? Who do I want to be throughout this situation?

The first set of questions in Box 3.1 focuses on the ideas of duty, obligations and rights, and prompts the researcher to think about identifying the **right** course of action in the particular situation described. The questions reflect a long-standing tradition in ethics that many call deontological ethics (from the Greek *deon*, meaning duty), which emphasises acting out of duty, as opposed to pleasure, inclination or interest. This approach centres on universal principles (which hold irrespective of particular conditions); an example is Immanuel Kant's categorical imperative, one formulation of which states: 'act in such a way that you always treat humanity, whether in your own person or in the person of any other, never simply as a means, but always at the same time as an end' (1964: 96). In this tradition, ethical decision making tends to be deductive: it starts with principles (such as truthfulness, respect and beneficence), from which derive rules (such as 'don't deliberately distort your data', 'don't deceive', 'don't cause harm to participants'). Actual judgements refer to these rules, which are binding regardless of consequences. Deontological ethical approaches work well if there is a stock of rules based on absolute principles and values; if these rules are fair and widely accepted; if individuals and groups are prepared to uphold them regardless of immediate consequences; and if individuals and groups have access to guidance for the selection and application of rules, particularly in cases of conflict (such as possible conflict between truthfulness and beneficence).

The second set of questions in Box 3.1 focuses on the consequences of actions, and on the balance of benefits and harms arising from them. It aims to find the **best** course of action, that is, the one likely to result in the greatest good for all concerned. In teleological ethics (from Gr. *telos* – aim, purpose, end, destination), the focus shifts from duty and universals, to the outcomes or results of actions. Moral worth is determined by the consequences of an act; the nature of the act comes second to that. Good action aims to achieve the greatest good (health, happiness, welfare, knowledge) overall. This is the so-called 'greatest happiness' or utility principle: 'actions are right in proportion as they tend to promote happiness, wrong as they tend to produce the reverse of happiness' (Mill, 1863: 9–10). Other versions include achieving 'the greatest happiness of the greatest number' of people (Bentham, 1823: 9), 'the greatest possible balance of good over evil in the world' (Frankena, 1973: 34); maximising benefits and minimising harm for all those foreseeably affected by an action; and ensuring that action, including research, has a reasonable likelihood to bring about benefits and that no alternative of comparable effectiveness exists (WMA, 2000, Art. 19). Consequence ethics require comprehensive understanding of the facts of the situation, accurate prediction of likely consequences, and the ability to ensure justice while maximising good over harm.

The final set of questions moves away from the emphasis on universal principles and consequences towards actions arising out of particular dispositions in particular situations. The questions prompt scrutiny of one's own and others' ways of being and seek those dispositions or traits that embody moral excellence, or virtue, through their action. In other words, these questions seek the most **virtuous** ways of being and living. For aretaic ethics (from the Greek *arete* – virtue, value, excellence), acting ethically means acting in accordance with the traits, or dispositions, of the virtuous person. These may include intellectual impartiality, benevolence, honesty, or may refer to a more holistic concept of integrity and excellence in research. Virtuous action is based on moral wisdom and discernment, which includes an appreciation of the situation – that is, the capacity to understand the situation and to discern its morally salient issues. It is also an exercise of virtuosity – the skilful transposition of these dispositions into morally appropriate action. Ethically sound research cultures support virtuous research practice and the flourishing of virtuous researchers. There is no one principle or code to capture all this; at best, we only have rules of thumb and the examples of others to help us recognise, choose and sustain virtuous research. Thus, an aretaic approach is premised on the ability to recognise, understand and choose virtue, together with finely-tuned, sensitive reading(s) of the situation, including understanding of the self and of others (see, for example, Aristotle, and, in recent days, Elizabeth Anscombe, Alasdair MacIntyre, Martha Nussbaum and Linda Zagzebski).

Other approaches to research ethics also stress the importance of particular situations in defining and addressing ethical issues. Situated ethical approaches emphasise that ethical decisions are contextual and ethical problems are never neatly defined, nor fully resolved. They show that ethical concerns in research, like more general ethical debates in society, are more wide-ranging than can be covered by sets of rules. Applied feminist ethics has a sharp focus on the key themes of power, responsibility and accountability, and questions the notion of neutral expertise and the meaningfulness of ethical prescription that discounts standpoint, personal experience, emotion, nurturing and caring (Edwards and Mauthner, 2002; Usher, in Simmons and Usher, 2000).

3.3 Debates around ethics in research have a long history, but became more intense in the 20th century. These debates were fuelled by scandals around harmful and exploitative studies, in particular in medical research, such as the Tuskegee syphilis study on black males, the Willowbrook school hepatitis study on disabled children, and many horrific experiments on humans during the Second World War and the Cold War. Psychological and social research entered the fray too – for example, the Iowa stuttering study on orphan children, the Stanford prison experiment, and the Milgram (1974) experiments on obedience were subject to intense controversy. Reactions to such experiments led to the establishment of formal regulation on research ethics, such as the 1947 Nuremberg code, the 1964 Helsinki Declaration by the World Medical Association, the 1979 Belmont report in the USA, and a series of data protection and human experimentation acts worldwide. While many of the issues that were seen as controversial at the time of these debates would now be seen as unacceptable research practice, there are new difficult issues that have emerged since, as technologies available to researchers have become more complex. This has led to the development of new areas of research ethics (such as the ethics of geoengineering, virtual reality, stem cell or human enhancement research), but also to challenging areas of past consensus (such as those around research with disabled subjects). Thus research ethics continues to be a dynamic field.

Professional regulations and ethical codes, including those for research, tend to include detailed rules that are more specific and limited in scope than the philosophical principles that may be underpinning them. They may draw unevenly on different ethical traditions, often in favour of a deontological approach. They stipulate standards for conduct or 'proper' ways of behaving for members of a profession, as well as a range of conditions and procedures for their application. These standards, such as those concerning informed consent and confidentiality, are the product of negotiated agreement about acceptable practice in particular professional, occupational and institutional contexts. They add collective and institutional dimensions to ethical decision making in research. Their role is (a) to offer resources that can inform ethically acceptable decisions by researchers; and (b) to construct frameworks of consensus against which proposed and actual courses of action and research conduct can be judged and sanctioned by relevant bodies (for example, a committee granting or refusing 'ethical clearance', or an examiner deeming the approach described in a thesis as ethically acceptable or not). At the institutional level, the establishment of formalised mechanisms for ethical scrutiny also arises from a concern about litigation.

By way of example, Box 3.2 describes some of the better-known codes produced by professional associations and funding bodies in the field of educational research. Some of their prescriptions are especially stringent, as well as challenging, in research involving vulnerable populations, including children (defined in the United Nations Convention on the Rights of the Child as any person under the age of 18).

BOX 3.2

Ethical Codes and Regulation for Educational Research

The Australian Association for Research in Education's code of ethics (2005, www.aare.edu.au/ethics/ethcfull.htm) starts with detailed statements of principles, drawn eclectically from a range of ethical traditions. These principles include: consideration of the extent to which the consequences of research enhance general welfare; recognition of the variety of views about what counts as a good life and, thus, as educationally worthwhile; and prioritising respect for the dignity, worth and welfare of persons over considerations of public benefit or researchers' interests. The code then concentrates on procedural issues around minimising harm, informed consent and voluntary participation, confidentiality, integrity and social responsibility in carrying out, reporting and publishing research.

The American Educational Research Association's code (2011, www.aera.net/Portals/38/docs/About_AERA/CodeOfEthics(1).pdf) draws on principles of professional competence, integrity, responsibility and respect for people's rights, dignity and diversity. It seeks to set standards for different stages and contexts of research, from research planning to publication and use. The standards include academic practice (e.g. competence and training, contractual issues, conflicts of interests, publication and reviewing, authorship, and academic integrity) and stipulate in great detail the conditions for ensuring informed consent and confidentiality.

The ethical guidelines of the British Educational Research Association (2011, http://bera.dialsolutions.net/system/files/3/BERA-Ethical-Guidelines-2011.pdf) state the association's commitment to 'an ethic of respect for the person, knowledge, democratic values, the quality of educational research, and academic freedom'. They describe procedural requirements, in terms of researchers' responsibilities: to research participants (such as ensuring voluntary informed consent, privacy, the right to withdraw, and avoiding detriment); to sponsors of research; to the community of educational researchers (including appropriate conduct and recognition of authorship); and to educational professionals, policymakers and the general public.

Finally, various funding bodies have also issued ethical standards, which can be highly prescriptive – they go beyond signalling professional values and function as ethical regulation. The UK's Economic and Social Research Council's ethics framework (2012, www.esrc.ac.uk/_images/Framework-for-Research-Ethics_tcm8-4586.pdf) opens with a statement of six 'principles', which are a mixture of moral principles and procedural requirements. It then provides a detailed technical description of ethical procedures and minimum requirements for funded projects. Similarly, the European Commission (http://cordis.europa.eu/fp7/ethics_en.html) has developed an ethical framework that combines a concern for the principles of respect for human dignity, utility, precaution and justice with detailed legal and technical requirements.

3.4 Punch (1994) summarises the main ethical issues in social research as harm, consent, deception, privacy and confidentiality of data. Miles and Huberman (1994: 290–7) have a broader list of 11 ethical issues that typically need attention before, during and after qualitative studies, though many apply to quantitative studies also. Their list includes:

- **Issues arising early in a research project**: the worthiness of the project; competence to carry out the project; informed consent; benefits, costs and reciprocity;
- **Issues arising as the project develops**: harm and risk; honesty and trust; privacy, confidentiality and anonymity; intervention (for example, when wrongful or illegal behaviour is witnessed) and advocacy (for example, for participants' interests);
- **Issues arising later in, or after, the project**: research integrity and quality; ownership of data and conclusions; use and misuse of results.

More recently, Hammersley and Traianou (2012) focus their discussion on the following concerns: risk of harm; autonomy and informed consent; and privacy, confidentiality and anonymity. At the same time, they warn against the dangers of what they see as excessive 'moralism', or 'overdoing' ethics in research (p. 136): they see ethics as a set of values extrinsic to the researchers' core task, which is one of producing knowledge 'in ways that answer worthwhile questions to the required level of likely validity' (pp. 1–2). They recommend a primary focus on 'intrinsic' research virtues, such as objectivity, independence and dedication, as a way to resolve potential tensions between moral values and knowledge aims, or between 'virtue and validity' in research (Figueroa, in Simmons and Usher, 2000: 82).

This section discusses some of the most common requirements placed upon university-based research and highlights some of the ethical challenges in conducting research in educational settings. The discussion will focus on requirements and procedures for the treatment of participants, arising from principles of autonomy, confidentiality and beneficence. Further requirements, such as those concerning academic conduct and misconduct (falsification, plagiarism, exploitation, discrimination, unacceptable publication practice, conflict of interests, etc.), are not discussed here, but are covered at length in the ethical codes described in Box 3.2.

Autonomy

Access to a research setting and/or to secondary data is normally negotiated with relevant gatekeepers (such as, for example, a headteacher in a school). Responsible gatekeeping involves understanding research, sensitivity to the setting and care for the participants. For their part, researchers need to be aware of the complexities of gatekeepers' positions (Homan, 2004). A headteacher, for example, may have to take many factors into account when faced with a request for access to her school, in order to prioritise between competing demands on pupils' and teachers' time.

-EXAMPLE 3.1-

Challenges of Access and Consent

Burgess, R.G. (1989) Grey areas: Ethical dilemmas in educational ethnography. In: R.G. Burgess (ed.) *The Ethics of Educational Research.* **Barcombe: The Falmer Press.**

> 'On gaining access to teacher job interviews I reached an agreement with the head whereby he would either introduce me to all candidates or he will give me an opening to do this for myself. However, I soon found out that this rarely happened in a systematic way. In the first job interviews that I sat in on the head gave me an opportunity to introduce myself to candidates and to ask if they had any objections to me being present. Needless to say, neither of the candidates indicated any objection nor for that matter have any candidates since. However, it is dubious whether this kind of situation can be regarded as constituting informed consent given the power relations involved in the situation. What candidate would risk having me ejected from an interview when it was apparent that the head and the governors had invited me into the situation?' (p. 60)

Read the book: Burgess, R.G. (1983) *Experiencing Comprehensive Education.* **A study of Bishop McGregor School. London: Methuen.**

After access to a setting, the collection of primary data is normally carried out with the explicit consent of participants, or of their legal representatives, in the case of populations where the likelihood of direct consent is questionable, as in the case of children. This requirement is usually termed 'voluntary informed consent', meaning that participants agree freely to be part of research, that they understand what their participation entails and how it will be reported, and that they feel free to withdraw their agreement at any time throughout the research process. Consent can be given actively, through opt-in procedures (such as when participants actively sign and return a consent form at one or several points in the research process – for example, a teacher agreeing to take part in a face-to-face interview); or passively, through opt-out procedures (such as when participants or their representatives only return the form if they decline to take part – for example, parents opting out prior to a questionnaire being distributed to all children in a school).

This process may be more challenging in research conducted in settings where it may be unusual, undesirable or unfeasible to request written confirmation of verbal agreements, such as research in different cultural contexts, research with participants whose levels of literacy may not permit signed consent, or research in virtual environments (Eynon, Fry and Schroeder, 2008). Such research may require more creative ways of documenting consent, such as the recording of verbal agreement or using electronic markers of consent. While documenting consent is important, more important still is ensuring that consent is genuine and is monitored on an ongoing basis, rather than seen as a one-off event that subsequently may become a form of implicit constraint on the participants.

Research in schools and other educational settings comes with its own constraints around procedures for obtaining voluntary informed consent. Some of these complications arise from the asymmetrical nature of educational relationships, others from the variable ability, among potential participants, to offer informed consent. For example, will consent be entirely voluntary when given following a letter or a message from someone in a position of authority, such as the school's headteacher (see Example 3.1)? Will people feel that they are free to say 'no' or to withdraw at any time with no consequences for themselves? What if a teacher researches her own practice – will her pupils be in a position to withhold their assent?

Similarly, how much age-relevant information about a project ought to be offered to potential participants, and what kinds of checks need to be in place to ensure that they understood it, in order to assert confidently that the participants have made an informed decision? Both of these issues are heightened in research that involves children. In this case, common practice is to request consent from the parents or other legal representatives on behalf of the minor; many researchers also secure the minor's assent to participate, and develop protocols for continuous monitoring of assent (particularly in the case of very young children) and plans for taking action if, at any point, that assent is withdrawn.

EXAMPLE 3.2

Food for Thought: Hypothetical Examples

A headteacher gives permission to a researcher to carry out an observational study (involving no A/V recording) of morning assembly in her school, as she believes that the research would benefit teachers and pupils. However, she makes the researcher aware that writing to parents is likely to elicit negative reactions. Will the headteacher's permission suffice in order to carry out the study?

Read more about responsible gatekeepers and privileged access: Homan (1998)

A researcher plans to study primary school children's use of language to construct gender. She has concerns about the validity and authenticity of the study if its aims are disclosed to the children being observed and interviewed. Therefore she decides to seek permission from the teachers and informed consent from the parents (giving both groups full information about the aims and focus of the project), while presenting the study as being about games and friendships to the children. Is her decision justified?

Read more about children's assent and the limits of 'informed' consent/assent: Alderson and Morrow (2011, Chapter 8)

In planning a study set in a tightly-knit community with a strong oral culture and tradition, a researcher becomes aware that seeking individual consent from

(Continued)

(Continued)

members of the community once the consent of a main authority figure (gatekeeper) had been publicly granted might be seen as undermining that authority. In addition, she realises that seeking written consent in addition to verbal consent may be seen as a signal of distrust. Should she insist on documenting written, individual consent?

Read more about ethical challenges of research in different cultural settings: Gomm (2004)

Trust

In their work, researchers are entrusted with information about participants, much of which is of a personal and sensitive nature. There are very clear legal contexts for the recording, storage, archiving and use of some elements of personal data, such as, in the UK, the Data Protection Act 1998. These legal requirements apply to personal data collected for research purposes, as well as to data originally collected for other purposes, but that researchers may wish to access and use in new projects. Ethical regulation, such as that of the ESRC or of the European Commission (Box 3.2), includes detailed recommendations for the recording, storage and archiving of research data in compliance with current legislation.

EXAMPLE 3.3

Challenges of Trust and Confidentiality

Nathan, R. (pseudonym) (2005) An anthropologist goes under cover. *The Chronicle of Higher Education*, 9 July.

'Three years ago, while a tenured professor on sabbatical, I conducted research by enrolling as a freshman in my own university [...]. The semester after I finished my research, I was walking out of a building just as a student from one of my freshman task groups was walking in. We exchanged warm "how you doin'?" small talk. Then my friend asked where I was headed, and I told her that I was going to class.

"What is it?" she asked.

"Oh, an anthropology class ... actually I'm teaching it."

"No kidding!" she exclaimed. "How did you get to do that? I want to take it!"

"Well," I answered sheepishly, "it's 'cause I'm actually a professor, too. I was a student last year to do some research, but now I'm back to being a professor."

"I can't believe that," she responded and then paused. "I feel fooled."'

Read the book: Nathan, R. (2005) *My Freshman Year: What a professor learned by becoming a student*. New York: Cornell University Press.

However, the issues of privacy, anonymity and confidentiality cannot be reduced to mere compliance with predetermined sets of legal and technical requirements. Example 3.2 is based on research that had received ethical clearance, did not use any of the participants' real names and affiliations, and was originally published under a pseudonym, in an attempt to protect participants' identity. As it turned out, such measures were not enough: participants experienced psychological distress, while the cover of anonymity proved flimsy in the longer term.

Privacy refers to individuals' right to control the disclosure of what they deem personal or non-public information about themselves. There is legal provision in many countries to protect the right to privacy (for example, legislation around the disclosure of personal data). The right to privacy may be seen as people's right to be free from any research intervention that they may construe as unwelcome and intrusive, and to withhold any information that they deem personal or sensitive. However, the boundaries around what is considered private may vary in different cultures and across time, as well as in relation to individual life-histories and experience, and are particularly difficult to define in areas such as Internet research (Jones, 2011) or visual research (Wiles et al., 2008).

Researchers need to be alert to the fact that invasions of privacy are possible at all stages of research, from the choice of topic to publication and beyond (for example, in storing, archiving, following up and replicating research). The notion of secrecy, rather than privacy, is often used in relation to collective agents, such as groups, communities and organisations, particularly in situations where expectations of secrecy may clash with demands for public accountability.

Confidentiality arises from respect for the right to privacy, and functions as a 'precautionary principle' (Hammersley and Traianou, 2012: 121). Research interactions, from questionnaires to interviews and observations, are based on respondents' choice to disclose information to the researchers, some of which may be sensitive. In most cases, this disclosure happens in confidence: that is, on the basis of researchers' assurance that the connection between the individual respondent and the information disclosed will not be made known to third parties by the researcher, nor will it be able to be inferred from the research report. In order to achieve this, researchers may decide to only offer aggregate, composite (e.g. 'typical' or 'average' respondents) or fictionalised accounts of the data. They will also make sure that data are stored securely and that access to them is tightly controlled, over the duration of the project and beyond.

However, maintaining confidentiality is not always straightforward. Gatekeepers and other members of a community may use a wide range of contextual clues to infer the identity of people quoted in a research report; for example, a headteacher may be able to infer the identity of individual subject teachers from her school. There may also be situations when keeping information to oneself may be too emotionally challenging for the researcher, or when the researcher may experience conflict between continuing to seek knowledge (thus maintaining secrecy) and refusing to connive with participants at what she sees as morally unacceptable behaviour. Confiding to others in such cases may lead to breaks of confidentiality. In some situations, when the researcher comes across information about criminal activity or dangerous behaviour, for example, she may be legally required to disclose this information to the relevant authorities.

One of the strategies used by researchers to ensure confidentiality (and protect participants from harm) is to remove any information from the data they store and analyse that may make individual respondents easily traceable and identifiable. This strategy is known as *anonymisation*. Commonly-used anonymisation techniques include: deleting personal information (such as names, job title, place of work, name of school, dates and places of crucial events, detailed institutional descriptors, and other information that the researcher deems relevant) from the data or replacing it with aliases and more generic categories; using numerical identifiers; and storing any personal information completely separately from the data.

However, anonymity, in some forms of qualitative research in particular, is often a matter of degree, rather than being clear-cut (Hammersley and Traianou, 2012). For example, in some closed-question survey research that collects no identifying information from the respondents, anonymity (including anonymity to the researchers) can be almost complete. Meanwhile, it is very difficult, if not impossible, to guarantee it in, say, face-to-face in-depth interview research or in visual research. In such cases, non-traceability, rather than full anonymity, may be a more realistic aim. A further complication arises in research situations when participants may actually prefer to be named in the research report, either personally or institutionally. This might be the case when they assert a level of ownership of the material they produced (for example, in some online research or in action research – Simons, 2009), or when there is a concern about possible misrepresentation of participants through anonymised, aggregated or fictionalised accounts (such as in some ethnographic research on personally, institutionally or politically sensitive issues – see Pendlebury and Enslin, 2001 and Walford, 2005).

EXAMPLE 3.4

Food for Thought: Hypothetical Examples

While conducting research with children and their families, a researcher comes across evidence of violent treatment in the home and decides to break the confidentiality agreement and inform the relevant authorities.

Read more about whistle-blowing and disclosure: McNamee and Bridges (2002, Chapter 8), Holmes (1998)

A study of young people's gap year experiences uses blog data. The researcher reasons that – as the blogs are publicly available – no consent procedures are required, but is concerned that some of the bloggers may have written about personal issues and given personal details while not fully aware of how public the information would be once online. She decides that blog URLs and bloggers' names should not be given in her thesis. However, she wonders whether using unattributed quotes may go against some bloggers' likely wish to be recognised for what they wrote in the blog.

Read more about the boundaries between public and private data online: Snee (2010)

Beneficence

Research is commonly expected to minimise the risk of causing harm (*non-malefi-cence*), to carry out worthwhile and potentially beneficial work (*beneficence*) and to distribute any benefits and risks non-discriminatorily throughout a research project and beyond (*fairness*). (For critiques of rationalist, distributive justice models of ethical practice, see Edwards and Mauthner, 2002). Sometimes these aims may pull in different directions, however; for example, an intervention design may at the same time withhold or delay potential benefits from a control group and/or expose the intervention group to unknown risks. Balancing these risks may involve a detailed risk assessment, coupled with identifying an alternative set of benefits to be offered to the control group.

There are many different types of *harm* (or damage) that may be associated with research, such as, at the individual level, physical, psychological, social and reputa-tional, and practical and occupational harm (Hammersley and Traianou, 2012). Those exposed to the risk of harm may be individual participants, their peers, families or acquaintances, but also individual researchers and members of their net-works. Organisations, communities and professions may also be at risk: for example, research and the publication of its outcomes may pose economic threats to an organisation, or bring a professional group into disrepute. The threshold for what counts as more or less severe and long-lasting harm, thus for the perceived accept-ability of different research practices, may vary, historically, culturally and contextu-ally. In addition, not all harms connected to research may be the full responsibility of the researcher; for example, damage may arise from subsequent, hard-to-antici-pate uses of research. Assessing and monitoring risks, seeking consent and confiden-tiality as ongoing rather than one-off events, and taking relevant insurance may help minimise the risk of harm and contain its impact. However, none of these strategies is foolproof; it is not feasible to anticipate and deflect all potential risks, and there may be differences of opinion about the likelihood and seriousness of particular risks among those involved in a project (Example 3.3).

EXAMPLE 3.5

Challenges in Anticipating Harms

Sikes, P. and Piper, H. (2010) *'A courageous proposal, but ... this would be a high risk study': Ethics review procedures, risk and censorship.* In: Sikes and Piper (2010).

'The primary purpose of the ethics procedure that we were subject to is stated to be the protection of potential research participants (and researchers). In our case those participants were specific teachers who had been accused of sexual abuse, members of their families, their colleagues, and people associated with their

(Continued)

---

schools. However, we were being taken to task for failing to protect unknown and, most significantly, hypothetical children who were to play no part in the research process. While we appreciate and accept the need to attempt to anticipate unforeseen consequences arising in the course of, or subsequently to, an actual project, we feel that it is quite another matter to have to try to predict future damage to people who are entirely unconnected to and uninvolved in that research. Such forecasting and pre-empting of problems is, we would suggest, beyond the scope of most mortals. Also, seeking to obviate all possible risk could lead to a situation where only the most anodyne of projects would receive clearance.' (pp. 29–30)

Read the book: Sikes, P. and Piper, H. (2010) *Researching Sex and Lies in the Classroom: Allegations of sexual misconduct in schools.* **Abingdon: Routledge.**

The concept of *benefits* is also complex and situated. Research takes time and effort, and some of that time and effort belongs to the participants, whether they are children and young people, teachers and headteachers, administrators or policymakers. Does the expected outcome of research, both in terms of advancement and corroboration of knowledge and of practical collective or individual benefit, justify the burden placed on participants?

Arguably, the most important benefit of research is the creation of valuable knowledge (Hammersley and Traianou, 2012). As Denzin (1997) argued in relation to ethnography, the act of writing itself, as well as the sharing of the writing with others, can be powerful acts of moral discovery and social and political transformation. Further potential benefits include: learning and educational outcomes and support; therapeutic effects of research; enjoyment and sense of belonging and empowerment; relationships and networking; or services provided by researchers in the setting, for example, in some forms of participatory research (e.g. language teaching, extra-curricular activities, writing and filing documents, driving). Common practices aimed at protecting children and other vulnerable groups are to avoid offering any financial incentives for participation in research (reimbursement of travel expenses does not fall into this category) and to scrutinise carefully the use of any other inducements to recruit and retain participants. Some forms of post-participation *reward*, such as book tokens or participation in educationally worthwhile activities, may be deemed acceptable, depending on circumstances. Certificates of participation in research or stickers (in the case of children), thank you letters or cards, or, as appropriate in light of confidentiality agreements, acknowledgment in publications may also be acceptable forms of non-financial *recognition*. In research with children, regardless of potential benefits, there is an expectation that risk and burden would both be minimal in relation to an ideal 'no harm' situation.

The positioning of the researcher within, or relative to, the field of her research is also important. For example, asks Figueroa, how do researchers' personal values affect their approach to the research, their interpretations and their judgements about ethical courses of action? Further, is it ethical to research a community with which you cannot empathise? (Figueroa, in Simmons and Usher, 2000: 88). Personal values and lack of empathy may make it difficult for researchers to avoid silencing or marginalising particular concerns of the participants (McNamee and Bridges, 2002). Reflexivity in analysis and writing and participant involvement may help alleviate some of these issues.

Depending on the approach taken to research, participants can be engaged in checking interpretations of the data, in seeking alternative interpretations and in exploring their implications. Sometimes, such as in the case of research conducted with vulnerable participants or in disadvantaged communities, it can be very tempting to extend the role of the researcher into political activism, advocacy and support; in other words, to prioritise reciprocity and voice over the articulation and communication of knowledge. This can be a very fulfilling personal project for the researcher, but may make it more difficult to produce and publish a report from the work – hence, to gain a PhD, in the case of doctoral research – and to disengage from the field after the end of a project. The question is how to maintain a balance between rigour in research and care for the participants and their setting.

EXAMPLE 3.6

Food for Thought: Hypothetical Examples

A researcher is working with adolescent girls who had been victims of abuse. She is committed to telling participants' stories in an authentic, credible and convincing way. She sees her role as enabling the voices of these young women to be heard in professional arenas. Her participants see her as empathetic and trustworthy and speak openly to her; the interviews have a therapeutic tone. However, despite her best intentions, after the publication of the report some of the participants feel exposed and experience psychological distress, a sense of betrayal, hurt and outrage.

Read more about activism and voice: Thomson (2008)

An intervention study uses random allocation of 7-year-olds from one school to experimental and control groups. The experimental group receives 6 months of intensive supplementary support for reading, delivered by a trained assistant and using an electronic platform, while the control group continues as before, with no supplementary support. The researchers see this design as a highly efficient way of generating good data, but are concerned about issues of fairness involved in withholding support from the control group for the duration of the intervention.

Read more about benefits to participants: Eynon, Fry and Schroeder (2008)

(Continued)

(Continued)

A researcher uses photographs taken by children in their community. Children and parents have consented to participation in the project and have assigned copyright over the images to the researcher, on the formal understanding that all the faces in the photographs will have been blurred prior to being stored on the researchers' computer. The researchers wish to use the images in the following contexts: (a) in a presentation about research, with no handouts; (b) in the published report; (c) as part of a qualitative data archive, for other researchers to use. They feel that each of these contexts raises distinctive ethical issues and end up using the images on the basis of the original consent in (a), seeking further, image-by-image, consent for (b), and deciding against (c).

Read more about ethical responsibilities in visual research: Wiles et al. (2008).

The ethics of student research as situated deliberation

3.5 Ethical codes vary in structure and content. For example, they may engage more or less explicitly with the moral underpinnings of procedural requirements. In terms of content, they may vary, for example, in how they balance generic rules for academic conduct with principles and rules guiding the relationship between researchers or research institutions and participants and beneficiaries. No code is perfect, and no attempt to apply it to real-life research situations is entirely straightforward.

Therefore, codes leave important spaces for institutions, teams and individual researchers to deliberate about what would be an ethically acceptable course of action in particular research situations and contexts. The link between abstract and general principles and standards and concrete and particular situations is the responsibility of the researchers, who interpret them in the light of values specific to research as a form of practice focused on generating knowledge (Pring, 2004). Hammersley and Traianou see research ethics as 'a form of occupational ethics: it is about what social researchers ought, and ought not, to do *as researchers*, and/or about what count as vices and virtues *in doing research*' (2012: 36).

As explained in this chapter, thinking about ethics in research involves constant questioning of both the aims and means of research, drawing on first-hand understanding of the particular actors and circumstances of a research situation as it unfolds. Justifying ethical decisions is a matter of principled reasoning as well as of active commitment – an ongoing process throughout which researchers need to pay attention to the situation and the ways in which it shapes their judgement. To paraphrase McNamee (McNamee and Bridges, 2002: 13), it is *this* particular researcher (or team) in *this* particular set of circumstances who needs to exercise context-sensitive judgement and embed it in her practice. That is to say, the researcher must identify the ethically salient aspects of a situation and connect

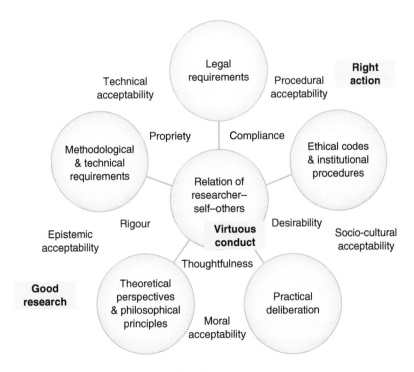

FIGURE 3.1   Research ethics as situated deliberation

them, as appropriate, with principles, rules, outcomes and other cases, in order to act ethically throughout the life span of a research project.

The relationships between the researcher herself (or himself) and others (including relevant communities of research practice) are at the centre of situated ethical deliberation. A researcher may enter a research situation with a range of roles and aims that may be in conflict with each other and which, therefore, need to be negotiated in her research practice. This practice may be subject to many, sometimes contradictory, demands. Figure 3.1 illustrates some of the different demands placed upon research, the criteria of acceptability shaping it and the ethical traditions framing it. To start with, research is subject to legal requirements; it is guided by ethical codes, institutional procedures (such as ethical clearance requirements in universities) and methodological and technical requirements; in the case of student research, it is shaped by course requirements, including definitions of success and assessment criteria. As a form of practice, it is also expected to articulate with other practices, including, in the case of education research, teaching, learning and policymaking. Further, by virtue of its being research, rather than any other form of professional practice, it has epistemic aims and draws on methodological and substantive theories and philosophical approaches. These demands form a space of values that is specific to research, as distinct from other practices. Research that negotiates these different positions and demands successfully while maintaining integrity is deemed 'acceptable' in a range of ways: procedurally, technically, epistemologically, morally and socio-culturally.

The complexity of the contexts and demands illustrated in Figure 3.1 and of the judgements, including moral, required to navigate them suggests that research ethics is more than the linear application of specific rules to get out of dilemmas and to comply with institutional requirements. It involves reflective deliberation that draws on a rich understanding of concrete situations and can employ ways of reasoning and doing that may be associated with more than one tradition of ethics. It can also be experienced as an emotionally-charged process, fraught with indecision, frustration or, sometimes, a sense of guilt. As research ethics concerns not only the treatment of others (from participants and gatekeepers, to peers), but also the self, the ways in which researchers recognise and make sense of these emotions is part of the overall ethical texture of a research project.

Further discussion of ethical issues, focusing specifically on research and the Internet, can be found in Chapter 13.

Chapter summary

- Ethical action in research arises from rich, context-sensitive deliberation at the intersection of practical wisdom, theoretical understanding and principled reasoning.
- Different traditions in philosophical ethics, including duty, consequence, virtue and situated ethics, may help researchers identify the ethically salient aspects of a research situation, reflect on the relative worth of different courses of action available to them, and act ethically throughout the research process.
- Ethical codes and guidelines may offer further resources for ethical deliberation, as well as providing the procedural framework for institutional sanctioning of researchers' chosen courses of action and actual conduct.
- For individual researchers, it is important not just to achieve technical compliance (thus ethical 'approval' or 'clearance') of their projects with ethical codes and other procedural requirements, as stipulated in checklists, guidebooks and forms, but also to develop their personal understanding of ethical principles and contexts, their commitment to ethical research, and the ability to act wisely in ethically complex situations.

KEY TERMS

Ethics: the study of what are good, right or virtuous courses of action; can be approached from different points of view

Deontological ethics: emphasises acting out of duty, as opposed to pleasure, inclination or interest. What is the right course of action in this situation?

Teleological ethics: emphasises choosing the best course of action, using the 'greatest happiness' or 'utility' principle. What course of action in this situation is likely to result in the greatest good for all concerned?

Aretaic ethics: emphasises the most virtuous ways of being and living. What course of action in this situation accords with the traits or dispositions of the virtuous person?

Situational ethics: emphasises that ethical decisions are contextual, and are never neatly defined or fully resolved

Ethical codes: negotiated agreements from professional associations about acceptable practice in particular professional, occupational and institutional contexts; tend to include detailed rules for conducting research

Principle of Autonomy: the obligation on the part of the investigator to respect each participant as a person capable of making an informed decision regarding participation in the research study

Principle of Trust: the obligation of investigators to safeguard the information entrusted to them by participants in the research; includes the principles of confidentiality, privacy and anonymity

Principle of Beneficence: the obligation on the part of the investigator to attempt to maximise benefits for the individual participant and/or society, while minimising risk of harm to the individual

Research ethics as situated deliberation: researchers need to interpret ethical codes – which often include abstract principles and standards – in the context of particular research situations

Exercises and study questions

1. Describe what is meant by these:
   - Deontological approach to ethical issues
   - Teleological approach to ethical issues
   - Aretaic approach to ethical issues
   - Situational approach to ethical issues

2. Apply each of these four approaches to the six hypothetical examples shown in the two boxes labelled 'Food for Thought' (p. 59 and p. 65). What conclusions do the different approaches lead to for each of the six situations?

3. What similarities do you see in these four approaches? What differences do you see?

4. Study one of the codes of ethics for education research referred to in Box 3.2. How helpful would this code be in resolving ethical issues in your proposed research? What difficulties would it lead to?

5. Read through the codes of ethics for research in another area of social science – for example, The British Sociological Association (www.britsoc.co.uk/media/27107/StatementofEthical-Practice.pdf) or The American Psychological Association (www.apa.org/ethics/code/index.aspx). To what extent do you think they are helpful? What difficulties do you think they might lead to? Does anything you read there surprise you?

Further reading

Alderson, P. and Morrow, V. (2011) *The Ethics of Research with Children and Young People: A Practical Handbook*. London: SAGE.

Hammersley, M. and Traianou, A. (2012) *Ethics in Qualitative Research*. London: SAGE.

Jones, C. (2011) *Ethical issues in online research*. British Educational Research Association online resource. www.bera.ac.uk.

Simons, H. (2009) 'Whose data are they?' In: *Case Study Research in Practice*. London: SAGE.

Snee, H. (2010) *Using Blog Analysis*. NCRM Realities Toolkit 10. Online at http://eprints.ncrm.ac.uk/1321/2/10-toolkit-blog-analysis.pdf.

Walford, G. (2005) 'Research ethical guidelines and anonymity', *International Journal of Research and Method in Education*, 28(1): 83–93.

Wiles, R., Prosser, J., Bagnoli, A., Clark, A., Davies, K., Holland, S., and Renold, E. (2008) *Visual Ethics: Ethical Issues in Visual Research*. ESRC National Centre for Research Methods Review Paper. Southampton: NCRM. Online at: http://eprints.ncrm.ac.uk/421/1/MethodsReviewPaper NCRM-011.pdf.

World Medical Association (WMA) (2000) *Declaration of Helsinki*.

four
RESEARCH QUESTIONS

Contents

As a finished product, a piece of empirical research needs to demonstrate both conceptual clarity and a good fit between its different component parts, especially between its questions and its methods. For the report of completed research, the order in which things were done does not matter, only that there is this conceptual clarity and good fit. This can be achieved in different ways – the questions can be developed first, and the methods aligned; or the research might begin with only a general approach to its topic, and then develop focus in the questions and methods as things proceed; or there might be a mixture of these two, where the researcher cycles backwards and forwards between questions, methods and some initial data.

Because empirical research is driven by research questions, the next two chapters describe a model of research with well-developed research questions 'up front'. This is a good model for learning about research, making it easy to see the connections between questions, concepts and data, and thereby promoting fit and conceptual clarity. As a model, it is worth aiming at – if it is rejected as not appropriate, the reasons for that rejection are helpful in understanding the area, and in tailoring a more suitable approach. This helps to clarify where on the continuum of structure the researcher wants to be. This position can then be articulated to ensure that the approach to design and data fits with it.

Miles, Huberman and Saldana (2013) point out that developing research questions is a valuable defence against the confusion and overload that is possible in the early stages of research. Often, also, the researcher can make considerable progress towards identifying specific research questions, particularly when professional knowledge about the topic is brought to the research. However, when research questions emerge during the project rather than in advance of it, the need for conceptual clarity and fit still arises, and therefore the issues in these next two chapters remain relevant. They do not disappear, they simply arise later.

A hierarchy of concepts

4.1 One advantage of planning research in terms of research questions is that it makes explicit the idea of levels of abstraction in research. We can distinguish five levels of concepts and questions, which vary in levels of abstraction, forming an inductive–deductive hierarchy:

- research area;
- research topic;
- general research question(s);
- specific research questions;
- data collection questions.

To say these five things form a hierarchy is to say that they vary systematically in levels of abstraction and generality, and that they need to be connected to each other logically, by induction and deduction, across these levels. The top level is the most general and the most abstract. The bottom level is the most specific and the most concrete.

Thus, from the top down, the research area is more general than the research topic, which itself is more general than the general research question(s), which are more general than the specific research questions, which in turn are more general than the data collection questions. Another way of saying this, and now moving from the bottom up, is that the data collection questions follow on from the specific research questions, which in turn follow on from the general research questions, and so on up the hierarchy.

A benefit of thinking this way, and of planning and organising research this way, is that it exposes and highlights the links between these different levels of abstraction. It is necessary to have tight logical links between these levels for the research to have internal consistency, coherence and validity. This is what is meant by 'follow on from' in the paragraph above. The processes involved here are deduction and induction. We move downwards in the hierarchy by deduction, and upwards by induction. Both processes are governed by logic.

Not all research projects can be organised or planned in this way. In particular, those that have a more unfolding design would not fit easily with this prestructured approach. There are also issues about 'generalising' versus 'particularising' research questions (Maxwell, 2012),[1] and the intended emphasis on one of these types of questions or the other in a particular study. At the same time, however, very many projects do fit well into this approach, and, in any case, this hierarchy of concepts is useful both pedagogically and practically. Not only does thinking in these terms help to organise the developing proposal, it also helps you to communicate clearly about your research, and to write the proposal (and, later on, the dissertation).

Research areas and topics

4.2 Research areas are usually stated in a few words, and sometimes just one word. Topics similarly are a few words, but usually more than those describing the research area. The topic falls within the area. It is an aspect, or part,

TABLE 4.1   From research area to research topics

Research area
Youth suicide.

Four possible research topics
1 Suicide rates among different groups.
2 Factors associated with the incidence of youth suicide.
3 Managing suicide behaviour among teenagers.
4 Youth culture and the meaning of suicide.

Note
Topics 1 and 2 imply a predominantly quantitative approach.
Topics 3 and 4 imply a predominantly qualitative approach.

of the area; a step towards making the general area more specific. It is included in the area, but it is, of course, not the only topic within the area.

Examples of research areas are absenteeism from school, youth culture, job satisfaction, workplace conflict, change in organisations, decision making, emotional dissonance and youth suicide. Four possible research topics within the research area 'youth suicide' are shown in Table 4.1. This chapter shows how to develop topics and research questions for the research area. Let's take, for example, the area of youth suicide.

Identifying first the research area, and then the topic within the area, immediately gives a first level of focus to the research, a first narrowing of the possibilities. Of course, any research area includes many topics, so two decisions are involved here – the first is the selection of an area, the second is the selection of a topic within the area. Most of the time students have little difficulty with the first decision, the area. They know generally what research area they are interested in. Often, they have rather more difficulty with the second decision: With all these possible topics within this area, which should I choose?

A valuable consequence of identifying the research area is that it enables you as the researcher immediately to connect your work to the literature. It defines a body of literature as relevant to this piece of research. Identifying a topic within an area gives still more specific direction to the literature. It enables a more specific body of literature to be identified as centrally relevant to the research.

General and specific research questions

4.3 General and specific research questions bring things down to the next level of specificity, further narrowing the focus of the proposed research. The distinction between them is in terms of specificity. General research questions are broader, more general, more abstract and (usually) are not themselves directly answerable because they are too general. Specific research questions are more specific, detailed and concrete. They are directly answerable because they point directly

TABLE 4.2   From research topic to general research questions

Research topic:
Factors associated with the incidence of youth suicide.
General research question 1
What is the relationship between family background factors and the incidence of youth suicide?

General research question 2
What is the relationship between school experience factors and the incidence of youth suicide?

Note
More general research questions are possible. These are only two examples. As noted in Table 4.1, this topic and these general questions have a quantitative bias.

at the data needed to answer them. This point is elaborated in Section 5.1 in the next chapter.

General research questions guide our thinking, and are of great value in organising the research project. Specific research questions follow from, and fit in with, the general question(s). They direct the empirical procedures, and they are the questions that are actually answered directly by the data in the research. It is useful in planning to identify and separate the general and the specific research questions.

Just as there are many research topics within a research area, so there are many possible general research questions within a research topic. Specific research questions take the deductive process further, subdividing a general question into the specific questions that follow from it.

A general question is normally too broad to be answered directly, too broad to satisfy the empirical criterion for research questions (see Section 5.1). Its concepts are too general. It therefore requires logical subdivision – or 'unpacking' – into several specific research questions. The general research question is answered indirectly by accumulating and integrating the answers to the corresponding specific research questions. A study may well have more than one general research question. In that case, each will require analysis and subdivision into appropriate specific research questions. Tables 4.2 and 4.3 illustrate this process with the research area 'youth suicide'.

This distinction is really a matter of common sense, and, in the practical business of planning research, is not difficult to make. And, as already noted, while the description here is presented deductively, it is by no means necessary for things to proceed that way. They may also proceed inductively, and, as is probably most common, by some cyclical and iterative mixture of induction and deduction.

In practical terms, a good way to distinguish general from specific research questions is to apply the empirical criterion (see Section 5.1) to each question, as it is developed. This criterion asks: Is it clear what data will be required to answer this research question? If the answer for each research question is yes, we can proceed from questions to data and methods. If the answer is no, one thing probably needed is further specificity. This criterion is also a good check on deciding whether we have reached a set of researchable questions.

Genereal research question
What is the relationship between family background factors and the incidence of youth suicide?

Specific research question 1
What is the relationship between family income and the incidence of youth suicide?
or
Do youth suicide rates differ between families of different income levels?

Specific research question 2
What is the relationship between parental break-up and the incidence of youth suicide?
or
Do youth suicide rates differ between families where parents are divorced or separated, and families where they are not?

Note
More specific research questions are possible. These are only two examples

At the heart of this discussion is the process of making a general concept more specific by showing its dimensions, aspects, factors, components or indicators. In effect, you are defining a general concept 'downwards' towards its data indicators – you are unpacking it. Of the several terms shown above (dimensions, aspects, factors components, indicators), I prefer the term *indicators* because of its wide applicability across different types of research. It applies in quantitative and qualitative contexts, whereas the terms dimensions, factors and components have more quantitative connotations.

A caveat, more likely to be needed in qualitative studies, is that the research may proceed upwards in abstraction from indicators to general concepts, rather than downwards in abstraction from general concepts to indicators. To repeat, the important thing is not which way the research proceeds. You can proceed downwards, using deduction, from general concept to specific concept to indicators, or you can proceed upwards, using induction, from indicators to specific and general concepts. Or deduction and induction can both be used. The important thing is that the finished product as a proposal (and, ultimately, as a piece of research) shows logical connections across the different levels of abstraction.

Data collection questions

4.4 At the lowest level in this hierarchy come data collection questions. They are questions at the most specific level.

The reason for separating out data collection questions here is that students sometimes confuse research questions with data collection questions. A research question is a question the research itself is trying to answer. A data collection question is a question that is asked to collect data to help answer the research question. In this sense, it is more specific still than the research question. In this sense too, more than one data collection question, sometimes several and sometimes many, will be involved in assembling the data necessary to answer one research question.[2]

What does this hierarchy of concepts mean for research proposal development? I have gone into this detailed analysis because it is often a central aspect of the pre-empirical, setting-up stage of the research, and because it shows clearly the differing levels of abstraction. Understanding this hierarchy of concepts is important, but it is unlikely to be applicable, formula-like, in proposal development. As already noted, the question development stage is likely to be messy, iterative and cyclical, and it can proceed in any way at all.[3] But if you are aware of this hierarchy, you can use it to help disentangle and organise the many questions that serious considera-tion of almost any research area and topic will produce.

Developing research questions

4.5 One way to get to research questions is to identify a research area and topic, and then develop questions within that area and topic, working deductively from general to specific questions. Another is more inductive – to begin with some specific questions, and to work from these back to more general questions.

Sometimes the more abstract concepts of research area and topic, and general and specific research questions, are not enough to get the process of identifying and developing research questions started. When that happens, it is good to focus on the question 'What are we trying to find out?' The focus on this question almost always shows that there is 'much more here than meets the eye'. The topic expands, and many questions are generated. What perhaps seemed simple and straightforward becomes more complicated, many-sided and full of possibilities. This can happen whether the researcher proceeds deductively or inductively. On the one hand, any research area, when fully analysed, will yield many research questions, general and specific. On the other, any research question, when carefully considered, will gener-ate others, and they in turn will generate more.

What sort of work is this, in the question development stage? First, it is generat-ing possibilities. Answers to the question 'What are we trying to find out?' are pro-visional at this stage. We do not want to get to a final set of questions too quickly, because we might overlook possibilities. Generating possibilities should not be end-less, but we do want to allow enough time to see what the possibilities are. Second, it is a mixture of question subdivision, where we split a general question into its component parts, and of disentangling the different questions from each other. Third, it is ordering these questions, and progressively developing focus.

It is usually an iterative process to get a stable view of what one is trying to find out. There are benefits to doing some of this work with others – another student, or a small group, which might include supervisor(s), colleagues or other researchers. Others will often see possible questions that the individual researcher might miss, and discussion with others can also be a stimulus to think more deeply, and perhaps differently, about the topic.

What generally happens after a period of question development is that the whole thing has expanded, sometimes greatly. This can cause anxiety, but for most projects it should happen. In fact, if it does not, we should probably be concerned, since it may be a sign of insufficient question development work. Therefore, it is to be encouraged, within reason, as an important stage. Probing, exploring and seeing other possibilities within a topic can be valuable before reaching closure on the specific directions for a project.

When a small set of starting questions has multiplied into a larger set, disentangling and ordering are required. Disentangling is necessary because one question will often have other questions within it. Ordering involves categorising, and the grouping of questions together. This will soon become hierarchical, and general and specific research questions begin to be distinguishable from each other.

The final stage then involves bringing the project down to size, since it has usually become too big. In fact, it probably suggests a research programme with several research projects by now. How is this trimming done? It is important to decide which questions are manageable within the practical constraints of this project, and which seem the most important. There are of course limits around any project – even if that project involves a grant and a team of researchers. The principle here is that it is better to do a smaller project thoroughly than a larger project superficially. Trimming a project down to size is a matter of judgement, and experience in research has a big role to play here. Once again, therefore, this stage is best done in collaboration with others.

How many research questions should there be? There are practical limitations on any one project, and, as stated above, it is better to have a small job done thoroughly than a large job done only superficially. More than about three or four general research questions, assuming that each is subdivided into (say) two or three specific questions, tests the upper limit of what can be done in one study.[4]

This question development stage is pre-empirical, in the sense that we are not yet really focusing on issues of method, which come later. As far as possible, we are following the rule to put substantive or content issues before methodological issues. Method questions will always intrude to some extent, but there is value during this stage in keeping them at arm's length. The questions 'How will I do this?' or 'Should I use this method or that method?' are important, but the point here is that they can come too early.

During this planning stage, there is benefit to 'hastening slowly'. Since research questions almost never come out right the first time, several iterations are often required, and we only reach an answer to the question 'What are we trying to find out?' after careful thought. This question development stage needs time – time to see the possible questions buried in an area and to see related questions that follow from an analysis of particular questions. The setup stage of the research is important, for the decisions taken here will influence what is done in later stages. This does not mean that the decisions cannot be varied, as when iteration towards the final research questions goes on during the early empirical stages of the project. But varying them should not be done lightly if considerable effort has been invested in reaching them during the setup stage.

Focusing on what we are trying to find out is useful not only at this stage, but at all stages of research. It helps to keep things focused during planning, design and execution of the project – especially during data analysis – and it helps in the writing-up of the research report.

The role of research questions

4.6 Research questions are central. They do five main things:

- they organise the project, and give it direction and coherence;
- they delimit the project, showing its boundaries;
- they keep the researcher focused during the project;
- they provide a framework for writing up the project;
- they point to the data that will be needed.

The third point (keeping focused during the project) requires a comment. Research can get complicated, and it is therefore easy for any of us to get lost on the way through a project. Clearly stated research questions have great value in bringing the research back on track in those situations when complications or side issues threaten to take it off course. Being able to step back from the complications and details, and to refer again to research questions, can be of great assistance.

The last point above, indicating what data will be necessary in the project, is the empirical criterion, to be discussed in Chapter 5. The idea is that a well-asked question itself indicates what data will be necessary to answer it. This brings up again the distinction between a research question and a data collection question. A research question is a question that guides the project, and which the research is designed to answer. A data collection question is more specific again, and is a question that is asked (very often in a survey questionnaire or interview) to provide data relevant to a research question.

Chapter 5 also discusses conceptual frameworks. The conceptual framework shows the conceptual status of the factors, variables or phenomena we are working with, usually in diagram form. Developing the research questions often involves developing a conceptual framework for the research as well. These two things do not have to go together, but it can be very useful when they do. This is because developing the questions often brings into focus the (implicit) conceptual framework we are using in our thinking about the topic. When this is the case, it is a good idea to make this framework explicit. The research questions then operationalise the conceptual framework, pointing ahead to the data. In quantitative research, this is usually very clear, and it is taken for granted that the conceptual framework for the study will be shown. Developing a conceptual framework can be very useful in qualitative research as well, focusing and delimiting the study, and giving direction to the sampling decisions that will be required. Examples of conceptual frameworks are given in Chapter 5.

To this point, this chapter has dealt with identifying and developing the research questions, and their central role in a project. It is time now to consider the hypothesis, and what role it has in research.

Hypotheses

4.7 Complicated definitions of the hypothesis can be found in some of the older social science research methodology literature (Brodbeck, 1968; Nagel, 1979; Kerlinger, 1999), but these will not be used here. Instead, I will use the simple definition of the hypothesis as a predicted answer to a research question. To say we have a hypothesis is to say we can predict what we will find in answer to a question. We make this prediction before we carry out the research – *a priori*. A specific research question states what we are trying to find out. The hypothesis predicts, *a priori*, the answer to that question.

On what basis can we make such a prediction? Why do we expect to find this (what we predict), rather than something else? In general, there are only two answers to this last question. One is: Because another researcher did some similar research and this is what was found. While this answers the question, it does not explain the prediction. The other answer to 'Why predict this?' involves an explanation. Propositions are put forward which explain why the predicted answer (the hypothesis) can be expected. We can call this set of propositions a 'theory'. It fits the description of substantive theory given in Chapter 2 (Section 2.2).

In this case, we have a theory, which explains the hypothesis, and from which the hypothesis follows, by deduction, as an if–then proposition. If the theory is true, then the hypothesis follows. So, in executing the research and testing the hypothesis, we are actually testing the theory behind the hypothesis. This is the classical hypothetico-deductive model of research. In passing, we should note that it shows why theories cannot be proved, only disproved. We cannot prove the 'if' part (the theory) by validating the 'then' part (the hypothesis).[5] This is why it is often pointed out that scientific knowledge develops by disproving its theories (Popper, 2002).

Two points follow from viewing the structure of knowledge and the structure of inquiry in this way. The first concerns the role of hypotheses in empirical research. We should only have hypotheses when it is appropriate to do so. When is that? When we do have an explanation (a theory) in mind behind our hypotheses. If this is the case, we should by all means formulate hypotheses as predicted answers to research questions, and test them. If not, we can ignore hypotheses and proceed with research questions. After all, there is no logical difference between research questions and research hypotheses, when it comes to their implications for the empirical operations of design, data collection and data analysis.

Therefore there is a simple procedure for determining whether it is appropriate to have hypotheses. Once we have specific research questions, we can routinely ask, of each one, and before carrying out the research: 'What answer do we expect (or predict) to this question?' If we cannot predict with any confidence, we need go no further into the matter of hypotheses, and we can proceed instead with research questions. If we can predict, we next ask: 'Why do we predict this (and not something else)?' If the only answer to that question is 'Because some other researcher found it to be true', again we do not need to propose hypotheses. If, however, we really do have some explanation in mind, from which the predicted answer(s) follow, then there is value in proposing hypotheses, and exposing and analysing the theory behind them. In testing the hypotheses, we are then testing the theory. The hypothesis has a central role in the testing of theories, and it should not be divorced from this role. This means that there is no point in putting forward hypotheses for testing unless we can also put forward the theory behind them.

The second implication of this way of seeing the hypothesis concerns the overall structure of scientific knowledge, and takes us back to the diagram about that shown in Figure 2.1 in Chapter 2. The structure shown in that diagram illustrates the point made above, that a hypothesis is derived from, and explained by, the higher order theory above it. It also shows the hierarchical structure of knowledge, with increasing levels of power, abstraction and generality towards the top of the diagram, and the central role of empirical generalisations. This view of the hypothesis, its relationship to research questions and to the theory behind it, shows, in microcosm, the same structure. This underlines the point that there are concepts and propositions at different levels of abstraction in a research project, and therefore that there need to be logical links between these different levels of abstraction.

Hypotheses are given a very prominent place in some research methods books, especially quantitative ones (for example, see Burns, 2000), but that is not the case here. The sequence of ideas shown above helps in understanding the role and place of the hypothesis, and enables judgements about the appropriateness of hypotheses in a study. If appropriate, we can use them. If not, the study is better kept at the level of research questions. There is no point in simply having hypotheses for their own sake. What is useful in all cases is to go through the above questioning sequence, once the research questions are settled, asking whether the answer to each research question can be predicted, and, if so, on what basis.

A simplified model of research

4.8 Whether or not hypotheses are appropriate, organising research around research questions, and insisting that each question conforms to the empirical criterion described in the next chapter, leads to the simple model of the research process shown in Chapter 1, but now with two versions, as shown in Figure 4.1.

This simplified model of research stresses:

- framing the research in terms of research questions;
- determining what data are necessary to answer these questions;
- designing research to collect and analyse these data;
- using the data to answer the questions.

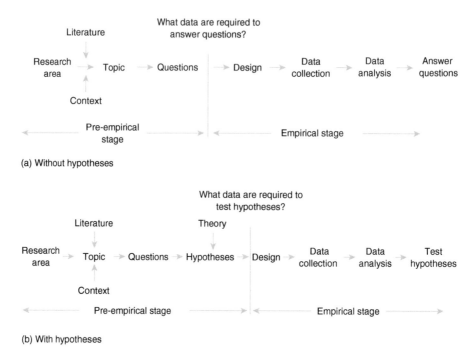

Figure 4.1 Simplified model of research

The model in the upper part of the diagram shows research questions without hypotheses. The model in the lower part shows research questions with hypotheses. The model is essentially the same in both cases.

Based on this model of research, we can see that two overall questions guide the research planning process. They are also the questions around which the research proposal can be written, and later and with some additions, the research report. The questions are the straightforward ones of:

- **What? (What questions is the research trying to answer? What is the research trying to find out?)**
- **How? (How will the research answer these questions?)**

This chapter and the next deal with ways of answering the 'What' question. Chapters 7 to 12 concentrate on the 'How' question, first for qualitative research, then for quantitative research. There is also a third question:

- **Why? (Why are these questions worth answering? Why is this research worth doing?)**

This question concerns the justification for doing the research, and is discussed in Chapter 15. This model of research helps to organise the planning, execution and writing up of the research. Especially during planning, it also helps to counter overload and possible confusion. It is effective with quantitative, qualitative and mixed methods research. It needs modification where prespecified research questions are not possible or desirable, and where the plan is that they will be developed as the early empirical work provides focus. In those cases, as noted earlier, it is still worth keeping this model in mind, in order to see where and why it is not appropriate. When research questions are developed as the research becomes more focused, the analytic process described in this chapter is delayed. It comes after some empirical work, not before. When this happens, question development will be influenced by the initial data. Otherwise, it is much the same process, and just as important for ensuring the fit between the parts of the research.

The role of the literature

4.9 The appropriate point in the planning process at which to concentrate on the literature is something that may well vary in different styles of research. In a traditional model of research, the literature is reviewed (often comprehensively) as part of the research planning and question development stage. The literature itself becomes an input to the analysis and planning during this stage. This is the recommended way to proceed in many research situations, and it has been the model typically followed in quantitative research and in some types of qualitative research. At the other end of the scale, we might have, for example, a grounded theory study, where the literature coverage is deliberately delayed until directions emerge from the early analysis of data. The literature is brought in later, and treated as further data for analysis. The reason for this, as explained in Chapter 7, is that the researcher wants categories and concepts to emerge from the data – to be fully grounded in the data – rather than to be brought to the data from the literature. If these two examples are the two ends of a scale, there are obviously points in between, which combine elements of the two approaches.

It is a matter of judgement at what point to concentrate on the literature. Factors involved in this judgement include the style of the research, the overall research strategy, what the objectives of the proposed study are, the nature of the substantive problem and how much is known about it, how well developed the literature in the area is, and how closely this study wants to follow the directions established by this literature. A further important factor is the professional or experiential knowledge that the researcher already has, especially when the research topic comes from practice or experience.

In different areas of social science research, many topics and questions come from the world of professional practice, and are often set in organisational, institutional, community or public settings. Often, also, the researcher is a professional practitioner, or closely connected with professional practice, in this setting. In such a situation, the researcher has considerable knowledge about the topic, before commencing the research. This knowledge can be used as a starting point for the question development work described earlier. This involves exploring and articulating that knowledge, an activity that will often be valuable to the individual in encouraging reflection about the issue. For the research itself, this knowledge is a valuable input to the research planning process. Maxwell (2012) offers some specific suggestions for dealing with 'experiential knowledge', and gives the example (pp. 32–34) of an 'experience memo' on the subject of diversity.

In such cases, there is often some benefit in delaying for a while the use of the literature, during the question development stage. There is benefit, in other words, to doing a certain amount of work on developing the questions (and perhaps the conceptual framework) before consulting the literature. This is because the literature will usually influence this process, and we may want to minimise or delay this influence. Of course, the literature can be a fruitful source of concepts, theories and evidence about a topic, but it can also influence how we look at a topic, thereby precluding the development of some new way. Chapter 6 deals with searching and reviewing the literature. Before that, Chapter 5 discusses the relationship between research questions and data.

Chapter summary

A hierarchy of concepts can help in planning and organising research. From most general to most specific, the hierarchy is:

- Research area
- Research topic
- General research question(s)
- Specific research questions
- Data collection questions.

- Planning research can proceed downwards through the hierarchy (by deduction), upwards through it (by induction), or both. Good research shows tight logical links between the different levels in the hierarchy.
- Developing research questions is usually a process of generating possible questions, subdividing them, then disentangling and ordering them. Careful work through this pre-empirical stage helps build internally consistent research.
- A hypothesis can be defined as a predicted answer to a research question. It stands in an if–then relationship to explanatory theory. This leads to a straightforward questioning sequence to determine when hypothesis-testing research is appropriate.
- A simple but robust model of research can be built around two key questions: What questions is the research trying to answer? How will it answer these questions?
- Very often, a literature review precedes and is part of the development of research questions. At other times, it may be better to delay reviewing literature until a more appropriate stage of the research planning.

KEY TERMS

Hierarchy of concepts: research area; research topic; general research question(s); specific research questions; data collection questions

Levels of abstraction: different levels of generality and specificity – more general means more abstract, more specific means more concrete

Deduction: from a more general to a more specific level

Induction: from a more specific to a more general level

Data collection questions: survey and interview questions to collect data

Hypotheses: predicted answers to research questions

Hypothesis-testing research: research which aims to test hypotheses, which ideally are derived from an explanatory theory

Exercises and study questions

1. What does 'hierarchy' in 'hierarchy of concepts' mean? What is its relationship to induction and deduction?
2. Identify four different areas of research in your field of social science.
3. This chapter shows how to develop topics and research questions for the research area of youth suicide. Follow this example to develop topics and research questions for the research areas you have identified in (2) above.
4. Identify different specific dimensions for these general concepts: educational achievement, job satisfaction, alienation from the workplace, self-esteem, leadership style.
5. What are data collection questions, and how do they differ from research questions?
6. Take one of the general concepts in exercise 4 above. Using the dimensions you identified, formulate one or more research questions for each dimension. Then develop some data collection questions for (a) qualitative interviews and (b) quantitative surveys which can help you answer the research questions.
7. Why are research questions important in a research proposal?
8. What is a hypothesis, and what is its relationship to theory? Describe hypothesis-testing research.
9. What examples of theory–hypothesis relationships can you find in your field of social science?

Further reading

Babbie, E. (2012) *The Practice of Social Research*. 13th edn. Belmont, CA: Wadsworth.

Brewer, J. and Hunter, A. (2005) *Foundations of Multimethod Research: A Synthesis of Styles*. Thousand Oaks, CA: SAGE.

Campbell, J.P., Daft, R.L. and Hulin, C.L. (1982) *What to Study: Generating and Developing Research Questions*. Beverly Hills, CA: SAGE.

Clark, A.W. (1983) *Social Science: Introduction to Theory and Method*. Sydney: Prentice-Hall.

Marshall, C. and Rossman, G.B. (2010) *Designing Qualitative Research*. 5th edn. Thousand Oaks, CA: SAGE.

Maxwell, J.A. (2012) *Qualitative Research Design: An Interactive Approach*. 3rd edn. Thousand Oaks, CA: SAGE.

Miles, M.B., Huberman, A.M. and Saldana, J. (2013) *Qualitative Data Analysis*. 3rd edn. Thousand Oaks, CA: SAGE.

Neuman, W.L. (2010) *Social Research Methods: Qualitative and Quantitative Approaches.* 7th edn. Harlow: Pearson.

Punch, K.F. (2006) *Developing Effective Research Proposals.* 2nd edn. London: SAGE.

Notes

1. A generalising question seeks nomothetic knowledge–universalised law-like statements applying generally across a class of people, situations, events or phenomena. A particularising question seeks ideographic knowledge – local, case-based, specific propositions.

2. This does not apply literally to all data collection questions that might be used in a study. Thus some data collection questions might themselves be quite general questions – for example, introductory or 'grand tour' questions in a qualitative research interview. But the point being made here is that the role of most data collection questions is to operate at the most specific level. As Maxwell (2012) says, research questions identify what you want to understand; interview questions, as data collection questions, provide the data you need to understand these things. The same is true of survey questions in quantitative research. Being the most specific level of questions, the actual data collection questions will probably not be shown in a proposal.

3. Locke et al. (1993: 99) give examples of this question development process, including inductively and deductively. Maxwell (2012), writing for qualitative research, makes distinctions between research questions (generalising–particularising, instrumentalist–realist, variance–process). He also gives an example of the development of research questions and gives an exercise to assist in this (pp. 83–86).

4. Miles and Huberman are more ambitious: they suggest that asking more than a dozen or so general research questions is 'looking for trouble' (1994: 25).

5. To claim to do so is to commit the logical fallacy of 'affirming the consequent'.

five
FROM RESEARCH QUESTIONS TO DATA

Contents

The empirical criterion

5.1 The essential idea of the empirical criterion for research questions is that a well-stated research question indicates what data will be necessary to answer it. It is useful to apply this criterion to all research questions, as they are developed. Another way of saying this is that 'a question well asked is a question half answered' – the way a well-asked research question is stated indicates what data will be necessary to answer it. Since empirical research means collecting data, we will not know how to proceed if the research questions do not give clear indications of the data needed to answer them.

This criterion applies most clearly to prespecified research questions. What about when there are no clearly prespecified research questions – where, instead, the research strategy is for the questions to emerge? There still has to be a close fit between questions and data, but now, rather than questions leading to data, we may have data leading to questions. In fact, it is more likely that there will be a 'reciprocal interaction' between the questions and the data. In this sort of unfolding situation, the question identification and question development processes are delayed. Instead of before the research, these processes come in later, with the data influencing the way the questions are identified and developed. But it is still important that the questions and the data fit with each other.

Linking concepts and data

5.2 Empirical research requires the linking of data to concepts, which means connecting a concept to its empirical indicators. In quantitative research, where the concepts are variables, this idea is described as operationalism. Variables have conceptual definitions, where they are defined using abstract concepts, followed by operational definitions, where they are connected by means of empirical operations to data indicators. The same idea applies in qualitative research, but comes up in the analysis of data.

The empirical criterion stresses the link between research questions and data, and between concepts and their empirical indicators. This link is an important part of the fit between the different parts of a research project. It is also part of the overall logical chain within a piece of research. Tight logical connections are needed between all levels of abstraction in this chain. Figure 2.1 in Chapter 2 shows the different levels of abstraction in theories, empirical generalisations and first order facts. First order facts are very concrete, whereas empirical generalisations use abstract concepts, and theories use even more abstract concepts. There must be firm connections between concepts at each level of abstraction in this hierarchical structure.

We can illustrate these points using Charters' example in his discussion of the hypothesis, remembering that a hypothesis is a predicted answer to a research question. Charters (1967) shows propositions at different levels of generality, and demonstrates the need for logical links between those levels.[1]

Theoretical Proposition: Aggression occurs when a person is frustrated in getting to his *[sic]* goals. That is, whenever a person is prevented from getting something he wants, an aggressive urge arises within him that induces him to behave aggressively towards the party responsible for his frustration.

Conceptual Hypothesis: Elementary school children who are prevented by their teacher from going to recess on a sunny day will express greater hostility in their remarks to the teacher during the remainder of the school day than elementary school children who are not prevented by the teacher from going to recess, other things being equal.

Operational Hypothesis: The ratio of 'hostile' to 'non-hostile' remarks made by pupils and classified as 'directed towards teacher', based upon the observation of classroom interaction by a trained observer between 2.00 and 3.30 in the afternoon of sunny days, will be significantly lower under Condition A (27 second grade pupils in Hawthorne School whose teacher said, 'You may go to recess now') than under Condition B (36 second grade pupils in Hawthorne School whose teacher said, 'Instead of going to recess today, I think we had better work some more on spelling').

In a tightly prefigured quantitative study such as is used in this example, the linking of concepts and data is done ahead of the empirical work of data collection and analysis. The link is made *from concepts to data*. In the language of quantitative research, the variables are operationally defined. In a more 'open-ended' qualitative study, say a grounded theory study, this linking is done during the empirical work. In fact, one purpose of such a study is to develop concepts linked to, or grounded in, the data. In this sort of study, the link is made *from data to concepts*. Earlier, in the comparison between theory verification and theory generation research, I used Wolcott's theory-first or theory-after description. Here, it is concepts-first or concepts-after. Whenever it is done, before or during the empirical part of the research, the careful linking is necessary, and the principles are the same. These same points are stressed by Lewins (1992).

It is useful to apply the empirical criterion to all research questions. When all questions satisfy this criterion, we are ready to move from content to method.

When research questions fail the test of this criterion, one of two situations will usually apply. Either we have more conceptual–analytic question–development work to do, which means that the questions are most likely still not specific enough. This is typical of questions that are being developed deductively, from the general to the specific. Or we have research questions that are faulty in some way. This leads to the topic of good and bad research questions.

Good and bad research questions

5.3 It follows from Chapter 4 that good research questions are:

- clear – they can be easily understood and are unambiguous;
- specific – their concepts are at a specific enough level to connect to data indicators;
- empirical, in the sense that they are answerable with data – we can see what data are required to answer them and how the data will be obtained;
- interconnected – they are related to each other in some meaningful way, rather than being unconnected;
- substantively relevant – they are interesting and worthwhile questions for the investment of research effort.

Bad research questions fail to satisfy one or more of these criteria. Often, this is because they are either unclear and not specific enough, or they fail on the test of the empirical criterion, which is expressed in the second and third points above. If we cannot say how we would answer each research question, and what data would be required to answer it, we cannot proceed.

While there are many different ways in which research questions can be inappropriate or unsatisfactory, two types of problems often occur. The first concerns value judgements, the second concerns causation. Both raise important philosophical issues, both are problematic for empirical research and both have been prominent in the paradigm discussions referred to earlier.

Value judgements

5.4 Value judgements are moral (or ethical) judgements or statements. They are statements about what is good or bad, right or wrong (or any synonyms of these words), not in the sense of instrumental values (means) but in the sense of terminal values (ends). They are often described as statements of 'ought' (or 'should'), and are contrasted with statements of 'is'.[2] Whereas 'is' statements are statements of fact, 'ought' statements are statements of value. The problem is that it is not clear how (or whether) we can use empirical evidence (that is, facts) to make such value judgements. There are two main positions on this important issue.

One main position is that we cannot use empirical evidence in the making of value judgements, because of the so-called 'fact-to-value gap'. The fact-to-value gap maintains that there is a fundamental difference between facts and values, and that because of this difference there is no logical way to get from statements of fact to statements of value. If this is true, it means that evidence is irrelevant to the making of value judgements, and that value judgements cannot be justified by evidence. Some other basis will be required for their justification. For proponents of this view, science must remain silent on value judgement questions, since scientific research, being based on empirical data, can deal only with the facts. This is not a small problem, since value judgements are among the most important judgements people (individually and collectively) must make. In this view, science has no role in making these value judgements. Nor do value judgements have any place in scientific inquiry. This is the conventional, positivist, 'science-as-value-free' view, and it has a long history (see, for example, O'Connor (1957), especially Chapter 3).

The other main position is that this so-called gap is based on a mistaken dualism which sees facts and values as quite different things. In this view, such a distinction is invalid, and the fact-to-value gap is therefore a misleading fallacy. The reasoning behind this view is not easy to summarise, but it is described by Lincoln and Guba (1985: Ch. 7). In that chapter, they indicate the many possible meanings of values, they show why the fact-value dualism is discredited, they stress the value-ladenness of all facts, and they show the four main ways in which values have a direct impact on the research. They end their chapter with the following plea that we discontinue the fallacious dichotomy between facts and values, and stop trying to exclude values from research:

> At this point, at a minimum, we should be prepared to admit that values do play a significant part in inquiry, to do our best in each case to expose and explicate them ... and, finally, to take them into account to whatever extent we can. Such a course is infinitely to be preferred to continuing in the self-delusion that methodology can and does protect one from their unwelcome incursions. (1985: 186)

This rejection of the positivist view comes from several quarters. Feminist scholars, for example, have repeatedly challenged the 'persistent positivist myth' (Haig, 1997) that science is value-free, and critical theorists and feminists alike regard the distinction between facts and values as simply a device that disguises the role of conservative values in much social science research. Instead of value-free research, critical theorists especially argue that research should be used in the service of the emancipation of oppressed groups – in other words, that it should be openly ideological (Hammersley, 1993).

> The attempt to produce value-neutral social science is increasingly being abandoned as at best unrealisable, and at worst self-deceptive, and is being replaced by social sciences based on explicit ideologies. (Hesse, 1980: 247)

While the positivist value-free position has a long history, opposition to it has grown strongly in the past 30 years. Ironically, the positivist position is itself a statement of values, and many see it as discredited in maintaining that inquiry can be value-free. A problem with the rejection of the value-free position, however, is that it is not clear where this leads. This can complicate the development of research questions, since the area of value judgements is controversial. In the face of these difficulties, I suggest three points to keep in mind, when planning research. First, we should be aware that there are different positions on this issue of value judgements, and therefore not be surprised if we encounter different reactions to it. Second, we should recognise when value statements are being made, and be careful about phrasing research questions in value judgement terms – to admit the value-ladenness of facts does not itself justify the making of sweeping value judgements. We should be aware of synonyms for 'good–bad' and 'right–wrong', which may camouflage the value judgements, but do not remove the issue[3]. Third, if value judgement terms are used in questions, we can first determine whether they are being used in the instrumental or terminal sense. If instrumental, we can rephrase the question to get rid of the value judgement term(s). If terminal, we should indicate how the evidence will be used in relation to the value judgements.

Causation

5.5 Scientific research has traditionally sought the causes of effects (or events or phenomena). Indeed, a useful definition of scientific research in any area is that it seeks to trace out cause–effect relationships. In this sense, science reflects everyday life. The concept of causation is deeply ingrained in our culture, and saturates our attempts to understand and explain the world. On the everyday level, we find it a very useful way to organise our thinking about the world – the word 'because', for example, is one of the most central in our language and in our world-view. As Lincoln and Guba (1985) point out, our preoccupation with causation may be related to our needs for prediction, control and power. Whether this is true or not, the concept of causation is deep-seated, and perhaps built into the way we think about the world.

But causation is also a difficult philosophical concept. What does causation mean, and how do we know when we have a cause (or the cause, or the causes) of something? The definitional question about causation has no easy answer. For example, Lincoln and Guba (1985: Ch. 6) review six main formulations of the concept of causation. Similarly, Brewer and Hunter (2005) discuss different types of causes. Without going into the definitional details, one way to simplify this complicated issue is to see the difference between two of the main views of causation – the constant conjunction view and the necessary connection view.

The constant conjunction view of causation

In the constant conjunction view, to say that X (for example, watching violence on television) causes Y (for example, the development of anti-social attitudes) is to say that every time X occurs, Y occurs. This means simply that Y always follows X, that there is a constant conjunction between them. This view is clear enough, but it has a problem. Night always follows day, there seems to be a constant conjunction between them, yet we don't want to say that day causes night. Therefore constant conjunction alone does not seem to be enough to define causation.

The necessary connection view of causation

On the other hand, in the necessary connection view, to say that X causes Y is to say not only that X is followed by Y, but that X *must be* followed by Y. In this view causation means that the variables are *necessarily* connected. The problem with this view is that we cannot observe that X *must be* followed by Y. We can only observe whether or not X is followed by Y. We cannot observe the must or the necessity part. Since we cannot observe it, we can only infer it. Thus causation, in this view, is not observable, it can only be inferred. It is, in other words, a metaphysical concept, not an empirical concept.

The necessary connection view of causation therefore leads to this question: Under what conditions is it plausible to infer that an observed relationship is a causal one? This is a difficult question, precisely because the world is full of relationships we can observe, but most of them are not causal. It is a question to which many answers have been proposed (see, for example, Rosenberg, 1968; Lincoln and Guba, 1985; Brewer and Hunter, 2005). Without attempting here a full treatment of this question, some of the main conditions for inferring that X (watching violence on television) causes Y (the development of anti-social attitudes) are:

- The variables X and Y must be related, and this relationship must be demonstrated empirically.
- A time order between the variables must be demonstrated, with the cause X preceding the effect Y; if the time order cannot be established, the 'relative fixity and alterability' of the variables must support the proposed causal inference – see Rosenberg (1968).
- There must be a plausible theory showing the links by which the variables are causally related – that is, the missing links which bring about the causal connection must be specified.
- Plausible rival hypotheses to the preferred causal one must be eliminated.

Perhaps no topic has received more attention in quantitative research design than this. For a long time, and in some quarters still, the experiment has been the preferred empirical research design, precisely because, by systematically eliminating rival hypotheses, it is the safest basis we have for inferring causal relationships between variables. We will see this in Chapter 10. More recently, there have been advances in design for inferring causation, both in quantitative research through the development of quasi-experimental and non-experimental designs, and also in qualitative research (see, for example, Miles, Huberman and Saldana, 2013).

Different researchers have different views of causation (Huberman and Miles, 1994: 434), and the credibility of causal claims depends on the view one holds. Despite the resistance to the concept and terminology of causation among some

TABLE 5.1   Substitute terms for cause and effect

Cause	Effect
Independent variable	Dependent variable
Treatment variable	Outcome variable
Predictor variable	Criterion variable
Antecedents	Consequences
Determinants	

'Correlates' is sometimes used for both causes and effects. Sometimes 'cause–effect relationship' is replaced by 'functional relationship'.

qualitative researchers, and despite the view of Lincoln and Guba (1985) that the concept may have outlived its usefulness, it seems a safe assumption that many researchers will continue to want to think causally about the world. But it is important to be careful about the way we use the word cause(s). In particular, we need to remember that causation can only be inferred, according to the necessary connection view described above. This is one reason that the word cause(s) itself is not often used among experienced researchers. Other words are substituted. We therefore need to be careful about such statements in a proposal as 'In this research we will find the cause(s) of . . .'. We must be even more careful of such statements in a finished report as 'In this research we have found the cause(s) of . . .'.[4]

On the assumption that we will retain the idea of causation, I suggest that we proceed as follows. First, when we are thinking causally, we replace the words cause and effect with other terms, choosing from those shown in Table 5.1, especially in quantitative studies. Second, we proceed to study the extent to which, and the ways in which, things are interconnected and variables are interrelated, according to whatever design we have chosen. Third, we reserve any causal description of observed relationships until it is time to interpret the results. It is one thing to observe, describe and report a relationship. It is another to interpret it, to say how the relationship came about. If the interpretation we prefer is a causal one, we are on safe ground if we point out that this interpretation is an inference, and then argue for this inference on the basis of the sorts of conditions mentioned earlier.

The distinction in the third point just made is important, and will come up again later in this book. It is the difference between observing and describing a relationship between variables (or a connection between things) on the one hand, and interpreting this relationship, or explaining it and saying how it came about, on the other. The difficulty in research is not normally in showing that a relationship exists. The difficulty is more likely to lie in interpreting the relationship. (A well-known example of this is 'correlation is not causation'. Correlation is about showing the relationship. Causation is about interpreting it.) Later chapters will show that there has been much work done on this issue in both the quantitative and qualitative approaches. For now, it is important to see clearly this distinction between describing a relationship and interpreting it.

What terms can we substitute for cause and effect? In a quantitative context, instead of cause, we use the term 'independent variable'. Instead of effect, we use 'dependent variable'. These are the most common terms used in research. Other synonyms for these are 'treatment' or 'predictor' variable for independent variable, and 'outcome' or 'criterion' variable for dependent variable. In still other contexts, 'antecedents' and 'determinants' are used for causes, 'consequences' for effects, and 'correlates' for both. The main thrust of these terms is to get away from the metaphysical part of the term 'cause' itself.

Two other points are made before leaving this topic of causation. The first is more applicable to quantitative research, the second to qualitative research. Both have implications for research design and for the analysis of data.

Multiple causation

The discussion in this section so far has been simplified, by talking basically about one cause and one effect. In social science research today, especially quantitative research, single cause-and-effect thinking is uncommon, and multiple causation is seen as much more realistic. Multiple causation means that there will likely be more than one cause, and probably several causes, for any particular effect. Effects are thought to have several causes, and these causes can act together in various ways, and can fluctuate in importance in how they bring about the effect. The terms 'multiple causes' and 'multiple causation' express these ideas. While the discussion in this chapter has been simplified, and put in terms of one cause and one effect, everything we have said about the nature of causes and the logic of causation holds for the more complicated case of multiple causation.

The same point also applies to effects. Much research has moved from a single effect to multiple effects. Multiple effects means that there will likely be several effects of any given cause, or set of causes. This move from single to multiple causes and effects has important consequences for research design, as shown in Figure 5.1. This diagram shows the various combinations of single and multiple causes and effects. In the top left-hand cell, there is the one-cause/one-effect design, now rather outmoded in social science research. In the top right-hand cell, there is the multiple-causes/one-effect design, the most common design in quantitative research, and the basis of the important multiple regression approach to be described in Chapters 10 and 12. The bottom left-hand cell shows the one-cause/multiple-effects design, while the bottom right-hand cell shows the multiple-causes/multiple-effects design.[5]

Causation in qualitative research

The second point concerns causation in qualitative research. The term causation has positivist connotations (Hammersley and Atkinson, 2007), and this, combined with

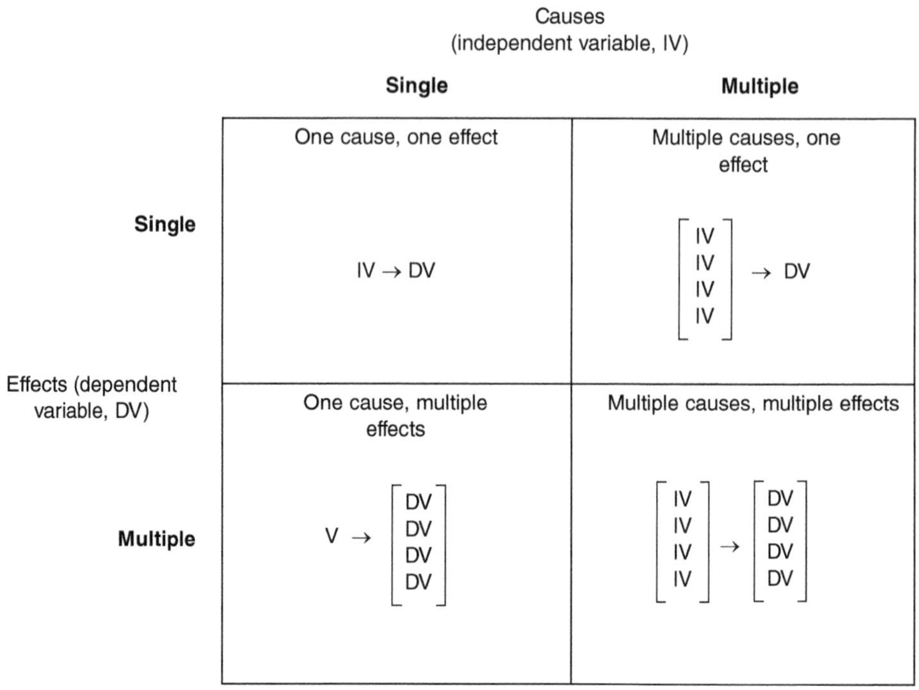

Figure 5.1 Cause-effect combinations and designs

the difficulty of assessing causal claims, makes some qualitative researchers reluctant to use the concept. Some postmodernists, for example, as pointed out by Neuman (1994), reject the search for causation because they see life as too complex and rapidly changing. Thus causation has typically been a preoccupation of quantitative research.

However, as Hammersley and Atkinson (2007) point out, causal theories and models are common in ethnographic work, even if they are used implicitly. Similarly, Miles, Huberman and Saldana (2013) make clear the importance of causation in qualitative research. Indeed, they claim that qualitative studies are especially well suited to finding causal relationships. Qualitative studies can:

> look directly and longitudinally at the local processes underlying a temporal series of events and states, showing how these led to specific outcomes and ruling out rival hypotheses. In effect, we get inside the black box; we can understand not just that a particular thing happened, but how and why it happened. (Huberman and Miles, 1994: 434)

and further,

> We consider qualitative analysis to be a very powerful method for assessing causality . . . Qualitative analysis, with its close-up look, can identify *mechanisms*, going beyond

sheer association. It is unrelentingly *local*, and deals well with the complex network of events and processes in a situation. It can sort out the *temporal* dimension, showing clearly what preceded what, either through direct observation or *retrospection*. It is well equipped to cycle back and forth between *variables* and *processes* showing that stories are not capricious, but include underlying variables, and that variables are not disembodied, but have connections over time. (Miles and Huberman, 1994: 147; emphasis in original)

In *Qualitative Data Analysis*, Miles and Huberman show how causal networks can be developed to model qualitative data, just as causal path diagrams model quantitative data.

Conceptual frameworks

5.6 A conceptual framework is a representation, either graphically or in narrative form, of the main concepts or variables and their presumed relationship with each other. It is usually best shown as a diagram. Some sort of conceptual framework is often implicit, as the question development stage described in Chapter 4 proceeds. It can help in the development of the research questions to make this conceptual framework explicit. In these cases, development of both the research questions and the conceptual framework goes hand in hand. The direction of thinking may be from the conceptual framework to the research questions, or vice versa, or they may interact with each other in some reciprocal way. Developing both together, like the questions themselves, is usually an iterative process.

Whether or not it is appropriate to have a predetermined conceptual framework depends on how much prior knowledge and theorising are brought to the research. In discussing the development of research questions, it was pointed out that there is often considerable prior knowledge, and the same point applies to the conceptual framework. It is useful to get our prior knowledge and theorising out on to the table, and organising this into a conceptual framework as research questions are developed can bring several benefits:

- it brings clarity and focus, helping us to see and organise the research questions more clearly;
- it helps to make explicit what we already know and think about the area and topic;
- it can help considerably in communicating ideas about the research; therefore it can simplify the preparation of the research proposal, and can also make it more convincing;
- it encourages selection, and assists in focusing and delimiting thinking during the planning stage.

In quantitative research, where well-developed research questions are typical, the conceptual framework is common, usually in diagram form. The diagram(s) will typically show the variables, their conceptual status in relation to each other and the hypothesised relationships between them. In qualitative research, there is, as usual, more of a range. Conceptual frameworks have generally been less common in qualitative research, but, as Miles, Huberman and Saldana (2013) and Maxwell (2012) make clear, a strong case can be made for their usefulness there too. Example 5.1 refers to conceptual frameworks for both quantitative and qualitative studies.

EXAMPLE 5.1

Conceptual Frameworks

Quantitative

- Neuman (1994: 47) shows five conceptual frameworks to represent possible causal relationships between variables.
- Rosenberg (1968: 54–83) shows numerous conceptual frameworks to represent intervening and antecedent variable relationships.
- Calder and Sapsford (1996) show a variety of multivariate conceptual frameworks.

Qualitative

- Miles and Huberman (1994: 18–20) show conceptual frameworks for their studies on disseminating educational innovations, and on school improvements.
- Miles and Huberman (1994: 21) also show two conceptual frameworks used by other qualitative researchers: one an ethnographic study of minority children's school experience, the other an emergent conceptual framework for the study of the creation of a new school.

From research questions to data

5.7 Once we have stabilised our research questions, and they are satisfactory in terms of the empirical criterion and the other criteria listed in Section 5.3, we can move from content to method. The connection from content to method is through data – what data will be needed and how they will be collected and analysed. Before we get down to details of method, therefore, we need to consider further the nature of data.

What, exactly, are data? As noted earlier, synonyms for data are evidence, information and empirical materials. The essential idea is first-hand observation and information about, or experience of, the world. Obviously, this could include all sorts of things, so data is a very broad term, and is subdivided into quantitative and qualitative. Both are empirical.

5.7.1 Quantitative data

The key concept here is quantity, and numbers are used to express quantity. Therefore quantitative data are numerical – they are information about the world, in the form of numbers.

Information about the world does not occur naturally in the form of numbers. It is we, as researchers, who turn the data into numbers. We impose the structure of the number system on the data, bringing the structure to the data. This means there is nothing 'God-given' about the numerical structure we impose – on the contrary, that structure is very much 'man-made'. It is therefore not inevitable, nor essential, that we organise our empirical data as numbers. The question is whether we find it useful to impose this structure on the data. If we find it useful (and if it is feasible), we should do it. If not, we are not at all bound to do it.

Measurement is the process by which we turn data into numbers. Measurement involves assigning numbers to things, people, events or whatever, according to particular sets of rules, as will be discussed in Chapter 11. Therefore to collect quantitative data is to collect measurements. By definition, quantitative data collected with measuring instruments are prestructured, falling at the left-hand end of the structuring continuum presented in Chapter 2. The numerical structure is imposed on the data, ahead of the research.

Two types of operations produce numbers – counting and scaling. *Counting* is such a common everyday occurrence that we don't think twice about it. We do it automatically, it is straightforward and not problematic, and we find it extremely useful in dealing with the world. When we count, we are counting with respect to something. There is a dimension of interest, some scale or quantity we have in mind, which gives meaning to the counting.

Scaling is rather different,[6] though again we do it all the time. The basic idea here is that we have in mind some characteristic, or property or trait – we will use trait – and we envisage a continuum, or scale, ranging from a great deal (or perhaps 100%) of this trait, to very little (or perhaps 0%) of this trait. Further, we envisage different locations along this continuum, corresponding to different amounts or quantities of this trait. We use this sort of thinking and describing very frequently in everyday language, and it is not difficult to find many examples. Nor do we normally consider it a problem to do this. In other words, the idea of scaling (though we do not normally call it that) is deeply ingrained into our world-view and into our language. This needs stressing because of the controversies that can arise with this same operation in a research situation. As a final step, in actual measurement, we assign numbers to represent these different locations along the scaled continuum. We do not normally make this last step in everyday life, and it seems to be here that the controversies exist. The idea of a scale is useful to us in everyday life because it helps us to be systematic in our thinking, and because it helps us to compare things (or events or people) in some sort of standardised way. Making standardised comparisons is something we often want to do, and measurement formalises these comparisons, enabling us to make them more precise and systematic.

To summarise, quantitative data are data in the form of numbers, either from counting, scaling or both. Measurement turns data into numbers, and its function is to help us make comparisons. Although measurement is a technical tool, it is a technical tool with very many similarities to what we do with great frequency in everyday life. It is important to stress this point because the process of measurement itself has been at the centre of much of the debate between quantitative and qualitative researchers. Measurement seems also to have fostered entrenched positions in this debate. One entrenched position has been slavishly devoted to measurement, and believes only in research where the data are quantitative. The other has been just as slavishly anti-measurement, distrusting all quantitative research. In this book, I want to avoid such entrenched positions about measurement, which we can do by asking two questions. First, will it help us to measure what we want to study – that is, will it be useful for the comparisons we wish to make? Second, if it is helpful, is it in fact possible to measure in this particular situation? We will return to this latter question in Chapter 11.

Counting and scaling are part of measurement, and it is variables that are measured. The concept of a variable (something that varies) is central to quantitative research. Quantitative research design, together with its associated conceptual framework, shows how the variables are seen and organised with respect to each other. Quantitative data collection is about how the variables are to be measured, and quantitative data analysis is about how the measurements of the variables are to be analysed. Thus both the concept of a variable, and the measurement of variables, are essential to the way quantitative research proceeds.

5.7.2 Qualitative data

We have defined quantitative data as empirical information in the form of numbers. Qualitative data can therefore be defined as empirical information about the world, not in the form of numbers. Most of the time in social science research, as noted earlier, this means words.

This definition covers a very wide range, and qualitative data do indeed include many different types of things. Denzin and Lincoln (2011) use the term 'qualitative empirical materials' and point out that this includes interview transcripts, recordings and notes, observational records and notes, documents and the products and records of material culture, audio-visual materials and personal experience materials (such as artefacts, journal and diary information, and narratives). The qualitative researcher thus has a much wider range of possible empirical materials than the quantitative researcher, and will typically also use multiple data sources in a project. For some qualitative researchers, literally everything is data. In this book, we concentrate on qualitative data from observation (and participant observation), interviews and documents – or, as Wolcott (1992) puts it – on qualitative data from 'watching, asking or examining'.

We saw that quantitative data have a predetermined structure, being at the left-hand end of the structure continuum. What about qualitative data? As with research questions and research designs, qualitative data can fall anywhere along this continuum. Thus, they can be towards the left-hand end, and well structured, as in the case of standardised interview questions with predetermined response categories, or observations based on a predetermined observation schedule. On the other hand, qualitative data can be relatively unstructured at the point of collection, as in the transcript of an open-ended interview or field notes from participant observation.

In this case, there would be no predetermined categories or codes. Rather, the structure in the data will emerge during the analysis. The basis of this structure is codes and categories, and they are typically derived from the data in the initial stages of analysis, as is described in Chapter 9.

Earlier, we saw comparisons between theory-before and theory-after, between concepts-before and concepts-after, and between research questions-before and research questions-after. Here it is a case of structure-before or structure-after in the data. But here, with data, another point emerges. 'Structure-before' means that the researcher imposes codes, categories or concepts on the data – these are researcher-imposed concepts. Measurement in quantitative research is a clear example of concepts and structure imposed on the data by the researcher. By contrast, 'structure-after' allows respondents in research to 'tell it in their own terms' to a much greater extent. This is often a big issue in a research project. A common criticism of prestructured data is on this very point – that prestructuring the data does not permit people to provide information using their own terms, meanings and understandings. On the other hand, when we collect data using people's own terms and meanings, it can be difficult to make standardised comparisons. This is an example of the sort of choice often facing the researcher. Like all other such choices, it needs to be analysed, and there are advantages and disadvantages of each way of doing it. Thus, it will often seem good to begin with the data in respondents' own terms and concepts. But the systematic comparisons that structure and measurements permit are also valuable, and they require that the same terms and concepts be used across different respondents – that they be standardised. This suggests combining the two approaches in such a way as to retain the advantages of each. Some ways of doing that are given in Chapter 14.

Open-ended qualitative data are often appealing to researchers who are keen to capture directly the 'lived experience' of people. But unstructured qualitative data require some processing to prepare them for analysis. Therefore the data themselves represent a text constructed by the researcher. It is one thing to experience (some aspect of) the world. It is another thing to represent that experience in words. Once data are put into words, it is the researcher-constructed text that is used in the analysis. It is inevitable that the words we use to record data from the field will reflect, to some extent, our own concepts. Thus, as Miles, Huberman and Saldana (2013) write, behind the apparent simplicity of qualitative data there is a good deal of complexity,[7] requiring care and self-awareness from the researcher. In this sense, too, qualitative research is similar to quantitative – in both, the researcher brings something to the data.

Combining quantitative and qualitative data

5.8   We can now summarise these sections on the nature of data. Quantitative data are information about the world in numerical form, whereas qualitative data are (essentially) information about the world in the form of words.

Quantitative data are necessarily structured in terms of the number system and reflect researcher-imposed constructs. Qualitative data may range from structured to unstructured, and may or may not involve researcher-imposed constructs. The basic difference between the two types of data lies in the process of measurement, which has often engendered rigid positions about research and which has been at the centre of debates between proponents of the two approaches.

To move past the rigid positions often adopted in these debates does not of course mean that we must combine the two types of data – only that we can do so when appropriate. Thus there are three possibilities for any empirical study:

- it can have all quantitative data;
- it can have all qualitative data; or
- it can combine both types of data in any proportions.

Which of these three should apply is not a matter for rules. The type of data we finish up with should be determined primarily by what we are trying to find out, considered against the background of the context, circumstances and practical aspects of the particular research project. Concentrating first on what we are trying to find out means that substantive issues dictate methodological choices. The 'substantive dog' wags the 'methodological tail', not vice versa.

This topic of combining quantitative and qualitative data is discussed again in mixed methods research in Chapter 14. Before that, we have to look in detail at each of the two different types of data – the designs which produce them, the methods for collecting them and how they can be analysed. For ease of presentation, we now separate out the qualitative and quantitative approaches, and deal with them separately. Thus Chapters 7, 8 and 9 deal with qualitative research and Chapters 10, 11 and 12 with quantitative research. In both cases, we deal first with design, second with the collection of data and third with the analysis of data. The two approaches are brought together again in Chapter 14. Before all of that, Chapter 6 discusses literature searching and reviewing.

Chapter summary

- The idea behind the empirical criterion is that a well-stated research question indicates what data are necessary to answer it.
- Careful linking of concepts with data is necessary for internal consistency in research. This fits in with the importance of logical connections across different levels of abstraction in the research.
- Value judgements are moral judgements or statements, and are statements of value(s). They are often contrasted with statements of fact. Some writers maintain that the 'fact-to-value' gap cannot be bridged logically, and that empirical evidence therefore has no place in making value judgements. Others maintain that the 'fact-to-value' gap is a misleading fallacy.
- The necessary connection view of causation is generally preferred to the constant conjunction view. However, an implication of this is that causation must be inferred and cannot be

directly observed. This has led to the use of substitute terms for cause and effect in research language – 'independent variable' and 'dependent variable' are the most common substitute terms.

- A conceptual framework shows the main concepts or variables in the research and their presumed relationships with each other. Conceptual frameworks are very common in quantitative research, and can also be useful in qualitative research.
- Quantitative data are numbers, which come from measurement – either through counting or scaling. Quantitative researchers impose the structure of the number system on the data.
- Qualitative data are mostly words, which come from watching, asking or examining. Qualitative data can vary in their level of structure, but are often much more open-ended.
- The question of whether or not to measure in a piece of research should be answered by looking at the usefulness and feasibility of measuring in the particular research situation. Usefulness and feasibility should also be used to decide whether or not to combine quantitative and qualitative data in a piece of research.

KEY TERMS

Empirical criterion: a well-stated research question indicates what data are required to answer it

Value judgement: a moral or ethical judgement about what is good or bad, right or wrong, etc.

Fact-to-value gap: the view that statements of fact are fundamentally different from statements of value, and that there is no logical connection between the two

Cause as constant conjunction: to say X causes Y means that every time X occurs, Y follows

Cause as necessary connection: to say that X causes Y means that not only is X followed by Y, but that X *must be* followed by Y

Independent variable: the most common substitute term for cause

Dependent variable: the most common substitute term for effect

Multiple causation: phenomena of interest in social science research very often have many causes

Conceptual framework: usually in diagram form, a conceptual framework shows the concepts or variables in the research and their relationship to each other

Measurement: the process which turns data into numbers; includes counting and scaling

Exercises and study questions

1. What is the empirical criterion for research questions? How do we know when it is satisfied?
2. What are values, and what are value judgements? What is meant by the fact-to-value gap? In your opinion, is it an important distinction or a misleading fallacy?

3. Are the following questions empirical questions? If not, how can they be changed into empirical questions? (hint: concentrate on the word 'should')

   - Should teachers know the IQ of students?
   - Should teachers use corporal punishment for students' delinquent behaviour?
   - Should nurses wear white uniforms?
   - Should managers use democratic, authoritarian or laissez-faire leadership styles?

4. What difficulties are there in using the terms 'causation' and 'cause' in empirical research?
5. What are three substitute terms for cause, and three for effect? Which pair of substitute terms is most common?
6. List several possible 'causes' (i.e. independent variables) for differential school achievement (as dependent variable). List several possible 'effects' (i.e. dependent variables) of the introduction of co-educational schooling (as independent variable) into a previously single-sex school system.
7. What is a scale, and what does it mean to scale a variable? What are some of the issues involved in scaling these variables: students' attitudes towards school; beliefs about immigration; teachers' use of questioning; managers' leadership styles?
8. In general, when is measurement appropriate in research? When is it not appropriate?

Further reading

Blalock, H.M., Jr (1982) *Conceptualization and Measurement in the Social Sciences*. Beverley Hills, CA: SAGE.

Brewer, J. and Hunter, A. (2005) *Foundations of Multimethod Research: Synthesizing Styles*. 2nd edn. Thousand Oaks, CA: SAGE.

Charters, W.W., Jr (1967) 'The hypothesis in scientific research'. Unpublished paper, University of Oregon, Eugene, OR.

Davis, J.A. (1985) *The Logic of Causal Order*. Beverley Hills, CA: SAGE.

Guba, E.G. and Lincoln, Y.S. (1989) *Fourth Generation Evaluation*. Newbury Park, CA: SAGE.

Hage, J. and Meeker, B.F. (1988) *Social Causality*. Boston, MA: Unwin Hyman.

Lieberson, S. (1992) *Making It Count: The Improvement of Social Research and Theory*. 2nd edn. Berkeley, CA: University of California Press.

Miles, M.B., Huberman, A.M. and Saldana, J. (2013) *Qualitative Data Analysis*. 3rd edn. Thousand Oaks, CA: SAGE.

Rosenberg, M. (1968) *The Logic of Survey Analysis*. New York: Basic Books.

Notes

1. This paper by Charters is a valuable discussion of the functions, anatomy and pathology of the hypothesis. However, to my knowledge it has never been published.
2. Terminal values are ends in themselves. Instrumental values are means towards achieving those ends. For a discussion of value judgements in science, see Broudy et al. (1973: 502–8) and also Brodbeck (1968: 79–138).
3. Examples are 'worthwhile–worthless', 'effective–ineffective' and 'efficient–inefficient'.

4. Sometimes, words other than 'cause' are used, but the causal connotations remain. Some examples are 'due to', 'affects', 'contributes to', 'has an impact on', 'is a function of' and 'determines'.

5. Quantitative research also accommodates more than one direction for causal influences. The ideas of mutual causation and reciprocal influences between variables can be built into causal path models, which specify the networks of causal influences among a set of variables (see, for example, Asher, 1976; Davis, 1985).

6. Scaling is used here to mean placing on a scale or continuum. In Chapter 11 the more general term 'measurement' is used. Here scaling, along with counting, is seen as one type of measurement. In general, the term 'scaling' is used more often in psychology, the term 'measurement' more often in educational research.

7. This complexity has another aspect too, centring on the use of language and the analytic status of qualitative data, discussed in Chapter 8.

six

LITERATURE SEARCHING
AND REVIEWING

Contents

After studying this chapter you should be able to:

- Describe the difference between empirical research literature and theoretical literature
- State the central purpose which guides a review of the empirical research literature
- Identify and explain the purposes of a literature review in a dissertation
- Describe five main stages in carrying out a literature review
- Explain what it means to be critical in a literature review
- Recognise and critically appraise different types of systematic reviews of research

Higher-degree dissertations, especially at the doctoral level, are expected to demonstrate mastery of the relevant literature. This chapter first distinguishes between empirical research literature and theoretical literature, and then considers the purposes of a literature review in a dissertation. It next describes the conduct of a literature review in five main steps – searching; screening; summarising and documenting; organising–analysing–synthesising; and writing. Following this, there are sections on being critical in reviewing literature, and on some common problems in writing a literature review for a dissertation. Systematic literature reviews are then discussed, and the final section draws attention to the research journal literature.

In this chapter, as in Chapter 2, the distinction is made again between methodology, on the one hand, and content or substance, on the other. The former concerns the methods used in the research, and the latter concerns the content and subject matter of the research. For empirical research literature, judgements are required about its methodological soundness, as is described in Sections 6.1 and 6.4.2. In addition, for both empirical research and theoretical literature, judgements are required about its substantive relevance. In a dissertation literature review, the focus is on the substantively relevant literature. The dissertation literature review should concentrate on the literature that is most centrally relevant to the topic and research questions. Less attention is paid to literature that is only marginally relevant. Thus 'review of the literature' really means 'review of the relevant literature'.

Earlier chapters, and especially Chapter 4, have concentrated on the central role of research questions, locating them in this five-part hierarchy: research area, research topic, general research question(s), specific research questions, data collection questions. For some types of research, reading and reviewing literature takes place before the development of research questions. Indeed, the literature can be important in identifying the research topic within an area, and in developing research questions. When this is the case, the initial reading of the literature is usually more exploratory. However, the dissertation reporting the research will still need a formal literature review. In the interests of clarity, therefore, this chapter is written as though the research topic and general research question(s) are both clearly identified. Using the above hierarchy, the chapter first focuses at the level of general research question to discuss reviewing empirical research literature. It then goes to the topic level, to discuss reviewing theoretical literature. The terms empirical research literature and theoretical literature now need definition.

Empirical research literature

6.1 The empirical research literature is literature that reports empirical research results. Once the topic and general research question have been identified, we can use them as a guide in identifying the relevant empirical research literature. We then need to screen this literature methodologically, as described in Section 6.4.2 below.

The review of the empirical research literature relevant to the research question focuses on this central issue:

> **What previous empirical evidence is there about this question, and what does the empirical evidence tell us about the answer to this question? In other words, based on previous research, what is known – and not known – about this question?**

The process to deal with this problem is therefore to assemble the previous research evidence and, after appropriate methodological screening (see Section 6.4.2), to determine to what extent a coherent picture emerges from the evidence in answer to the question. Very often the picture that emerges from the research literature is not especially coherent or consistent, and various gaps, tensions and inconsistencies are revealed. When this happens, it provides a convenient way to locate your study in relation to the literature: your study may then aim to address gaps or inconsistencies in the evidence. Thus the review of research literature concentrates on previous empirical evidence. Not surprisingly, most of the empirical research evidence is reported in the research journal literature.

Theoretical literature

6.2 Lifting the focus from research question to research topic brings the theoretical literature into view. Whereas empirical research literature concentrates on findings from empirical research, theoretical literature includes relevant concepts, relevant theories and theoretical contexts, and discursive and analytical literature that contains ideas and information relevant to the topic. Thus the use of the term 'theoretical' here is rather broad, and includes both substantive and methodological elements.

In social science research, it is sometimes difficult to find large bodies of systematic empirical evidence on topics of interest, so that sometimes the relevant research literature is quite small. However, it is quite common for different writers and researchers to approach a social science research topic from different points of view.

In addition, sometimes different sets of concepts are used, sometimes different substantive theories are used, and sometimes different methodologies and paradigms of inquiry are used. This writing forms part of the theoretical literature for a topic, and the dissertation is expected to deal with it. The theoretical literature for most social science research topics is therefore usually quite broad, as is reflected in this definition of a literature review:

> The selection of available documents (both published and unpublished) on the topic, which contain information, ideas, data and evidence written from a particular standpoint to fulfill certain aims or express certain views on the nature of the topic and how it is to be investigated, and the effective evaluation of these documents in relation to the research being proposed. (Hart, 1998: 13)

The theoretical literature review is thus much broader than the review of empirical evidence, and now includes 'information' and 'ideas', and also acknowledges different 'particular standpoints'.

To summarise, we can say:

> Reviewing theoretical literature means reviewing the ideas, thinking and discussion about a topic or question,
>
> whereas
>
> Reviewing empirical research literature means reviewing the evidence about a topic or question.

This description has drawn a sharp distinction between empirical and theoretical literature, and both need to be covered in a dissertation. But it is a matter of judgement in writing the review whether they should be presented separately or together.

Purposes of a literature review

6.3 We can now identify three purposes to the literature review in a dissertation. One relates to the empirical research literature, one to the theoretical literature, and one to the relationship of your study to all of this literature.

Empirical research literature

The purpose of this part of the review is to describe current knowledge, by bringing together and summarising the empirical evidence about this research question, no matter how incomplete or inconsistent the picture from previous empircal evidence may be. As indicated, the issue that guides this part of the review is: To what extent can empirical evidence about this question be accumulated and integrated into a coherent overall picture? Other related problems concern the quality of available research, and the need for new research (Fink, 2005: 227), and such methodological issues as what approaches have been used in research on this question, what methodological issues arise and what methodological gaps exist.

Theoretical literature

The purpose of this part of the review is broader – to assess critically the overall state of knowledge on this topic, and the state of research, thinking and theorising on this topic. This includes understanding the history of research on the topic. Following Hart (1998: 14), examples of particular issues which can guide this part of the review are:

- **What are the key theoretical and philosophical sources on which scholars have drawn in discussing this topic?**
- **What are the major issues and debates about the topic?**
- **What are the political standpoints?**
- **What are the origins and definitions of the topic?**
- **What are the key concepts, theories and ideas?**
- **What are the epistemological and ontological grounds for the discipline?**
- **What are the main questions and problems that have been addressed to date?**
- **How is knowledge on the topic structured and organised?**

And, in an overall sense,

- **How have our approaches to these questions increased our understanding and knowledge?**

Relationship of your study to the literature

The purpose here is to locate your study in relation to the literature. The central issue now is: What is the relationship of my research to the literature being reviewed? A focus on this issue helps to integrate the literature review into your dissertation. A common criticism of dissertation literature reviews is that they are unconnected to the rest of the dissertation – we could remove the literature review section and the dissertation would lose nothing. A focus on this issue ensures the literature review is integrated with and connected to the research you have conducted and are reporting. This works in the early chapters of the dissertation, in locating the research in relation to its literature, and can be an important element in justifying the research. It also works in the later stages, when findings are being reported. Findings can be interpreted and discussed in relation to the study's literature. Both strategies help to give the dissertation internal coherence and consistency.

Carrying out a literature review

6.4 A literature review can be divided into five main stages – searching, screening, summarising and documenting, organising–analysing–synthesising, and writing.

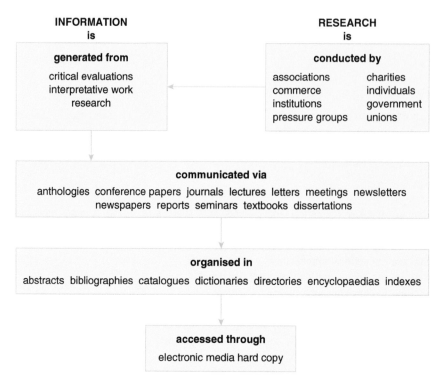

INFORMATION
is

generated from

critical evaluations
interpretative work
research

RESEARCH
is

conducted by

associations	charities
commerce	individuals
institutions	government
pressure groups	unions

communicated via

anthologies conference papers journals lectures letters meetings newsletters
newspapers reports seminars textbooks dissertations

organised in

abstracts bibliographies catalogues dictionaries directories encyclopaedias indexes

accessed through

electronic media hard copy

FIGURE 6.1   The generation and communication of research knowledge and information
Source: Hart, 1998: 4

6.4.1 Searching

An understanding of the structure of the research world, and of the production of research literature, helps in directing your search for the empirical research and theoretical literature relevant to your topic and research question. For some topics, the policy literature will also be relevant (Wallace and Poulson, 2003: 21). The diagram from Hart (1998: 4) summarises the generation and communication of research information (see Figure 6.1).

The university library is obviously a central location for finding the literature needed for review. Today, university libraries typically have three main search domains – the main library catalogue, the journals catalogue and the electronic resources index. The graduate student needs to be familiar with all three, but should pay special attention to the research journal literature. Social science has a very large number of research journals, and knowing the main ones for your area and topic is essential at this level of work. The top international refereed research journals have always been the main outlet used by leading researchers for their work, and they are a crucial source both of empirical research findings and of important theoretical discussions. Electronic databases are of great assistance here, as more and more research journals go online. Citation indexes, such as Scopus and Web of Science, and tools like Google Scholar can enable you to identify and follow chains of relevant references, including books, for example by looking at the sources cited in a particular article or at more recent texts that cite it.

While the social science research journals are of primary importance for literature reviewing, also important within the electronic databases are the thesis and dissertation collections for different countries, and collections of abstracts. Examples of dissertation collections are Theses Canada, Dissertation Abstracts International (for North America), Digital Access to Research Theses (for Europe), British Library Electronic Theses Online Service (for the United Kingdom) and Education Research Theses (for Australia). Examples of collections of abstracts, which are often brought together by discipline, are ERIC (Education Resources Information Center), British Education Index, Education Abstracts, Social Science Abstracts, Psychological Abstracts, Sociological Abstracts, and Applied Social Sciences Index and Abstracts (ASSIA). In addition, the main research conferences in different social science areas, usually held annually, publish programmes that summarise the papers to be delivered. Some particularly significant conferences publish full conference proceedings.

In short, there are multiple sources for locating the relevant literature, and technology has substantially facilitated the literature-searching process. Judgements of relevance in this literature searching are guided by the research question for the research literature and by the topic for the broader theoretical literature.

This richness of sources may seem daunting, but it can be managed with a well-planned and well-documented search strategy. Drawing on Phelps, Fisher and Ellis's summary (2007), the strategy can include:

- Clarifying the purposes and timetable of the search;
- Conceptualising your search: identifying key terms (and their synonyms, variations in form, and overlapping and connected concepts);
- Deciding how the key terms will be combined and used. The key techniques listed in Box 6.1 may yield different results, so it is worth experimenting with a range of techniques;
- Keeping a record of your searches, so that you can repeat them in the future, but also to avoid veering off-track or unnecessarily duplicating effort. In addition, efficient record-keeping helps you to assess the relative value of different databases for your purposes, to manage your references and to describe clearly your approach to identifying relevant literature in your dissertation;
- Saving your search results: good reference management (for example, using software packages such as Mendeley, RefWorks or EndNote) and a clear, well backed-up and easily accessible filing system are required;
- Monitoring the databases for new literature: this can be done manually, for example by repeating some of the searches at a later stage, or automatically, for example by subscribing to journal content monitoring services, table of contents services or news feeds.

Electronic searches: key techniques for combining and entering search terms (adapted from Phelps, Fisher and Ellis, 2007)

1. Using Boolean logic: combining terms by using the connectors AND, OR and NOT
2. Using phrase searching: using particular strings of words as search terms, for example by placing phrases in quotation marks
3. Using proximity operators: depending on the functionality of the database, using terms that are NEAR, SAME or come WITH, the key terms entered
4. Using truncators and wildcards: replacing parts of the terms with special characters such as * to include different spellings, suffixes, words with the same root, and so on
5. Determining which fields in the database are relevant to search: most databases offer a choice of several fields by which searches can be carried out – including author, title, abstract, publication date, subject area or the full text of a document
6. Limiting searches by, for example, date of publication, language, country of publication or type of material (conference paper, journal article, etc.).

6.4.2 Screening

Two types of screening are needed, as research and theoretical literature is located and read – substantive or content screening and methodological screening.

Substantive (or content) screening

Content screening applies to both types of literature, and is important because your dissertation literature review needs to concentrate on literature centrally relevant to your topic and question. Marginally relevant literature should not receive as much attention and often may only be noted in passing. The topic and research question are your reference points for this substantive screening.

Methodological screening

This applies to the empirical research literature. Its purpose is to assess critically the methodological quality of the research that has produced the evidence and the findings. The issue here is: How much confidence can we have in the evidence reported and the findings claimed in a piece of published research? There are different ways a piece of research can fail the test of quality, and Chapter 14 considers in detail the evaluation of research quality. But two general points are relevant here. The first is that research reported in the top-quality international refereed journals will have been through stringent peer review, which means that its methods have been carefully scrutinised by experts in the field (see Section 6.8). One implication of this is that we can have confidence in the quality of research reported in international refereed journals. Another implication is that 'findings' reported in journals or at conferences that do not have expert peer review have to be very carefully assessed, with respect to the methods used. The second general point is that the main themes to use in assessing methodological quality are those that guide our discussion of research methods throughout the remainder of this book. Specifically:

- *Design* – is the design appropriate to answer the research questions? Have weaknesses in the design been identified and controlled? Have ethical issues been addressed?
- *Sample* – is the sample or case appropriate for the research described? To what extent are findings likely to be generalisable (or transferable), based on this sample? To what extent is the case typical or unique?
- *Data collection* – are the data collected of sufficient quality to allow confidence in the findings? Quality control in data collection is an important theme in Chapter 8 (for qualitative data) and Chapter 11 (for quantitative data) in this book.
- *Data analysis* – similarly, is the data analysis appropriate and sufficiently thorough to allow confidence in the findings?

Systematically using these general evaluation questions (and the more specific evaluation questions in Chapter 14) as you read enables you to make judgements about how much confidence to place in evidence and findings reported. It also has two other benefits. It shows that you are critically assessing research literature as you review it, an expectation you need to meet in your literature review (see Section 6.5). And it enables you to comment analytically on the methodological approaches used in research on this topic and question. Both contribute to your demonstration of mastery of the relevant literature.

6.4.3 Summarising and documenting

Summarising is an essential activity in literature reviewing. It is also an essential part of managing the literature and provides the basis for the organising, analysing and synthesising which follow. However, while summaries are important building blocks, the review itself needs to go well beyond mere summarising. A literature review is not merely a serialised or chronological summary of what others have done – it is not, in other words, an annotated bibliography. Reviewing literature at this level requires building an argument based on themes, which in turn requires organisation and structure, and analysis and synthesis, as discussed in the next section. Literature summaries are the building blocks for this organising, analysing and synthesising.

Summarising concentrates on capturing the main points of a paper, both substantively and methodologically. The task in summarising is to shorten significantly, without significant loss of information. For research reports, summaries of the main substantive points can focus on the topic and research question(s), the context, the data and the findings for each piece of research. Summaries of the main methodological points can focus on the design, the sample, the data collection, the data analysis and the theoretical basis and orientation of each piece.

At the time of summarising, setting up a documenting, indexing and filing system is important. It is part of organising and should include full bibliographic details in addition to the substantive and methodological summary points noted. Summarising literature as you read is an important first step in literature reviewing. Doing it systematically, with complete bibliographic details and organised filing, always pays later dividends. Your completed literature review will need to have all referencing and bibliographic details correct, and this becomes a particularly onerous task if the details are not recorded as the review work progresses.

6.4.4 Organising, analysing and synthesising

These activities are not sequential. They overlap, and will typically occur more or less simultaneously as literature is read and summarised. Together with summarising, they help you to manage the literature you read. Developing an organising framework for dealing with the literature, often in terms of main themes, is part of reading critically and analytically. It will often help with developing a conceptual framework for your own study. It will also help to make the literature review you write both thematic (rather than merely a summary of what others have done) and integrated with your own study. Your study needs to be connected to its literature, so that there is some point to the literature review.

Organising the material in your literature summaries helps to develop a structure. A completed review needs a structure, because the alternative to a structured review is an amorphous mass of unstructured writing, which makes it difficult for the reader to navigate and comprehend. Structure in reviewing is usually developed through main themes and sub-themes, and structure in the presentation of the review is provided by sections and subsections. These can be tied together by short 'advance organisers' and interconnecting summaries. Integration and synthesis of the literature will normally suggest a structure for writing the review.

Analysing here means breaking the literature into its constituent parts and describing how the parts relate to each other (Hart, 1998: 110). When you subject the methodology of a piece of research to the questions suggested under screening above, you are analysing it methodologically. Similarly, when you comment on methodological trends, inconsistencies or gaps in a body of research literature, you are dealing with it analytically. A substantive analysis of the literature means critically reflecting on its organisation, completeness, coherence and consistency. The questions suggested by Hart and shown earlier in the theoretical literature part of Section 6.3 can help in dealing analytically with the substance or content of the literature.

In contrast to analysing, *synthesising* involves making connections between the parts identified, and showing new patterns and arrangements among them (Hart, 1998: 110). Thus synthesising involves consideration of the convergence and divergence of the findings, theories, methods and sometimes of the implications that are found in the literature. Burton and Steane (2004: 131–2) suggest the dialectical process of thesis–antithesis–synthesis as a framework for developing synthesis in a literature review. They use the metaphor of tapestry to illustrate synthesising in a review, stressing the weaving together and integration of threads contained in previous writing on the topic. This sort of process is closely connected to building an argument – indeed synthesising is one important way of building an argument. Such a focus while writing the literature review ensures that it is much more than a summary or annotated bibliography. Synthesis of the contents of the literature also assists in evaluating its quality. A critical stance throughout the literature review ensures that evaluation is an on-going theme. In addition to this, some summary evaluative statements are an effective way to conclude a synthesis, and at the same time they present another opportunity to show the connections of your study to the literature. The synthesis of course needs a clear exposition, which leads to the next stage of writing the review.

6.4.5 Writing

Writing the literature review brings it all together. This writing task is often seen by the graduate student as formidable or daunting, but it is also an opportunity to display your mastery. A tried and tested writing plan for literature reviews has three main parts:

- developing a structure;
- writing a first draft;
- revising and writing subsequent and final drafts.

Structure is needed in the way you write your review, and this means that sections and section headings within the review are important. Sometimes, too, subsections will be required, but they should not be overdone. A great benefit of sectionising the literature review is that the writing becomes modularised. Instead of one formidable task (writing the review) you have broken it into a series of manageable ones (writing each section). Interconnecting paragraphs, which bind the review together, can be added in the later stages of writing the review.

Also useful, but often written in the final stage, are appropriately placed 'advance organisers' where you briefly describe the structure and argument of the material to come, providing the reader with a 'road map' for navigating the review. The most important advance organiser comes at the start of the review, where the aims of the review are stated and the structure is overviewed. The statement of aims is developed iteratively with the structure to follow in the review, so that the finished statement of aims leads naturally to the structure and fits seamlessly with it. The section and subsection headings, when listed as a table of contents, should have a logical progression, and should give indications of the argument that binds the review together.

An important part of writing is the referencing process. Academic writing consists of original ideas and ways of saying things, but it also, fundamentally, builds on others' ideas. These ideas (and not just particular phrases and sentences quoted) need to be properly attributed to their authors and to the texts in which they were found. This attribution might be done by direct citation, by paraphrasing or by indirect use.

Faced with the writing task, four useful points to keep in mind are:

- Recognise that all research has a history, both methodological and theoretical–substantive, and that this history provides the body of your review.
- Use the review not only to demonstrate your mastery of literature, but also to justify your study and its approach. Specifically, use the review as a substantive and methodological

rationalisation for your study. This means building your argument through the literature review and beyond. This will ensure satisfactory connections between your study and the literature review.

- Acknowledge the sources of ideas taken from the literature, and mark them clearly relative to your own ideas.
- Be critical.

Being critical

6.5 In higher-degree dissertations especially, the literature review is expected to be critical, not simply descriptive. Being critical means, among other things, not simply accepting what is written at face value, but instead subjecting it to careful analysis and evaluation. Therefore it is important to adopt a critical stance from the beginning, in reading and summarising the literature. More specifically, Wallace and Poulson (2003: 6) define being critical as:

- adopting an attitude of scepticism or reasoned doubt;
- habitually questioning the quality of claims to knowledge;
- scrutinising claims to see how far they are convincing;
- respecting other people at all times;
- being open-minded;
- being constructive.

If the piece of literature in question is a research journal article, and in addition to what has been said earlier (see Section 6.4.2), the following questions can help in achieving and maintaining a critical orientation as you read and review literature:

- Has the author identified a topic or formulated a problem or an issue, with research questions that follow from it to guide the investigation?
- Is it clearly defined? Is its significance clearly established?
- What is the author's research orientation or perspective? Could the problem have been more effectively approached from another perspective?
- What is the author's theoretical framework? Are the main concepts clearly defined and consistently used?
- Has the author evaluated the literature relevant to the problem? Has the literature been dealt with thoroughly and even-handedly?
- If an empirical study, how good are the basic components – the design, the sampling, the quality of the data collected, the data analysis? Are the conclusions justified by the data?
- How does the author structure the argument behind the research? Can you 'unpack' the flow of argument to see if it holds together logically?
- Is the paper appropriately written?
- In what ways does this paper contribute to our understanding of the problem? In what ways is it useful for practice? What are the strengths and the limitations?
- How does this paper relate to the research I am developing and proposing?

Interrogating the literature this way helps you to develop and maintain an appropriate critical focus. In addition, as noted earlier, Section 14.5 shows evaluative criteria that can be used for assessing empirical research reports. In summarising, Wallace and Poulson (2003: 27–8) see a high-quality literature review as focused, structured, critical, accurately referenced, clearly expressed, reader-friendly, informative and balanced.

6.6 One question that often occurs in dissertation reviews of social science literature is: Does the review need to be comprehensive and exhaustive, covering all the literature? Or, to what extent can it be selective? The first part of the answer to this question is to stress again that 'literature' here means 'relevant literature'. As literature is read and summarised, classifying it as centrally relevant, marginally relevant or only of background and contextual relevance is useful. The second part of the answer is to recognise that, for some topics, the volume of related literature is so great that a single dissertation literature review cannot be comprehensive, covering everything. This is especially true for those topics where more than one body of literature is relevant, as is often the case in the applied social sciences. In these cases, the researcher is forced to be selective. When this occurs, the writer should indicate the basis on which the selection is made, and why it is being done. Here is where previous reviews of the literature, if available and reasonably recent, can be extremely valuable. If you find a good literature review, you can make use of it, of course with appropriate acknowledgements. It is worth remembering that completed dissertations normally contain a literature review. Finding a recent dissertation on (or close to) your topic can save you a lot of time and work.

At the opposite end of the continuum, beware of claiming that there is no relevant literature for your research question(s). Raising the level of abstraction – from specific research question to general research question, and sometimes from general research question to topic – can help to show its connections to the literature. An example is given in Box 6.2.

BOX 6.2

Using the Literature: Levels of Abstraction

Assume the specific question for the research concerns the educational performance of Aboriginal children in Narrogin, Western Australia. In all probability, there is no literature or previous research on this specific topic. However, Aboriginal children are an indigenous ethnic minority group; Narrogin is a rural community. Now the search for relevant literature is broader: the educational performance of indigenous ethnic minority children in rural communities.

LITERATURE SEARCHING AND REVIEWING   105

Six other common problems are presented as a 'list of don'ts' in Box 6.3.

Don'ts for Reviewing Literature

In reviewing literature, be careful NOT to:

- Quote in excess. Judgement, experience and the reactions of supervisor(s) about the amount of quoting are useful, but too many direct quotes, or direct quotes that are too long, raise doubts about your mastery of the literature. Rudestam and Newton have good advice: 'Restrict the use of quotations to those with particular impact or those that are stated in a unique way that is difficult to recapture' (2000: 59).
- Rely too much on secondary sources. At this level of work, you are expected, where possible, to study primary sources. Secondary sources are acceptable where the primary source is not available or accessible, or where the secondary source adds significantly to the discussion. Again, however, over-reliance on secondary sources raises doubts about your knowledge and mastery of the literature for your topic.
- Neglect practitioner-oriented literature. While the research literature on your topic is obviously important, there is often practitioner-oriented literature that is relevant and useful.
- Give in to the temptation to include and report everything you know or have read. Your review needs to be selective, on an appropriate basis. As Rudestam and Newton put it, 'build an argument, not a library' (2000: 59).
- Rely too much on 'old' literature. Two judgements are involved here. First, how old is too old? Second, what about very important older literature? These judgements are related. The age of a classic piece of literature or research is not important. Thus, for example, Piaget's work (from the 1950s and earlier) or the Coleman report (Coleman et al., 1966) remain important today, despite their age, and there is no problem referring to them. But for the vast majority of research literature, which does not fall into the 'classic' category, going back more than 15 or certainly 20 years can be problematic. The advice really comes down to this: Don't produce a dissertation literature review where the great majority of the references are to literature more than say 15–20 years old.
- Fail to reference properly ideas taken from the literature. Good citation practice is not just a technicality but is an essential element of academic work, part of the process of building and critically testing knowledge. It is thus important to make sure that you acknowledge appropriately the sources of ideas that you may be using, whether you quote them verbatim, paraphrase them or just refer to them in passing.

Systematic reviews

6.7 All reviews of the literature need to be systematic in their searching, documenting and summarising of the literature, as well as in their analysis, synthesis and presentation. The term 'systematic review' has, however, a further, more technical, sense. It refers to a particular approach to inquiry, the development of which was strongly stimulated by the evidence-based movement in professional practice and policy. In this sense, systematic reviews of the literature can be research projects in their own right: they seek to answer specific research questions using explicit and rigorous methods, and they communicate their findings to a range of audiences. Gough, Oliver and Thomas (2012) define systematic reviews as a form of research that identifies, describes, appraises and synthesises the available research literature 'using systematic and explicit accountable methods' (p. 5). The aims of reviews, these authors argue, may be anywhere on a continuum from aggregative synthesis (that is, reviews that add up or pool data from primary studies to answer a question) to configurative synthesis (that is, reviews that organise and interpret data without necessarily adding them up). Using the example of education research, some databases are comprised of such systematic reviews; some of them (such as the What Works Clearinghouse and the Campbell Collaboration) may prioritise aggregative reviews of quantitative research, in particular of randomised control trials, in order to show 'what works' in particular areas of intervention. The topics covered by the systematic reviews included in these databases are very diverse (Box 6.4).

BOX 6.4

Examples of Recent Systematic Reviews in Education Research

- Childhood obesity and educational attainment (an EPPI-Centre narrative synthesis of empirical literature – Caird et al., 2011).
- Interventions to increase school attendance among chronic truant students (a Campbell Collaboration critical meta-analysis – Maynard et al., 2012).
- Teacher competences and pupil achievement (a Danish Clearinghouse of Educational Research literature mapping and narrative synthesis – Nordenbo et al., 2008).

In this technical sense, systematic reviews are ways of addressing substantive research questions in their own right. Their main aim is not to provide the background against which a particular empirical or theoretical project can be presented and understood, but to pull together and integrate all the high-quality research evidence available on a particular question. Considerable time, effort (often by a team of experienced researchers who are able to check each other's interpretations) and resources may be required to achieve this aim. This may make systematic reviews of this kind difficult to carry out by individual students, although in principle it is possible to produce a dissertation based on systematic reviewing methodologies, as a project in its own right. Most students can, however, use some of the systematic reviewing techniques to develop an initial mapping of the literature relevant to their dissertations.

Regardless of the particular methodology adopted, systematic reviews of this kind have in common a series of steps and principles. They use prespecified protocols and formalised tools for searching, screening, coding, weighting and integrating the literature. They place great emphasis on the repeatability and reliability of all the processes involved. They aim to produce evidence syntheses that are not only rigorous in the scholarly sense, but also relevant to practitioners and policymakers. To achieve this aim, they may involve 'users' right from the start of the project, in defining the review question and developing its specification. The review stages are pre-defined, and although the names and descriptions of these stages may vary according to the methodology adopted, they include in some form the steps listed in Box 6.5.

BOX 6.5

Steps in a Systematic Review

1. Initiate the review, including the creation of the team and engagement with stakeholders and specifying the aims and context of the review.
2. Formulate the review question(s) and develop a conceptual framework and a protocol for carrying out the review.
3. Decide on the nature and method of the review, develop inclusion/exclusion criteria and a search strategy (inclusion and exclusion criteria for relevance and acceptability of the literature to be reviewed; these may include: the types of studies, population, key variables, research methods, cultural and linguistic range, time frame, publication types).
4. Carry out a comprehensive search, keeping logs, and screen the results using the inclusion criteria.
5. Develop data extraction and coding tools or adopt/adapt standardised ones, and extract data from the studies included.
6. Apply quality criteria to appraise the studies included.
7. Analyse and synthesise the data extracted, and carry out checks for the quality of the review itself (for example, in terms of reliability, bias, appropriateness of any aggregation techniques, etc).
8. Interpret and communicate the findings to the relevant audiences in a report and via other means.

Although more directly applicable to quantitative empirical literature, pre-defined systematic review methods have also been refined for use with qualitative findings and conceptual literature. Thus thematic and narrative reviews, and other forms of synthesising qualitative literature (for example, meta-ethnography), aim to weave together insights from the literature into a richer and more textured account than can come from individual studies alone. Meta-ethnographies, proposed by Noblit and Hare (1988), attempt to translate concepts from one ethnographic or more widely qualitative study to another and to develop further interpretations of them, in order to organise the different 'lines of argument' into a 'wider narrative' (Gough, Oliver and Thomas, 2012: 199).

In quantitative research, a particular type of systematic review that draws on results from the literature is the specialised technique of meta-analysis. First proposed in education research (Glass, 1976), it is now widely used in other areas of research. It uses formal statistical techniques to combine separate studies into a larger 'meta' study, taking as its data the results and findings of quantitative studies that survive methodological screening. Descriptions of meta-analysis can be found in Glass, McGaw and Smith (1981), Wolf (1986) and Hunter and Schmidt (2004). Numerous examples of meta-analyses in education research can be found in the journal *Review of Educational Research*, and the book *Visible Learning* (Hattie, 2008) synthesises more than 800 meta-analyses on the factors influencing achievement in school-aged students (Box 6.6).

—BOX 6.6—

Example of Quantitative Synthesis: 'Visible Learning'

Visible Learning (Hattie, 2008) is one of the best-known syntheses of research evidence in the field of education. It is a quantitative synthesis of over 800 meta-analyses of education research – that is, of quantitative studies that aggregate information about the effectiveness of different methods and strategies that teachers can use to enable learning. In 2012, the author produced a companion book aimed at students and teachers, which connects the findings with the challenges of everyday teaching practice and communicates them in accessible language and charts.

Beyond the qualitative–quantitative distinction, systematic reviews can also be historical, conceptual and/or theoretical. Examples of these, again from the field of education research, can be found in the *Review of Educational Research*, published by the American Educational Research Association. This journal is published four times each year and is now past its 80th year. It is a top-quality international refereed journal, which publishes reviews of literature on important education research topics. It publishes different types of reviews, including quantitative meta-analyses and qualitative narrative or meta-narrative reviews, but also critical reviews of theoretical literature, and conceptual and interpretative syntheses. Box 6.7 gives several examples of critical and theoretical reviews published in RER. Another journal that specialises in such reviews is The British Educational Research Association's journal, *Review of Education*.

Examples of Critical, Historical and Conceptual-Theoretical Reviews (from recent editions of RER)

- Academic development in higher education (a conceptual review, Amundsen and Wilson, 2012).
- Student homelessness (a critical thematic review, Miller, 2011).
- Class-based theories of student resistance in education (a theoretical review, McGrew, 2011).
- The impact of technology on learning (a critical second-order meta-analysis, Tamim, Bernard, Borokhovski, Abrami, and Schmid, 2011).
- Distance and online education (a state of the art historical review – Larreamendy-Joerns and Leinhardt, 2006).

The research journal literature

6.8 Social science researchers need to be aware of the social science research journal literature, which is the primary publication outlet for professional researchers. There are a very large number of such journals. However, as in any academic field, international refereed (i.e. peer reviewed) journals are the most important, and publish the best quality research. Stringent peer review is central to achieving and maintaining this status. Papers published in top-quality international refereed journals are reviewed by experts in the field, and normally go through one or more revisions after review.

In addition to the use and transparent description of the expert peer review process, there are other indicators to use in identifying which journals are top-quality international refereed journals. For example, such journals:

- are usually published by leading publishers, and are often university-based;
- have an international editorial and advisory board;
- have both international contributors and an international readership;
- publish, in each edition, statements of both publication and review policy;
- provide clear guidelines for authors.

Chapter summary

- Empirical research literature refers to literature which reports empirical research results. The central question guiding a review of the research literature is: What previous empirical evidence is there about this question, and what does the empirical evidence tell us about the answer to the question?.

- Theoretical literature refers to theories and concepts, and discursive and analytical literature relevant to the topic. Whereas reviewing research literature means reviewing the evidence, reviewing the theoretical literature means reviewing the thinking, theorising and discussion about a topic.
- A dissertation needs to review both relevant empirical research literature and relevant theoretical literature, and to relate the present study to this literature.
- Five stages in reviewing literature are searching, screening, summarising, organising–analysing–synthesising, and writing.
- At all stages, the literature review needs to be critical, subjecting the relevant literature to careful analysis and evaluation.
- Some common problems in reviewing literature, and some dos and some don'ts are noted.
- Systematic reviews, as a method of inquiry, developed in response to the evidence-based movement in professional practice and policy, and general steps for carrying out a systematic review are described. Meta-ethnographies (qualitative) and meta-analyses (quantitative) are specific examples of systematic reviews, but there are also historical, conceptual and theoretical reviews.

KEY TERMS

Empirical research literature: literature which reports empirical research results about the topic or research question under consideration

Theoretical literature: literature which includes concepts, theories, discussions and analyses relevant to the topic

Substantive screening: screening to concentrate on both empirical research and theoretical literature which is centrally relevant to the topic and research question

Methodological screening: screening to assess critically the methodological quality of reported research

Summarising: shortening significantly by capturing the main points of a paper, both substantively and methodologically

Organising: developing a structure for the literature being reviewed; organising requires themes, sections and subsections

Analysing: breaking the literature into its constituent parts and showing how the parts relate to each other

Synthesising: making connections between the parts and showing new patterns and arrangements among them

Being critical: subjecting the literature to careful analysis and evaluation, rather than simply accepting it at face value

Systematic review: a particular approach to inquiry which can be a research project in its own right; stimulated by the evidence-based movement in professional policy and practice

Exercises and study questions

1. Why is mastery of the relevant literature expected in a doctoral dissertation?
2. What central issue guides the review of empirical research literature?
3. What are three purposes of a literature review in a dissertation?
4. What does it mean to be critical in a literature review, and why is it important?
5. How can we tell if a research journal is a top-quality international refereed journal?
6. Find a literature review on a topic you are interested in in any recent review journal in your area of social science. Analyse the review, focusing on its structure, its level of critical assessment, its degree of analysis and synthesis, and its usefulness to researchers in the field.
7. Critically assess the literature review in a recent dissertation from your university or department library.
8. Locate the relevant social science research journal section of your library. Spend time browsing:

   i. journal titles held there;
   ii. journal policy statements;
   iii. journal article titles;
   iv. article abstracts.

Discuss what you learned from this activity.

Further reading

Gough, D., Oliver, S. and Thomas, J. (2012) *An Introduction to Systematic Reviews*. London: SAGE.

Hart, C. (1998) *Doing a Literature Review: Releasing the Social Science Research Imagination*. London: SAGE.

Hart, C. (2001) *Doing a Literature Search: A Comprehensive Guide for the Social Sciences*. London: SAGE.

Ridley, D. (2012) *The Literature Review: A Step-by-Step Guide for Students*. London: SAGE.

Wallace, M. and Poulson, L. (2003) *Learning to Read Critically in Educational Leadership and Management*. London: SAGE.

seven

QUALITATIVE RESEARCH DESIGN

Contents

After studying this chapter you should be able to:

- Describe the main components of research design, and how questions, design and data are connected
- Describe and explain the strategies behind case studies, ethnography, grounded theory and action research
- Discuss the strengths and weaknesses of case studies, ethnography, grounded theory and action research
- Discuss the potential contribution of case studies, ethnography, grounded theory and action research
- Compare and contrast case studies, ethnography, grounded theory and action research, as qualitative research designs

We begin this chapter by looking at research design in general, in order to set a context both for qualitative design in this chapter and quantitative design in Chapter 10. We then focus on four common designs used in qualitative research – case studies, ethnography, grounded theory and action research.

What is research design?

7.1 Three uses of the term 'research design' can be distinguished in the literature, roughly ordered from general to specific. *At the most general level* it means all the issues involved in planning and executing a research project – from identifying the problem through to reporting and publishing the results. This is how it is used by Ackoff (1953) and Miller and Salkind (2002), for example. By contrast, *at its most specific level* the design of a study refers to the way a researcher guards against, and tries to rule out, alternative interpretations of results. *Between these two* there is the general idea of design as situating the researcher in the empirical world, and connecting research questions to data (Denzin and Lincoln, 2011). The first view is too broad for our purposes in this chapter, and the second will come up as we go through this chapter and Chapter 10. Here, we will focus on the third use of the term, since we need a way of thinking about design which is general enough to accommodate both qualitative and quantitative approaches.

In this view, research design situates the researcher in the empirical world, and connects the research questions to data, as shown in Figure 7.1. The research design is the basic plan for a piece of research, and includes four main ideas. The first is the strategy. The second is the conceptual framework. The third is the question of who or what will be studied. The fourth concerns the tools and procedures to be used for collecting and analysing empirical materials. Research design thus deals with four main questions, corresponding to these ideas.

Research design

Data collected and analysed:
- Following what strategy?
- Within what framework?
- From whom?
- How?

Research questions → [Research design] ← Data

FIGURE 7.1   Research design connects research questions to data

The data will be collected (and analysed):

- Following what strategy?
- Within what framework?
- From whom?
- How?

These questions overlap, especially the first two. Also the second question, in particular, is more typical of quantitative designs, although it does apply in some qualitative research. We will now look briefly at each of the four questions.

Following what strategy?

At the centre of the design of a study is its logic or rationale – the reasoning or the set of ideas by which the study intends to proceed in order to answer its research questions. The term 'strategy' refers to this. Thus, in qualitative research, a multiple case study design involves strategy (for example: 'the detailed investigation, using multiple sources of data, of a small number of deliberately chosen cases, guided by research questions which focus on comparisons between the cases'). Ethnography and grounded theory are different sorts of strategies the qualitative researcher might use, as is explained in Sections 7.4 and 7.5. Similarly, in quantitative research, the experiment includes a strategy designed to achieve certain comparisons. So does the correlational survey. Answers to the question 'following what strategy?' will differ according to whether the approach is qualitative, quantitative or mixed methods. If qualitative, is the strategy case study, ethnography, grounded theory, action research or some combination of these? If quantitative, is the strategy experimental, quasi-experimental or non-experimental? If there is a combination of quantitative and qualitative approaches, what is the mixture of strategies? Associated with this question of strategy is another important question: To what extent will the researcher manipulate or organise the research situation, as against studying it naturalistically? In other words, to what extent will the researcher intervene in the research situation, contriving it and constructing it for research purposes, as against studying it as it occurs? Qualitative research design is generally non-interventionist. Quantitative research design can vary from extremely interventionist to non-interventionist.

Strategy is important because it drives the design. Or, put another way, behind the design lies a logical rationale for answering the research questions – this is the strategy. In Chapter 14, on mixed methods research (Section 14.4), it is recommended that a short paragraph describing the strategy and design of a study be included in a proposal (and in a dissertation). This same advice applies to all qualitative and quantitative studies.

Within what framework?

Framework here means conceptual framework – the conceptual status of the things being studied and their relationship to each other. Quantitative designs typically have well-developed prespecified conceptual frameworks, showing variables and their relationship to each other, whereas qualitative designs show much more variability. While many qualitative studies proceed without a conceptual framework, there is often a role for conceptual frameworks in qualitative research – Miles and Huberman (1994: 18–22) give examples. A conceptual framework may be developed ahead of the study, or it may emerge as the study unfolds. Together with the strategy, it is the conceptual framework that determines how much prespecified structure a study will have.

From whom will the data be collected?

This question concerns the sampling for the research. In this form, the question is biased towards quantitative studies. The more general question 'Who or what will be studied?' (Denzin and Lincoln, 2011) covers qualitative, quantitative and mixed methods approaches.

How will the data be collected and analysed?

This question asks about the tools and procedures to be used in data collection and analysis, topics dealt with in Chapters 8 and 9 for qualitative research and Chapters 11 and 12 for quantitative research.

Together, these four components of research design situate the researcher in the empirical world. Design sits between the research questions and the data, showing how the research questions will be connected to the data, and what tools and procedures to use in answering them. Therefore design needs to follow from the questions and fit in with the data. Design must be driven by strategy. The starting point is the strategy – the logic of the approach by which the data will be used to answer the research questions. Design implements, or formalises, this strategy.

In this book, qualitative and quantitative approaches are both presented under the same three main headings – design, data collection and data analysis. Before considering these headings for qualitative research, the next section looks at the complex nature of this field, stressing its diversity.

7.2 In sharp contrast with quantitative research, which seems relatively methodologically unidimensional despite its internal technical debates, a dominant feature of present-day qualitative research is its diversity. Early in their *Handbook*, Denzin and Lincoln (1994: ix) wrote:

> It did not take us long to discover that the 'field' of qualitative research is far from a uni-fied set of principles promulgated by networked groups of scholars. In fact, we have discovered that the field of qualitative research is defined primarily by a series of essen-tial tensions, contradictions and hesitations. These tensions work back and forth among competing definitions and conceptions of the field.

Qualitative research methods is a complex, changing and contested field – a site of multiple methodologies and research practices. 'Qualitative research' therefore is not a single entity, but an umbrella term that encompasses enormous variety.

Four aspects of this diversity concern paradigms, strategies and designs, approaches to data, and methods for the analysis of data. The last three of these are dealt with in this book in Chapters 7, 8 and 9 respectively. This section comments on the diver-sity of paradigms and perspectives in qualitative research. We need to be aware of the differences between qualitative and quantitative research on this issue.

Paradigm debate and diversity has not been a typical feature of quantitative research. In general, quantitative research has been mainly based on positivism – as Tesch (1990) points out, the whole approach of constructing concepts and measuring variables is inherently positivistic.[1] The situation in qualitative research is quite differ-ent, with several different paradigm positions, and much paradigm discussion and debate. By comparison with quantitative research, the field of qualitative research is multidimensional and pluralistic with respect to paradigms. The main alternative para-digms within qualitative research include positivism, post-positivism, critical theory and constructivism, but there are finer distinctions than these and more detailed sub-divisions. Furthermore, paradigm developments within qualitative research continue, so that we do not yet have a final picture, although some convergence now seems to be taking place (see Section 2.1). It is important to be aware of this range of paradigm possibilities within qualitative research, especially when reading the literature.

One effect of these developments within qualitative methodology has been to highlight the political nature of much social science research – the recognition that research, like other things people do, is a human construction, framed and presented within a particular set of discourses (and sometimes ideologies), and conducted in a social context with certain sorts of social arrangements, especially involving fund-ing, cognitive authority and power. Both the substantive concepts and the methods research uses are ways of describing the social world for particular purposes, not just abstract and neutral academic tools. In other words, social science research is in part a political process, and always has been. Thus Apple (1991, in Lather, 1994: vii) stresses the inescapably political contexts in which we speak and work, and points out that all of our discourses are politically uninnocent. Or, as Punch (1994) puts it, politics suffuses all social science research, from the micropolitics of personal relations in a research project, to issues involving research units, universities and university departments, and ultimately government and its agencies.

Some aspects of the political nature and context of research are discussed by Sapsford and Abbott (1996), and by the various writers in *Beyond Methodology* (Fonow and Cook, 1991). A collection of readings edited by Hammersley (1993) considers the politics of research in relation to development studies in the third world, feminism, critical theory, evaluation studies and to methodology and data themselves. Hammersley (1995) also presents a comprehensive review of the changes in the nature of ideas about social research, with reference to political issues and concerns. In Chapter 6 of that book, he undertakes a detailed analysis of the question 'Is social research political?'

Research methods and styles themselves can be seen from this 'politicised' perspective. Sapsford and Abbott (1996) note the argument that choices about research styles are choices that have political elements. Research styles are not neutral, but embody implicit models of what the social world is or should be like, and of what counts as knowledge and how to get it. A consequence of this is that a large area of knowledge is suppressed as 'non-scientific' by the limitations of prevailing research methodologies. Research methods themselves, as a field of study, can be analysed and understood using the approaches and techniques developed within the field to study other things. The politics of research methods, and the university contexts in which choices about methods often occur, are discussed by Jayaratne and Stewart (1991) and by Eisner (1991).

Feminism and *postmodernism* are two perspectives from which the political aspects of research have received a great deal of attention. The former stresses the role of power in research, especially in the traditional hierarchical relationship between researcher and researched. Like critical analysis, and some types of class, race and ethnic studies, feminism also often has emancipation as its goal. The latter perspective often 'foregrounds' power directly, insisting that research is no more immune from the power–knowledge connection than any other human activity (Lather, 1991). Such perspectives apply to virtually every part of the research process – the conception of research itself, the purposes of research, the role of the researcher, approaches to design, data collection and analysis, ethical considerations and evaluative criteria.

7.2.1 Common themes within the diversity

While qualitative research is much more diverse than quantitative research, there are at the same time important recurrent features in qualitative research.

The first is that a major characteristic of qualitative research, reflected in its strategies and designs, is that it is naturalistic, preferring to study people, things and events in their natural settings. While much quantitative research (for example, an experiment) is not at all naturalistic, quantitative research can be naturalistic also, in studying people in their natural settings, without artificially contriving situations for research purposes. Some observational studies and correlational surveys fall into this category, but they are likely to have a prefigured conceptual framework and design, with prestructured data. Qualitative designs are more likely to delay conceptualising and structuring of the data until later in the research. They are also much less likely to contrive or create a situation for research purposes.

Beyond this main characteristic, there are several attempts to classify the many varieties of qualitative research by identifying its common features (for example, Tesch, 1990; Wolcott, 1992). A summary of the recurrent elements in qualitative research is given by Miles and Huberman (1994: 6–7) and is reproduced here:

- Qualitative research is conducted through an intense and/or prolonged contact with a 'field' or life situation. These situations are typically 'banal' or normal ones, reflective of the everyday life of individuals, groups, societies and organisations.
- The researcher's role is to gain a 'holistic' overview of the context under study: its logic, its arrangements, its explicit and implicit rules.
- The researcher attempts to capture data on the perceptions of local actors 'from the inside', through a process of deep attentiveness, of empathetic understanding and of suspending or 'bracketing' preconceptions about the topics under discussion.
- Reading through these materials, the researcher may isolate certain themes and expressions that can be reviewed with informants, but that should be maintained in their original forms throughout the study.
- A main task is to explicate the ways people in particular settings come to understand, account for, take action and otherwise manage their day-to-day situations.
- Many interpretations of this material are possible, but some are more compelling for theoretical reasons or on grounds of internal consistency.
- Relatively little standardised instrumentation is used at the outset. The researcher is essentially the main 'instrument' in the study.
- Most analysis is done with words. The words can be assembled, subclustered, broken into semiotic segments. They can be organised to permit the researcher to contrast, compare, analyse and bestow patterns upon them.

Many of these features will come up in different ways in this and the next two chapters. They provide a good background against which to look at some main qualitative research designs. Against this background, this chapter now describes case studies, ethnographies, grounded theory and action research, as strategies and designs commonly used in qualitative research. There will often be overlap between these four – any particular qualitative study will not necessarily be only one thing or the other. While recognising this, it is still useful to consider each separately.

Case studies

7.3 Case studies are now discussed under four headings – the general idea of case studies, some main characteristics, case studies and generalisability, and preparing a case study. Some classic case studies in social science research are shown in Example 7.1.

Examples of case studies

Beachside Comprehensive: A Case Study of Secondary Schooling (Ball, 1981), a study of mixed-ability teaching in a comprehensive school, utilised comparisons of lesson observations between those of the research and those provided by teachers.

Street Corner Society: The Social Structure of an Italian Slum (Whyte, 1955) is a classic example of a descriptive case study. It describes an Italian–American subculture, 'Cornerville', covering one neighbourhood in Boston in the 1940s. Issues of low-income youths and their ability (or inability) to break with neighbourhood ties are discussed.

In Search of Excellence: Lessons from America's Best-Run Companies by Peters and Waterman (1982) is based on more than 60 case studies of large-scale successful American businesses. The text contains cross-case analyses with each chapter dealing with characteristics associated with organisational excellence.

TVA and the Grass Roots: A Study of Politics and Organization, a classic study by Selznick (1949) of the Tennessee Valley Authority (TVA), describes the political behaviour and organisational decentralisation that occurred as a result of the TVA Act. Under this Act the TVA was charged with the duty to plan for the proper use, conservation and development of the natural resources of the Tennessee River drainage basin and its adjoining territory.

7.3.1 The general idea

What is a case study? The basic idea is that one case (or perhaps a small number of cases) will be studied in detail, using whatever methods and data seem appropriate. While there will be specific purposes and research questions, the general objective is to develop as full an understanding of this case as possible. We may be interested only in this case, or we may have in mind not just this case we are studying, but others like it. That raises the question of generalisablilty, which we will look at later.

In keeping with other approaches in qualitative research, the case study aims to understand the case in depth, and in its natural setting, recognising its complexity and its context. It also has a holistic focus, aiming to preserve and understand the wholeness and unity of the case. Therefore the case study is more a strategy than a method. As Goode and Hatt (1952: 331) pointed out many years ago: 'The case study then is not a specific technique; it is a way of organising social data so as to preserve the unitary character of the social object being studied.' This strategy for understanding contrasts strongly with the reductionist approach of some quantitative research.

What then is a case? It is difficult to give a full answer to this question, since almost anything can serve as a case, and the case may be simple or complex. But, with Miles, Huberman and Saldana (2013), we can define a case as a phenomenon of some sort occurring in a bounded context. Thus, the case may be an individual, or a role, or a small group, or an organisation, or a community or a nation. It could also be a decision, or a policy, or a process, or an incident or event of some sort, and there are other possibilities as well. Brewer and Hunter (2005) list six types of units that can be studied in research – individuals, attributes of individuals, actions and interactions, residues and artefacts of behaviour, settings, incidents and events, and collectivities. Any of these may be the focus of case study research.

Just as there are different types of cases, there are also different types of case studies. Stake (1994) distinguishes three main types:

- the *intrinsic case study*, where the study is undertaken because the researcher wants a better understanding of this particular case;
- the *instrumental case study*, where a particular case is examined to give insight into an issue, or to refine a theory; and
- the *collective case study*, where the instrumental case study is extended to cover several cases, to learn more about the phenomenon, population or general condition.

The first two of these are single case studies, where the focus is within the case. The third involves multiple cases, where the focus is both within and across cases. It is also called the *multiple case study* or sometimes the *comparative case study*.

Because of the great variation, it is not easy to define the case study. Stake gives a 'pretty loose definition' (1988: 258) – a case study is 'a study of a bounded system, emphasising the unity and wholeness of that system, but confining the attention to those aspects that are relevant to the research problem at the time'. Yin (2013) stresses that a case study is an empirical inquiry that:

- investigates a contemporary phenomenon within its real-life context, when
- the boundaries between phenomenon and context are not clearly evident, and in which
- multiple sources of evidence are used.

A dictionary of sociological terms defines a case study as:

a method of studying social phenomena through the thorough analysis of an individual case. The case may be a person, a group, an episode, a process, a community, a society, or any other unit of social life. All data relevant to the case are gathered, and all available data are organised in terms of the case. The case study method gives a unitary character to the data being studied by interrelating a variety of facts to a single case. It also provides an opportunity for the intensive analysis of many specific details that are often overlooked with other methods. (Theodorson and Theodorson, 1969)

These definitions highlight four main characteristics of case studies.

7.3.2 Four characteristics of case studies

- The case is a 'bounded system' – it has boundaries. Yin points out that the boundaries between the case and the context are not necessarily clearly evident. Nonetheless, the researcher needs to identify and describe the boundaries of the case as clearly as possible.
- The case is a case of something. This may seem obvious, but it needs stressing, to give focus to the research, and to make the logic and strategy of the research clear. Identifying what the case is a case of is also important in determining the unit of analysis, an important idea in the analysis of data.
- There is an explicit attempt to preserve the wholeness, unity and integrity of the case. The word 'holistic' is often used in this connection. At the same time, since not everything can be studied, even about one case, specific focus and within-case sampling are required. Research questions help to define this focus.
- Multiple sources of data and multiple data collection methods are very likely to be used, typically in a naturalistic setting. Many case studies will use sociological and anthropological field methods, such as observations in natural settings, interviews and narrative reports. But they may also use questionnaires and numerical data. This means that the case study is not necessarily a totally qualitative technique, though most case studies are predominantly qualitative.

7.3.3 Case studies and generalisability

A common criticism of the case study concerns its generalisability: 'This study is based on only one case, so how can we generalise?' Because this reaction is so common, we need to take this question seriously.

The first point is to ask whether we would want to generalise from a particular case study. There are two types of case study situations where generalisation would not be the objective. *First*, the case may be so important, interesting or misunderstood that it deserves study in its own right. Or it may be unique in some very important respects, and therefore worthy of study. These are examples of Stake's intrinsic case study. It is not the intention of such a study to generalise, but rather to understand this case in its complexity and its entirety, as well as in its context. *Second*, a strong argument can often be made about studying the 'negative case'. This is where a particular case seems to be markedly different from the general pattern of other cases, perhaps even completely opposite to them, creating the need to understand why this case is so different. The logic is that we can learn about the typical by studying the atypical, as when we study disease in order to learn about health. This is Stake's second type of case study, the instrumental case study. Therefore, whether a case study should even seek to generalise, and claim to be representative, depends on the context and purposes of the particular project. Generalisation should not necessarily be the objective of all research projects, whether case studies or not (Denzin, 1983).

Aside from these two situations, however, there are many case studies where we do have in mind more than just the case being studied, and where we do want to find something more broadly applicable. How can a case study produce something that might be generalisable? There are two main ways that a case study can produce potentially generalisable results. Both depend on the purposes of the case study, and especially on the way its data are analysed. *The first is by conceptualising*, the *second is by developing propositions*. In both instances, the findings from a case study can be put forward as being potentially applicable to other cases.

To *conceptualise* means that, on the basis of the disciplined and in-depth study of this case, and using methods for the analysis of data that focus on conceptualising rather than on describing (for example, those described in Chapter 9 under grounded theory analysis), the researcher develops one or more new concepts to explain some aspect of what has been studied. Indeed, to develop such new concepts may require the sort of in-depth study that is only possible in a case study. To *develop propositions* means that, based on the case being studied, the researcher puts forward one or more propositions – they could be called hypotheses – about concepts or elements or factors within the case. These can then be assessed for their applicability and transferability to other situations. This turns the traditional model of research around. In traditional quantitative research, we often begin with propositions or hypotheses – they are inputs into the research. In this view of case study research, we end with them – they become outputs of the research.

In neither of these instances will the one case study have proved the generalisability of its findings. But it can certainly suggest such generalisability, putting forward concepts or propositions for testing in further research. Clearly, every case that can be studied is in some respects unique. But every case is also, in some respects, similar to other cases. The question is whether we want to focus on what is unique about a particular case, or on what is common with other cases. At different times we need to do each of these, and we need to be aware of when we are doing each. This is a matter to be addressed in the purposes and research questions that are developed to guide a case study. When generalisability is a goal, and we are focusing on the potential common elements in a case, it is necessary for the analysis of the case study data to be conducted at a sufficient level of abstraction. The more abstract a concept, the more generalisable it is. Developing abstract concepts and propositions raises the analysis above simple description, and in this way a case study can contribute potentially generalisable findings.

The generalisation process is not mechanical, though this is more freely recognised in qualitative research than in quantitative research. There have been some attempts to see the complexity of generalisation in the quantitative context (for example, Bracht and Glass, 1968), but it is still widely regarded there as generalisation from a sample to a population. In fact, however, as Firestone (1993) points out, there are three levels of generalisation – generalisation from sample to population, analytic or theory-connected generalisation, and case-to-case transfer. Similarly, Stake (1988: 260) distinguishes between scientific generalisation, arrived at by experimentation and induction, and naturalistic generalisation, where general understandings are furthered by case studies and experience in individual events.[2]

While on this lack-of-generalisability criticism of case study research, which is often a 'knee jerk' reaction to the case study, we should note the central role given to the case method of teaching in professional schools of business, medicine and law, as well as nursing, public administration, social work and psychoanalysis (Reinharz, 1992). In these training situations, historical cases are studied in great detail and are used to train managers, doctors, lawyers, and so on, to deal with situations they will encounter in the future. This clearly underlines the potential generalisability of knowledge built from case studies. If every case were totally unique, there would be no transferability of knowledge from one case to another, and little point in the case method of training.

Case studies have had an ambiguous place in social science research (Reinharz, 1992), and historically there has often been a disapproving attitude towards the case study. This attitude is usually based on the generalisability criticism and is expressed in the condescending remark 'that's only a case study'. This book takes a different view. Properly conducted case studies, especially in situations where our knowledge is shallow, fragmentary, incomplete or non-existent, have a valuable contribution to make in social science research, in three main ways:

> The *first* is what we can learn from the study of a particular case, in its own right. As noted, the case being studied might be unusual, unique or not yet understood, so that building an in-depth understanding of the case is valuable. This might cover all of the three types of case study described by Stake.

> *Second*, only the in-depth case study can provide understanding of the important aspects of a new or persistently problematic research area. This is particularly true when complex social behaviour is involved, as is the case in much social science research. Discovering the important features, developing an understanding of them and conceptualising them for further study, is often best achieved through the case study strategy. Following this line of argument, it may be that too much research has tried to go straight to measurement and quantitative mapping, without a fuller understanding of the phenomena and processes involved that are best achieved by case studies.

> *Third*, the case study can make an important contribution in combination with other research approaches.

For example, a case study ahead of a survey can give direction to this survey not otherwise possible without the understanding built from the case study. Similarly, a survey could be followed by, or done in conjunction with, one or more case studies. Because of the limitations of the survey, the case study can 'flesh out' the picture in a way that is both crucial to our understanding, and not possible using more superficial techniques. In addition, the case study may be particularly appropriate in a student project or dissertation, where there are limited resources, including time.

These potential contributions of the case study counter the disapproving attitude described above. At the same time, this critical attitude can have validity, especially when a case study is standing alone, not integrated with other approaches to its subject matter and simply descriptive, or when more is claimed from its findings than the data can bear. Therefore, because of these criticisms, and because of the diversity within case study research, it seems especially important to be clear on the rationale behind the case study and on its purpose(s). That means clarifying the strategy of the case study and developing research questions to guide the study, either ahead of it or as focal points in the case become clear.

7.3.4 Preparing a case study

We can now summarise what has been said into a set of guidelines for preparing a case study. A case study research proposal would need to:

- be clear on what the case is and on what it is a case of, in a way that anticipates and connects to the strategy behind the research;
- be clear on the need for the study of this case and on the general purpose(s) of this case study;
- translate this general purpose into specific purposes and research questions (these may emerge during the early empirical work);
- identify the overall strategy of the case study, especially whether it is one case or multiple cases, and why;
- show how the strategy leads to the case(s) selected for study;
- show what data will be collected, from whom and how;
- show how the data will be analysed.

The last point will come up again, in Chapter 9 especially when we look at levels of abstraction in the analysis of qualitative data. Similarly, the first point, on identifying and bounding the case, has implications for the unit of analysis in the study and for the analysis of the study's data.

Ethnography

7.4 This section has three parts. First, it summarises the introduction to ethnography given by Hammersley and Atkinson in their well-known textbook on the subject. Second, it identifies some important features of the ethnographic approach to research. Third, it makes some general comments about the place of ethnography in social science research. Examples of ethnographic studies are shown in Example 7.2. The term ethnography itself comes from cultural anthropology. 'Ethno' means people or folk, while 'graphy' refers to describing something. Thus ethnography means describing a culture and understanding a way of life from the point of view of its participants – ethnography is the art and science of describing a group or culture (Fetterman, 2010; Neuman, 1994). Fielding (2008) discusses the origins of ethnography and surveys the history of its use in British colonial and American research.

7.4.1 Introduction

Hammersley and Atkinson (2007) take a 'fairly liberal' view of ethnography, whereby the ethnographer participates, overtly or covertly, in people's daily lives for an extended period of time, watching what happens, listening to what is said, asking questions and collecting any other relevant data. They point out ethnography's connection to naturalism, a way of doing social research developed by ethnographers in the face of the difficulties they saw with positivism. In naturalistic research, unlike other approaches, the social world is studied as far as possible in its natural state, undisturbed by the researcher. Research uses methods that are sensitive to the nature of the setting, and the primary aim is to describe what happens in the setting, and how the people involved see their own actions, others' actions and the context.

Drawing especially on symbolic interactionism (see Box 7.1), but also on phenomenology and hermeneutics, naturalism sees social phenomena as quite different in character from physical phenomena. The basic ideas here are that human behaviour is based upon meanings that people attribute to and bring to situations, and that behaviour is not 'caused' in any mechanical way, but is continually constructed and reconstructed on the basis of people's interpretations of the situations they are in.

BOX 7.1

Symbolic Interactionism

There is a natural affinity between ethnography and symbolic interactionism. But symbolic interactionism is also of great general importance in qualitative research, beyond ethnography. Symbolic interactionism is a general theory about human behaviour which stresses that people define, interpret and give meaning to situations, and then behave in response to these definitions, interpretations and meanings. It is the 'actor's definition of the situation', or the insider's view, which is important in accounting for human behaviour, not some 'objective' reality of the situation itself. The insider's view and the meanings of situations and actions to the participants are paramount, and symbolic interactionist researchers want access to this view and these meanings. Theoretical treatments of symbolic interactionism are given by Blumer (1969) and Woods (1992). (Examples of the use of symbolic interactionism in education research can be found in van den Berg, 2002; Evans, 2007; and O'Donoghue, 2007.)

Therefore, to understand behaviour, we need an approach that gives access to the meanings that guide behaviour. It is the capacities we have all developed as social actors – the capacity to do participant observation (see Chapter 8) – which can give us this access. As participant observers we can learn the culture or subculture of the people we are studying, and learn to understand the world as they do. Classic anthropological studies demonstrate how this approach is used to study societies other than our own, but it can be used for the study of all societies, including our own. This is because there are many different layers of cultural knowledge within any society, especially modern industrialised society.

Thus ethnography:

> exploits the capacity that any social actor possesses for learning new cultures, and the objectivity to which this process gives rise. Even where he or she is researching a familiar group or setting, the participant observer is required to treat this as anthropologically strange, in an effort to make explicit the presuppositions he or she takes for granted as a culture member. In this way, it is hoped, the culture is turned into an object available for study. Naturalism proposes that through marginality, in social position and perspective, it is possible to construct an account of the culture under investigation that both understands it from within and captures it as external to, and independent of, the researcher: in other words, as a natural phenomenon. Thus, the *description* of cultures becomes the primary goal. (Hammersley and Atkinson, 2007: 9)

The concept of culture is central in ethnography. *Culture* can be thought of as a shared set of meanings or a cognitive map of meanings (Spradley, 1980). The cultural knowledge that any group of people have is their knowledge of this map. Ethnography has developed within anthropology as the central strategy to study culture, and many anthropologists consider cultural interpretation to be ethnography's main contribution. A full discussion of the concept of culture is beyond our scope here, but useful references are Keesing (1976), Haviland et al. (2013) and Howard (1997). Derived from culture, the concept of subculture has great applicability in social science research. Any stable group of people develops over time a shared set of meanings, and in this way a subculture develops. Drawing on this, research can study ethnographically the subculture of any stable group, whether children or adults.

We can summarise this introduction to ethnography using the words of a prominent educational ethnographer:

> Ethnography means, literally, a picture of the way of life of some identifiable group of people. Conceivably, those people could be any culture-bearing group, in any time and place. In times past, the group was usually a small, intact, essentially self-sufficient social unit, and it was always a group notably 'strange' to the observer. The anthropologist's purpose as ethnographer was to learn about, record, and ultimately portray the culture of this other group. Anthropologists always study human behaviour in terms of cultural context. Particular individuals, customs, institutions, or events are of anthropological interest as they relate to a generalised description of the life-way of a socially interacting group. Yet culture itself is always an abstraction, regardless of whether one is referring to culture in general or to the culture of a specific social group. (Wolcott, 1988: 188)

7.4.2 Some main characteristics

The overarching characteristic of the ethnographic approach is its *commitment to cultural interpretation*. The point of ethnography is to study and understand the cultural and symbolic aspects of behaviour and the context of this behaviour, whatever the specific focus of the research. This specific focus is typically either some group of people, or a case (or a small number of cases), focusing on culturally significant behaviour. In addition to this central characteristic, we can identify six important and interrelated features of the ethnographic approach.

1. When studying a group of people, ethnography starts from the assumption that the *shared cultural meanings of the group* are crucial to understanding its behaviour. This is part of its commitment to cultural interpretation. As Goffman (1961: ix–x) says: 'any group of persons – prisoners, primitives, pilots or patients – develop a life of their own that becomes meaningful, reasonable and normal once you get close to it. . . .' The ethnographer's task is to uncover that meaning.

2. The ethnographer is sensitive to the *meanings* that behaviour, actions, events and contexts have, in the eyes of the people involved. What is needed is the *insider's perspective* on those events, actions and contexts. As Spindler and Spindler (1992: 73) point out: 'Sociocultural knowledge held by social participants makes social behaviour and communication sensible. Therefore a major part of the ethnographic task is to elicit that knowledge from informant participants.' The ethnographic study will be designed, and its data collection techniques organised, in line with this.

3. The group or case will be studied in its *natural setting.* A true ethnography therefore involves the researcher becoming part of that natural setting (Fielding, 2008). This explains why participant observation, discussed in Chapter 8, is the favoured method in ethnographic research. To understand any group, or any culturally significant act, event or process, it is necessary to study behaviour in its natural setting, with special reference to the symbolic world associated with this behaviour.

4. An ethnography is likely to be an *unfolding and evolving sort of study,* rather than a prestructured one. As part of developing a focus for the study, it will not normally be clear what to study in depth until some fieldwork has been done. While specific research questions and perhaps hypotheses will be used in the research, they are more likely to develop as the study proceeds, rather than to be formulated ahead of the research. This point also applies to data collection procedures. Data collection in ethnography may use several techniques, but any structuring of the data, or of data collection instruments, will be generated in situ, as the study unfolds.

5. From the point of view of *data collection techniques,* ethnography is *eclectic,* not restricted. Any techniques might be used, but fieldwork is always central. An ethnographic fieldwork continuum would range from direct non-participant observation to participant observation, then to ethnographic interviewing with one or more informants, and then to the words of the people themselves (often called, in ethnographic writing, the 'voices of the natives'). Data collection may well range across this whole continuum in an ethnography, and it may be further supplemented by anything that gives a fuller picture of the live data, such as film or audio records, documents, diaries, and so on. It may also use structured and quantitative questionnaires, with scaled variables, though these would be developed as the study proceeds.

6. Ethnographic *data collection* will typically be *prolonged and repetitive*. There is both a general and a specific reason for this. The general reason is that the reality being studied, the meanings, symbolic significance and cultural interpretation, exists on several levels. It takes time for a researcher to gain access to the deeper and most important levels of this reality (Woods, 1992). The specific reason is that the ethnographic record needs to be comprehensive and detailed, and typically focuses on things that happen again and again. The ethnographer therefore needs to observe this a sufficient number of times. Closure is achieved by recognising the point at which nothing new about its cultural significance is being learned.

7.4.3 General comments

While ethnography is a distinctive strategy, there is no one design for an ethnographic study. Its design may overlap, in whole or in part, with other designs. Thus, for example, it may use elements of the case study or grounded theory approaches, which are consistent with its orientation. It can also be used in combination with field experimentation and with surveys. Whatever the specific design, ethnography typically uses relatively unstructured empirical materials, a small number of cases and a style of analysis and writing that stresses description and interpretation (Atkinson and Hammersley, 1994). Ethnography is also both process and product. 'Process' means that it is a particular approach to research and has a particular distinctive way of going about it. 'Product' means that a certain type of research report (sometimes called the ethnographic record or a full ethnographic description) will be produced. The term 'an ethnography' illustrates the idea of ethnography as a product.

A full-scale ethnography means carrying out a detailed and demanding study, with fieldwork and data collection running over a long period of time. Where these demands exceed the time and resources of one project, there is nonetheless great value in bringing the ethnographic approach to the topic. Thus elements of the ethnographic approach, or 'borrowing ethnographic techniques' (Wolcott, 1988), are used in some social science research projects, rather than producing full-scale ethnographies. Borrowing from ethnographies is also helpful in qualitative social science research through the study of subcultures, as noted.

When would the ethnographic approach be most appropriate? In general, when we need to understand the cultural context of behaviour, and the symbolic meaning and significance of the behaviour within this context. The ethnographic approach, being a method of discovery, is particularly useful when we are dealing with something new, different or unknown. It is an excellent way of gaining insight into a culture, sub-culture or social process, particularly those in complex behavioural settings, and particularly those involving other cultures and subcultures, including those of the organisations and institutions of the modern world. The ethnographic approach can sensitise us to the cultural context and symbolic significance of behaviour we need to understand, in a way that other research approaches cannot. As Fielding (2008: 265) points out, it is often pathbreaking, and, 'as a means of gaining a first insight into a culture or social process, as a source of hypotheses for detailed investigation using other methods, it is unparalleled'.

With the culture and subculture of different groups, and of different institutions and organisations, there is both ample scope and an important contribution for the ethnographic approach in social science research. Some prominent ethnographic studies are shown in Example 7.2.

EXAMPLE 7.2

Ethnographies

Translated Woman: Crossing the Border with Esperanza's Story (Behar, 1993) is the life story of a Mexican Indian woman who was reputed to have bewitched her former husband for abusing her and leaving her for another woman. Rumours of her witchcraft powers were reinforced when her husband suddenly went blind.

When Prophecy Fails: A Social and Psychological Study of a Modern Group that Predicted the Destruction of the World, a participant observation study by Festinger et al. (1964), was carried out opportunistically with two small groups who claimed to have received messages from a planet, 'Clarion', predicting a catastrophic flood in three months. The researchers and some hired observers joined the group and conducted intensive investigations before the predicted disaster and afterwards during the period of disconfirmation.

The National Front (Fielding, 1981) is an ethnography of an extreme right racist organisation. The researcher joined the group as a member and conducted participant observation at meetings and interviews with party officials and opponents of the party, as well as content analysis of party documents.

McLaren's (1986) ethnographic study, *Schooling as a Ritual Performance: Towards a Political Economy of Educational Symbols and Gestures*, is of an inner-city Catholic school in Toronto, Canada, where the school population is largely made up of Portuguese and Italian students. McLaren analyses body postures and gestures of students and generates a theoretical framework for conceptualising embodied meaning and power.

The Man in the Principal's Office: An Ethnography is Wolcott's (1973) inquiry into the behaviour of one elementary school principal. The researcher spent two years following a typical school principal in all of his professional and many of his private activities.

Grounded theory

7.5 As a research strategy, grounded theory is specific and different. At the same time it cuts across the other strategies and designs discussed in this chapter, and is 'currently the most widely used and popular qualitative research method across a wide range of disciplines and subject areas' (Bryant and Charmaz, 2007a: 1). This book has two sections on grounded theory, one in this chapter and one in Chapter 9. This is because grounded theory is both a strategy for research and a way of analysing data. Chapter 9 (Section 9.5) deals with grounded theory analysis. In this chapter we deal with grounded theory as a strategy under six headings:

- What is grounded theory?
- A short history of grounded theory
- Theory generation research versus theory verification research
- Theoretical sampling: data-collection/data-analysis relationships
- The use of the literature in grounded theory
- The place of grounded theory research

Examples of grounded theory studies are shown below in Example 7.3, and more are noted in Chapter 9.

EXAMPLE 7.3

Examples of grounded theory studies

Using a database of 33 interviews with academic department chairpersons, Creswell and Brown (1992) in 'How chairpersons enhance faculty research: a grounded theory study' developed a grounded theory relating categories of chair influence to faculty scholarly performance.

Fresh Starts: Men and Women after Divorce (Cauhape, 1983) describes the processes by which men and women rebuild their social worlds after mid-life divorce. Participants were upwardly mobile professional men and women, who were originally from non-professional backgrounds.

Awareness of Dying (Glaser and Strauss, 1965) was the fist publication reporting the original grounded theory studies. Those studies (and this book) focus on the process of dying: what happens when people die in hospitals, how hospitals manage the situation, and the interaction between staff and patients. The research was carried out at six hospitals in San Francisco.

Time for Dying (Glaser and Strauss, 1968) was the second report of the grounded theory study. This book is based on intensive fieldwork combining observation and interviewing in the six hospitals. The focus again is on the organization of terminal care in hospitals, and the aim in the book is to describe the temporal features of dying, seeing dying itself as a social process.

From Practice to Grounded Theory (Chenitz and Swanson, 1986: Chapters 14 to 19) describes six grounded theory studies dealing with topics such as 'Getting around with emphysema' and 'Entry into a nursing home as status passage'.

The focus in Davis's (1973) study *Living with Multiple Sclerosis: A Social Psychological Analysis* was on patients with multiple sclerosis who, in certain circumstances, took the initiative in furthering the continuity of their care.

7.5.1 What is grounded theory?

The first point to make is that grounded theory is not a theory at all. It is a research strategy, or, from some points of view, a research approach or method.

Grounded theory is a research strategy whose purpose is to generate theory from data. 'Grounded' means that the theory will be generated on the basis of data; the theory will therefore be grounded in data. 'Theory' means that the objective of collecting and analysing the research data is to generate theory to explain the data. The essential idea in grounded theory is that explanatory theory will be developed inductively from data. Grounded theory, then, is an overall strategy for doing research. To implement this strategy, grounded theory has a particular set of techniques and procedures. As well as the grounded theory strategy, we can therefore talk also about grounded theory analysis – that style of analysis which uses procedures to develop a theory grounded in the data, as described in Chapter 9.

7.5.2 A short history of grounded theory

A brief look at the history of grounded theory helps in understanding it, and in seeing its present place in social science research. Its early history can be traced primarily through five key publications. In the 1960s, Glaser and Strauss began collaborative work in medical sociology, and published two landmark studies of dying in hospitals (Glaser and Strauss, 1965, 1968). These books had an important impact, and represented a different style of empirically based sociology. In response to numerous 'how did you do it?' requests from readers after *Awareness of Dying* was published, the authors wrote a book that detailed the methods they had developed and used in the dying studies. This book, published in 1967 under the title of *The Discovery of Grounded Theory*, was the first description of the method and the first key publication about grounded theory. According to Strauss and Corbin (2008: 326), *The Discovery of Grounded Theory* had three purposes – to offer a rationale for theory that was grounded, to suggest the logic for and specifics of grounded theories, and to legitimate careful qualitative research. In the years after its publication, first Glaser and then Strauss taught a grounded theory-style seminar in qualitative analysis at the University of California in San Francisco.

While a good deal of research using grounded theory to investigate a variety of phenomena was published by numerous graduates of this programme, the next methodological work, and the second key publication, came 11 years later with Glaser's *Theoretical Sensitivity*, published in 1978. Its purposes were to update methodological developments in grounded theory and to help analysts develop theoretical sensitivity. Once again, while studies reporting grounded theory research continued to be published, it was another nine years before the next methodological statement. This was Strauss's *Qualitative Analysis for Social Scientists*, published in 1987, and the third key grounded theory publication. In this book the focus is broadened to qualitative analysis in general, but grounded theory still plays the central role. It is described as 'a handbook of sorts for the better understanding of social phenomena through a particular style of qualitative analysis of data (*grounded theory*). That mode of doing analysis . . . is designed especially for *generating and testing theory*' (p. x emphasis in original).

The fourth key publication came in 1990, with Strauss and Corbin's *Basics of Qualitative Research*, subtitled 'Grounded Theory Procedures and Techniques'. It is addressed to researchers in various disciplines who aim to build theory through the analysis of qualitative data. It presents the analytic mode of grounded theory, and stresses that skill in this method of analysis is learnable by anyone who takes the trouble to study its procedures. This provoked, in response, the fifth key publication – Glaser's critique of the Strauss and Corbin book – titled *Basics of Grounded Theory Analysis* subtitled 'Emergence vs Forcing' (Glaser, 1992). In this book Glaser sets out to correct what he takes to be the misconceptions about grounded theory evident in the Strauss and Corbin book.

These five publications give the early history of the development of grounded theory. They are not the only methodological statements on grounded theory from that period, but they are the main ones. Since the early 1990s, however, there has been considerable further development and diversification of grounded theory approaches and methods. Main recent features include constructivist grounded theory (Charmaz, 2006) and the 2007 publication *The Sage Handbook of Grounded Theory* (Bryant and Charmaz, 2007b). As Bryant and Charmaz point out in Chapter 1 of the *Handbook*, grounded theory methods now seem to have taken on a life of their own. A basic three-way classification within the present-day diversification of grounded theory would include: (a) 'traditional' or 'classical' grounded theory, as practised by Glaser and his followers, (b) followers of the Strauss and Corbin approach, and (c) followers of Charmaz's constructivist grounded theory. On the other hand, on a more detailed level, Denzin identifies seven versions. Thus grounded theory is best viewed today not as one method, but as a family of methods (Bryant and Charmaz, 2007a: 10).

7.5.3 Theory generation versus theory verification

Grounded theory has as its explicit purpose the generation of theory from data. This raises the contrast between research that aims to generate theory and research that aims to verify theory. As pointed out in Chapter 2, this contrast represents a difference in research styles. Traditionally, much research, especially quantitative research, has followed the theory verification model, as indicated in the importance it has traditionally given to the role of the hypothesis. Many research methods texts insisted that hypotheses were central to research and that, since the hypothesis was deduced from some more general theory, the point of the research was the testing of theory.

As noted in Chapter 4, this book takes a different view of the hypothesis, recommending that it be included only when appropriate. In the grounded theory approach, which aims to generate theory, no 'up-front' theory is proposed, and no hypotheses are formulated for testing ahead of the research. The research does not start with a theory from which it deduces hypotheses for testing. It starts with some research questions and an open mind, then it moves to data, aiming to end up with a theory. This emphasis was developed deliberately by Glaser and Strauss as a reaction to the exclusive insistence on theory verification research, especially in the American sociology of the 1950s.

It is useful to make this theory generation-vs-verification contrast sharply, in order to highlight the difference in research styles. But in fact, in practice, the distinction is not so sharp. For while we may start without a theory, and have the objective of creating one, it is not long into the theorising process before we are also wanting to test theoretical ideas that are emerging. So, in fact, theory generation depends on progressive verification, as well. Another way of saying this is that grounded theory is essentially an inductive technique, but it uses deduction as well. It stresses induction as the main tool for theory development, but, in developing the theory, deduction will also often be necessary.

7.5.4 Theoretical sampling: data-collection/data-analysis relationships

Grounded theory has a specific approach to this topic, which is different from many other approaches. (It is not unique, however – see Hughes (1958) and Becker (1971).)

In the traditional view of research, data collection is a discrete stage in the research, usually to be completed before data analysis begins. In grounded theory, the pattern is different. Guided by some initial research questions, the researcher will collect a first set of data, often quite small. At this point, analysis of the data begins, using the procedures to be described in Chapter 9. The second set of data will be collected after the first analysis of data, guided by emerging directions in this analysis. This is the principle of theoretical sampling – the idea that subsequent data collection should be guided by theoretical developments that emerge in the analysis of previously collected data. This cycle of alternation between data collection and analysis will not stop at two repetitions. It continues until theoretical saturation is achieved – that is, until new data are not showing new theoretical elements, but are rather confirming what has already been found. This pattern is shown in Figure 7.2.

It is becoming more common to find this sort of data-collection/data-analysis relationship in qualitative research today. It is different from traditional research, but it resembles what we normally do in everyday life, when we encounter a puzzling situation. Like much else in grounded theory, it models the way humans have always learned. In this respect, grounded theory is faithful to its philosophical roots in pragmatism (Glaser and Strauss, 1967).

FIGURE 7.2   Theoretical sampling: data-collection/data-analysis relationships

7.5.5 The use of the literature in grounded theory

Grounded theory also has a different perspective on this matter from other research approaches. The difference lies in how the literature is dealt with, and when it is introduced, and follows from the stress that grounded theory places on theory generation.

If a satisfactory theory already exists on a particular topic, there is no point in mounting a study to generate a new theory about the topic. The rationale for doing a grounded theory study is that we have no satisfactory theory on the topic, and that we do not understand enough about it to begin theorising. In this case, we will want to approach the data as open-mindedly as possible, guided by research questions. While a general comment on the literature may be necessary to orient a study, and to show the lack of satisfactory theory, the problem with a detailed substantive review of the literature in advance of a study is that it can strongly influence us when we begin working with the data.

As is detailed in Chapter 9 we want to begin the analysis by finding categories and concepts within the data, not by bringing them to the data, from the literature or from anywhere else. In such a case, it makes sense to delay the literature-reviewing stage of the work, at least until conceptual directions within the data have become clear. We will introduce the literature later than would normally be done, seeing the relevant literature as further data for the study. This is the key concept in using the literature in grounded theory – the literature is seen as further data to be fed into the analysis, but at a stage in the data analysis when theoretical directions have become clear. This use of the literature is consistent with the overall logic of grounded theory research. The whole approach is organised around the principle that theory that is developed will be grounded in data.

7.5.6 The place of grounded theory research

It is not surprising that grounded theory has become a widely used approach in qualitative research. I think there are five main reasons for this:

1. While much is said in the research methodology literature about the need to generate theory in research, very little is said about *how* to do this. Grounded theory explicitly addresses this question.
2. It represents a coordinated, systematic but flexible overall research strategy, in contrast to the ad hoc and uncoordinated approaches that have sometimes characterised qualitative research.
3. It brings a disciplined and organised approach to the analysis of qualitative data. In the qualitative research context, with its history of a lack of well-formulated methods for the analysis of data, this point has great appeal.
4. There are impressive demonstrations of what the grounded theory approach can produce in a research area. These began with the dying studies of Glaser and Strauss, and have continued, initially in the area of medical sociology, and now much more broadly (Bryant and Charmaz, 2007b).

5. A fifth reason has to do with the identification of research problems from professional practice, and from organisational and institutional contexts. In these situations, a traditional hypothesis-testing approach is not appropriate. Many of these problems confronting social science researchers, especially in applied areas, are substantively new, because they come from new developments in professional practice and/or from newly developing organisational contexts. Empirical research, much of it qualitative, is needed in these areas, and the theory verification approach would be inappropriate. The theory generation approach of grounded theory has much to recommend it in these substantively new areas, where there is a lack of grounded concepts for describing and explaining what goes on. Grounded theory appeals because it concentrates on discovering concepts, hypotheses and theories.

Action research

7.6 Early in *The Handbook of Action Research*, editors Reason and Bradbury (2007: 1) tell us that there is no short answer to the question 'What is action research?' Rather, the term is used for a family of related strategies that share certain important common ideas, while differing in details of their approach to the research. The differences have led to a variety of names by which such researchers describe their approach – technical action research, practical action research, emancipatory action research, participatory action research and collaborative action research are examples, along with feminist action research – but the generic term action research probably encompasses most of the approaches (Kemmis and McTaggart, 2000: 567). This section concentrates on the main common ideas behind the different strands of action research.[3]

The central idea is conveyed by the term 'action research' itself. Action and research are brought together: action researchers 'engage in careful, diligent inquiry, not for purposes of discovering new facts or revising accepted laws or theories, but to acquire information having practical application to the solution of specific problems related to their work' (Stringer, 2004: 3). Action research brings together the acting (or the doing) and the researching (or the inquiring). In contrast to the ideas of inquiry for its own sake and building knowledge for its own sake, action research aims to design inquiry and build knowledge for use in the service of action to solve practical problems. Therefore, in action research, the inquiry deliberately starts from a specific practical or applied problem or question. Its whole purpose is to lead to action to solve this practical problem or answer this practical question. As Reason and Bradbury (2008: 1) say, action research 'seeks to bring together action and reflection, theory and practice, in participation with others, in the pursuit of practical solutions to issues of pressing concern to people'. And again (2008: 2): 'A primary purpose of action research is to produce practical knowledge that is useful to people in the everyday conduct of their lives.' In a similar vein, Stringer's five-part action research sequence shows 'basic research' in four parts (research design, data gathering, data analysis, communication), with action research adding a fifth part – action itself – to these.

Stringer's five-part action research sequence shows clearly that research itself is central in the sequence. That is, systematic, disciplined inquiry – research – is brought to bear on a practical problem that requires a solution – action. All of this is done in a carefully organised framework. This systematic, disciplined inquiry – this research – is, of course, empirical. Therefore it draws on the approaches to research covered in this book. Thus action research may involve quantitative data methods and designs, qualitative data methods and designs, or mixed methods data and designs. While action research is usually thought of as a qualitative approach, and is included here under qualitative research designs, it does not rely only on qualitative data. On the contrary, it uses quantitative data whenever they are appropriate and available. It is like case study research in this respect.

An important characteristic of action research, which sets it apart from other designs, is that it is usually *cyclical* in nature, reflecting the fact that people usually work towards solutions to their problems in cyclical, iterative ways. The words 'cycle', 'spiral' and (less often) 'helix' are used by writers on action research to describe this. They convey the idea that the one piece of research leading to the one set of actions is not the end of the process, but rather the start of a cycle or spiral. The research produces outcomes that lead to the taking of action, but this in turn generates further questions for research, which in turn generates further action, and so on. Kemmis and McTaggart (2000: 595–6) diagram the action research spiral, and write that, while difficult to describe the process as a series of steps, participatory action research is generally thought to involve a spiral of self-reflective cycles of:

- planning a change;
- acting and observing the consequences of the change;
- reflecting on these processes and consequences, and then;
- replanning;
- acting and observing;
- reflecting, and so on.

Stringer begins with the action research cycle, then broadens this to the action research helix and then spiral. Whichever version we consider, the main idea here is that action research is repetitive, continuing and cyclical.

For many people, the spiral of cycles of self-reflection, involving planning, acting and observing, reflecting, replanning and so on, has become the dominant feature of action research as an approach. For Kemmis and McTaggart, however, there are seven additional important features of participatory action research – it is a social process, participatory, practical and collaborative, emancipatory, critical, recursive, and it aims to transform both theory and practice.

Just as action research does not separate inquiring from doing, neither does it separate the researcher from the researched. An older version of action research, especially in education research in the 1970s, located the two roles in the one person – the teacher became the action researcher. This led to credibility problems for action research, since most teachers did not have the research skills to communicate effectively to an often-sceptical research community. Now the action and the research are seen as different roles, and are typically done by different people, but collaboration and participation between the different people are stressed. Stringer (2004) distinguishes practitioner research in education from action research in education on this very point. When the teacher steps back, reflects, collects information, observes classroom interaction and so on, this is practitioner research. When the teacher engages others in the process of inquiry, with the intent of solving an educational work problem together, this is action research. Collaborative participation becomes central.

Similarly, Kemmis and McTaggart (2000: 595) believe that, while some action research depends on solitary processes of systematic self-reflection by the action researcher, the steps in the self-reflection spiral are best undertaken collaboratively by co-participants in the research process. This is why they prefer the term *participatory action research*. Their formulation highlights the role of participation and collaboration in some types of action research. When participation and collaboration are involved, action research develops new research relationships, and often works towards building a community of learners. Whether this happens or not, the researcher and the researched become co-researchers, collaborating participants in the action research.

Action research has diverse origins. Many writers trace it back to the social experiments of Kurt Lewin in the 1940s, but Reason and Bradbury (2007: 2–4) identify other important influences as well. These include the contemporary critique of positivist science and scientism, Marxism ('the important thing is not to understand the world but to change it'), the liberating perspectives on gender and race, the practices of experiential learning and psychotherapy, and some types of spiritual practices. Kemmis and McTaggart (2000: 568) also note the connection of participatory research to liberation theology and Third World movements aimed at social transformation. In education, action research became popular in the 1970s, but then declined in popularity and credibility in the 1980s, only to re-surface strongly in the 1990s. An indication of its present popularity in education research is the vast literature on action research in education (Stringer, 2004). An indication of its present prominence in social science research in general comes from the recent and already mentioned *Handbook of Action Research* (Reason and Bradbury, 2007).

Chapter summary

- Research design connects research questions to data. It is based on a strategy, often involves a conceptual framework, and shows from whom, and how, data will be collected and analysed.
- Multiple paradigms, perspectives and strategies and designs characterise present-day qualitative research. At the same time, there are important common features across this diversity.
- In case study research, one case (or a small number of cases) is studied in depth, in context, in its natural setting and holistically. There should be a logic behind case selection, and research questions and multiple sources of data are normally involved.

- Ethnography focuses on the way of life of some group of people, which can only be understood from the insider's perspective. Culture – as a shared set of meanings – is the central concept, and multiple sources of data, mostly qualitative, are used by the ethnographer to uncover cultural meanings.
- Grounded theory is a research strategy whose objective is to generate explanatory theory grounded in data. It has evolved today into a family of methods, with distinctive concepts and approaches.
- Action research is a family of related approaches which stress the bringing together of action and research, in a cyclical pattern directed at solving practical problems, often in a participative situation.

KEY TERMS

Research design: connects research questions to data; design is based on a strategy, and shows from whom, and how, data will be collected and analysed

Case study: the detailed, holistic and in-context study of one case or a small number of cases

Ethnography: a research strategy which focuses on uncovering the shared meanings which develop among any stable group of people

Culture: the set of meanings shared by a group of people, without which their behaviour and actions cannot be understood

Symbolic interactionism: a general theory which stresses that people behave in terms of the way they define (or interpret, or give meaning to) situations

Insider's perspective: the definition, interpretation or meaning given to a situation by the participants in that situation

Grounded theory: a research strategy for generating theory grounded in data

Theoretical sampling: later stages of data collection are guided by theoretical developments emerging from earlier data

Action research: a research strategy which combines action and research in cyclical spirals to focus on the solution to a problem

Exercises and study questions

1. List four questions that can help us understand research design. What is the function of research design?
2. What is meant by research strategy, and what is its relationship to research design?
3. What is a case study, and what are its strengths and weaknesses as a research strategy?
4. Outline the strategy and design for the study of a case (an individual, a group, an organisation, a decision, etc.) with which you are familiar. Follow the points given in Section 7.3.4.

5. What does ethnography mean? What is its connection to anthropology, and to the concept of culture?
6. How can ethnography be applied in social science research?
7. What is meant in research by the insider's perspective?
8. Why did Glaser and Strauss use the term 'grounded' to describe the grounded theory method they developed?
9. What does it mean to say that grounded theory is best seen as a family of methods?
10. What is theoretical sampling?
11. What key characteristics of action research make it a distinct research strategy?

Further reading

Case studies

Ragin, C.C. and Becker, H.S. (eds) (1992) *What is a Case? Exploring the Foundations of Social Inquiry*. New York: Cambridge University Press.

Stake, R.E. (1988) 'Case study methods in educational research: seeking sweet water', in R.M. Jaeger (ed.), *Complementary Methods for Research in Education*. Washington, DC: American Educational Research Association. pp. 253–300.

Stake, R.E. (1994) 'Case studies', in N.K. Denzin and Y.S. Lincoln (eds), *Handbook of Qualitative Research*. Thousand Oaks, CA: SAGE. pp. 236–47.

Stake, R.E. (2006) *Multiple Case Study Analysis*. New York: Guilford Press.

Yin, R.K. (2013) *Case Study Research: Design and Methods*. 5th edn. Thousand Oaks, CA: SAGE.

Ethnography

Agar, M. (1986) *Speaking of Ethnography*. Beverly Hills, CA: SAGE.

Atkinson, P. and Hammersley, M. (1994) 'Ethnography and participant observation', in N.K. Denzin and Y.S. Lincoln (eds), *Handbook of Qualitative Research*. Thousand Oaks, CA: SAGE. pp. 248–61.

Atkinson, P., Delamont, S., Coffey, A., Lofland, J. and Lofland, L. (eds) (2007) *Handbook of Ethnography*. London: SAGE.

Crang, M. and Cook, I. (2007) *Doing Ethnographies*. London: SAGE.

Fetterman, D.M. (2010) *Ethnography Step by Step*. 3rd edn. Thousand Oaks, CA: SAGE.

Gobo, G. (2007) *Doing Ethnography*. London: SAGE.

Hammersley, M. and Atkinson, P. (2007) *Ethnography: Principles in Practice*. 3rd edn. London: Routledge.

Spindler, G. and Spindler, L. (1992) 'Cultural process and ethnography: an anthropological perspective', in M.D. LeCompte, W.L. Millroy and J. Preissle (eds), *The Handbook of Qualitative Research in Education*. San Diego, CA: Academic Press. pp. 53–92.

Wolcott, H.F. (1988) 'Ethnographic research in education', in R.M. Jaeger (ed.), *Complementary Methods for Research in Education*. Washington, DC: American Educational Research Association. pp. 187–249.

Woods, P.H. (1986) *Inside Schools: Ethnography in Educational Research*. London: Routledge & Kegan Paul.

Grounded theory

Bryant, A. and Charmaz, K. (eds) (2007) *The Sage Handbook of Grounded Theory*. Thousand Oaks, CA: SAGE.

Charmaz, K. (2006) *Constructing Grounded Theory*. Thousand Oaks, CA: SAGE.

Glaser, B. (1978) *Theoretical Sensitivity*. Mill Valley, CA: Sociology Press.

Glaser, B. (1992) *Basics of Grounded Theory Analysis: Emergence vs Forcing*. Mill Valley, CA: Sociology Press.

Glaser, B. and Strauss, A. (1967) *The Discovery of Grounded Theory: Strategies for Qualitative Research*. Chicago: Aldine.

Strauss, A. (1987) *Qualitative Analysis for Social Scientists*. New York: Cambridge University Press.

Strauss, A. and Corbin, J. (1994) 'Grounded theory methodology: an overview', in N.K. Denzin and Y.S. Lincoln (eds), *Handbook of Qualitative Research*. Thousand Oaks, CA: SAGE. pp. 273–85.

Strauss, A. and Corbin, J. (2008) *Basics of Qualitative Research: Grounded Theory Procedures and Techniques*. 3rd edn. Thousand Oaks, CA: SAGE.

Action research

Herr, K. and Anderson, G.L. (2005) *The Action Research Dissertation*. London: SAGE.

Kemmis, S. and McTaggart, R. (2000) 'Participatory action research', in N.K. Denzin and Y.S. Lincoln (eds), (2011), *Handbook of Qualitative Research*. 4th edn. Thousand Oaks, CA: SAGE.

Reason, P. and Bradbury, H. (eds) (2007) *Handbook of Action Research*. 2nd edn. London: SAGE.

Sagor, R. (2004) *Action Research Guidebook*. London: SAGE.

Stringer, E. (1996) *Action Research: A Handbook for Practitioners*. Thousand Oaks, CA: SAGE.

Stringer, E. (2007) *Action Research in Education*. 2nd edn. Upper Saddle River, NJ: Pearson.

Taylor, C., Wilkie, M. and Baser, J. (2006) *Doing Action Research*. London: SAGE.

Notes

1. We should be careful, however, about labelling all quantitative research positivistic, for two reasons. One is that the term 'positivism' has many different interpretations (Blaikie, 1993); the other is that some researchers (for example, Marsh, 1982) point out that some quantitative work is not positivist.

2. Stake also reports a personal communication from Julian Stanley: 'When I want to find out something important for myself, I often use the case study approach' (1988: 262). This statement is worth bringing to the attention of critics of case study research, coming as it does from a respected quantitative researcher, and a major contributor to its literature.

3. Kemmis and McTaggart (2000: 568–72) identify seven approaches within the general area of participatory action research. They are: participatory research, critical action research, classroom action research, action learning, action science, soft systems approaches and industrial action research.

eight
COLLECTING QUALITATIVE DATA

Contents

After studying this chapter you should be able to:

- Identify and describe the main types of research interviewing
- List the practical issues involved in managing qualitative interviews
- Describe the strengths and weaknesses of structured and unstructured interviewing and observation
- Describe participant observation and explain its relationship to ethnography
- Identify opportunities for using documentary data in social science research
- Explain how data collection procedures can affect the quality of interview data
- Explain the role of sampling in qualitative research and the need for a sampling strategy

Qualitative social science researchers study spoken and written representations and records of human experience, using multiple methods and multiple sources of data. Several types of data collection might well be used in the one qualitative project. In this chapter, we deal with some of the main ways of collecting qualitative data – the interview, observation, participant observation and documents.

The interview

8.1 The interview is the most prominent data collection tool in qualitative research. It is a very good way of accessing people's perceptions, meanings, definitions of situations and constructions of reality. It is also one of the most powerful ways we have of understanding others. As Jones (1985: 46) puts it:

> In order to understand other persons' constructions of reality, we would do well to ask them . . . and to ask them in such a way that they can tell us in their terms (rather than those imposed rigidly and a priori by ourselves) and in a depth which addresses the rich context that is the substance of their meanings.

While interviewing is basically about asking questions and receiving answers, there is much more to it than this, especially in a qualitative research context. Consider this description:

> Interviewing has a wide variety of forms and a multiplicity of uses. The most common type of interviewing is individual, face-to-face verbal interchange, but it can also take the form of face-to-face group interviewing, mailed or self-administered questionnaires, and telephone surveys. Interviewing can be structured, semi-structured, or unstructured. It can be used for marketing purposes, to gather political opinions, for therapeutic reasons, or to produce data for academic analysis. It can be used for the purpose of measurement or its scope can be the understanding of an individual or a group perspective. An interview can be a one-time, brief exchange, say

Structured interviews	Focused or semi-structured interviews	Unstructured interviews

←———→

Standardised interviews	In-depth interviews	In-depth interviews
Survey interviews	Survey interviews	Clinical interviews
Clinical history taking	Group interviews	Group interviews
		Oral or life history interviews

FIGURE 8.1 The continuum model for interviews

Source: Minichiello et al., 1990: 89

> **five minutes over the telephone, or it can take place over multiple, lengthy sessions, sometimes spanning days, as in life-history interviewing. (Fontana and Frey, 1994: 361)**

In short, there are many different types of interviews.

8.1.1 Types of interviews

Much has been written on the topic of different types of interviews. For example, Patton (2002) distinguishes three main types of interview – the informal conversational interview, the general interview guide approach and the standardised open-ended interview. Minichiello et al. (1990) provide a useful continuum of interviewing methods, based on the degree of structure involved. It is shown in Figure 8.1, and is similar to the typology Fielding (1996a) describes, using the terms standardised, semi-standardised and non-standardised. Similarly, Fontana and Frey (1994) use a three-way classification of structured, semi-structured and unstructured interviewing, and they apply that to individual and group interviews. This section draws on their work.

Whichever typology we use, important dimensions of this variation are the degree of structure in the interview, and how deep the interview tries to go. At the left-hand end of the continuum, interviews are tightly structured and standardised. Here, interview questions are planned and standardised in advance, precoded categories are used for responses, and the interview itself does not attempt to go to any great depth. At the right-hand end, by contrast, interviews are unstructured and open-ended. Interview questions are not preplanned and standardised, but instead there are general questions to get the interview going and to keep it moving. Specific follow-up questions will then emerge as the interview unfolds, and the wording of those questions will depend upon directions the interview takes. There are no pre-established categories for responding.

With so many different types, the interview is a data collection tool of great flexibility, which can be adapted to suit a wide variety of research situations. Different types of interview have different strengths and weaknesses, and different purposes in research. The type of interview selected should therefore be aligned with the strategy, purposes and the research questions, as Fontana and Frey (1994: 373) write:

Clearly, different types of interviewing are suited to different situations. If we wish to find out how many people oppose a nuclear repository, survey research is our best tool, and we can quantify and code the responses and use mathematical models to explain our findings (Frey, 1993). If we are interested in opinions about a given product, a focus group interview will provide us with the most efficient results; if we wish to know and understand about the lives of Palestinian women in the resistance (Gluck, 1991), we need to interview them at length and in depth in an unstructured way.

Thus we begin by first recognising that there are many different types of interview, and then we select the interview type based on research purposes and questions. The type of interview we select will influence the practical aspects of the interview, and how we manage the process.

Structured interviews

In structured interviews the respondent is asked a series of pre-established questions, with pre-set response categories. There is little room for variation in response, though open-ended questions may sometimes be used as well. All respondents receive the same questions in the same order, delivered in a standardised manner. Flexibility and variation are minimised, while standardisation is maximised. In this sort of interview, the interviewer attempts to play a neutral role, and a neutral manner and demeanour are encouraged in executing that role. The stimulus–response nature of this type of interview stresses rational and factual responses, rather than emotional responses (Fontana and Frey, 1994). The standardised interview schedule is described in detail by Wilson (1996), and Fielding (1996b) gives suggestions for developing structured and semi-structured interview schedules.

Group interviews – focus groups

Group interviewing is a general term, where the researcher works with several people simultaneously, rather than just one. The focus group was originally a particular type of group interview used in marketing and political research, but now the terms 'focus group interview' and 'group interview' are used more interchangeably. Group interviewing is now popular in social science research, though it is not new.

There are several different types of group interview, and like other interviews they can be unstructured, semi-structured or highly structured. Since different types of group interviews have different purposes, which type should be used in a particular research situation depends on the context and research purposes. Fontana and Frey (1994) tabulate the characteristics of five different types of group interviews, and Morgan (1988) and Shamdasani and Rook (2006) also discuss the characteristics of different types of group interviews, along with their purposes, strengths and weaknesses.

The role of the researcher changes in a group interview, functioning more as a moderator or facilitator, and less as an interviewer. The process will not be one of alternate question and answer, as in the traditional interview. Rather, the researcher will be facilitating, moderating, monitoring and recording group interaction. The group interaction will be directed by questions and topics supplied by the researcher. This means particular skills are required of the group interviewer (Merton et al., 1990; Fontana and Frey, 1994).

Group interviews can make an important contribution in social science research. Writing about focus groups, Morgan (1988: 12) points out that 'the hallmark of focus groups is the explicit use of the group interaction to produce data and insights that would be less accessible without the interaction found in a group'. Well-facilitated group interaction can assist in bringing to the surface aspects of a situation that might not otherwise be exposed. The group situation can also stimulate people in making explicit their views, perceptions, motives and reasons. This makes group interviews an attractive data gathering option when research is trying to probe these aspects of people's behaviour. They are inexpensive, data-rich, flexible, stimulating, recall-aiding, cumulative and elaborative. But there can also be problems associated with group culture and dynamics, and in achieving balance in the group interaction (Fontana and Frey, 1994).

The data from group interviews are the transcripts (or other records) of the group's interaction. They might be used as the only data gathering technique in a study or, frequently, in conjunction with other qualitative or quantitative techniques. As in mixed methods research (see Chapter 14), it is becoming increasingly common today to see group interviews used in conjunction with surveys, sometimes to assist in developing questionnaires, and sometimes used after the survey, to 'flesh out' views and information on topics surveyed. The numerous specific practical issues that need to be considered in planning the use of group interviews are dealt with in the two monographs by Morgan (1997) and by Shamdasani and Rook (2006). The latter includes a useful typology of focus group questions.

Unstructured interviews

There is a wide range indeed when it comes to unstructured interviewing. The traditional type of unstructured interview is the non-standardised, open-ended, in-depth interview, sometimes called the ethnographic interview. It is used as a way of understanding the complex behaviour of people without imposing any a priori categorisation which might limit the field of inquiry. It is also used to explore people's interpretations and meanings of events and situations, and their symbolic and cultural significance. Fontana and Frey discuss seven aspects of unstructured interviewing, and use a variety of examples from the research literature to illustrate each aspect. These aspects provide a useful checklist of things to think about when planning data collection by unstructured or ethnographic interview:

- accessing the setting;
- understanding the language and culture of respondents;
- deciding on how to present oneself;

- locating an informant;
- gaining trust;
- establishing rapport;
- collecting the empirical materials.

How each is handled will vary with the nature of the situation and respondents. There is, and needs to be, flexibility in the unstructured interview situation (what Douglas (1985) calls creative interviewing), especially for oral history and life history projects. The unstructured interview is a powerful research tool, widely used in social science research and other fields, and capable of producing rich and valuable data. A successful in-depth interview has many of the characteristics of a prolonged and intimate conversation. Skill in this sort of interviewing, and especially in probing meanings, interpretations and symbolic significance, does not come naturally, and most of us need at least some training to develop this skill.

8.1.2 Feminist perspectives on interviewing

Feminist research makes great use of the semi-structured and unstructured interview: 'The use of semi-structured interviews has become the principal means by which feminists have sought to achieve the active involvement of their respondents in the construction of data about their lives' (Graham, quoted in Reinharz, 1992: 18).

Feminist research also redefines the interview in significant ways. This is because the feminist perspective sees traditional interviewing as a masculine paradigm, embedded in a masculine culture, stressing masculine traits and excluding sensitivity, emotionality and other traits culturally viewed as feminine. Oakley (1981) identifies the contradiction between scientific positivistic research requiring objectivity and detachment, and feminist interviewing requiring openness, emotional engagement and the development of trust in a potentially long-term relationship.

A primary consideration for feminists concerns the researcher's role. The feminist preference is typically for non-hierarchical research relationships. The traditional interview is seen not only as paternalistic, condescending in its attitudes towards women and not accounting for gendered differences, but also as based on a hierarchical relationship with the respondent in a subordinate position. As Fontana and Frey (1994) point out, there are both moral and ethical objections to this, and methodological ones as well – better data are at stake. Minimising status differences between interviewer and respondent, and developing a more equal relationship based on trust that includes both self-disclosure by the researcher and reciprocity, can avoid the 'hierarchical pitfall' (Reinharz, 1992), enabling greater openness and insight, a greater range of responses, and therefore richer data. In this perspective, as Haig (1997) points out and as the above quote from Graham suggests, researcher and researched become co-creators of data through the interview. Feminist redefinition of the interview situation transforms interviewers and respondents into co-equals, who are carrying on a conversation about mutually relevant, often biographically critical, issues (Denzin and Lincoln, 1994: 354).

Reinharz (1992) points out that there is no single uniform perspective in feminism on such topics as researcher–interviewee relationships and self-disclosure. Rather there is openness to different possible meanings of these things in different research situations. Feminist-based interview research has already modified social science concepts, and created important new ways of seeing the world. By listening to women, understanding women's membership in particular social systems, and establishing the distribution of phenomena accessible only through sensitive interviewing, feminist researchers have uncovered previously neglected or misunderstood worlds of experience. (Reinharz, 1992: 44). Reinharz points out also that feminist researchers are likely to continue to refine and elaborate the method of interviewing, as more and more experience with it is built up.

Sharing some of the same concerns as feminists, postmodern ethnographers have been concerned with moral aspects of the traditional researcher–subject interview, with the controlling role of the interviewer, and with the influence of the interviewer on data and reporting. As well as gender, they stress the importance of race (Stanfield, 1985), and the perspectives of the decolonialised, the disadvantaged and the disempowered. Fontana and Frey (1994) note several directions in which postmodern researchers take account of these matters. They include polyphonic interviewing, interpretive interactionism, critical ethnography and oralysis, specialist topics beyond our scope in this book.

8.1.3 Practical aspects of interviewing

A major decision has been made once the type of interview has been selected, in accordance with the research strategy, paradigm considerations (if relevant), purposes and questions of the study. Practical aspects of interviewing then include the selection of interview respondents, managing the interview and recording.

Interview respondents

The main issues that need to be considered here are:

- Who will be interviewed and why?
- How many will be interviewed, and how many times will each person be interviewed?
- When and for how long will each respondent be interviewed?
- Where will each respondent be interviewed?
- How will access to the interview situation be organised?

All of these issues depend on the type of interview selected, where it falls on the structured–unstructured continuum shown earlier, and the perspective from which the research is being conducted. The first two questions relate to the sampling plan for the project, which itself depends on the research questions and purposes. The next two questions, concerning time and location, are obvious things that need organising, but their influence on the quality of the data can be decisive. Recognising the importance of these questions, and careful consideration of the alternatives in any particular research situation, enables decisions to be made that maximise the quality of the data, in the light of ethical responsibilities towards those being interviewed. The last point concerns gaining access. Much is written on this (for example, Lofland et al., 2004; Hammersley and Atkinson, 2007), and how it is done depends on the particular research project, its setting and context. How interviewers make contact with respondents, and organise access, can affect all stages of the interviewer–interviewee relationship, and with that the quality, reliability and validity of interview data.

Managing the interview

A general checklist for managing the interview includes:

- preparation for the interview – the interview schedule;
- beginning the interview – establishing rapport;
- communication and listening skills;
- asking questions – the sequence and types of questions;
- closing the interview.

The importance of each of these, and how each is handled, is determined by the type of interview selected. Thus, a highly-structured interview requires a schedule, which will need developing and pre-testing. If practical, trialling of the process and situation for this type of interview is also recommended, since the quality of the preparation will influence the quality of the data. On the other hand, an unstructured interview would have only a general sense of the questions or topics to be discussed, would be kept deliberately open-ended, and there would be no attempt at standardisation.

The more unstructured the interview, the more communication skills in general, and listening and follow-up questioning in particular, are important. Considerable literature exists on this topic – see, for example, Woods (1986), Keats (1988) and McCracken (1988) – which is useful in developing the skills involved. In particular, Minichiello et al. (1990) show 16 subskills of listening which they recommend researchers practise in order to improve their listening competency.

Question-asking is at the centre of interviewing, and has been analysed extensively in research methods literature. This analysis includes the way questions are delivered, the wording that is used, and the sequence and types of questions that can be asked. This latter topic in particular has been the subject of classification systems. For example, Patton (2002) classifies questions into experience/behaviour, opinion/belief, feeling, knowledge, sensory and demographic/background. Patton also goes on to discuss and classify probing questions, providing a useful checklist of questions that will often be necessary at different stages during the interview. Other classifications are described by Sudman and Bradburn (1982) and by Foddy (1993).

Finally, ways of closing the interview may also require attention, and six strategies for closing the interview are described by Minichiello et al. (1990). The applicability of these points, and of much of the literature cited, depends very much on the perspective, on the approach taken to interviewing in a particular project, and on the type of interview selected.

Recording

How the interview data are to be recorded needs to be considered in planning the research. For highly-structured interviews, which use pre-coded response categories, recording of responses is probably a simple matter of making checkmarks on a response sheet. For more open-ended interviews, the possibilities include tape recording, video recording and/or note taking. Although the literature is not unanimous on the point (see, for example, Lincoln and Guba, 1985; Patton, 2002), there are important advantages to tape recording open-ended interviews, which are spelled out by Seidman (2013). It may be that the situation dictates the recording method. If, for example, interviewing is being done in the field, there may be no opportunity for electronic recording. But other situations will differ. The various possibilities need to be assessed in relation to the practical constraints of the situation, the cooperation and approval of the respondent, and the type of interview selected. Whatever recording method is chosen, some preparation work is involved. If electronic recording is involved, the researcher must be adept at working the equipment (Minichiello et al., 1990; Patton, 2002). If note taking is involved, note-taking skills need to be developed. After the interview is completed, the data will need to be transcribed.

8.1.4 The analytic status of interview data: the role of language

The great variety and flexibility of the interview as a research tool give it wide applicability, with different types of interview suited to different situations. In some respects, however, interview data are problematic, since they are never simply raw, but are always situated and textual (Silverman, 2011).

> [T]he interview is a conversation, the art of asking questions and listening. It is not a neutral tool, for the interviewer creates the reality of the interview situation. In this situation answers are given. Thus the interview produces situated understandings grounded in specific interactional episodes. This method is influenced by the personal characteristics of the interviewer, including race, class, ethnicity and gender. (Denzin and Lincoln, 1994: 353)

The analytic status of interview data is discussed by, among others, Mishler (1986), Silverman (1985, 2011) and Fielding (2008). The discussion in this section follows mainly that of Fielding.

The general question is how to interpret the responses received in the research interview. On a technical level, this is an issue about the validity of interview responses, aspects of which include the possibility of interviewer bias and effects, the accuracy of respondents' memories, people's response tendencies, dishonesty, self-deception and social desirability. The special situations of cross-cultural research raise further problems in interpreting interview responses. But, as Fielding points out, these technical issues can usually be countered by careful design, planning and training. The more difficult problem concerns the correspondence between verbal responses and behaviour, the relationship between what people say, what they do and what they say they do, and the assumption that language is a good indicator of thought and action.

What is the relation between interviewees' accounts and the worlds they describe, and are such accounts potentially true or false, or do these concepts not apply? Silverman (1993: 90–8) describes the positivist answer to these questions (where interview data are seen as giving access to facts about the social world) and the symbolic interactionist answer (where the interview is seen as a social event based on mutual participant observation, and the primary issue is to generate data, using no fixed format or questions, which gives authentic insight into people's experiences). There are other theoretical positions as well on this issue of the analytic status of interview data. However, some researchers are so doubtful about the status of such data that they abandon any concern with the content of response in favour of examining its form. Thus, for ethnomethodologists, interview data are not a report on external reality, but a reality constructed by both parties as they contrive to accomplish an interview, and can be studied as such. In focusing on form rather than content, they treat interview data as a topic, not as a resource (Fielding, 1996a; see also Silverman, 2011; Hammersley and Atkinson, 2007). This point applies not only to interview data, but to any accounts by people of their world. These accounts can be advocated, deconstructed or subjected to the same 'topic vs. resource' distinction noted here (Hammersley and Atkinson, 1995: 124–6). The analytic status of interview data is an example of the analytic status of qualitative data generally.

Another aspect of this issue centres on language itself. An older view of language is that it represents a transparent medium to reality, that the words are used to transmit information about the world 'out there', based on a correspondence between the words used, their meanings and the aspects of the world they describe. That view is no longer tenable since a number of important ideas have changed the way we see language and especially its relation to social life (Wooffitt, 1996). These ideas have come from philosophy, linguistics and sociology. Wittgenstein, in particular, emphasised the importance of language use, showing that the meaning of words derives largely from their use, and that language is a central feature of the socio-cultural situation in which it is used, not merely a system of symbols to represent the world 'out there'. Similarly, the linguist Saussure stressed that the signs of language, like all signs, derive meaning from their relation with other signs. A correspondence view of language is thus replaced by a relational view. Language use is itself a form of social action, and descriptions are actions – they do not merely represent the world, they do specific tasks in the world (Wooffitt, 1996: 297).

This change in the way of seeing language, and especially seeing language use itself as a form of social action, has opened up important new perspectives in qualitative analysis. Examples include conversation analysis in sociology (with its connections to ethnomethodology), discourse analysis, semiotics and deconstruction. Conversation analysis concentrates on oral talk, but the others can be applied as much to written language as to spoken language (and, for that matter, to all types of verbal and textual material). Whether applied to spoken or written language, the transcript or text is not reduced to a secondary status in the research. We return to these topics in Chapter 9.

Observation

8.2 Observation has a long tradition in the social sciences, and it has been especially extensively employed by education researchers (Foster, 1996b) and by psychologists (Irwin, 1980; Brandt, 1981; Liebert, 1995). Like interviews, observation as a data collection technique can, to varying degrees, be structured or unstructured.

8.2.1 Structured and unstructured approaches to observation

In naturalistic observation, observers neither manipulate nor stimulate the behaviour of those whom they are observing – the situation being observed naturalistically is not contrived for research purposes. This is direct or non-participant observation, in contrast to participant observation, which we discuss in Section 8.3.

In the literature on observation as a data collection technique, the terms 'quantitative' and 'qualitative' are frequently used. The terms 'structured' and 'unstructured' are more appropriate in this book, because observational data can be highly structured without necessarily being turned into numbers. The issue is not whether the observational data will be turned into numbers, but rather how much structure the observations will involve.

Quantitative approaches are highly structured, and require predeveloped observation schedules, usually very detailed. If this approach is chosen, decisions will be required from the researcher as to whether already existing observational schedules will be used, or whether an observation schedule will be specially developed. This is similar to the decision in Chapter 11 about whether to use already existing measuring instruments, or to develop them specifically for a study, and similar considerations to those given in Chapter 11 can guide the choice here. Examples of highly-structured observation schedules are shown in Foster (1996b: 52–60).

Qualitative approaches to observation are much more unstructured. In this case, the researcher does not use predetermined categories and classifications, but makes observations in a more natural and open-ended way. Whatever the recording technique, the behaviour is observed as the stream of actions and events as they naturally unfold. The logic here is that categories and concepts for describing and analysing the observational data will emerge later in the research, during the analysis, rather than be brought to the research, or imposed on the data, from the start.

When the observational strategy is unstructured, the process of observation typically evolves through a series of different activities. It begins with selecting a setting and gaining access to it, then starting the observing and recording. As the study progresses, the nature of the observation changes, typically sharpening in focus, leading to ever-clearer research questions that require more selected observations. The observational data gathering continues until theoretical saturation is reached (Adler and Adler, 1994). Silverman (2011) suggests five stages in organising an initially unstructured observational study:

- beginning the research (where a set of very general questions is proposed);
- writing field notes (usually beginning with broad descriptive categories, but later developing more focused codes and categories);
- looking as well as listening;
- testing hypotheses and;
- making broader links.

Where focus and structure emerge during the fieldwork, the analogy of the funnel is useful (Spradley, 1980; Silverman, 2011). As Hammersley and Atkinson (1995: 206) comment:

> Ethnographic research should have a characteristic 'funnel' structure, being progressively focused over its course. Over time the research problem needs to be developed or transformed and eventually its scope is clarified and delimited and its internal structure explored. In this sense, it is frequently well into the process of inquiry that one discovers what the research is really about, and not uncommonly it turns out to be about something rather different from the initial foreshadowed problems.

This theme of structure that is imposed, or structure that emerges, is familiar. In this case it illustrates the specific point to be made in Chapter 9 about holistic and reductionist approaches to data. Structured observation, based on predetermined categories, breaks behaviour up into small parts. Unstructured observation, by contrast, can focus on the larger patterns of behaviour, more holistically and more macroscopically. There are advantages and disadvantages in both approaches. With smaller units of behaviour, we lose the larger picture, but recording and analysing are easier and more standardised. The more holistic approach keeps the larger picture in view, but the logistics of recording and, especially, of analysing the data will be more demanding. As with other issues, this does not need to be an either/or matter. Combinations of the two approaches are possible, depending on the research purposes and context.

8.2.2 Practical issues in observation

There are two main practical issues in planning the collection of observational data – approaching observation, and recording.

Approaching observation (Foster, 1996b) means establishing the focus of the observations, selecting the cases for observation and, as appropriate, selecting within cases for observation. In other words, the researcher has to decide what will be observed, and why. These are sampling decisions, and they need to be made with reference to the research questions. The issue of structure applies here too. At the highly-structured end, approaching the observation in terms of focus and cases is organised ahead of data collection. In unstructured observation, focus and cases may only become clear as observations are made. Gaining access is also part of the practical business of approaching observation. In some settings this will involve negotiation with gatekeepers, and different types of research may well require different types of negotiation and access.

The general possibilities for *recording observational data* range from the use of video and audio-visual equipment to the use of field notes.[1] There may be advantages to combining these different methods. The choice here is influenced by the extent to which the data are structured or unstructured – although increasingly, with today's sophisticated recording equipment, there is value in recording everything and, even if structured observation schedules are involved, using these in the analysis stage. These different recording methods each have their strengths and their limitations (Foster, 1996b). The observational researcher's task is the usual one of analysing these in relation to the purposes and context of the research, and then choosing accordingly.

Before leaving direct observation and moving to participant observation, a central method for data collection in ethnography, we should note the importance of direct observation in ethnography: 'The requirement for direct, prolonged on-the-spot observation cannot be avoided or reduced. It is the guts of the ethnographic approach. This does not always mean participant observation' (Spindler and Spindler, 1992: 63). And again: 'Above all else is the requirement that the ethnographer observe directly. No matter what instruments, coding devices, recording devices or techniques are used, the primary obligation is for the ethnographer to be there when the action takes place, and to change that action as little as possible by his or her presence' (1992: 64). Thus direct observation, as well as participant observation, is important in ethnography. This is a timely reminder to balance a possible over-emphasis – especially in symbolic interactionist studies – on perceptions, perspectives and meanings. There are dangers in replacing direct observation with data about perceptions (Silverman, 2011). In other words, as well as studying perceptions, we should also be sure to study what people do. Thus a good strategy in qualitative research is to combine observational and interview data collection techniques – for example, recording the behaviour of people and then using the observational data to inform and guide qualitative ethnographic interviewing with these people can lead to very rich, high-quality data.

Ethnographic observation has a special flavour, the flavour of ethnography itself. As Wolcott (1988: 193) puts it:

We are ethnographic observers when we are attending to the cultural context of the behaviour we are engaging in or observing, and when we are looking for those mutually understood sets of expectations and explanations that enable us to interpret what is occurring and what meanings are probably being attributed by others present.

Data collection techniques in ethnography need to be aligned with this viewpoint. This means that it is both the behaviour (or situation) itself which is of interest in ethnography, and also the meaning of this behaviour or situation as seen by the people involved in it.

Participant observation

8.3 The main characteristics of ethnography were described in Chapter 7. The essential idea is captured again in this quote from Spradley (1980: 5):

> The essential core of ethnography is this concern with the meaning of actions and events to the people we seek to understand. Some of these meanings are directly expressed in language; many are taken for granted and communicated only indirectly through word and action. But in every society people make constant use of these complex meaning systems to organise their behaviour, to understand themselves and others, and to make sense out of the world in which they live. These systems of meaning constitute their culture; ethnography always implies a theory of culture.

Participant observation is the central data collection technique in ethnography. It differs from direct or non-participant observation in that the role of the researcher changes from detached observer of the situation, to both participant-in and observer-of the situation. This raises a general question about the role of the researcher in observation research: How far distant or removed will the researcher be from the behaviour being studied? Or, to what extent will the researcher be involved in the behaviour? There is a continuum of possibilities here, as summarised in the literature by the frameworks of Gold (1958), Adler and Adler (1994) and Wolcott (1988).

Gold's analysis cross-classifies participant and observer, as shown in Figure 8.2. Adler and Adler modify this, and describe three membership roles for the observer–researcher: the complete-member-researcher, the active-member-researcher and the peripheral-member-researcher. Wolcott distinguishes between the researcher's opportunity to be an active participant, a privileged observer and a limited observer. Whichever classification is used, these possibilities for the researcher have different consequences for the level of obtrusiveness or unobtrusiveness involved in ethnographic data collection. This refers to the extent to which the researcher intrudes into the situation during data collection. This in turn influences the level of reactivity in the observation or participant observation data.[2]

These frameworks help us to think about the role of the researcher in participant observation, and possible effects of this role on the data. The actual fieldwork role in research may be a blending of these possibilities. Whatever the role, full-scale participant observation – 'prolonged immersion in the life of a group, community

| Mainly participant | • Complete participant |
| | • Participant as observer |

←———————————————————————————→

| Mainly observer | • Observer as participant |
| | • Complete observer |

FIGURE 8.2 Typology of naturalistic research roles

Source: Gold, 1958

or organization in order to discern people's habits and thoughts as well as to deci-pher the social structure that binds them together' (Punch, 1994: 84) – is a demanding and specialised form of data collection. To take the role of the other, to 'go native', to obtain the insider's perspective by becoming part of the natural set-ting, is not straightforward, and raises a number of issues. They include the ethical issues associated with this method of data collection, the conceptual issues of the importance of the researcher's prior picture and the role of exploration and inspec-tion in participant observation (Blumer, 1969), and the more practical issues of gaining access to the situation, overt versus covert observation, 'front management' or the researcher's presentation of self, and how to record what is being observed (Fielding, 1996a).

It is difficult to codify the steps involved in participant observation, but Sprad-ley's framework is useful. He analyses participant observation (and ethnography) into a sequence of 12 developmental tasks (his 'Developmental Research Sequence'), the end product of which is a written ethnography (Spradley, 1980). For Spradley, participant observation, together with ethnographic interviewing, produces ethnographic description. Ethnographic interviewing uses questions designed to discover the cultural meanings people have learned. Spradley shows how descriptive questions, structural questions and contrast questions are used in this way, as part of the step-by-step account he gives of participant observation. On the other hand, Hammersley and Atkinson (2007) are less directive – ethnographers do not decide beforehand the questions they want to ask, though they may enter the interview with a list of issues to be covered.

Wolcott (1988) writes more generally about seven types of interviews anthro-pologists may use, in conjunction with participant observation. They are: key informant interview, life history interview, structured or formal interview, informal interview, questionnaire, projective techniques, and standardised tests and related measuring instruments. Much of this has been covered in Section 8.1, but key informant interviewing and life history interviewing require a brief comment. Empirical work in anthropology and sociology has often depended on the key informant – 'an individual in whom one invests a disproportionate amount of time because that individual appears to be particularly well informed, articulate, approachable or available' (Wolcott, 1988: 195). It is an approach that can often be adapted for social science research. In ethnography, key informant interviewing is appropriate because people differ also in their cultural sensitivity, and therefore in their ability to contribute culturally meaningful data. Life history interviewing, where it is possible, can help greatly with understanding how the social context gets played out in individual lives. The depth of data possible in such an interview helps in getting a full understanding of the participant's view of the world (Fetterman, 2010).

Documentary data

8.4 Documents, both historical and contemporary, are a rich source of data for social science research. Indeed, a distinguishing feature of our society may well be the vast array of 'documentary evidence' that is routinely compiled and retained. Yet much of this is neglected by researchers, perhaps because the collection of other sorts of research data (experiments, surveys, interviews, observations) has become more fashionable. This is ironic, since the development of social science depended greatly on documentary research (MacDonald and Tipton, 1996: 187). For example, in sociology, Marx, Durkheim and Weber worked primarily from documents; similarly, Chicago School sociology was often based on written documents (Hammersley and Atkinson, 2007). These points have particular application in institutional and organisational research. For example, organisations such as schools, colleges, universities, as well as companies and government departments, hospitals and many other types of organisations, routinely produce a vast amount of documentary data. Unfortunately, much of it is neglected by researchers.

Documentary sources of data might be used in various ways in social science research. Some studies might depend entirely on documentary data, with such data the focus in their own right. Some types of policy analysis are examples of this, as is the exercise suggested by MacDonald and Tipton (1996), where students are asked to research financial scandals using documentary sources. In other research, for example case studies or grounded theory studies, documentary data may be collected in conjunction with interviews and observations. In conjunction with other data, documents can be important in triangulation, where an intersecting set of different methods and data types is used in a single project (Denzin, 1989). Finally, documentary products are especially important for the ethnographer, providing a 'rich vein for analysis' (Hammersley and Atkinson, 1995: 173). The ethnographer will make use of all manner of written resources, and of any other materials that will help in documenting either the immediate natural and detailed behaviour of participants (Spindler and Spindler, 1992: 74) or the cultural and symbolic context and significance of this behaviour. Sociologists point out that documentary evidence does not mean only words – it can also include audio and visual evidence.

The range of documents that might be used by researchers includes diaries, letters, essays, personal notes, biographies and autobiographies, institutional memoranda and reports, government pronouncements and proceedings (Jupp, 2006) and policy documents and papers. And this list does not include documentary quantitative evidence, such as files, statistics and records, which are also of interest. Writers have classified this bewildering variety (Hammersley and Atkinson, 2007). For example, MacDonald and Tipton (1996) use this broad four-way classification:

public records, the media, private papers and visual documents. Other distinctions used are primary–secondary sources, direct–indirect uses (Finnegan, 2006), classification according to referent, and whether or not the document(s) was/were produced with this research in mind – the witting–unwitting distinction. The latter is a type of unobtrusive measure, where the observer is removed from the interactions or events being studied (Webb et al., 1966; Jupp, 2006).

Scott's two-way typology of documents is based on authorship and access (Scott, 1990; Jupp, 2006). Authorship refers to the origin of the document (in three categories – personal, official–private, official–state), while access refers to the availability of documents to people other than the authors (in four categories – closed, restricted, open-archival and open-published). This 12-cell typology suggests four key questions in evaluating documentary data (Jupp, 2006): its authenticity (whether it is original and genuine), its credibility (whether it is accurate), its representativeness (whether it is representative of the totality of documents of its class) and its meaning (what it is intended to say).

MacDonald and Tipton (1996: 199) stress that in documentary research, nothing can be taken for granted, and they recommend Denzin's triangulation framework to ensure that everything is checked from more than one angle. Finnegan (2006) points out that thinking about and checking how documents have come into existence generates eight other useful questions:

1. Has the researcher made use of the existing sources relevant and appropriate for his or her research topic?
2. How far has the researcher taken account of any 'twisting' or selection of the facts in the sources used?
3. What kind of selection has the researcher made in her or his use of the sources and on what principles?
4. How far does a source that describes a particular incident or case reflect the general situation?
5. Is the source concerned with recommendations, ideals or what ought to be done?
6. How relevant is the context of the source?
7. With statistical sources: what were the assumptions according to which the statistics were collected and presented?
8. And, finally, having taken all the previous factors into account, do you consider that the researcher has reached a reasonable interpretation of the meaning of the sources?

For ethnographers, documentary products provide a rich source of analytic questions, which include: How are documents written? How are they read? Who writes them? Who reads them? For what purposes? On what occasions? With what outcomes? What is recorded? What is omitted? What does the writer seem to take for granted about the reader(s)? What do readers need to know in order to make sense of them? (Hammersley and Atkinson, 2007). Such questions as these point ahead to textual analysis, the analysis of documentary data, outlined in Chapter 9. How the document has come into existence – its social production – is one of its main themes. Others are the social organisation of the document and the analysis of its meaning.

8.5 Whether qualitative data collection involves interviews, observation, participant observation or documents, there are four common-sense things we can do to maximise the quality of the data:

- Think through the rationale and logistics of the proposed data collection, and plan carefully for data collection.
- Anticipate and simulate the data collection procedures; this will show the value of pilot testing any instruments (if appropriate) and the procedures for using them.
- When approaching people for data collection, ensure that the approach is both ethical and professional; how access and cooperation are negotiated can have an important effect on the quality of data.
- Appreciate the role of training in preparing for data collection, both for ourselves and others; for example, if we are doing unstructured (or focus group) interviews, we should not just assume we will be good at this, but prepare for it, undertaking activities designed to develop the skills involved; if others are to be involved in collecting the data, they will need training for the data collection; if special equipment is involved (for example for recording), we should ensure that the appropriate skills to use the equipment have been mastered.

Very often, the point of a qualitative study is to look at something holistically and comprehensively, to study it in its complexity, and to understand it in its context. These points correspond to three criticisms of quantitative social science research – that it is too reductionist in its approach to the study of behaviour, thereby losing sight of the whole picture; that it oversimplifies social reality, in its stress on measurement; and that it strips away context from the data. For the qualitative researcher, the 'truth' about human behaviour is not independent of context; it is not context-free. Therefore it is important for the qualitative researcher to be able to convey the full picture. The term often used to capture this is 'thick description'. There are two parts to this idea. First, the description (of the group, or the case, event or phenomenon) must specify everything a reader needs to know in order to understand the findings. Second, the research report needs to provide sufficient information about the context of the research so that a reader can judge the transferability or generalisability of its findings (Lincoln and Guba, 1985). The exact nature of the thick description will vary from project to project, but both parts of this idea acknowledge and emphasise the context around any project and its findings. But we cannot *give* the full picture unless we *have* the full picture. This is an important aspect of the quality of data in qualitative research.

Sampling in qualitative research

8.6 Sampling is just as important in qualitative research as it is in quantitative research – as noted by Miles and Huberman (1994: 27) 'you cannot study everyone everywhere doing everything'. Sampling decisions are required not only about which people to interview or which events to observe, but also about settings and processes. Even a case study, where the case selection itself may be straightforward, will require sampling within the case. We cannot study everything about even one case. A qualitative study based on documents will also, in most cases, face sampling issues.

However, there is a major difference in sampling in the two approaches. In quantitative research, an important focus tends to be on people sampling. The basic concept very often used is probability sampling directed at representativeness – measurements of variables are taken from a sample, which is chosen to be representative of some larger population. Because of the representativeness, findings from the sample will then be inferred back to the population. Qualitative research would rarely use probability sampling, but rather some sort of deliberate sampling – 'purposive sampling' is the term often used. It means sampling in a deliberate way, with some purpose or focus in mind.

There are no simple summaries of strategies for sampling in qualitative social science research, because of the great variety of research approaches, purposes and settings. Thus Miles, Huberman and Saldana (2013) show 16 qualitative sampling strategies in a typology, and refer to more in their discussion. These strategies are reproduced here in Table 8.1. Patton (2002), Johnson (1990) and Janesick (1994) contribute still others. The basic ideas behind the specific sampling strategies vary considerably, and reflect the purposes and questions guiding the study. For example, a maximum variation sampling plan would deliberately seek as much variation as possible, whereas a homogeneous sampling would seek to minimise variation. Some social science research situations would require the former, some the latter. Similarly, there are some situations where convenience sampling would be appropriate, where advantage is taken of cases, events, situations or informants that are close at hand. Others would require extreme-case sampling, for example when the strategy is to learn from unusual or negative manifestations of the phenomenon. In ethnography and participant observation research especially, informant sampling will be involved, and this may be sequential, in the sense that several steps might be needed to locate information-rich informants. In case study research, qualitative sampling involves identifying the case(s) and setting the boundaries, where we indicate the aspects to be studied, and constructing a sampling frame, where we focus selection further. After that, however, general descriptions of sampling are difficult, because there is great variability. As another example, within-case sampling involves selection of focus within the case being studied, whereas multiple case sampling is directed more at replication across similar and contrasting cases.

Across the various qualitative sampling strategies, there is a clear principle involved, which concerns the overall validity of the research design, and which stresses that the sample must fit in with the other components of the study. There must be an internal consistency and a coherent logic, across the study's components, including its sampling. The sampling plan and sampling parameters (settings, actors, events, processes) should line up with the purposes and the research questions of the study. If it is not clear which cases, aspects or incidents to study, it is usually

TABLE 8.1   Sampling strategies in qualitative inquiry

Type of Sampling	Purpose
Maximum variation	Documents diverse variations and identifies important common patterns
Homogeneous	Focuses, reduces, simplifies, facilitates group interviewing
Critical case	Permits logical generalisation and maximum application of information to other cases
Theory based	Finds examples of a theoretical construct and thereby elaborates and examines it
Confirming and disconfirming cases	Elaborates initial analysis, seeks exceptions, looks for variation
Snowball or chain	Identifies cases of interest from people who know people who know what cases are information-rich
Extreme or deviant case	Learns from highly unusual manifestations of the phenomenon of interest
Typical case	Highlights what is normal or average
Intensity	Examines information-rich cases that manifest the phenomenon intensely, but not extremely
Politically important	Attracts desired attention or avoids attracting undesired attention cases
Random purposeful	Adds credibility to sample when potential purposeful sample is too large
Stratified purposeful	Illustrates subgroups, facilitates comparisons
Criterion	Considers all cases that meet some criterion, useful for quality assurance
Opportunistic	Follows new leads, takes advantage of the unexpected
Combination or mixed	Features triangulation, flexibility, meets multiple interests and needs
Convenience	Saves time, money and effort, but at the expense of information and credibility

Source: Miles and Huberman (1994: 28)

worth devoting more work to developing the research questions. If the research purposes and questions do not provide any direction at all about sampling, they probably require further development.

This principle is helpful when we are prespecifying the sampling plan. But what about when the sampling plan evolves during the course of the study? Here again there needs to be a logical basis to the way it evolves, and the same principle applies. Decisions about the sampling directions must be coherent, and consistent with the study's logic, rather than arbitrary or ad hoc. A clear example of this principle in operation as a study's sampling plan evolves is theoretical sampling, as was discussed in Section 7.5.4. Theoretical sampling is:

> the process of data collection for generating theory, whereby the analyst jointly collects, codes and analyses his data and decides what data to collect next and where to find them, in order to develop his theory as it emerges. The process of data collection is controlled by theoretical sampling according to the emerging theory. (Glaser, 1992: 101)

Both theoretical sampling as a study develops, and theory-driven sampling ahead of the research, are examples of the more general concept of purposive sampling.

Miles, Huberman and Saldana (2013) suggest six general questions against which to check a qualitative sampling plan. The first of these is the one we have just considered:

- Is the sampling relevant to your conceptual frame and research questions?
- Will the phenomena you are interested in appear? In principle, can they appear?
- Does your plan enhance generalisability of your findings, either through conceptual power or representativeness?
- Can believable descriptions and explanations be produced, ones that are true to real life?
- Is the sampling plan feasible, in terms of time, money, access to people and your own work style?
- Is the sampling plan ethical, in terms of such issues as informed consent, potential benefits and risks, and the relationship with informants?

Finally, as with quantitative research, we should note also the growing importance of secondary analysis with qualitative data, as primary research becomes more and more expensive. In the UK, for example, the Economic and Social Data Service (ESDS) is a national data service that, among other things, houses the UK Data Archive. The archive provides continuous access to the UK's largest collection of digital research data in the social sciences, and holds thousands of data collections for social science research and teaching (quantitative and qualitative). Data are typically acquired via the Economic and Social Research Council (ESRC) Datasets Policy that requires all research grant award holders to offer data collected during the course of their research for preservation and sharing through the ESDS. ESDS Qualidata works closely with data creators to ensure that high quality and well-documented qualitative data are produced. The service provides both general guidance and a dedicated advisory service for data creators and depositors. For further information on the ESDS, see http://www.esds.ac.uk/news/publications/qualleaflet. pdf and for further information on the data archive, see http://www.data-archive. ac.uk/about/projects. A short discussion of secondary analysis, with directions to further reading, is given in Section 11.12.

Chapter summary

- The interview is the most widely used data collection technique in qualitative research; there are different types of interview, especially with respect to the degree of structure, and the type of interview used should align with the purposes, questions and overall strategy of the research.
- Careful planning for managing the numerous practical issues involved in collecting data by interview will increase the quality of the interview data.
- Like interviews, observation as a data collection technique can vary from highly structured to totally unstructured; again, the type of observation used should fit with the purposes, questions and strategy of the research.

- The main practical issues in collecting observational data are approaching the observation (including case and within-case selection) and recording the observation.
- Participant observation is the central data collection technique in ethnography; instead of being detached from the situation, the participant observation researcher is both a participant in, and observer of, the situation.
- Ethnographic interviewing aims to discover the cultural meanings people have learned, and is often used in conjunction with participant observation.
- Documents are a rich – and too often neglected – source of data for social science research; many projects are enriched by including documentary data alongside interview and/or observational data.
- Maximising the quality of the interview, observational and documentary data collected requires careful planning, anticipation of issues which might arise, professionally negotiated access to the data collection situation, and training.
- Sampling is important in qualitative research, and the sampling strategy used should fit with the purposes, questions and overall strategy of the research; various sampling strategies are possible, but qualitative research sampling would mostly be deliberate or 'purposive' in some way.

KEY TERMS

Structured interview: pre-established questions are used, with pre-set response categories; there is little room for variation in the questioning

Unstructured interview: a flexible method of data collection, sometimes called the open-ended or in-depth interview; any pre-set questions are very general, no pre-set responses are used, and subsequent questions depend on the responses to earlier questions; probing and follow-up questioning are very important

Focus group interview: several people are interviewed as a group, rather than individually; the researcher functions more as a moderator and facilitator, and less as an interviewer

Structured observation: predeveloped observation schedules are used to study behaviour, often with very detailed categories which break up behaviour into small parts

Unstructured observation: focuses on larger patterns of behaviour, more holistically and macroscopically; does not use predetermined categories and captures behaviour in a more natural and open-ended way

Participant observation: the researcher is no longer a detached observer of the situation, but becomes both a participant in, and observer of, the situation; much used in ethnography, to investigate the meanings of actions and events to participants

Documentary data: a general term for any sort of already existing documentary evidence, formal or informal

Probability sampling: very often used in quantitative research, where sampling is mainly directed at representativeness; sometimes called random sampling

Deliberate (or purposive) sampling: sampling for representativeness is not the main criterion; rather, samples are selected deliberately, according to some criterion drawn from the overall logic and strategy of the study; many different deliberate sampling strategies are possible

Exercises and study questions

1. What are the strengths and weaknesses of:
   - structured interviewing
   - unstructured interviewing
   - structured observation
   - unstructured observation

2. For what sorts of research situations and research questions would focus group interviewing be a useful data collection method?
3. How can interviews and observation be combined in the collection of qualitative data?
4. In planning the case study of a school or college or university (with suitable research questions), what existing documentary data about the school, college or university would be useful?
5. In what way(s) can the negotiation with respondents for access and cooperation influence the quality of data? (Consider especially unstructured in-depth qualitative interviews with, for example, a sample of small business managers.)
6. Why is sampling important in qualitative research? What is meant by a sampling strategy, and the logic of a sampling strategy?

Further reading

Adler, P.A. and Adler, P. (1994) 'Observational techniques', in N.K. Denzin and Y.S. Lincoln (eds), *Handbook of Qualitative Research*. Thousand Oaks, CA: SAGE. pp. 377–92.

Atkinson, P. and Hammersley, M. (1994) 'Ethnography and participant observation', in N.K. Denzin and Y.S. Lincoln (2011) (eds), *Handbook of Qualitative Research*. 4th edn. Thousand Oaks, CA: SAGE.

Babbie, E. (2012) *The Practice of Social Research*. 13th edn. Belmont, CA: Wadsworth.

Denzin, N.K. (1989) *The Research Act*. 3rd edn. Englewood Cliffs, NJ: Prentice-Hall.

Fielding, N. (2008) 'Qualitative interviewing', in N. Gilbert (ed.), *Researching Social Life*. 3rd edn. London: SAGE. pp. 138–52.

Finnegan, R. (1992) *Oral Traditions and the Verbal Arts: A Guide to Research Practices*. London: Routledge.

Finnegan, R. (2006) 'Using documents', in R. Sapsford and V. Jupp (eds), *Data Collection and Analysis*. 2nd edn. London: SAGE. pp. 138–52.

Foddy, W. (1993) *Constructing Questions for Interviews and Questionnaires: Theory and Practice in Social Research*. Cambridge: Cambridge University Press.

Fontana, A. and Frey, J.H. (1994) 'Interviewing: the art of science', in N.K. Denzin and Y.S. Lincoln (eds), *Handbook of Qualitative Research*. Thousand Oaks, CA: SAGE. pp. 361–76.

Foster, P. (1996) *Observing Schools: A Methodological Guide*. London: Paul Chapman.

Greenbaum, T.L. (1998) *The Handbook for Focus Group Research*. Thousand Oaks, CA: SAGE.

Hammersley, M. and Atkinson, P. (2007) *Ethnography: Principles in Practice*. 3rd edn. London: Routledge.

Krueger, R.A. (2008) *Focus Groups: A Practical Guide for Applied Research*. 4th edn. Thousand Oaks, CA: SAGE.

Kvale, S. (1996) *Interviews: An Introduction to Qualitative Research Interviewing*. Newbury Park, CA: SAGE.

MacDonald, K. and Tipton, C. (1996) 'Using documents', in N. Gilbert (ed.), *Researching Social Life*. London: SAGE. pp. 187–200.

Minichiello, V., Aroni, R., Timewell, E. and Alexander, L. (1990) *In-depth Interviewing: Researching People*. Melbourne: Longman Cheshire.

Morgan, D.L. (1997) *Focus Groups as Qualitative Research*. 2nd edn. Thousand Oaks, CA: SAGE.

Plummer, K. (1983) *Documents of Life*. London: Allen and Unwin.

Scott, J. (1990) *A Matter of Record: Documentary Sources in Social Research*. Cambridge: Polity Press.

Silverman, D. (1985) *Qualitative Methodology and Sociology*. Farnborough: Gower.

Silverman, D. (2011) *Interpreting Qualitative Data: Methods for Analysing Talk, Text and Interaction*. 4th edn. London: SAGE.

Spradley, J.P. (1979) *The Ethnographic Interview*. New York: Holt, Rinehart and Winston.

Spradley, J.P. (1980) *Participant Observation*. New York: Holt, Rinehart and Winston.

Stewart, D., Shamdasami, P. and Rook, D. (2006) *Focus Goups: Theory and Practice*. 2nd edn. Thousand Oaks, CA: SAGE.

Notes_____

1. Making and taking field notes raises questions of what to record, when and how. For the 'what', Spradley (1980) suggests a basic checklist to guide field notes, using nine headings (space, actor, activity, object, act, event, time, goal and feeling). The 'when' and 'how' of making field notes in observation and participant observation research are discussed by Hammersley and Atkinson (1995: 175–86).

2. These issues, and especially the connection between obtrusiveness and reactivity, were highlighted in the book by Webb et al. (1966). They are considered again in Chapter 11.

nine
ANALYSING QUALITATIVE DATA

Contents

In Chapter 7 the diversity of qualitative research was noted. Perhaps nowhere is that diversity more apparent than in approaches to the analysis of qualitative data. Indeed, the term 'data analysis' itself has different meanings among qualitative researchers, and these interpretations lead to different methods of analysis. We begin this chapter by looking at the present-day diversity in qualitative analysis. This is followed by a description of some of the main ideas and approaches in qualitative data analysis. The chapter ends with some general advice about writing the analysis of data section in a qualitative research proposal, in view of the multiple methods available.

Diversity in qualitative analysis

9.1 Qualitative research in social science concentrates on the study of human behaviour and of social life in natural settings. Its richness and complexity mean that there are different ways of analysing social life, and therefore multiple perspectives and practices in the analysis of qualitative data: 'There is variety in techniques because there are different questions to be addressed and different versions of social reality that can be elaborated' (Coffey and Atkinson, 1996: 14). The different techniques are often interconnected, overlapping and complementary, and sometimes mutually exclusive – 'irreconcilable couples' (Miles and Huberman, 1994: 9). But whether complementary or contrasting, there are good reasons for the existence of the many analytic strategies, since any set of qualitative data can be looked at from different perspectives. A repertoire of analytic techniques thus characterises qualitative research today, and different techniques can be applied to the same body of qualitative data, illuminating different aspects of it (Example 9.1).

┌─ EXAMPLE 9.1 ─┐

Different Analytic Techniques

Feldman (1995) applies the four techniques of ethnomethodology, semiotics, dramaturgical analysis and deconstruction to the one body of qualitative data, drawn from a single study of a university housing office. The different techniques illuminate different aspects of the data.

Despite this variety, some writers have sought to identify the common features of qualitative data analysis. For example, Miles and Huberman (1994: 9) suggest a 'fairly classic set' of six moves common across different types of analysis – these are shown in this book in Appendix 1. Similarly, Tesch (1990: 95–7), while concluding that no characteristics are common to all types of analysis, nevertheless identifies ten principles and practices that hold true for most types of qualitative analysis. But Tesch also identifies no fewer than 26 different approaches to the analysis of qualitative data in her survey of methods.

This variety of approaches underlines the point that there is no single right way to do qualitative data analysis – no single methodological framework. Much depends on the purposes of the research, and it is important that the proposed method of analysis is carefully considered in planning the research, and is integrated from the start with other parts of the research, rather than being an afterthought. In the expanding literature on qualitative analysis, terms such as 'transforming', 'interpreting' and 'making sense of' qualitative data are prominent, and it is the different ways of doing these things that lead to the diversity in methods of analysis. This diversity is valuable, but scholarly rigour and discipline are also important. In their book *Making Sense of Qualitative Data*, Coffey and Atkinson (1996: 3) stress: 'What links all the approaches is a central concern with transforming and interpreting qualitative data – in a rigorous and scholarly way – in order to capture the complexities of the social worlds we seek to explain.' A similar point about the need for discipline is made by Silverman (2011).

These recent concerns for disciplined methods of analysis echo this well-known quote from more than 40 years ago:

> **The most serious and central difficulty in the use of qualitative data is that methods of analysis are not well formulated. For quantitative data, there are clear conventions the researcher can use. But the analyst faced with a bank of qualitative data has very few guidelines for protection against self-delusion, let alone the presentation of unreliable or invalid conclusions to scientific or policy-making audiences. How can we be sure that an 'earthy', 'undeniable', 'serendipitous' finding is not, in fact, wrong? (Miles, 1979: 591)**

Methods for the analysis of data need to be systematic, disciplined and able to be seen (and to be seen through, as in 'transparent') and described. A key question in assessing any piece of research is: How did the researcher get to these conclusions from these data? If there is no answer to this question – if the method of analysis cannot be described and scrutinised – it is difficult to know what confidence to have in the findings put forward.

All empirical research has to deal with this problem. One strength of quantitative research is that methods for the analysis of its data are well known and transparent. This enables reproducibility in the analysis – a second analyst, working with the same quantitative data and using the same statistical operations as the first, should get the same results.[1] For qualitative research, the relevance of the criterion of reproducibility is a matter of debate in the literature. But there have been great developments in the analysis of qualitative data in the past 40 years, and the concept of the 'audit trail' through the data analysis is now realistic for much qualitative research.[2]

For the individual researcher, this problem comes alive at the point of sitting in front of the collected qualitative data – perhaps interview transcripts, and/or field notes from observations and discussions, and/or documents. At this point, what, exactly, does the researcher do? Deciding what to do can cause bewilderment, as Feldman's vivid description shows (1995: 1).

Despite progress in the development of analytic methods, it would be wrong to assume that all developments in qualitative analysis have been directed at this issue. For one thing, there are researchers who would reject the view of knowledge on which the ideas of reproducibility and the audit trail are based – for example, those devoted to a relativist epistemology rooted in a postmodernist and constructivist philosophy (Kelle, 1995). For another, some more recent developments in qualitative analysis have taken the field in quite new directions, where this criterion has seemed both less central and less problematic. This will be seen in later sections of this chapter.

A survey of methods of analysing qualitative data suggests a division of analytic approaches into general and specialised. The next three sections (9.2., 9.3, 9.4) describe some important general approaches to the analysis of qualitative data, which can be applied across a wide variety of social science research situations. Section 9.5 deals with the specialised approach of grounded theory analysis, and Section 9.6 then overviews some of the other more specialised approaches.

Analytic induction

9.2 In the search for regularities in the social world, induction is central. Concepts are developed inductively from the data and raised to a higher level of abstraction, and their interrelationships are then traced out. But while induction is central, deduction is needed also, since, as noted in Chapter 7, theory generation involves theory verification as well. This sort of qualitative data analysis is a series of alternating inductive and deductive steps, whereby data-driven inductive hypothesis generation is followed by deductive hypothesis examination, for the purpose of verification (Kelle, 1995).

The fact that much qualitative analysis depends on induction suggests 'analytic induction' as a useful general term. But this term also has a more specific meaning. The method of analytic induction was developed by Znaniecki (1934), and was originally identified with the search for 'universals' in social life, where universals are properties that are invariant (Ragin, 1994: 93). Today, it is often used to refer to the systematic examination of similarities between cases to develop concepts or ideas (Example 9.2). It has been described by, for example, Lindesmith (1968), Cressey (1950, 1971) and Hammersley and Atkinson. This is the description given by Hammersley and Atkinson (1995: 234–5):

1. An initial definition of the phenomenon to be explained is formulated.
2. Some cases of this phenomenon are investigated, documenting potential explanatory features.
3. A hypothetical explanation is framed on the basis of analysis of the data, designed to identify common factors across the cases.
4. Further cases are investigated to test the hypothesis.
5. If the hypothesis does not fit the facts from these new cases, either the hypothesis is reformulated or the phenomenon to be explained is redefined (so that the negative cases are excluded).
6. This procedure of examining cases, reformulating the hypothesis and/or redefining the phenomenon is continued until new cases continually confirm the validity of the hypothesis, at which point it may be concluded that the hypothesis is correct (though this can never be known with absolute certainty).

EXAMPLE 9.2

Analytic Induction

Bloor (1978) used analytic induction in his study of surgeons; the study is summarised in Silverman (1993).

Cressey (1950) used analytic induction to study 'trust violation'.

Lindesmith (1947) used analytic induction to study drug addiction.

The Miles and Huberman framework for qualitative data analysis

9.3 *Qualitative Data Analysis* (2013), by Miles, Huberman and Saldana, is a comprehensive sourcebook, describing analysis that is directed at tracing out lawful and stable relationships among social phenomena, based on the regularities and sequences that link these phenomena. They label their approach 'transcendental realism', and their analysis has three main components:

- data reduction;
- data display;
- drawing and verifying conclusions.

They see these as three concurrent streams or activities, interacting throughout the analysis, as shown in Figure 9.1.

1. *Data reduction:* Data reduction occurs continually throughout the analysis. It is not something separate from the analysis, it is part of the analysis. In the early stages, it happens through editing, segmenting and summarising the data. In the middle stages, it happens

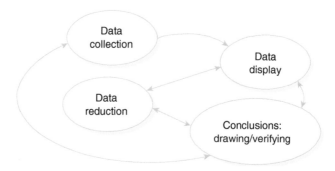

Figure 9.1   Components of data analysis: interactive model
Source: Miles and Huberman, 1994: 12

through coding and memoing, and associated activities such as finding themes, clusters and patterns. In the later stages, it happens through conceptualising and explaining, since developing abstract concepts is also a way of reducing the data. In the need to reduce data, qualitative analysis is not different from quantitative analysis, and the parallels in conceptual structure are shown in the levels of abstraction diagram in Section 9.4 of this chapter. In both quantitative and qualitative analysis, the objective of data reduction is to reduce the data without significant loss of information. In qualitative analysis, an additional important component of not losing information is not to strip the data from their context.

2. *Data display:* Data displays organise, compress and assemble information. Because qualitative data are typically voluminous, bulky and dispersed, displays help at all stages in the analysis. Miles and Huberman regard displays as essential, often using the phrase 'You know what you display'. They see better displays as a major avenue to valid qualitative analysis (1994). There are many different ways of displaying data – graphs, charts, networks, diagrams of different types (Venn diagrams, causal models, etc.) – and any way that moves the analysis forward is appropriate. Displays are used at all stages, since they enable data to be organised and summarised, they show what stage the analysis has reached and they are the basis for further analysis. The message is clear: good qualitative analysis involves repeated and iterative displays of data. The same point is made in the grounded theory literature.

3. *Drawing and verifying conclusions:* The reasons for reducing and displaying data are to assist in drawing conclusions. While drawing conclusions logically follows reduction and display of data, in fact it takes place more or less concurrently with them. Thus possible conclusions may be noted early in the analysis, but they may be vague and ill-formed at this stage. They are held tentative pending further work, and sharpened during it. They are not finalised until all the data are in and have been analysed. Conclusions will be in the form of propositions, and once they have been drawn, they need to be verified.

Conclusion drawing and verifying is the third part of this analysis. It involves developing propositions, and is conceptually distinct from the other stages, but again is likely to happen concurrently with them. Miles and Huberman give a list of 13 tactics for drawing meaning and conclusions from displayed data. Since conclusions need also to be verified, they give a second list of 13 tactics for testing and confirming findings. The two lists are shown here in Appendix 1.

This stage in the analysis is the most difficult to describe, because it typically involves a number of different analytical processes, which may be used simultaneously rather than sequentially, and which cut across and combine with each other. In other words, several things are going on at once. This work starts from the point where ordering and integration of the previous analysis is required. After coding and memoing (see Sections 9.3.1 and 9.3.2), there are many labels, at different levels of abstraction, and piles of memos of various kinds. The aim of this stage is to integrate what has been done into a meaningful and coherent picture of the data. The two lists of tactics give an overview of the activities involved, and, as noted, are shown in Appendix 1.

These three overall components are interwoven and concurrent throughout the data analysis. The first two, data reduction and display, rest mainly on the operations of coding and memoing. In virtually all methods for the analysis of qualitative data, coding and memoing are the two basic operations that get the analysis going. I discuss them here in general terms, and deal with them separately. In practice, they happen together and are closely related.

9.3.1 Coding

Coding is the starting activity in qualitative analysis and the foundation for what comes later. For analysis directed at discovering regularities in the data, coding is central.

What is coding, and what are codes? Codes are tags, names or labels, and coding is therefore the process of putting tags, names or labels against pieces of the data. The pieces may be individual words, or small or large chunks of the data. The point of assigning labels is to attach meaning to the pieces of data, and these labels serve a number of functions. They index the data, providing a basis for storage and retrieval. The first labels also permit more advanced coding, which enables the summarising of data by pulling together themes, and by identifying patterns. In view of the volume and complexity of much qualitative data, these early labels become an essential part of subsequent analysis. So basic coding is both the first part of the analysis and part of getting the data ready for subsequent analysis. Advanced coding is the same activity – labelling and categorising – applied at higher levels of abstraction with the data. The type of coding done – that is, what sorts of labels are attached to the data – depends upon the method of analysis being used.

In the Miles and Huberman approach, there are two main types of codes – descriptive codes and inferential (or pattern) codes. Early labels may be *descriptive* codes, requiring little or no inference beyond the piece of data itself. These are especially valuable in getting the analysis started, and in enabling the researcher to get a 'feel' for the data. Glaser and Strauss use the term 'in vivo' codes in the same way, in grounded theory coding. In Example 9.3 Richards uses the term 'topic coding' in much the same way. First level coding mainly uses these descriptive, low inference codes, which are very useful in summarising segments of data, and which provide the basis for later higher order coding. Later codes may be more interpretive, requiring some degree of inference beyond the data. Thus second level coding tends to focus on pattern codes. A pattern code is more inferential, a sort of 'meta-code'. *Pattern* codes pull together material into a smaller number of more meaningful units. A good way to understand pattern codes is by analogy with factor analysis in quantitative research (Section 12.6). A factor is a concept at a higher level of abstraction, which brings together less abstract variables. Similarly, a pattern code is a more abstract concept that brings together less abstract, more descriptive codes.

There is the usual range of possibilities, when it comes to bringing codes to the data or finding them in the data. At one end of the continuum we can have prespecified codes or more general coding frameworks. At the other end, we can start coding with no prespecified codes, and let the data suggest initial codes. This decision is not independent of other such decisions concerning research questions, conceptual framework and the structuring of data generally. Neither, as before, does it need to be an either/or decision. Thus, even when guided by an initial coding scheme, we can be alert to other labels and categories suggested by the data. Similarly, we might start with a 'tabula rasa', derive a first set of codes from the data and then draw on a coding scheme after the initial analysis.

There is another similarity, in this sort of coding of data, with quantitative research. It concerns operational definitions:

> Whether codes are prespecified or developed along the way, clear operational definitions are indispensable, so they can be applied by a single researcher over time and multiple researchers will be thinking about the same phenomena as they code. (Miles and Huberman, 1994: 63)

Operational definitions, in a quantitative context, mean the definition of a variable in terms of the operations necessary to measure it. This quote makes clear the applicability of the same concept in this style of qualitative analysis. There must be clear links between data indicators and the conceptual labels (or codes) given to the data. These links enable check coding and tests of inter-coder reliability in qualitative analysis. They are important in establishing the audit trail through the analysis.

In Example 9.3, Coffey and Atkinson (1996: 33–44) illustrate coding using an interview with an academic anthropologist. Miles, Huberman and Saldana (2013) give coding examples from several different studies and settings, and show some coding frameworks and lists. In the third item in Example 9.3, Richards (2005: 87–8) illustrates another useful general approach to coding, using the terms 'descriptive coding', 'topic coding' and 'analytical coding'.

Coding

- Coffey and Atkinson (1996: 33–44) illustrate coding using an interview with an academic anthropologist.
- Miles and Huberman (1994: 55–72) give coding examples from several different studies and settings, and show some coding frameworks and lists.
- Richards (2005: 87–8) gives the following example, using the terms 'descriptive', 'topic' and 'analytic' coding.

  Descriptive coding involves coding and storing information about the cases being studied.

  Topic coding, the 'hack work' of qualitative research, labels pieces of text according to its subject.

  Analytic coding goes further and is central to qualitative inquiry. It involves both the interpretation of data, and the conceptualising and theorising of data.

A passage of text will normally require all three types of coding. Consider the following data:

> *'A man interviewed is discussing the need for community action in the local council elections, in which a schoolteacher is a candidate. This man says that he never listens to gossip about the schoolteacher, it's women's stuff. But he does worry that she is standing for local council, when she is obviously not a responsible person.'*

- Descriptive coding: First, store the information about the speaker, perhaps about three attributes: gender, age and job – *male, 45 years and tradesman*
- Topic coding: Now, what topics are being discussed in this passage? *The need for community action and the schoolteacher; perhaps we need to code for her multiple roles*

In two ways the coding has described the passage: what sort of person offered these ideas, and what they were about.

- Analytic coding: Now, what's going on in the statement about the schoolteacher? *Several themes there that need noting, about patriarchal assumptions, the credibility of 'gossip', the informal networks of women, the authority of the schoolteachers and the interplay of inter-personal and political relations.*

Richards notes that such coding leads the researcher to ask further useful questions: *Did men always deny they gossiped? Are the negative attitudes towards the schoolteacher coming mainly from the over-forties? And how do they relate to attitudes to community action?*

Different writers use different terminology to describe the levels and types of coding, and this can produce confusion when reading the literature. Yet both the main ideas involved in coding and the main types of coding have similarities, despite the different terms used. Box 9.1 illustrates this, using the Miles and Huberman, Richards and grounded theory (Section 9.5) approaches to coding.

BOX 9.1

Terminology in Coding

There are many descriptions of coding in the literature, and considerable variation in terminology. Even the three types of coding described in Sections 8.3–8.5 of this chapter use different terms, but the similarities between them are important. Comparing Miles and Huberman (Section 8.3.1) and Richards (Example 8.3):

Miles and Huberman	Richards
Descriptive codes	Topic codes
Pattern codes	Analytic codes

Descriptive and topic codes focus on identifying and labelling what is in the data. *Pattern and analytic codes* go further, interpreting and/or interconnecting and/or conceptualising data.

Grounded theory coding (Section 9.5) is similar, but more detailed. Thus:

- In vivo codes focus on what is in the data
- Open codes raise the conceptual level of the data
- Axial codes focus on interconnections between open codes
- Selective codes raise the conceptual level of the data again

The important point in all of these is that a first level of coding is descriptive, whereas second and higher levels are analytic. These higher levels take the analysis of the data from a descriptive level to a conceptual or theoretical level, and there are several ways of doing this (finding patterns, abstracting–conceptualising, interpreting, etc.).

In summary, coding is the concrete activity of labelling data, which gets the data analysis under way, and which continues throughout the analysis. Initial coding will typically be descriptive and low-inference, whereas later coding will integrate data by using higher-order concepts. Thus there are two main types of codes – low inference descriptive codes and higher inference pattern or conceptual codes. While coding is central, basic to all analysis, and goes on throughout the analysis, analysis is not only coding. It also involves memoing.

9.3.2 Memoing

Memoing is the second basic operation of qualitative data analysis, but this does not necessarily mean that it is the second stage. The operations are not sequential – memoing begins at the start of the analysis, along with coding.

While the researcher is coding, at whatever level, all sorts of ideas will occur. These become the stuff of memos, which record the ideas. Glaser's definition of a memo is widely used:

> A memo is the theorising write-up of ideas about codes and their relationships as they strike the analyst while coding . . . it can be a sentence, a paragraph or a few pages . . . it exhausts the analyst's momentary ideation based on data with perhaps a little conceptual elaboration. (Miles and Huberman, 1994: 72; Glaser, 1978: 83–4)

These memos can cover many things. They may be substantive, theoretical, methodological or even personal. When they are substantive and theoretical, these memos may suggest still deeper-level concepts than the coding has so far produced. Thus they may point towards new patterns and a higher level of pattern coding. They may also elaborate a concept or suggest ways of doing this, or they may relate different concepts to each other. This last type of memo produces propositions.

As with the higher levels of coding, the important thing about substantive and theoretical memos is that *they have conceptual content and are not simply describing the data*. They help the analyst move from the descriptive and empirical to the conceptual level. They are therefore especially important in induction, since they move the analysis towards conceptualising and developing propositions. Memoing links coding with the developing of propositions. It is important in qualitative analysis to balance discipline with creativity, and it is in memoing where creativity comes in. We can think of coding as the systematic and disciplined part of the analysis (though creativity and insight are also needed to see patterns and connections), whereas memoing is the more creative–speculative part of the developing analysis. This speculative part of course needs verification.

Together, coding and memoing provide the building blocks for this style of qualitative analysis. While the initial analysis might be mainly concerned with coding, it is not long before memoing is involved. We have said earlier that the analysis of qualitative data cannot be reduced to rules. But there is one exception to this one rule (Glaser, 1978: 83): *Record all ideas, as they happen, as memos. When an idea occurs during coding, stop the coding and record the idea.* Later, the memos can be indexed for storage and subsequent use. Miles and Huberman (1994: 72–5) show several memos taken from different projects, and Charmaz (2006: 72–95) describes and discusses memoing, and gives several examples of memo-writing.

Abstracting and comparing

9.4 The sort of qualitative analysis so far described requires many different intellectual tools and activities, but two activities stand out as fundamental – abstracting and comparing.

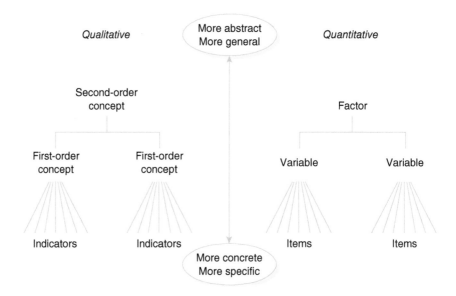

FIGURE 9.2   Levels of abstraction in data analysis

Abstracting

The essential point here is that some concepts are at a higher level of abstraction than others. The terms 'concrete to abstract' describe this continuum of abstraction, as do the terms 'specific to general'. The diagram in Figure 9.2 shows this idea, as does the original diagram in Chapter 2.

This diagram shows the levels of abstraction in both the qualitative and quantitative contexts, and the close similarities between the two. At the lowest level of abstraction, the most concrete or specific or descriptive level, we have indicators (qualitative) and items (quantitative). At the next level, the first level of abstraction, we have first-order concepts (qualitative) and variables (quantitative). As will be shown in Chapter 11, latent trait theory in measurement formalises this idea. At the next level, the second order of abstraction, we have second-order concepts (qualitative) and factors (quantitative). Again, factor analysis (and cluster analysis) in quantitative work formalise this idea. The process of abstraction does not need to stop there. Still more abstract and general concepts are possible, in both approaches, but two levels of abstraction show the idea and encompass much of what we do.

Two things stand out from this diagram. First, the conceptual structure, in terms of the continuum from concrete-to-abstract and specific-to-general, is remarkably similar in both qualitative and quantitative approaches to the analysis of data. Therefore, the general nature of this sort of analysis, developing higher-order concepts to summarise and integrate more concrete levels of data, is also similar in both approaches. Second, quantitative analysis has formalised the way it moves from one level to the next to a much greater extent than qualitative analysis. Thus quantitative analysis aggregates items into variables, to move to the first level of abstraction, and derives factors from variables, to move to the second level of abstraction. By the nature of its data, qualitative analysis cannot be formalised to the same extent, but the role of abstraction explains the central importance of tree diagrams in qualitative data analysis (O'Leary, 2004: 258; Richards, 2005: 104–21).

Comparing

Comparison is fundamental to all systematic inquiry, whether the data are qualitative or quantitative. In quantitative research we don't often think explicitly about comparison, since comparison is built into all stages of quantitative inquiry. Thus measurement encapsulates the concept of comparison, quantitative design is developed to permit comparison, and the various data analysis techniques are based on comparison. So we are comparing automatically when we use the techniques of quantitative research.

Comparison is not so automatically integrated into qualitative analysis, and it therefore needs stressing. Comparing is essential in identifying abstract concepts, and to coding. At the first level of coding, it is by comparing different indicators in the data that we arrive at the more abstract concepts behind the empirical data. Thus it is comparison which leads to raising the level of abstraction, to the 'one-upping' (Glaser, 1978) so essential to conceptual development. The same is true for coding at a higher level. Comparing concepts and their properties at a first level of abstraction enables us to identify more abstract concepts. The systematic and constant making of comparisons is therefore essential to conceptual development at all levels in the analysis of qualitative data.

Tesch (1990), in her comprehensive survey of methods used in qualitative data analysis, sees comparison as the central intellectual activity in analysis. Glaser and Strauss (1967), co-founders of grounded theory, saw comparison as so important that they described grounded theory analysis as the 'constant comparative method'. Thus comparing is at the heart of grounded theory analysis.

Grounded theory analysis

9.5 Grounded theory is both an overall approach to research and a set of procedures for developing theory through the analysis of data. The overall approach was described in Chapter 7. This section deals with the basic ideas of grounded theory analysis. This analysis aims directly at generating abstract theory to explain what is central in the data. All of its procedures are oriented to this aim, and from the start of its coding it recognises both the central role of conceptual abstraction and the hierarchical structure of theoretical knowledge.

How does the analyst go about generating theory from data? What follows now is an overview of grounded theory analysis, then a description of open, axial and selective coding.

9.5.1 Overview

The ultimate idea in discovering a grounded theory is to find a core category, at a high level of abstraction but grounded in the data, which explains and accounts for what is central in the data. Grounded theory analysis does this in three steps, which are conceptually distinct but not necessarily sequential. The first is to find conceptual categories in the data, at a first level of abstraction. The second is to find relationships between these categories. The third is to conceptualise and account for these relationships at a higher level of abstraction. This means there are three general types of codes – substantive codes (produced by open coding), which are the initial conceptual categories in the data; theoretical codes (produced by axial coding), which connect these categories; and the core code (produced by selective coding), which is the higher-order conceptualisation of the theoretical coding, around which the theory is built.

Thus the first objective is to find the substantive codes in the data. These are categories generated from the empirical data, but at a more abstract level than the data themselves. In this first level of analysis, some of these substantive codes will appear as more central in the data than others. The second objective is to bring the main substantive codes together, to interconnect them using theoretical codes. These statements of interconnection are propositions or hypotheses about the data, to be integrated into the grounded theory. The third objective is thus to find a higher-order, more abstract construct – the core category – which integrates these hypotheses into a theory, and which describes and explains them.

At the heart of grounded theory analysis is coding – open coding, axial coding and selective coding. These are not necessarily done sequentially – rather, they are likely to be overlapping and done concurrently. But they are conceptually distinct operations. Open coding finds the substantive codes. Axial coding uses theoretical codes to interconnect the main substantive codes. Selective coding isolates and elaborates the higher-order core category.

9.5.2 Open coding

Open coding constitutes a first level of conceptual analysis with the data. The analyst begins by 'fracturing' or 'breaking open' the data. This is why the term 'open' in open coding is used. The idea is to open up the theoretical possibilities in the data. The purpose is to use the data to generate abstract conceptual categories – more abstract than the data they describe – for possible later use in theory building. These are the substantive codes. Open coding necessarily involves a close examination of (some of) the data, identifying conceptual categories implicit or explicit in the data, and the theoretical possibilities the data carry. What makes grounded theory analysis different from other forms of qualitative analysis is its insistence, from the start, on generating abstract conceptual categories to account for the data being studied. Therefore grounded theory coding is *not* centrally concerned with simple description, or with thematic analysis or interpretation of the data, though

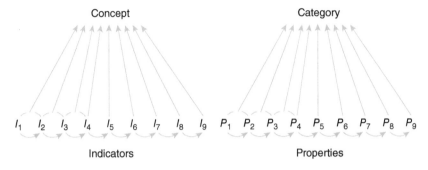

FIGURE 9.3   Concept–indicator diagram

Source: Glaser, 1978: 62

these may assist the analyst in the open coding. It *is* centrally concerned with 'rendering the data theoretically' (Glaser) or 'converting the data analytically' (Strauss). These phrases mean using the data to generate more abstract categories. The focus is on generating grounded abstract concepts, which can become the building blocks for the theory.

The key to understanding both open coding and grounded theory analysis in general is the concept–indicator model. It is shown again in Figure 9.3. It is the same model that we saw earlier, in the discussion of levels of abstraction in Section 9.4, and that we will see later, in latent trait theory in measurement (Section 11.3). As Glaser (1978: 62) points out, this model directs the coding of empirical indicators in the data.

A concept can have many different possible empirical indicators. When we infer a concept from an indicator in the data, we are abstracting – going upwards from a piece of empirical data to a more abstract concept. Because a concept has many indicators, the indicators are interchangeable with each other for the purposes of inferring the concept. This means that I_1 (indicator 1) is an indicator of the concept, and so is I_2 (and I_3, I_4, etc.). We compare indicator with indicator, assessing their similarities and differences, in order to infer the more abstract concept. We also ask, constantly, what more abstract concept this piece of empirical data indicates.

Thus the process of labelling in open coding is guided by two main activities – making comparisons and asking questions. The first means that different pieces of data, as indicators, are constantly compared with each other to help generate abstract categories. For the second, one type of question is constantly asked which is distinctive of grounded theory analysis. It has three forms:

- **What is this piece of data an example of?**
- **What does this piece of data stand for, or represent?**
- **What category or property of a category does this piece of data indicate?**

Open coding, like all coding, is labelling, putting labels on pieces of data. Sometimes these labels will be descriptive, low-inference labels, and sometimes they will be '*in vivo*' labels, but mostly they will be labels that involve a first level of inference.

In grounded theory open coding, the labelling is guided by the model and questions shown above. Codes (labels) at this early stage of the analysis are provisional, and a piece of data may have several labels. Closure on final codes is delayed until substantial coding has been done, and until the analyst has a stable view of what is central in the data. Potentially central categories are also being noted as the open coding proceeds, but closure is delayed here also.

Open coding is about using the data to generate conceptual labels and categories for use in theory building. Its function is to expose theoretical possibilities in the data. It is not about bringing concepts to the data, and no a priori coding scheme is used. Using only concepts and categories generated by the data ensures that they are grounded in the data, and that any concepts to be used in the theory have earned their conceptual status. Thus the analyst starts with no preconceived conceptual categories, but uses only those generated by the data. Open coding is not centrally concerned with summarising data, or with describing data, or with finding synonyms for words in the data or with interpreting data. It may do these things indirectly, or as part of generating abstract categories, but these things are not the objective – the objective is to conceptualise the data.

Successful open coding generates many provisional labels quickly from even a small amount of data, but this sort of coding does not go on indefinitely. The objective of open coding is not the endless generation of conceptual labels throughout the data. This process of labelling therefore needs to be balanced by two other processes. One is to keep an overview of the data in mind, and to keep looking broadly across the data, rather than to only do the intensive coding. This is what Glaser (1992) calls 'dip and skip', where you intensively code some parts (dip), while at the same time skimming the data using comparisons to look for possible conceptual patterns, and for concepts that tie together different pieces of the data and different incidents in the data (skip). The other is deliberately to step back from the data and to make judgements about what seems to be central and basic in the data, over and above all the coding labels generated. This judgement is made by focusing on such questions as:

- What centrally seems to be going on here?
- What are these data mainly about?
- What is the basic social problem people here are facing, and what is the basic social process they use for dealing with it?

In grounded theory analysis, it is important to find and focus on what is central in the data. The whole process is about successively integrating the data into a smaller set of more abstract concepts and categories. Therefore the focus is on possible integrating concepts right from the start. Ultimately, a grounded theory will be built around a core category, which accounts for most of the variation in the data, and integrates other parts of the data around it. Therefore coding procedures at all stages are aligned with this purpose of reducing the data through abstracting, of seeking to discover the conceptually central aspects of the data. The outcome of open coding is a set of conceptual categories generated from the data. There will also be some ordering and classification of these categories, and some sense of what is central in the data. There may be some initial views of possible core categories, but whether this has happened or not at this stage, a small number of important categories will have emerged.

EXAMPLE 9.4

Open Coding

Strauss and Corbin (2008) illustrate open coding using observational data from a restaurant setting.

Strauss (1987: 40–64 and 82–108) demonstrates open coding in a seminar with students, with Strauss himself as leader, using observational data from a study of pain management in a cardiac recovery unit.

Corbin (1986: 102–20) describes open coding on observational data from a nurse in a paediatric unit studying children's responses to hospitalisation.

Alder (2002) uses open coding in a study examining how caring relationships develop between middle school students and their teachers.

9.5.3 Axial (or theoretical) coding

Axial coding is the name given to the second operation in grounded theory analysis, where the main categories that have emerged from open coding of the data are interconnected with each other. The word 'axial' is used by Strauss and Corbin, and is intended to denote the idea of putting an axis through the data, where an axis connects the categories identified in open coding. Glaser (1978) uses the more general term 'theoretical coding' to describe this stage. Its meaning is made clear below.

If open coding breaks the data apart, or 'runs the data open' (Glaser, 1978), in order to expose their theoretical possibilities and categories, axial coding puts categories back together again, but in conceptually different ways. Thus axial coding is about interrelating the substantive categories that open coding has developed.

How is this done? To do the interrelating, we will need some concepts that connect things to each other. These connecting concepts are called theoretical codes, which is why Glaser uses the term theoretical coding rather than axial coding. Strauss and Corbin also use the term 'coding paradigm' to describe a set of concepts used for making the connections between things. All of these terms mean the same thing.

We know from quantitative analysis that there are many different ways in which connections between things can occur. For example, causes and consequences is one way; seeing things as different aspects (or dimensions or properties) of a common category is another; seeing things as parts or stages of a process is a third; a stimulus–response association is a fourth; and so on. Some of the ways things can be connected are covered by Miles and Huberman, in their list of tactics noted earlier, and two comprehensive treatments of this topic are by Glaser and Rosenberg. Glaser (1978: 72–82) discusses 18 ways these connections between things can occur. He calls them 'coding families'. Rosenberg (1968: 1–21), writing more from the quantitative perspective, classifies relationships between variables (the quantitative equivalent of connections between things) into three main types (symmetrical, reciprocal and asymmetrical) and then gives several subtypes within each of these classifications.

Strauss and Corbin (2008) write exclusively about the interactionist coding paradigm. This identifies causal conditions, phenomenon, context, intervening conditions, action/interaction strategies and consequences as a way of interrelating categories in the data – these are theoretical concepts used to interconnect the data. Thus, if the interactionist paradigm is used, the outcome of axial coding is an understanding of the central phenomenon in the data in terms of the conditions that give rise to it, the context in which it is embedded, the action/interaction strategies by which it is handled, managed or carried out, and the consequences of those strategies.

This idea of theoretical codes is important, but not esoteric – it is about the ways in which things are interconnected with each other. We will see in quantitative analysis (Chapter 12) that there are two conceptually distinct stages in studying relationships between variables. One is finding and describing the relationship. The other is interpreting the relationship, or saying how the relationship has come about, or giving meaning to the relationship. It is the same here, in qualitative analysis. The three sources indicated above, Glaser (1978), Rosenberg (1968) and Miles, Huberman and Saldana (2013), together give a comprehensive description of possible ways things can be related. These descriptions overlap, and all draw upon ideas on this topic from quantitative research.

EXAMPLE 9.5

Axial Coding

Strauss and Corbin (2008) illustrate axial coding using pain management data.

Strauss (1987: 64–8) demonstrates axial coding around the category 'monitoring', in a study of medical technology in a cardiac care unit.

Swanson (1986: 121–32) gives several examples of developing categories in axial coding, using as data nurses' accounts of their learning experiences.

Alder (2002) uses axial coding in a study examining how caring relationships develop between middle school students and their teachers.

9.5.4 Selective coding

Selective coding is the third operation in grounded theory analysis. The term 'selective' is used because, for this stage, the analyst deliberately selects one central aspect of the data as a core category, and concentrates on this. When this selection is made, it delimits the theoretical analysis and development to those parts of the data that relate to this core category, and open coding ceases. The analysis now proceeds around the core category, and the core category becomes the centrepiece of the grounded theory.

In selective coding, therefore, the objective is to integrate and pull together the developing analysis. The theory to be developed must have a central focus, around which it is integrated. This will be the core category of the theory. It must be a central theme in the data, and in order to integrate the other categories in the data, the core category will have to be at a higher level of abstraction. Potential core categories are noted right from the start of the analysis, though final decisions about the core category should not be made too early in the analysis.

Thus selective coding uses the same techniques as the earlier open and axial coding, but at a higher level of abstraction. The focus now is on finding a higher-order concept, a central conceptual category at a second level of abstraction. Selective coding deals with what is central in the data analytically, not simply descriptively. All aspects of grounded theory analysis focus on conceptualising and explaining the data, not on describing the data. For Glaser (1992), in true grounded theory analysis, the core category will emerge from the constant comparisons that have driven the earlier coding. Once the core category is clear, it is elaborated in terms of its properties, and systematically related to other categories in the data. Relationships are then validated against the data. This stage also shows those categories where further data are required, and thus directs further theoretical sampling. In grounded theory language, this stage is called the systematic densification and saturation of the theory.

EXAMPLE 9.6

Selective Coding

Strauss and Corbin (2008) illustrate the steps involved in selective coding using data about how women with chronic illness manage pregnancy.

Strauss (1987: 69–75) illustrates selective coding using nursing work in a cardiac recovery unit.

Corbin (1986: 102–20) illustrates selective coding using memos relating to pregnancy in situations of chronic illness.

The objective throughout is to construct abstract theory about the data, which is grounded in the data. The concepts the theory will use are not brought *to* the data and are not obvious *in* the data. They need to be inferred *from* the data by induction. This inductive inference is the process of abstraction. By showing a particular piece of data to be an example of a more abstract (first-order) concept, the analyst raises the conceptual level of the data. By showing that first-order concept to be a particular instance, or property, of a more general second-order concept, the conceptual level of the data is raised again. Thus this abstracting is done twice, following the conceptual

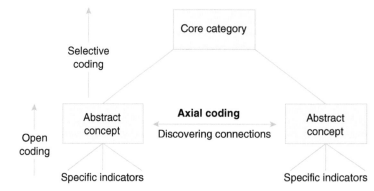

Open coding: discovering abstract concepts in the data; raising the conceptual level of the data.
Axial coding: discovering, in the data, connections between abstract concepts.
Selective coding: selecting the core category by concentrating on the basic social process evident
                     in the data; raising the level of abstraction again to the core category; elaborating
                     the core category.

FIGURE 9.4   Diagrammatic representation of grounded theory analysis

structure shown in the levels of abstraction diagram (Figure 9.2). By way of summary, a diagrammatic representation of grounded theory analysis is shown in Figure 9.4.

This description has not covered all aspects of grounded theory analysis. Among topics not dealt with here, but covered in the grounded theory literature, are theoretical sensitivity, sampling and saturation, the difference between substantive and formal theories, elaboration and the densification of a grounded theory, basic social problems and processes, and the implications of the grounded theory approach for the study of social processes. As noted in Chapter 7, there has also been considerable recent diversification of grounded theory methods. Further reading on all of these topics can be found in the *Handbook of Grounded Theory* (Bryant and Charmaz, 2007b) and Charmaz (2006).

EXAMPLE 9.7

Grounded Theory

Grounded Theory in Practice (Strauss and Corbin, 1997) is an edited collection of readings of grounded theory studies, from former students of Strauss. The editors provide commentaries for each paper.

Examples of Grounded Theory: A Reader (Glaser, 1993) is an edited collection of 25 grounded theory papers from both quantitative and qualitative projects.

Other analytic approaches in qualitative analysis

9.6 A dilemma for grounded theory, according to Denzin, is how to be subjective, interpretive and scientific at the same time (Lonkila, 1995: 46). This is one reason for recent diversification in grounded theory, and especially for the development of constructivist grounded theory (Charmaz, 2006). The difficulty in doing this may also be one reason for the development of other approaches in qualitative analysis. We will now look briefly at five of these, the first more interpretive, and the other four more focused on language.

9.6.1 Narratives and meaning

Data analysis approaches based on segmenting, coding and categorisation are valuable in attempts to find and conceptualise regularities in the data. But by no means do they exhaust the data or possibilities for the exploration of the data. Also, these approaches break the data into small pieces, fostering a 'culture of fragmentation' (Atkinson, 1992). In doing this, they can also decontextualise the data. Coffey and Atkinson (1996: 52) write:

> Our interview informants may tell us long and complicated accounts and reminiscences. When we chop them up into separate coded segments, we are in danger of losing the sense that they are accounts. We lose sight, if we are not careful, of the fact that they are often couched in terms of stories – as narratives – or that they have other formal properties in terms of their discourse structure. Segmenting and coding may be an important, even an indispensable, part of the research process, but it is not the whole story.

Miles and Huberman and the grounded theory writers are aware of the problem of fragmentation and decontextualisation, and they suggest ways of recombining and of recontextualising the data. But other approaches (such as the analysis of narratives and stories) deal more holistically with qualitative data right from the start. Much social science research data occurs 'naturally' in story form (for example, in participant observation research), and qualitative data can also be solicited and collected in story form, as in oral and life histories, and biographical interviewing. Even where data are not explicitly solicited in story form, they will often come with storied characteristics, as in unstructured interviews, where people may give narrative responses to an interviewer's questions. Thus there is a storied character to much qualitative data, and thinking about stories in the data can enable us to think creatively about collecting and interpreting data (Coffey and Atkinson, 1996).

Narratives and stories are also valuable in studying lives and lived experience, as is often demonstrated in studies concerned with empowerment. Contemporary anthropology and feminism often emphasise the study of lives from the narrator's viewpoint, with data seen as a shared production with the researcher (Manning and Cullum-Swan, 1994). Using stories as a way to capture the lived experience has occurred in many research settings – in medical and illness studies (Brody, 2002; Coles, 1989), in studies of major life events and trauma (Riessman, 1993), in studies in education from both students' point of view (Measor and Woods, 1984; Delamont, 1990, 2012) and teachers' points of view (Goodson, 1992), and in studies of life in organisations (Martin, 1990). Narratives of this sort can give a uniquely rich and subtle understanding of life situations, and the story is often a feasible way of collecting data just because it is such a common device in everyday interaction.

How can qualitative data in narrative and story form be analysed? Elliott (2005) points out that there is no single approach, and that researchers borrow ideas from literary studies and socio-linguistics to assist their analysis. She notes the three-part analytic framework used by Mishler (1986) – meaning, structure and interactional context, and the two-part framework used by Lieblich et al. (1998) – content and form. Structure itself is often analysed using the Labov and Waletzky (1997) model, using the concepts of abstract, orientation, complicating action, evaluation, resolution and coda.

The following brief description draws mainly on the writing of Coffey and Atkinson (1996), who use Denzin's framework from interpretive biography for thinking about narratives. They describe formal approaches to narrative analysis, where the focus is on identifying the structural features of narratives, and their arrangement – here, narrative analysis tends towards semiotics (Manning and Cullum-Swan, 1994).[3] They show also how narratives can be studied from the point of view of their function, using function as the unit of analysis. To illustrate the functional properties of narratives, they take the examples of success stories and moral tales, and of narratives as chronicles. The latter lead naturally to oral and life histories, and to biographies, autobiographies and personal experience methods generally (Clandinin and Connelly, 1994). Further avenues for the analysis of narratives are opened up by thinking about whose voices are telling the stories – in any storytelling context, the voices are differentiated and stratified – and by the social and cultural context in which the stories are told. In a general sense, stories are part of the representation of social reality as text, and narratives are therefore social constructions located within power structures and social milieux. In this respect, narrative analysis overlaps with discourse analysis.

In narrative analysis, form and content can be studied together, and a concern with narrative can illuminate how informants use language to convey particular meanings and experiences. How people convey their meanings through language can be looked at from a variety of complementary perspectives. We can examine, for example, how language is used figuratively. Coffey and Atkinson show how analysis can explore participants' use of imagery, and how such devices as metaphors reveal shared meanings and understandings. The more general exploration of the use of linguistic symbols to convey shared cultural meanings is referred to as 'domain analysis' (Spradley, 1980; Coffey and Atkinson, 1996).

People use metaphors constantly as a way of making sense of experience, and of expressing and conveying its meaning. Qualitative analysts will often do the same thing in making sense of data. Miles, Huberman and Saldana (2013) indicate some of the useful properties of metaphors in qualitative analysis – for example, they are data-reducing devices, pattern-making devices, decentring devices and ways of connecting findings to theory. Metaphors are one important way that people use language figuratively. They are a major type of trope (or literary device), comparing two things using their similarities but ignoring their differences. Other tropes often used are irony (the view from the opposite, sometimes incongruous or paradoxical side), synecdoche (linking instances to a larger concept) and metonymy (representing a whole in terms of one of its parts – Miles, Huberman and Saldana, 2013). Focusing on these concepts in analysing data for meaning links this sort of qualitative analysis with semiotics, as Coffey and Atkinson point out, and as is shown in Section 9.6.4. Example 9.8 shows two books that use narratives in education research.

Narrative Analysis

Connelly and Clandinin (1999) present stories from both teachers and administrators. The authors analyse and reflect upon these stories to make links between knowledge, context and identity, for both teachers and administrators.

The book by Cortazzi (1991) examines important aspects of primary teachers' experience by drawing on the author's analysis of nearly a thousand accounts of classroom events told by 123 teachers. Through their stories, a clear picture is built up of how teachers see teaching.

Gerstl-Pepin (2006) used narrative policy analysis to examine social justice narratives embedded within 'No Child Left Behind' with respect to economic inequities.

Bohanek (2008) examined the ways in which mothers and fathers scaffold conversations about past emotional events with their preadolescent children, using narratives of positive and negative shared family events.

Chapter 8 discussed the analytic status of interview data and the central role of language in qualitative research. This focus, together with the view of language as a form of social action rather than as a neutral medium for 'making pictures of the world out there', provides a convenient way to approach the following types of qualitative analysis.

9.6.2 Ethnomethodology and conversation analysis

Sociological interest in the study of language was stimulated by ethnomethodology, pioneered by Garfinkel (1967). Ethnomethodology sets out to understand 'folk' (ethno) methods (methodology) for organising the world (Silverman, 2011). The fundamental assumption of ethnomethodology is that people within a culture have procedures for making sense of their daily life. For ethnomethodologists, culture thus consists not of a stable set of things that members are supposed to know, but of processes for figuring out or giving meaning to the actions of members. The primary focus is on how central features of a culture, its shared meanings and social norms, are developed, maintained and changed, rather than on the content of those meanings and norms (Feldman, 1995: 8).

This focus on how the shared common world is created leads the ethnomethodologist to study activities that ordinary people engage in, often without thinking. Most of the time, especially when joint action and interaction are involved, language is central to these everyday activities. With so much of social life mediated through written and especially spoken communication, the study of language is at the heart of ethnomethodology. Thus conversation analysis becomes a central concern, as ethnomethodologists seek to understand people's methods for producing orderly social interaction.

As an earlier indication of its importance, Heath and Luff (1996) refer to a 1990 bibliography of ethnomethodological–conversation analytic studies which contains more than 1400 citations to articles in five different languages. The general purpose of such studies is to understand the social organisation of ordinary, naturally occurring human conduct, in which talk is a primary vehicle for the production and intelligibility of human actions. Where talk only is analysed, verbatim transcripts of actual conversations are used. If the data cover all interaction including conversation, a video recording is more likely to be used, as in interaction analysis (Heath and Luff, 1996).

Silverman (2011) summarises Heritage's account of three fundamental assumptions of conversation analysis. They concern the structural organisation of talk, the sequential organisation of talk and the need for the empirical grounding of the analysis. Following these assumptions, and using specialised transcription conventions, conversation analysis studies the situated production and organisation of talk (or action), developing a 'bottom-up' understanding of how context influences participants' production of the social reality. For example, with respect to sequential organisation, a part of that context is the immediately preceding utterance (or action). The next utterance is produced with respect to the immediately preceding utterance, and itself forms part of the context for the subsequent utterance(s). In this turn-taking, the conduct of participants in interaction is doubly contextual, both context-shaped and context-renewing (Heritage, 1984). Some of the tools and techniques used in conversation analysis are described by Coulthard (1985) and McCarthy (1991).

In this way, conversation analysis, like ethnomethodology generally, aims systematically to uncover and analyse the foundations of social life. Silverman (1993: 127–33) lists some of the features discovered so far in this microscopic analysis of ordinary talk. He concludes that conversation analysis, as an empirically based activity grounded in a basic theory of social action, generates significant implications from the analysis of previously unnoticed interactional forms, and goes on to show how conversation analysis can help in analysing and understanding the talk that occurs in organisations and institutions. Similarly, Heath and Luff (1996: 324) conclude that the naturalistic analysis of conversation and interaction has developed a substantial body of findings which delineate the interlocking social organisation of a wide range of ordinary social actions and activities.

Ethnomethodology and Conversation Analysis

Silverman (2011: 286–99) discusses conversational openings, obligations to answer, the structure of turn-taking and institutional talk.

Wooffitt (1996: 287–305) refers to data from various sources in discussing linguistic repertoires, the organisation of descriptive sequences and assembling descriptions.

Lynch (2006) argues that ethnomethodology and conversation analysis offer a path not taken in cognitive science – a viable research programme for investigating nominally 'cognitive' themes (memory, learning, perception, etc.) without trading in mentalistic notions of cognition.

Burns and Radford (2008) use conversation analysis to explore parent–child interaction within Nigerian families.

9.6.3 Discourse analysis

Another view of language looks above its words, sentences and linguistic features and focuses attention on the way language is used, what it is used for and the social context in which it is used. The term 'discourse' captures this broader focus, and refers to the general framework or perspective within which ideas are formulated (Abbott and Sapsford, 2006). Discourse inextricably permeates social life, since everything people do is framed within some sort of discourse – thus an ideology is framed within a discourse, so are accounts and descriptions (Wooffitt, 1996), and so is science itself (Gilbert and Mulkay, 1984).

Jupp (2006) cites Worrall's use of the term:

Discourse embraces all aspects of a communication not only its content, but its author (who says it?), its authority (on what grounds?), its audience (to whom?), its objective (in order to achieve what?). (Worrall, 1990: 8)

Discourse encompasses ideas, statements or knowledge that are dominant at a particular time among particular sets of people . . . and which are held in relation to other sets of individuals . . . Implicit in the use of such knowledge is the application of power . . . discourse involves all forms of communication, including talk and conversation . . . In the latter, however, it is not restricted exclusively to verbalised propositions, but can include ways of seeing, categorising and reacting to the social world in everyday practices. (Jupp, 1996: 300)

Discourse analysis is not a unified body of theory, method and practice. Rather, it is conducted within various disciplines, with different research traditions, and with no overarching unifying theory common to all types – being heterogeneous, it is difficult to define (Gee et al., 1992). Edley (2001: 189) notes that discourse analysis has become an umbrella term for a wide variety of different analytical principles and practices. In Taylor's view (2001: 5) it is best understood as a field of research rather than a single practice.

Coulthard (1985) gives an overview of its historical development, and shows the various disciplines that have contributed to it, while Potter and Wetherell (1994: 47) list at least four types of work that use the label 'discourse analysis'. The first is influenced by speech act theory, and is directed at accounts of the organisation of conversational exchanges. This type is similar to conversation analysis. The second, more psychological type focuses on discourse processes, such as the effect of discourse structure on recall and understanding. The third was developed from a sociology of knowledge perspective, studying specifically how scientists construct their talk and texts to present and validate their work and their actions. The fourth type derives from European social philosophy and cultural analysis, and attempts to show how institutions, practices and even the individual person can be understood as produced through the workings of a set of discourses. A similar classification is given by Gee et al. (1992)[4], and McCarthy (1991) identifies some differences between British and American discourse analysis. Our interest here is in the third and fourth types described by Potter and Wetherell (1994) – in discourse analysis for qualitative social research.

Despite the diversity and the many disciplinary perspectives, writers point to some fundamental principles and common features of discourse analysis. At the most general level, three principles inform all studies of discourse (Gee et al., 1992: 228): (a) human discourse is rule-governed and internally structured; (b) it is produced by speakers who are ineluctably situated in a socio-historical matrix, whose cultural, political, economic, social and personal realities shape the discourse; and (c) discourse itself constitutes or embodies important aspects of this socio-historical matrix. In other words, discourse reflects human experience and, at the same time, constitutes important parts of this experience. Thus, discourse analysis may be concerned with any part of human experience touched on or constituted by discourse.

At a similar general level, Jupp (1996: 305) identifies three features of discourse analysis as used by Foucault: (a) discourse is social, which indicates that words and their meanings depend on where they are used, by whom and to whom, consequently, their meaning can vary according to social and institutional settings and there is, therefore, no such thing as a universal discourse; (b) there can be different discourses, which may be in conflict with one another; (c) as well as being in conflict, discourses may be viewed as being arranged in a hierarchy – the notions of conflict and of hierarchy link closely with the exercise of power. The concept of power is vital to discourse analysis by way of the theoretical connection between the production of discourses and the exercise of power. The two are very closely interwoven and, in some theoretical formulations, are viewed as one and the same.

More specifically, Potter and Wetherell (1994: 48) point to three features that make the sort of discourse analysis they describe especially pertinent for qualitative social science research.

- First, it is concerned with talk and texts as social practices. As such it pays close attention to features that would traditionally be classed as linguistic *content* – meanings and topics – as well as attending to features of linguistic *form* such as grammar and cohesion. Indeed, once we adopt a discourse analytic approach, the distinction between content and form becomes problematic – content is seen to develop out of formal features of discourse and vice versa. Put more generally, the discourse analyst is after the answers to social or sociological questions rather than to linguistic ones.
- Second, discourse analysis has a triple concern with action, construction and variability (Potter and Wetherell, 1987). People perform actions of different kinds through their talk and their writing, and they accomplish the nature of these actions partly through constructing their discourse out of a range of styles, linguistic resources and rhetorical devices.
- A third feature of discourse analysis is its concern with the rhetorical or argumentative organisation of talk and texts. Rhetorical analysis has been particularly helpful in highlighting the way discursive versions are designed to counter real or potential alternatives (Billig, 1991). Put another way, it takes the focus of analysis away from questions of how a version relates to some putative reality and asks instead how this version is designed successfully to compete with an alternative.

Gee et al. (1992) discuss two main stances within discourse analysis research in education – one emphasises the study of discourse structure for its own sake, using analytic tools from linguistics (discourse as structure); the other studies discourse as it relates to other social, cognitive, political or cultural processes and outcomes (discourse as evidence). Potter and Wetherell (1994) distinguish two different complementary emphases in their style of discourse analysis. One studies the resources used to construct discourse and enable the performance of particular actions, and maps out the broad systems or 'interpretive repertoires' which sustain different social practices. The other studies the detailed procedures through which versions are constructed and made to appear factual. These different stances towards discourse analysis are often combined in research, but they produce different types of research questions, as shown in Example 9.10.

EXAMPLE 9.10

Research Questions in Discourse Analysis

Discourse as structure: Gee et al. (1992: 229a) list eight types of question that involve the study of discourse structure for its own sake.

Discourse as evidence: the same authors list seven types of questions researchers have used in the study of discourse in relation to social and cognitive processes (1992: 230).

A discourse–analytic research agenda from a critical perspective: Jupp (1996: 306) lists 12 questions that might guide a critical analysis of documents using discourse analysis.

Silverman (2011: 300–13) shows how a discourse–analytic perspective can change research questions dramatically.

Potter and Wetherell (1994: 55–63) point out that it is difficult to describe and codify explicit procedures that are used in discourse analysis, but they list five considerations that do recur, and they illustrate how each can operate in analysis. They are: using variation as a lever, reading the detail, looking for rhetorical organisation, looking for accountability and cross-referencing discourse studies. Gee et al. (1992) indicate some of the ways the analysis might proceed in the discourse-as-structure and discourse-as-evidence stances noted above, listing some of the tools linguists use when analysing discourse structure, and showing the categories they find useful in studying the social location of texts.[5] Tonkiss (1998: 250–60) discusses 'Doing Discourse Analysis' under the three broad headings of: selecting and approaching data; sorting, coding and analysing data; and presenting the analysis. Under the second heading – sorting, coding and analysing data – she adds two considerations to the list of five given by Potter and Wetherell above: using keywords and themes, and attending to silences.

Discourse analysis is an important development in qualitative research, starting as it does from the assumption that discourse at all levels, including people's accounts, is an important resource:

> In our view, people's texts are not trivial outcomes of communicative needs. Rather, they function at many levels and are the product of a person's entire set of political and psychological conditions and entities. Humans are constant creators of complex and multifaceted meanings. (Gee et al., 1992: 233)

Discourse analysis is sensitive to how spoken and written language is used, and how accounts and descriptions are constructed, and to the complex processes for producing social meanings (Tonkiss, 1998). At the microscopic level, it shares much in common with conversation analysis, and some writers (Coulthard, 1985; McCarthy, 1991) see conversation analysis as a particular type of discourse analysis. In a more macroscopic perspective, discourse analysis emphasises the interrelationships between accounts and hierarchies, power and ideology. Two important directions for this latter type of discourse analysis are critical discourse analysis (Blommaert and Bulcaen, 2000) and Foucauldian discourse analysis (Gubrium and Holstein, 2000). Critical discourse analysis aims to show 'non-obvious ways in which language is involved in social relations of power and domination, and in ideology' (Fairclough, 2001: 229). Foucault (1980) examines how historically and culturally located systems of power/knowledge construct subjects and their world. For Foucault, power operates in and through discourse as the other face of knowledge – thus the term power/knowledge. Discourse not only puts words to work, it gives them their meanings, constructs and perceptions and formulates understanding and ongoing courses of interaction (Gubrium and Holstein, 2000: 493–5). At this level, discourse analysis is similar to deconstruction, in dismantling constructed accounts to show connections with power and ideology. It has grown into a wide-ranging and heterogeneous discipline, which finds its unity in the description of language above the level of the sentence, and an interest in systems of meaning and in the context and cultural influences that affect language in use.

Discourse Analysis

Gee et al. (1992: 253–81) describe three examples of discourse analysis: sharing time in a first-grade classroom, reading with storybooks at home, and verbal analogy items in standardised test-taking.

   Potter and Wetherell (1994) use five extracts from their case study of the construction of a TV current affairs programme about cancer charities to illustrate discourse analysis.

   Jupp (2006) gives four case studies of discourse analysis, using different kinds of documents.

   Coulthard (1985) has many examples of micro-level discourse analysis in the language teaching context.

9.6.4 Semiotics

Language can be seen as a symbolic sign system, where a sign is something that stands for something else. In language, obviously, the signs are words. Semiosis is the process whereby something comes to stand for something else, and thus acquires the status of a sign (Anward, 1997). Semiotics, or the science of signs, lays out assumptions, concepts and methods for the analysis of sign systems. There are many sign systems (for example, mathematics, music, etiquette, symbolic rites, street signs) to which semiotics can be applied, and Eco (1976) points out that semiotics is concerned with everything that can be taken as a sign. At the same time, semiotics is based squarely on language, in line with the view that human linguistic communication can be seen as a display of signs, or a 'text to be read' (Manning and Cullum-Swan, 1994).

   The Swiss linguist Saussure and the American philosopher Peirce were the founders of semiotics. Peirce's basic point is that anything can be a sign. For Saussure, being a sign entails being part of a code, and he generated a method which showed that structures and words are inseparable (Silverman, 2011). Semiotics has thus been associated with the structural tradition in literary criticism, but the apparatus of semiotics also provides a way of thinking about any sign-mediated social activity.

   An essential idea in semiotics is that surface manifestations derive their meanings from underlying structures (Feldman, 1995). This makes semiotics especially useful in the analysis of language and of texts. Semioticians identify mechanisms by which meaning is produced (the most common ones are metaphor, metonymy and opposition), and have devised techniques using these mechanisms for interpreting qualitative data. Feldman (1995: 22–39) illustrates three of those techniques (semiotic clustering, semiotic chains and semiotic squares) in her analysis of data from her university housing office study. She provides an example of how the use of these techniques helped her to see relationships in the data of which she was not otherwise aware, thereby illuminating her data in a powerful way. As a rather different example, Manning and Cullum-Swan (1994) present a semiotic reading of the menus at McDonald's.

Semiotics can also be used for the analysis of texts, and we have noted already Silverman's (2011) use of semiotics to analyse narrative structures. With its focus on linguistic structures and categories, it can be used to develop a theory of texts and their constituent elements. This takes text analysis well past the earlier quantitative content analysis (Berelson, 1952) in an effort to get to the deeper meaning. Such meaning is to be found not only in words and phrases, but in the system of rules that structures the text as a whole. It is therefore this underlying structure and the rules it embodies that can tell the researcher what its cultural and social message is. While this semiotic emphasis is valuable, MacDonald and Tipton (1996) remind us that there are limits to the understanding we can develop using only the texts. A text also needs to be studied in its social context.

EXAMPLE 9.12

Semiotic Analysis

McRobbie (2000) demonstrates semiotic analysis using a magazine aimed at teenage girls.

Feldman (1995: 21–41) discusses semiotic cluster analysis using the example of 'buildings'.

Manning and Cullum-Swan (1994) present a semiotic analysis of a McDonald's menu.

Mavers (2007) conceptualises writing as a process of design to study how meaning is made by a 6-year-old child who uses semiotic resourcefulness in email exchanges with her uncle.

9.6.5 Documentary and textual analysis

We noted in Chapter 8 the availability and richness of documentary data for social science research. The analysis of such data shares characteristics with the approaches just described, but it also has some distinctive themes.

One theme focuses on the social production of the document, starting with how the document came into being. All documentary sources are the result of human activity, produced on the basis of certain ideas, theories or commonly accepted, taken-for-granted principles, and these are always located within the constraints of particular social, historical or administrative conditions and structures (MacDonald and Tipton, 1996; Finnegan, 2006). Words and their meanings depend on where they are used, by whom and to whom. Thus, as discourse analysts point out (for example, Jupp, 1996: 305), meaning varies according to social and institutional setting. Therefore documents and texts studied in isolation from their social context are deprived of their real meaning. Thus an understanding of the social production and context of the document affects its interpretation. Similar considerations apply also to the social production of an archive – what is kept, where and for how long, and what is thrown away (MacDonald and Tipton, 1996: 189).

A second, related, theme is the social organisation of the document. We saw these questions from Hammersley and Atkinson (2007) in Chapter 7: How are documents written? How are they read? Who writes them? Who reads them? For what purposes? On what occasions? With what outcomes? What is recorded? What is omitted? What does the writer seem to take for granted about the reader(s)? What do readers need to know in order to make sense of them? Silverman (2011) uses these questions to study the social organisation of documents, irrespective of their truth or error. Thus he shows how even such apparently 'objective' documents as organisational files are 'artfully constructed with a view to how they may be read'. He cites the work of Cicourel and Kitsuse in education, Garfinkel with coroners and Sudnow in hospital deaths and criminal statistics to show how the sociological analysis of statistics and files raises fundamental questions about the processes that produce them, quite apart from questions of the truth or error of the statistics themselves. In the same light, he also considers public records and visual images.

EXAMPLE 9.13

Analysis of the Social Organisation of Documents

Silverman (2011) applies textual analysis to files, statistical records, records of official proceedings and images, and includes illustrations from the work of others.

Woods (1979) analyses school reports, and shows the concepts and categories teachers use to make normative judgements about pupils.

A third theme concerns the more 'direct' analysis of text for meaning, this time including questions of truth and error. This analysis can focus on the surface or literal meaning, or on the deeper meaning, and the multi-layered nature of meaning is now much more widely understood and accepted (Finnegan, 2006). The surface meaning has often concerned historians, whereas sociologists have been more interested in ways of uncovering deeper meaning. Methods used range from interpretive understanding following the ideas of Dilthey (MacDonald and Tipton, 1996: 197) to more structural approaches, especially semiotics, as described above.

A fourth theme is the application of different theoretical perspectives to the analysis of texts and documents. As an example, Jupp (2006) describes the critical analysis of documents, seeing documents as media for discourses, and thus drawing on discourse analysis. Deconstruction is an approach that also has applicability in such a context. Thus, as Silverman points out, there are many ways of thinking about textual analysis, and many different theoretical perspectives that can be applied. Silverman (2011) is also convinced that sociologists make too little use of the great potential of texts as rich data, especially in light of their (often) relatively easy accessibility. The relevance of this point for social science research has been raised in earlier chapters.

Computers in the analysis of qualitative data

9.7 While the use of a computer is not appropriate for all of the approaches to analysis described, there are a number of programs to assist the qualitative researcher today. Computer Assisted Qualitative Data Analysis Software is now known among researchers as CAQDAS.

In choosing among the numerous packages available, several websites provide useful information. The website Text Analysis Info Page (www.textanalysis.info) has a comprehensive list of different sorts of packages available. CAQDAS (www.caqdas.soc.surrey.ac.uk) maintains a particularly useful site.

There are several factors to consider and questions to ask when a researcher is choosing among the packages. For example:

Compatibility with my analytic approach. Does this package enable me to do the sort of analysis I want to do?

Ease of use. Do I have a sense that I can master this software and work with it in ways that will promote my creativity?

Product support and upgrade path. Is this product well supported by a strong company and is it likely to be further developed and enhanced? This means that the product will continue to grow as my understanding and practice of qualitative research develops and as I grow as a researcher.

Does the product have previous versions?

Can I download and try out a trial copy? How does this trial cope and feel with some of my data?

Is the company active in its engagement with research and researchers?

Is there a supportive learning community?

Does the product have good quality tutorials?

Are there opportunities for training and workshops?

Is the product supported by a website and is there a discussion forum available?

Do people actively use this product around me in my context?

Does the research community in my area use this product? Are there frequent mentions of the product in the recent literature?

Costs of the software – not all the costs are in the purchase price:

Does it require specialised or higher-grade hardware?

Does the ongoing licence require further costs?

Are training and support expensive?

Who buys this software or does my institution provide a copy?

Qualitative software packages

Similar to SPSS and R, which help you analyse quantitative data, there are a number of software packages which can assist you in your qualitative data analysis. CAQDAS cannot interpret your data for you, but it can be extremely useful in helping you to manage and code your data and store it for easy retrieval.

As with quantitative packages, there is a range of options available to the qualitative researcher. Each package has strengths and weaknesses, though many have shared or similar functionality. Your choice of which software to use may be down to which package your university subscribes to. If you are in a position to choose for yourself, a good guide to the pros and cons and different functionality of each package can be found in *Using Software in Qualitative Data Analysis* by Ann Lewins and Christina Silver. A link to this book can be found on the companion website (www.sagepub.co.uk/punch3e).

NVivo is the most widely used software in most social sciences disciplines. On the companion website, you will find the full text of the first two chapters from Pat Bazeley and Kristi Jackson's book, *Qualitative Data Analysis with NVivo*. These chapters will help you to understand how NVivo supports qualitative data analysis and will help you to get started using the software. Links to additional resources are also provided.

ATLAS.ti is also a popular choice. For step-by-step guidance on using ATLAS.ti, see Susanne Friese's book, *Qualitative Data Analysis with ATLAS.ti* (a link to which is provided on the companion website).

Alternative software:

MAXQDA – http://www.maxqda.com/
Transana – http://www.transana.org/
Hyper Research – http://www.researchware.com/products/hyperresearch.html
Dedoose – http://www.dedoose.com/
Links to all of these softwares and additional resources can be found on the companion website (www.sagepub.co.uk/punch3e).

9.8 Students writing qualitative dissertation proposals often have difficulty with the section on the analysis of qualitative data. Faced with the many methods available, an effective way to proceed is:

1. Decide whether your project requires a specialised approach to data analysis. This should follow from the way your research and research questions have been framed and developed. For example, a grounded theory study will require grounded theory analysis, a discourse analysis will require some type of discourse analysis, and so on. If it is specialised, the proposal can then go on to describe the type of specialised analysis to be used, with appropriate support from the literature.

2. If a specialised approach is not involved, one of the more general approaches will be useful. (The Miles and Huberman approach is particularly good in this situation.) When identifying and describing the general approach selected, points to include are the basic operations of coding and memoing, and stressing that the data will be analysed, not just summarised and described. There are different directions the analysis itself might take – for example, it might be inductive, concerned with conceptualising the data, or interpretive, concerned with analysing meaning, or thematic and concerned with identifying patterns in the data. In all cases, ensure there is support from the reference literature.

3. In doing either (1) or (2), show how the proposed analysis fits with the overall logic of the research. This helps to make your proposal convincing, by strengthening its internal consistency and validity. (A common problem is the lack of fit between the data analysis section and other sections of the proposal.)

4. Show also how the analysis will be systematic, well-organised and thorough. This gives the proposal discipline, suggesting an audit trail through the analysis. In this way, you make your proposal more scholarly.

Chapter summary_____

- In contrast to the situation some 40 years ago, there are now multiple methods for the analysis of qualitative data. This means there is no single 'right' way to do qualitative data analysis. It also means that the analysis method selected needs to fit in with the purpose and strategy of the research.

- Induction as a general term is central to the search for regularities in the social world; analytic induction is a specific method to assist with the search for these regularities.

- The Miles and Huberman approach to qualitative data analysis is a very useful general framework, which works well in many situations; it has three main components – data reduction, data display, drawing and verifying conclusions.

- Coding and memoing are central concrete operations in all approaches to qualitative data analysis; different types of coding are associated with different approaches to analysis; more generally, abstracting and comparing are central intellectual activities in qualitative data analysis.

- Grounded theory analysis is an inductive method for the analysis of data, developed to fit in with the overall grounded theory research strategy; it can be described in terms of open coding, axial coding and selective coding.

• Other approaches to the analysis of qualitative data overviewed in this chapter are narrative analysis, ethnomethodology and conversation analysis, discourse analysis, semiotic analysis and documentary and textual analysis.

KEY TERMS

Audit trail: showing how the researcher analysed the data in order to reach conclusions; describing the methods used in the analysis to enable reproducibility

Analytic induction: a specific method for identifying regularities in the social world; concentrates on induction to raise the level of abstraction and to trace out relationships between concepts

Coding: assigning labels to pieces of data; different approaches in qualitative analysis use different types of coding

Memoing: recording all ideas (substantive, theoretical, methodological, etc.) that occur during coding

Abstracting: conceptualising data at higher and more general levels using induction; raising the level from more specific to more general, or from more concrete to more abstract

Comparing: systematically noting the similarities and differences between pieces of data or concepts

Grounded theory analysis: using open, axial and selective coding to discover or generate theory grounded in data

Open coding: discovering abstract concepts in the data

Axial coding: discovering connections between abstract concepts

Selective coding: raising the level of abstraction again to the core category, which is the central feature of a grounded theory

Narrative analysis: analysing data collected in storied or narrative form

Ethnomethodology: studies the procedures people follow for making sense of daily life, and how shared meanings and social norms are developed and maintained

Discourse analysis: studies the way language is used, what it is used for, and the social context in which it is used; this includes the structure of discourse, and its relationship to hierarchies, power and ideology

Semiotics: the science of signs; language as a sign system; how language produces meaning

Documentary analysis: the analysis of documents as qualitative data; includes their social production and organisation, as well as their content and meaning

Exercises and study questions

1. What has been the most fundamental development in the analysis of qualitative data in the past 40 or so years?
2. What is an 'audit trail' through the analysis?
3. What is induction, and why is it important in the analysis of qualitative data? (see Question 8).
4. Describe and discuss the three general components of the Miles and Huberman model for analysing qualitative data.
5. Study the three different parts of Appendix 1. Then write a paragraph, using your own words, to describe to someone not involved in research how qualitative data can be analysed.
6. What is coding? How can we briefly describe the two main levels of coding, and what is the fundamental difference between them?
7. Why is memoing important in analysing qualitative data?
8. What is meant by different levels of abstraction? (see Question 3). Illustrate by analysing the Charters' hypothesis example given in Section 5.2 (Chapter 5).
9. What is the objective of open coding? What are the three questions that can guide open coding?
10. What is the objective of (a) axial coding, and (b) selective coding?
11. What does it mean to say that grounded theory is essentially an inductive method?
12. Write a short paragraph to show that you understand each of:

- narrative analysis
- ethnomethodology
- discourse analysis
- semiotics.

Further reading

Narratives and meaning

Cortazzi, M. (1991) *Primary Teaching: How It is – A Narrative Account.* London: David Fulton.

Elliott, J. (2005) *Using Narrative in Social Research: Quantitative and Qualitative Approaches.* London: SAGE.

Fernandez, J.W. (1991) *Beyond Metaphor: The Theory of Tropes in Anthropology.* Stanford, CA: Stanford University Press.

Lakoff, G. and Johnson, M. (1990) *Metaphors We Live By.* Chicago: University of Chicago Press.

Plummer, K. (1995) *Telling Sexual Stories: Power, Change and Social Worlds.* London: Routledge and Kegan Paul.

Polkinghorne, D.E. (1988) *Narrative Knowing and Human Sciences.* Albany, NY: State University of New York Press.

Riessman, C.K. (1993) *Narrative Analysis.* Newbury Park, CA: SAGE.

Ethnomethodology and conversation analysis

Atkinson, J.M. and Heritage, J. (eds) (1984) *Structures of Social Action: Studies in Conversation Analysis.* Cambridge: Cambridge University Press.

Button, G. (ed.) (1991) *Ethnomethodology and the Human Sciences*. Cambridge: Cambridge University Press.

Garfinkel, H. (1967) *Studies in Ethnomethodology*. Englewood Cliffs, NJ: Prentice-Hall.

Gilbert, G.N. and Mulkay, M.J. (1984) *Opening Pandora's Box: A Sociological Analysis of Scientists' Discourse*. Cambridge: Cambridge University Press.

Heritage, J. (1984) *Garfinkel and Ethnomethodology*. Cambridge: Polity Press.

Psathas, G. (1994) *Conversation Analysis*. Thousand Oaks, CA: SAGE.

Wooffitt, R. (2008) 'Conversation analysis and discourse analysis', in N. Gilbert (ed.), *Researching Social Life*. London: SAGE. pp. 440–61.

Discourse analysis

Boden, D. and Simmerman, D.H. (1991) *Talk and Social Structure*. Cambridge: Polity Press.

Coulthard, M. (1985) *An Introduction to Discourse Analysis*. 2nd edn. London: Longman.

Fairclough, N. (1992) *Discourse and Social Change*. Cambridge: Polity Press.

Gee, J.P., Michaels, S. and O'Connor, M.C. (1992) 'Discourse analysis', in M.D. LeCompte, W.L. Millroy and J. Preissle (eds), *The Handbook of Qualitative Research in Education*. San Diego, CA: Academic Press. pp. 227–91.

Jupp, V. (1996) 'Documents and critical research', in R. Sapsford and V. Jupp (eds), *Data Collection and Analysis*. London: SAGE. pp. 298–316.

Potter, J. and Wetherell, M. (1987) *Discourse and Social Psychology: Beyond Attitudes and Behaviour*. London: SAGE.

Potter, J. and Wetherell, M. (1994) 'Analysing discourse', in A. Bryman and R.G. Burgess (eds), *Analysing Qualitative Data*. London: Routledge. pp. 47–66.

Tonkiss, F. (1998) 'Analysing discourse', in C. Seale (ed.), *Researching Society and Culture*. London: SAGE. pp. 245–60.

van Dijk, T. (ed.) (1985) *Handbook of Discourse Analysis*. Orlando, FL: Academic Press.

Wetherell, M., Taylor, S. and Yates, S.J. (eds) (2001) *Discourse as Data: A Guide for Analysis*: London: SAGE.

Semiotics

Barley, S.R. (1983) 'Semiotics and the study of occupational and organizational culture', *Administrative Science Quarterly*, 28: 393–413.

Eco, U. (1976) *A Theory of Semiotics*. Bloomington, IN: Indiana University Press.

Feldman, M.S. (1995) *Strategies for Interpreting Qualitative Data*. Thousand Oaks, CA: SAGE.

Fiol, C.M. (1989) 'A semiotic analysis of corporate language: organizational boundaries and joint venturing', *Administrative Science Quarterly*, 34: 277–303.

Manning, P.K. (1987) *Semiotics and Fieldwork*. Newbury Park, CA: SAGE.

Documentary and textual analysis

Hodder, I. (1994) 'The interpretation of documents and material culture', in N.K. Denzin and Y.S. Lincoln (eds), *Handbook of Qualitative Research*. Thousand Oaks, CA: SAGE. pp. 393–402.

Jupp, V. (1996) 'Documents and critical research', in R. Sapsford and V. Jupp (eds), *Data Collection and Analysis*. London: SAGE. pp. 283–316.

Jupp, V. and Norris, C. (1993) 'Traditions in documentary analysis', in M. Hammersley (ed.), *Social Research: Philosophy, Politics and Practice*. London: SAGE. pp. 37–51.

MacDonald, K.M. (1989) 'Building respectability', *Sociology*, 2(3): 55–80.

Silverman, D. (2011) *Interpreting Qualitative Data: Methods for Analyzing Talk, Text and Interaction*. 3rd edn. London: SAGE.

Notes

1. There is still, however, the question of the interpretation of those results: this comment applies only to the statistical operations performed on the data.
2. Procedures for setting up an audit trail are described by Schwandt and Halpern (1988); see also Lincoln and Guba (1985).
3. Similarly, Silverman (2011) shows the value of semiotics and the structuralist approach in the analysis of 'stories', ranging from Russian fairytales to contemporary political documents.
4. They identify four types of discourse analysis: an emphasis on linguistics, the analysis of talk from a sociological perspective, anthropological and socio-linguistic approaches, and discourse analysis in the explication of social, cultural and political institutions and relations.
5. Further descriptions of some of the linguistic tools can be found in Coulthard (1985), Brown and Yule (1984) and McCarthy (1991).

ten
QUANTITATIVE RESEARCH DESIGN

After studying this chapter you should be able to:

- Describe the similarities and differences between comparing groups and relating variables, as strategies in quantitative research
- Define independent, dependent and control variables
- Describe the basic characteristics of an experiment
- Show how the logic of experimental design extends to quasi-experimental and correlational survey designs
- Explain the key concept of accounting for variance
- Explain how multiple linear regression fits in with accounting for variance

In the most general terms, quantitative research does three main things:

- it conceptualises reality in terms of variables;
- it measures these variables; and
- it studies relationships between these variables.

Thus variables (and variance) are the central concepts in quantitative research.

Chapter 11 will deal with variables and their measurement. This chapter focuses on relationships between variables. From a quantitative design point of view, we can study relationships between variables either by comparing groups, or by relating variables directly. One theme of this chapter is therefore the broad division in the logic of quantitative design between comparing groups, on the one hand, and relating variables, on the other. We can see this by looking briefly at some methodological history in Section 10.2. Three main types of design follow from this broad division – experiments, quasi-experiments and correlational surveys. A second theme of the chapter is the shift from comparison-between-groups to relationships-between-variables, as a way of thinking, and to regression analysis as a strategy and design for implementing this shift. Running through both themes are the ideas of independent, control and dependent variables. We begin the chapter by reviewing the concept of research design, described in Chapter 7.

Research design

10.1 In Chapter 7 research design was described as the overall plan for a piece of research, including four main ideas – the strategy, the conceptual framework, the question of who or what will be studied, and the tools to be used for collecting and analysing data. Together, these four components of research design situate the researcher in the empirical world. Design sits between the research questions and the data, showing how the research questions will be

Research design

Data collected and analysed:
- Following what strategy?
- Within what framework?
- From whom?
- How?

Research questions ⟶ ⟵ Data

FIGURE 10.1   Research design connects research questions to data

connected to the data, and what tools and procedures to use in answering them. Therefore it needs to follow from the question and fit in with the data.

Thus, as in Chapter 7 and as shown again in Figure 10.1, in considering design we are moving from what data will be needed to answer the research questions (the empirical criterion, see Section 5.1) to how and from whom the data will be collected. The same four questions are used: the data will be collected:

1. **Following what strategy?**
2. **Within what framework?**
3. **From whom?**
4. **How?**

In quantitative studies, where variables are central, the design and conceptual framework tend to come together. The design shows how the variables are arranged, conceptually, in relation to each other. In other words, it shows diagrammatically the strategy behind the research. As stressed in Chapter 7, all research design is driven by strategy. The conceptual framework also shows the structure of the proposed study in terms of its variables. While quantitative research design tends to fall towards the tightly structured end of the structuring continuum, it varies in how much the situation is contrived for research purposes, as this chapter will show.

Some background

10.2 A brief sketch of some of the methodological history of quantitative research provides background both for this chapter and for Chapter 12, on quantitative data analysis.

Empirical social science research, as we know it today, began some 150 years ago (with the exception of economics, which has a much longer history). The early social scientists, especially in psychology and sociology, were impressed by the progress of the natural sciences, especially physics and chemistry, and set out to imitate their use of the scientific method in building knowledge. They saw the core of the scientific method as two things – the experiment and measurement. We describe the experiment later, but its central idea involves the artificial manipulation of some treatment variable(s) for research purposes, setting up controlled comparison groups. In the simplest case, the comparison groups are alike in all respects – that is, alike on all other variables – except for their differential exposure to the treatment variable. The other variables are controlled by the design. The aim is to relate the treatment variable(s) to outcome variable(s), having controlled the effects of other variables. The experiment was seen as the basis for establishing cause–effect relationships between variables, and its outcome (and control) variables had to be measured. Thus most early social science research was characterised by experimental design and by measurement.

In the 1950s and 1960s, quantitative researchers in social science began to broaden the scope of the experiment, partly because of its limitations. There was no questioning the logic of the experiment, but limitations to its applicability, both practical and ethical, forced this development. The logic of the experiment was extended first to quasi-experimental and then to non-experimental situations. These terms are explained in Section 10.5. This happened because many of the most important questions in social science research could not be studied by experimental design. Yet there were many examples of naturally occurring treatment groups (see Section 10.5), where the comparisons of interest were possible, but where they had not been set up specifically for research purposes. The development was therefore to apply the principles of experimental design to these quasi-experimental situations, studying these naturally occurring treatment groups. Since these comparison groups had not been set up for research, other (extraneous) variables were not controlled in the design. Therefore, it was necessary to develop techniques for controlling extraneous variables in the analysis of data, since, with the impossibility of true experimentation, they could not be controlled in the design. Put simply, what was developed was a statistical approximation to the desired experimental situation where the comparison groups were alike in all respects, on these other variables. This was done through the statistical control of extraneous variables in data analysis, rather than through the physical control of these variables in the design. These ideas are more fully described in Sections 10.4 through to 10.9. In these developments, measurement continued to be central – the introduction of more variables only accentuated the need for measurement.

These developments led to two main strands within the fields of quantitative design and data analysis:

- *First*, the comparison–between–groups strand, based on the experiment, and with the t-test and analysis of variance as its main statistical features;
- *Second*, the relationships–between–variables strand, based on non-experimental reasoning, with correlation and regression as its main features. I will call this second strand the correlational survey strand.

Comparing the direction of thinking behind these two strands is interesting. The true experiment looks 'downwards' or 'forwards', as it were, from the independent variable to the dependent variable, or from causes to effects. The central question here is: What is the effect of this cause? On the other hand, the correlational survey looks 'upwards' or 'backwards', from dependent variable to the independent variable, from effects to causes. The central question here is: What are the causes of this effect? Because this latter approach takes the world as a given, studying it after things have happened, it is sometimes called ex post facto research – that is, research that occurs after the fact. Mapping the variance in the dependent variable, and *accounting for variance in the dependent variable*, become two central notions in this way of thinking, and they are important themes in this and the next two chapters.

The above description is most typical of applied social science areas, especially those with a sociological bias, including education. The two strands developed in a different way in psychology and educational psychology, as Cronbach (1957) has pointed out. However, the end result is much the same. Cronbach called the two strands the 'experimentalists' and the 'correlationists'. The experimentalists create variation in the treatment variable, in order to study the consequences of doing this. They study how nature is put together, not through taking nature as it is, but through changing it and understanding the consequences of these changes. The correlationists, on the other hand, study the natural correlations occurring in nature. There is no manipulation to introduce changes, but rather the study of nature as it is (Shulman, 1988).

The two strands, the comparison-between-groups strand and the relationship-between-variables strand, are related to each other, particularly when it comes to the analysis of data. But they are also important distinct emphases, and a convenient way to present the material of this chapter. We will deal with the experiment first, and then move through the quasi-experiments to the correlational survey. This is because it is important to understand the logic of experimental design, and the developments which have flowed from it. Before that, however, we have to deal with some terminology.

Independent, dependent and control variables

10.3 Discussing causation in Chapter 5, I pointed out that technical research language avoids the use of the terms 'cause' and 'effect'. The most common terms substituted, and those that will mostly be used here, are *independent* variable (for cause) and *dependent* variable (for effect). However, they are not the only terms used, as shown in Table 5.1. In experimental design, common terms are also 'treatment' and 'outcome' variable, and the treatment variable is often also called the experimental variable. But 'independent' and 'dependent' variable are the most widespread terms, and apply in both the experimental and non-experimental (survey) situations. In addition to independent and dependent variables, we need now to introduce the idea of control variables.

A *control variable* is a variable whose effects we want to remove or control. We want to control this variable because we suspect that it might confound, in some way, comparisons we want to make or relationships we want to study. It is extraneous to the variables that we really want to study, but, at the same time, may influence these variables and the relationship between them (Rosenberg, 1968).

Therefore we want to remove its effects. Technical synonyms for 'remove its effects' are 'partial it out' or 'control it'. In addition, the term 'covariate(s)' is often used as a synonym for control variable(s), and analysis of covariance is the most general of the techniques for controlling variables. A description of ways of controlling these extraneous variables is given later in this chapter (Section 10.9) and in Chapter 12. For the moment, we are thinking only of the conceptual role of control variables in a research design.

Now we have three general categories or types of variables:

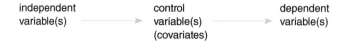

This shows the conceptual status of different variables in our thinking about research design. It is a general conceptual framework, showing the structure of a study in terms of these variables. The conceptual status for any variable may change from study to study, or from part to part within the one study. Thus, any particular variable may be an independent variable in one study, a dependent variable in another, and a control variable in a third. The researcher must of course make clear the conceptual status of each variable at each stage of the study.

The experiment

10.4 As noted in Section 10.2, one main strand in quantitative research design is the comparison-between-groups strand. The clearest case of this is the experiment. In research design, 'experiment' is a technical term with a precise meaning, which is made clear shortly. In discussing the logic of the experiment, we will use the simplest possible case of only two comparison groups.

The basic idea of an experiment, in social science research, is that two comparison groups are set up. Then we, as researchers, will do something (administer a treatment or manipulate an independent variable) to one of the groups. We call this group the experimental group or the treatment group. We do something different, or nothing at all, to the other group (we call this group the control group). We then compare the groups on some outcome or dependent variable. Our intention is to say that any differences we find in the outcome variable between the groups are due to (or caused by) the treatment or independent variable. In technical terms, we aim to attribute dependent (or outcome) variable differences between the groups to independent (or treatment) variable differences between the groups. This attribution is based on the important assumption that the groups are alike in all other respects. We will discuss this assumption shortly.

The experiment is based on comparisons between the groups. In the simplest case described above, the objective is to have the two groups alike in all respects, except that they receive different treatments – they have differential exposure to the independent variable. We then test for differences between them in the outcome (dependent) variable. If the only difference between the groups is in the treatment they received (that is, in their exposure to the independent variable), then, because the independent variable occurs before the dependent variable, we have the strongest possible basis for inferring that differences in the dependent variable are caused by the independent variable. This is why the experiment has traditionally been the preferred design among so many quantitative researchers, especially in educational psychology. Box 10.1 shows the conceptual equivalence of terms used in this description of the experiment.

The alike-in-all-respects criterion is the important assumption referred to earlier. How can this be achieved? How can the comparison groups be set up to be identical, except for differential exposure to the independent variable? Not easily, and historically different methods have been tried for achieving this. At one time, matching was favoured, whereby there was a deliberate effort to match the group members, one by one, in terms of relevant characteristics. However, one does not need many characteristics before this turns out to be impractical. Modern experimental design favours the random assignment of participants to comparison groups, as the way of meeting the alike-in-all-respects criterion.

This solution demonstrates a fundamental principle of quantitative reasoning. Random assignment of participants to treatment (or comparison) groups does not guarantee alikeness or equality between the comparison groups. Rather, it maximises the probability that they will not differ in any systematic way. It is an ingenious way to control for the many extraneous variables that could differ between the groups, and therefore could invalidate conclusions about relationships between the independent and dependent variables based on comparisons between the groups. Random assignment of participants to treatment groups is a form of physical control of extraneous variables. When physical control of these variables by random assignment of participants to treatment groups is not possible, researchers will resort to the statistical control of variables. This is where true experimental design gets modified into various quasi-experimental designs. This is described in Section 10.5.

To summarise, then, we have a true experiment if there is:

- the manipulation of one or more independent variables for the purposes of the research; and
- the random assignment of participants to comparison groups.

This description gives the essential logic of the experiment, but it is only an introduction to the topic of experimental design. Because situations in the real world are so variable, and because extraneous variables can influence experimental results in so many different ways, it has been necessary to modify and embellish this basic experimental design a great deal (see, for example, Kirk, 1995). Thus a wide variety of experimental designs has been developed, in order to ensure greater internal validity in different sorts of social science research situations. 'To ensure internal validity' here means to ensure better control of extraneous variables, or to eliminate rival hypotheses to the proposed causal one linking the independent and dependent variables. As a result of these developments, experimental design is a specialised topic in its own right. An important reference for the topic is the classic work by Campbell and Stanley (1963), in which they list the most common designs and the threats to the internal validity of those designs. Example 10.1 shows a number of research experiments.

EXAMPLE 10.1

Examples of Experiments

In 'Opinions and social pressure', Asch's (1955) classic experiment on compliance, male undergraduate students were recruited for a study of visual perception. Seven subjects were shown a large card with a vertical line on it and then asked to indicate which of three lines on a second card matched the original. Six of the group were accomplices of the researcher and gave false responses. The one 'real' subject was exposed to the subtle pressure of the other participants who presented a unanimous verdict.

Sherif et al. (1961) conducted a classic field experiment, *Intergroup Conflict and Cooperation: The Robber's Cave Experiment*, in which preadolescent American boys were brought into a summer camp in order to control and study the relations that developed among them.

In Project STAR (the Tennessee Student Teacher Achievement Ration experiment), Finn and Achilles (1990) studied the effect of reductions in class size on student academic achievement. Students were randomly assigned to classes of different sizes in 80 elementary schools.

Williams (1986) used the introduction of television into a remote Canadian community in the 1970s to study the effect of TV on children's cognitive skills.

Where it is possible to experiment, this design clearly provides the strongest basis for inferring causal relationships between variables. However, there are two problems that severely limit the applicability of the experiment in social science research. The first is practicality. It is simply not possible to investigate experimentally many of the questions of real interest and importance. Even with substantial funding, these questions remain out of reach, just on practical grounds. The second is ethics. Very often, questions of research interest are beyond the reach of the experiment, for a variety of ethical reasons.

However, despite these limitations, it is often still possible to make many of the comparisons we want to make, even if they are not set in a tight experimental design. There are situations where the comparisons that we want to make (and that we would have structured into an experiment were that possible) occur 'naturally', in the sense of not having been set up artificially for research purposes. These are called 'naturally occurring treatment groups'. How can we capitalise on these situations for research purposes? This question leads us to consider first quasi-experimental and then non-experimental designs. Both involve the extension of experimental reasoning to the non-experimental situation.

Quasi-experimental and non-experimental design

10.5 We can summarise the essential ideas here as follows:

- In the quasi-experiment, comparisons are possible because of naturally occurring treatment groups. These naturally occurring treatment groups are fairly clear-cut, though not set up for research purposes. Therefore the experimental treatment is not controlled by the researcher, but the researcher has some control over when to measure outcome variables in relation to exposure to the independent variable. Some quasi-experiments are shown in Example 10.2.
- In the non-experiment, because the comparison groups as such are either not at all clear-cut or non-existent, the concept of naturally occurring treatment groups is broadened to naturally occurring variation in the independent variable. The researcher has little control over when to measure outcome variables in relation to exposure to the independent variable. The non-experiment is really now equivalent to the correlational survey.

EXAMPLE 10.2

Examples of Quasi-Experiments

In 'Comparison of feminist and non-feminist women's reactions to variants of non-sexist and feminist counselling', Enns and Hackett (1990) addressed the issue of matching client and counsellor interests along the dimension of attitudes towards feminism. The hypothesis tested was that feminist subjects would be more receptive

(Continued)

(Continued)

to a radical feminist counsellor whereas non-feminist subjects would rate the non-sexist and liberal feminist counsellor more positively.

Glass's (1988) 'Quasi-experiments: the case of interrupted time series' described a number of quasi-experiments utilising time-series designs across serveral research areas: psychotherapy, road traffic accidents and fatalities, the stock market, self-esteem, anxiety, crime statistics and state school enrolments.

In *Experimental and Quasi-Experimental Designs for Research*, Campbell and Stanley (1963) described the formal characteristics, and the strengths and weaknesses, of ten different types of quasi-experimental designs.

In *Big School, Small School*, Barker and Gump (1964) studied the effects of school size on the lives of high school students and their behaviour, using samples of US schools of different sizes.

Shadish and Luellen (2006) report several education research examples using quasi-experiments with slightly different designs.

Thus there is a continuum of quantitative research designs here, where the true experiment is at the left-hand end, the non-experiment at the right-hand end, and the quasi-experiment in between. This continuum, shown in Figure 10.2, is about two things:

- The researcher's ability to control exposure to the independent variable, and therefore how clear-cut the comparison groups are. In the experiment, the researcher manipulates the independent variable, and has control over the groups' exposure to it. In the quasi-experiment and the non-experiment, the researcher has no such control.
- The researcher's ability to control when to take measurements on the dependent variable(s) in relation to exposure to the independent variable. Again, in the experiment the researcher can control this, taking dependent variable measurements at the most appropriate time. In the non-experiment, there is little opportunity to control this.

Thus, in both cases, researcher control is high at the left-hand end of this continuum, and low at the right-hand end.

We want to take advantage of naturally occurring treatment groups in a research situation. They provide the comparisons we want. But there is a logical difficulty in doing this, a clear threat to internal validity. It relates to the alike-in-all-respects criterion of the experiment. We may well find exactly the comparisons we want, in naturally occurring treatment groups, and we can certainly make the comparisons between these groups, with respect to one or more dependent (outcome) variables. But how can we be sure that there are not other differences between these naturally occurring comparison groups, over and above their differential exposure to the independent variable – differences that may themselves be responsible for any differences between the groups on dependent (outcome) variables? We have not been able to assign people randomly to these groups, to control variables physically, through the design. Therefore there is the real possibility of extraneous variable

Experiment	Quasi-experiment	Non-experiment (correlational survey)
• Manipulation of independent variable(s)	• Naturally occurring treatment groups	• Naturally occurring variation in independent variable(s)
• Random assignment to treatment groups	• Statistical control of covariate(s)	• Statistical control of covariate(s)

FIGURE 10.2   Continuum of quantitative research designs

influences – that is, of systematic differences between the groups, on factors relevant to the dependent (outcome) variable.

The strategy to deal with this problem is to remove the influence of such possible extraneous variables by identifying them, measuring them and extracting their effects statistically. We control them statistically, in the analysis, using the rationale shown in Chapter 12 (Sections 12.3.3 and 12.4.7). Logically, controlling variables in this way achieves a statistical approximation to the desired physical situation of the experiment, where the comparison groups are alike in all respects except for their differential exposure to the independent variable. These extraneous factors become the control variables, or the covariates mentioned earlier. A covariate is thus an extraneous variable which is likely to be related to the outcome variable, and to differ between the comparison groups. The analysis of covariance (ANCOVA) is the technical name given to the statistical technique for controlling covariates. Control variable analysis is the more general term for the statistical control of extraneous variables.

Control variable analysis, and covariance analysis in particular, is an important and widely used quantitative research strategy and design. It applies when there are one or more extraneous variables whose effects we want to remove, in order to get a clearer picture of relationships between independent and dependent variables. All control variables have to be identified and measured before the implementation of the treatment(s). We cannot control a variable, or co-vary out its effects, during the analysis of data unless we have measurements on this variable. And we won't have measurements on it unless we have anticipated its possible effects, and designed its measurement into the study. This is another example of the benefits of the careful question development work recommended in Chapters 4 and 5.

Random assignment of participants to treatment groups, as in the true experiment, is the strongest design for demonstrating causality. But, given the great difficulty of doing this in real world research, control variable analysis in general and covariance analysis in particular are valuable in many research situations. It is therefore a major concept in quantitative design and analysis. It will come up again in Chapter 12, but its essential logic can be expressed in a few sentences:

To co-vary out one or more variables from a comparison between groups is to reach a statistical approximation to the (desired) physical situation where the groups are the same on the covariate(s). If they are the same on the covariates, the covariates cannot be responsible for differences on the outcome variables. Therefore outcome variable differences are more likely to be due to independent variable differences.

I have put this in terms of comparison-between-groups, in order to see it clearly. It applies just as well in studying relationships-between-variables. This is taken up again in Section 10.9, on the physical and statistical control of variables.

What sorts of variables should be seen as covariates? As always, logical considerations prevail. Following the above description, a variable should be controlled or co-varied out if it:

- is known or suspected to differ between the comparison groups; and
- is related to either the independent variable, or, more importantly, the dependent variable.

As Chapter 12 will show, the logic of the statistical technique of covariance analysis is to extract from the dependent variable the variance it holds in common with the covariate(s), and then to see if the remaining variance in the dependent variable is related to the independent variable. Thus, covariance analysis, like everything else in quantitative design and analysis, works on relationships between variables. It is time now to deal directly with this theme. This means we move from the first main strand in quantitative design (the comparison-between-groups strand) to the second main strand (the relationships-between-variables strand).

Relationships between variables: the correlational survey

10.6 In the quasi-experiment, treatment groups are reasonably clear-cut. In the non-experiment – that is, the correlational survey – we move from discrete comparison groups to naturally occurring variation in the independent variable. Instead of talking about separate comparison groups who differ on some variable of interest, we are now talking about a whole range of naturally occurring differences on this same variable. Discrete comparison groups, whether two or more, are simply a special case of this more general situation.[1] From now on, I will use the term 'correlational survey' instead of 'non-experiment' for this research design.

The word 'survey' has different meanings. It is sometimes used to describe any research that collects data (quantitative or qualitative) from a sample of people. Another meaning, common in everyday language, is a simple descriptive study, usually concerned with individual pieces of information, which are studied one piece at a time. Variables as such may not be involved, and continuous variables, as will be described in Chapter 11, are unlikely. This is sometimes called a 'status survey' or a 'normative survey' or a 'descriptive survey', and its purpose is mainly to describe some sample in terms of simple proportions and percentages of people who respond in this way or that to different questions. Such surveys are common today, especially in market research and political research.

The term 'correlational survey' is used here to stress the study of relationships between variables, and some surveys of this type are shown in Example 10.3. These relationships are often studied using conceptual frameworks similar to those used in experimental design. Thus, in this sort of survey, we conceptualise different variables as independent, control (or covariate) and dependent, as shown earlier. This illustrates the point already made – the logic behind correlational surveys is based on the logic behind experimental design. Because we can only rarely experiment, research methodologists have applied the principles of experimental reasoning to the non-experimental research situation, developing logically equivalent non-experimental designs for those situations where variation occurs in the independent variables of interest, but where it is not possible to manipulate or control that variation for research purposes.[2] For this reason, it is important for researchers to understand the basic principles of experimental design, even if they are unlikely to design and use experiments.

EXAMPLE 10.3

Correlational Surveys

Bean and Creswell's (1980) study 'Student attrition among women at a liberal arts college' investigated factors affecting student dropout rates at a small religious coeducational liberal arts college in a Midwestern American city.

Blau and Duncan's (1967) influential book *The American Occupational Structure* looked at the movement from 'particularism' and 'ascription' to 'universalism' and 'achievement' by surveying occupational mobility in American society. The book included considerable material on the role of education in the intergenerational transmission of inequality. This was one of the first studies to use path analysis.

Equality of Educational Opportunity (Coleman et al., 1966) undertook the most comprehensive survey of the US school system, focusing mainly on the relationship between school characteristics and student achievement. Using a series of regression analyses, it produced the finding that school characteristics had little effect on student achievement. This led to the controversial conclusion that family background was more important than school characteristics in explaining differential achievement.

Peaker (1971) in his report, *The Plowden Children Four Years Later*, described a follow-up national survey of 3000 school-age children in the United Kingdom. Combined evidence from home and school from 1964 and 1968 is analysed and displayed.

Fifteen Thousand Hours: Secondary Schools and their Effects on Children (Rutter et al., 1979) is a large-scale study of 12 London secondary schools carried out over a three-year period. The study investigated whether schools and teachers have any effect on the development of children in their care.

We will now look at the relationships-between-variables strand of quantitative design, and see how that can be developed into an accounting-for-variance research design strategy.

Relationships between variables: causation and accounting for variance

10.7 To say that two variables are related is to say that they vary together, or co-vary, or share common variance. What variance means, and the different ways in which variables can vary together, will be explored in Chapters 11 and 12, but the essential idea of covariance is that the variables hold some of their variance in common. When two variables hold some of their variance in common, we can use the concept of accounting for variance and say that one variable accounts for (some of the) variance in the other. We can also say that one variable explains some of the variance in another, but accounting for variance is the more common description.

In Chapter 5 we took a brief philosophical look at the concept of causation, single and multiple. We saw how important this concept is in science, since we want to find the cause(s) of events or effects. But we saw that we cannot do this directly, because of the metaphysical element in the concept of causation. Therefore we may start with ideas of causation in mind, but we need to 'translate' these ideas to make them suitable for empirical research, rephrasing our research questions to replace causal language.

One way to do this is to change questions of the form 'What causes Y?' into 'What causes Y to vary?' and then into 'How can we account for variance in Y?' The first rephrasing introduces the term 'vary'. To vary means to show differences, so now we are looking for and focusing on differences in Y, on variance in Y. This is important – our strategy of inquiry in order to learn about Y is to look for variance in Y, for differences in Y. This simple conceptual step is fundamental to a great deal of empirical inquiry, and underlines the key importance of the concept of variance in research. This same point comes up again in different ways in measurement in Chapter 11 (see especially Section 11.8) and in data analysis in Chapter 12 (Section 12.4). Now we almost have a form of the question that we can operationalise, but we still have to get rid of the troublesome word 'cause'. So we rephrase a second time, and now the question is in terms of accounting for variance.

Thus accounting for variance becomes a crucial step in the way we proceed in empirical research, especially ex post facto research. Variance means differences – this is why it is often said that the scientific method works on studying differences. A main strategy of empirical science is to find out how some dependent variable of interest varies, and then to account for this variance. The idea of learning about a phenomenon by studying its variation and accounting for this variation applies also in qualitative research, as can be seen in some approaches to the analysis of qualitative data, and especially in grounded theory (see Chapter 9).

Returning to quantitative research, we now have a research strategy we can operationalise. This is because, if two variables are related, one can be said to account for (some of the) variance in the other. This is the crux of the matter. The way we account for variance in a dependent variable is to find the independent variables to which it is related.

As pointed out in Chapter 5, we have moved well past simple one-variable causation, accepting the idea of multiple causation for any particular dependent variable. This is the commonly occurring design shown in the top right-hand cell of Figure 5.1 in Chapter 5. We accept that several (maybe many) factors will be necessary to give us a full causal picture for this dependent variable. In the language of this chapter, we have several independent variables and one dependent variable. If we can account for most of the variance in our dependent variable with a particular set of independent variables, and if we know the importance of each of the independent variables in accounting for this dependent variable variance, then we understand the dependent variable very well – how it varies and how to account for its variance. Just as important, we would also have clear indications about which independent variables to concentrate on, in order to bring about changes in the dependent variable.

Multiple linear regression (MLR) is a research design that addresses these issues directly – which tells us how much of the variance in a dependent variable is accounted for by any group of independent variables, and which also tells us how important each independent variable is in accounting for this variance. In this chapter, we now look at MLR as a general strategy and design. In Chapter 12, we look at MLR as a general data analysis strategy.

Multiple linear regression (MLR) as a general strategy and design

10.8 Multiple linear regression – often abbreviated to MLR or just regression analysis – is basically a statistical technique for the analysis of data, but here I want to consider it as a strategy and design, as a way of conceptualising and organising quantitative research. It fits situations where we want to focus on a dependent variable, and to study its relationship with a number of independent variables. MLR is important because we want to do this sort of investigation very often. The conceptual framework is shown in Figure 10.3, and covariates may or may not be included. Of course, the conceptual framework is not limited to four independent variables. The general objective in the research is to account for variance in the dependent variable, and to see how the different independent variables, separately or in combination, contribute to accounting for this variance.

With MLR we can:

- Estimate how much of the variance in a dependent variable we can account for using a particular set of independent variables. When most of the variance is accounted for, we are well on the way to understanding the dependent variable. Conversely, if only a small proportion of the variance is accounted for, we still have a long way to go in understanding it.
- Determine the effects of the different independent variables on the dependent variable, by estimating the unique variance each independent variable accounts for.[3] We can say which independent variables are of most and least importance in accounting for variance in the dependent variable, and therefore in bringing about change in the dependent variable. This is important knowledge when it comes to recommending strategies for changing the dependent variable.

Many quantitative research problems fit into this design, and many other studies can be designed in this way. Figure 10.4 shows a well-used example of this in

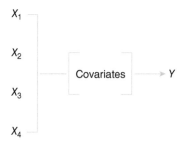

FIGURE 10.3   Conceptual framework for multiple linear regression

education research (with four independent variables and no covariates), and Figure 10.5 shows several multiple-independent-variable-one-dependent-variable designs from different social science areas. Whenever a researcher is interested in relationships between variables, a regression analysis design can be used. There are also benefits to thinking this way about an overall research area. When (as often) the focus is on some major dependent variable, MLR provides a coordinated overall approach to the topic, as well as a ready-made conceptual framework, strategy and design. The requirements are that the researcher must be able to specify, define and measure the independent variables, in addition of course to the dependent variable.

Sometimes, the focus in research may be more on a detailed study of the relationship between variables, than on accounting for variance. That is a strategic decision to be made in planning the research, but it is also a matter of emphasis in how we think about the question, since these are two sides of the same coin. We account for variance by studying relationships with other variables. Therefore, even when the focus is on relationships, we do well to use a regression analysis design, for two reasons – all aspects of the relationship can be studied within that design, as noted in Chapter 12; and knowing how much variance we can account for gives us a strong indication of how important the relationship is.

To sum up, the conceptual framework that goes with MLR is useful because it addresses directly questions of key substantive significance. It deals with central questions of social science research interest, those that derive directly from causation. It also has two other advantages. First, it is flexible, in being able to accommodate different conceptual arrangements among the independent variables, including their joint effects on a dependent variable. This applies particularly to covariance analysis, interaction effects and non-linearity. As Chapter 12 will show, these are three important areas of research interest. Second, it is not a difficult approach to understand, conceptually or operationally. In this chapter we have been stressing its relevance to designing research, and noting that it comes with a ready-made set of research questions and conceptual framework. That is why it is described here as a general strategy and design. In Chapter 12, we look at MLR as a general data analysis strategy.

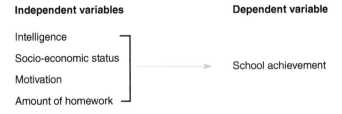

Independent variables   Dependent variable

Intelligence

Socio-economic status   School achievement

Motivation

Amount of homework

FIGURE 10.4   A regression analysis conceptual framework in education research

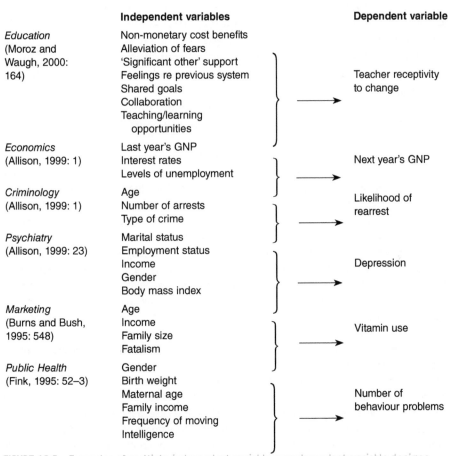

	Independent variables	Dependent variable
Education (Moroz and Waugh, 2000: 164)	Non-monetary cost benefits Alleviation of fears 'Significant other' support Feelings re previous system Shared goals Collaboration Teaching/learning opportunities	Teacher receptivity to change
Economics (Allison, 1999: 1)	Last year's GNP Interest rates Levels of unemployment	Next year's GNP
Criminology (Allison, 1999: 1)	Age Number of arrests Type of crime	Likelihood of rearrest
Psychiatry (Allison, 1999: 23)	Marital status Employment status Income Gender Body mass index	Depression
Marketing (Burns and Bush, 1995: 548)	Age Income Family size Fatalism	Vitamin use
Public Health (Fink, 1995: 52–3)	Gender Birth weight Maternal age Family income Frequency of moving Intelligence	Number of behaviour problems

FIGURE 10.5   Examples of multiple-independent-variable–one-dependent-variable designs

Controlling variables

10.9   The term 'control' has already come up a number of times and it is another central concept in quantitative research design. It is extraneous variables we want to control – variables that may either confound the relationship

TABLE 10.1   Strategies for controlling variables

In the design	In the analysis
Randomisation	Stratification
Restriction	Partial correlation
Matching	Analysis of covariance

we want to study or cause spurious interpretations of this relationship. To control such a variable means to remove its effects, or not to let it have any influence. There are two general ways variables are controlled in research – physical ways and statistical ways. In physical control, variables are controlled in the design. In statistical control, variables are controlled in the analysis of data. We will discuss each, in turn, and they are summarised in Table 10.1. Physical control is characteristic of experimental designs, whereas statistical control is more characteristic of correlational survey designs.

Physical control means that the variable is actually physically controlled, in the design of the study. There are three types of physical control:

- *Randomisation*, where a variable can be controlled by having it vary randomly, or non-systematically. The logic here is that the variable can have no systematic effect if it does not vary in a systematic way. Its effects will cancel each other out, because its variance is random. This idea is used when people are randomly assigned to treatment groups in a true experiment. As pointed out, this does not guarantee that the treatment groups will not differ from each other. Rather, it maximises the probability that they will not differ in any systematic way.
- *Restriction*, where a variable is controlled by physically restricting its variance and holding it constant in a study. Holding it constant means it has no variance in this piece of research. If it has no variance, it cannot have any covariance with other variables. This is the same as saying that it cannot show any relationship with other variables in the study, and therefore can have no effect on them. This second form of physical control is done in sample design and selection. For example, if gender was thought to be a possible extraneous or confounding factor in a study, one strategy would be to include in the study only either males or females. Because there is no variance in gender, it is controlled. The gain is clear – if only one sex group is included, then gender cannot be a factor in the relationships between other variables. But the loss is clear too – if only males are included, the study can have nothing to say about females (or vice versa). This sort of trade-off occurs frequently in research. In this case, a more complete answer might be possible. Both sexes could be included, and then the sample could be partitioned into sex groups during the analysis of the data. This would achieve both control of gender and generalisability to both sex groups. It also shifts control of the variable from physical to statistical.
- *Matching*, where group members are matched, one by one, on relevant characteristics. The problem, as noted, is that this quickly becomes impractical as the number of characteristics increases.

Statistical control means that the variable is not controlled in the design, but rather in the analysis of the data. Statistical control has to be designed into the study, in the sense that the variable to be controlled has to be measured. The logic of statistical control is that the analysis achieves a statistical approximation to the desired (but unattainable) physical situation where the comparison groups are the same on the control variable. There are three types of statistical control:

- Stratification, or test factor elaboration (Rosenberg, 1968), where the control variable, the test factor, is partitioned, and the analysis of the relationship between variables is conducted within each level of the control variable, as described in the case of gender above.
- Partial correlation, where the variable to be controlled is partialled out of the relationship between the other two variables; this is a suitable technique when all variables are continuous, and is discussed in Chapter 11.
- The analysis of covariance, where the control variable (the covariate) is extracted or co-varied out first, before the mainstream analysis is done.

The third of these ways, covariance analysis, has been described already, and is covered in more detail in Chapter 12, where it is incorporated into the MLR approach to data analysis. This third way is stressed here because it reflects the situation described in Sections 7 and 8 of this chapter – the very common situation in research, where there are several independent variables, one or more control variables and a dependent variable. While analysis of covariance is stressed, these three methods are logically equivalent to each other, in the sense that they are all designed to achieve the same thing – controlling the effects of unwanted or extraneous variables.

Chapter summary

- Research design sits between research questions and data, showing how the research questions will be connected to the data, and what tools and procedures to use in answering them; design is based on strategy.
- Quantitative research is fundamentally concerned with the relationship between variables; this is done either by comparing groups using experimental and quasi-experimental designs or by using non-experimental reasoning in correlational survey designs.
- Independent variables (treatment variables, or 'causes') are manipulated in experiments to study their effects on dependent variables (outcome variables, or 'effects'); more generally, an independent variable is seen as the cause, and the dependent variable as the effect, in any cause–effect relationship.
- Control variables, or covariates, are extraneous variables whose effects we want to remove or control, in order to see independent–dependent variable relationships more clearly.
- A true experiment involves the manipulation of one or more independent variables and the random assignment of participants to comparison groups.
- Quasi-experiments take advantage of naturally occurring treatment groups to study independent–dependent variable relationships, using the logic of experimental design.
- Non-experimental designs – correlational surveys – take advantage of naturally occurring variation in independent variables, to study their relationship with dependent variables.
- Variance is a central concept in quantitative research, and accounting for variance in a dependent variable is an important strategy for investigating causation.

- Multiple linear regression directly addresses the question of how much dependent variable variance is accounted for by a set of independent variables.
- Controlling variables is either done physically, through the research design, or statistically, through some form of covariance analysis.

KEY TERMS

Independent variable: the variable seen as the cause in a cause–effect relationship

Dependent variable: the variable seen as the effect in a cause–effect relationship

Control variable: an extraneous variable whose effects we want to remove or control; also called a covariate

Experiment: a technical research design term where one or more independent variables are manipulated to study their effect on a dependent variable, and where participants are randomly assigned to treatment or comparison groups

Quasi-experiment: a design which uses naturally occurring treatment groups to study independent–dependent variable relationships; uses the logic of experimental design

Correlational survey: a design which uses naturally occurring variation in independent variables to study relationships with dependent variables

Accounting for variance: a central strategy for quantitative research, which aims to account for the variation in a dependent variable through its relationships with independent variables

Multiple linear regression: a quantitative design with several independent variables and one dependent variable; estimates how much variance in the dependent variable is accounted for by these independent variables

Exercises and study questions

1. Define independent variable, dependent variable, control variable, and give examples of each.
2. Sketch the design of an education experiment to compare students' learning under a new method of teaching (used with an experimental group) with students' learning under an old method of teaching (used with a control group). What design issues arise? Which variables might need to be controlled?
3. What is a quasi-experiment, and what is meant by naturally occurring treatment groups? Illustrate by comparing (a) educational achievement in big classes versus small classes, and (b) self-concept in children from intact families versus broken families.
4. What does accounting for variance in a dependent variable mean? What is its relationship to causation and why is it a central strategy in quantitative research? In conceptual terms, how is it done?
5. Draw a diagram to show the conceptual framework of a study with six independent variables and one dependent variable. What technique is appropriate for analysing the data from such a design?

6. What are the advantages of multiple linear regression as a general research design strategy?
7. What does controlling a variable mean? Why is it important in quantitative research?
8. Explain the logic of each type of control shown in Table 10.1.

Further reading

Babbie, E. (2012) *The Practice of Social Research.* 13th edn. Belmont, CA: Wadsworth.
Blalock, H.M. (1969) *Theory Construction: From Verbal to Mathematical Formulations.* Englewood Cliffs, NJ: Prentice-Hall.
Brown, S.R. and Melamed, L. (1990) *Experimental Design and Analysis.* Newbury Park, CA: SAGE.
Campbell, D.T. and Stanley, J.C. (1963) *Experimental and Quasi-Experimental Designs for Research.* Chicago, IL: Rand McNally.
Cook, T.D. and Campbell, D.T. (1979) *Quasi-experimentation: Design and Analysis Issues for Field Settings.* Chicago, IL: Rand McNally.
Creswell, J.W. (2013) *Research Design: Qualitative and Quantitative Approaches.* 4th edn. Thousand Oaks, CA: SAGE.
de Vaus, D.A. (2013) *Surveys in Social Research.* 5th edn. London: Routledge.
Fowler, F.J. (1988) *Survey Research Methods.* Newbury Park, CA: SAGE.
Green, J.L., Camilli, G. and Elmore, P.B. (eds) (2006) *Handbook of Complementary Methods in Education Research.* Mahwah, NJ: Lawrence Erlbaum.
Keppel, G. (1991) *Design and Analysis: A Researcher's Handbook.* 3rd edn. Englewood Cliffs, NJ: Prentice-Hall.
Kerlinger, F.N. (1973) *Foundations of Behavioral Research.* New York: Holt, Rinehart and Winston.
Marsh, C. (1982) *The Survey Method: The Contribution of Surveys to Sociological Explanation.* London: George Allen and Unwin.
Sapsford, R. and Jupp, V. (1996) 'Validating evidence', in R. Sapsford and V. Jupp (eds), *Data Collection and Analysis.* London: SAGE. pp. 1–24.

Notes

1. This conceptual move, from discrete comparison groups to a continuum of variation, is actually an important and recurring theme in quantitative research. It comes up again in the discussion of measurement in Chapter 11.
2. Both simple descriptive surveys and correlational surveys are cross-sectional, with data collected from people at one point in time. Cross-sectional surveys need to be distinguished from longitudinal surveys, in which data are collected from people at different points over a period of time. Longitudinal research is an important specialised area – see Menard (1991).
3. In addition to estimating the unique contribution of variables, we can also estimate their joint contribution and any interaction effects.

eleven
COLLECTING QUANTITATIVE DATA

Contents

Quantitative data are numbers, and the measurement of variables is the process by which data are turned into numbers. This chapter describes the main ideas in the measurement of variables, and the application of these ideas in research situations. It was pointed out in Chapter 5 that data about the world do not occur naturally in the form of numbers, that measuring something involves imposing a structure on it, and that there is often a choice in research about whether to structure data quantitatively or not. This chapter therefore includes some comments on the general question of when measurement is appropriate in social science research. To simplify, the discussion throughout this chapter assumes that we are measuring the traits (or characteristics) of people. It generalises to measuring the characteristics of things or events, as well as people.

Types of variables

11.1 Variables can be classified in several ways. One fundamental way is to distinguish between categorical and continuous variables.

Categorical variables (also called discrete variables and discontinuous variables) vary in kind rather than in degree or amount or quantity. Examples include eye colour, gender, religious affiliation, occupation and most kinds of treatments or methods. Thus, if an education researcher wants to compare computerised and non-computerised classrooms, the categorical (or discrete) variable involved is the presence or absence of computers (Wallen and Fraenkel, 1991). For a categorical variable, the variance is between different categories, and there is no idea of a continuum or scale involved. People (or groups, or things) are classified into mutually exclusive categories, of which there may be any number. A dichotomous variable has two categories, a trichotomous variable has three, and so on.

Continuous variables (also called measured variables) vary in degree, level or quantity, rather than in categories. With differences in degree, we have first rank ordering, and then placing on a continuum or scaling. Ordering people into ranks means identifying the first, second, third and so on among them, according to some criterion, but it does not tell us how far apart the rankings are. Introducing an interval of measurement tells us this, and lifts the level of measurement from ordinal to interval. When this is done, the variable is continuous – we have a continuum, with intervals, showing less and more of the characteristic. Examples of such differences in degree are height, weight and age. As another example, we can assign numbers to students to indicate how much interest they have in a subject, with 5 indicating a great deal, 4 indicating quite a lot, and so on. In this case, we have constructed a continuous variable called 'degree of interest' (Wallen and Fraenkel, 1991).

This distinction between categorical and continuous variables is important, and is discussed in many places in the literature, usually in the context of levels of measurement – nominal, ordinal, interval and ratio (see, for example, Kerlinger, 1973). The distinction has historical significance and also practical significance, particularly in influencing how quantitative data are analysed. Because of this, we need to know always what sort of a variable we are dealing with.

Both types of variable are common in research. Sometimes there is no difficulty (or choice) in which type is involved, as when a variable has only categories and no continuum. Sometimes, however, the researcher has a choice as to how a particular variable will be used. Here, the question is whether to use discrete categories or a measured continuum to make the desired comparisons. The historical development, which had important consequences, was to prefer the measured continuum rather than discrete categories, wherever possible. We express the same preference in everyday language when we use 'varying shades of grey' to describe things, rather than using simply 'black versus white'.

To see something in discrete categories is to sharpen the comparisons, which is sometimes what we want. On the other hand, seeing that thing as a measured continuum is more flexible, which is also sometimes what we want. We saw an example of this same shift in the case of research design, when we moved from comparison-between-groups designs to relationships-between-variables designs. We will see the same shift again in the analysis of quantitative data. One implication now is that, while differences in degree can always be turned into differences in kind (as when we convert a set of continuous educational achievement scores into dichotomous comparison groups such as 'pass' or 'fail'), we often do better in research to retain them as differences in degree. We preserve information this way, which is valuable as long as the information is reliable. While each research situation should be assessed on its merits, a useful point to keep in mind is that continua or scales, rather than simple dichotomies or trichotomies, provide more information.[1]

The process of measurement

11.2 Measurement can be seen as the process of using numbers to link concepts to indicators, when a continuum is involved.[2] We can illustrate this process using the measurement of self-esteem as described by Rosenberg (1979) and summarised by Zeller (1996: 823–4) in three tasks:

1. *Defining self-esteem:* Rosenberg (1979: 54) defines self-esteem as a positive or negative orientation toward oneself. An individual of low self-esteem 'lacks respect for himself, considers himself unworthy, inadequate, or otherwise seriously deficient as a person'. On the other hand, persons of high self-esteem consider themselves to be persons of worth. High self-esteem carries no connotations of 'feelings of superiority, arrogance, conceit, contempt for others, overweening pride'.
2. *Selecting measures of self-esteem* – that is, selecting indicators to provide empirical representations of the concept. Having defined self-esteem theoretically, Rosenberg (1979: 291) then constructs indicators that he considers measure the concept. The indicators are statements about oneself, and subjects respond to these indicators by expressing strong agreement, agreement, disagreement, or strong disagreement. Some indicators are written with a positive description of self – 'On the whole, I am satisfied with myself', and 'I feel that I'm a person of worth, at least on an equal plane with others'. Other indicators are written with a negative description of self – 'I feel I do not have much to be proud of', and 'I wish I could have more respect for myself'. Rosenberg constructed five positive and five negative indicators of self-esteem.
3. *Obtaining empirical information* for those indicators: Rosenberg then obtains data for these indicators by asking adolescents to respond to each indicator in terms of the response categories.

A fourth task involves evaluating the validity of the indicators, assessing to what extent the indicators represent the concept of self-esteem empirically. We discuss validity in Section 11.8.

This view of the process shows that we actually construct a variable when measuring it, and anticipates the question of validity, which involves the inference from indicators to concepts. This description of measurement also helps in clarifying the question of when measurement is appropriate in social science research. This question is important because measurement has been at the centre of debates between quantitative and qualitative researchers, and because beginning researchers are sometimes puzzled about whether a study should be done quantitatively or qualitatively. Keeping this view of measurement in mind, I suggest the following ideas as a guide to thinking about when measurement might be appropriate:

- we have in mind a characteristic, or construct or trait of some sort, which we can define unidimensionally (or in terms of its unidimensional components – there may be more than one trait, but each one needs to be defined unidimensionally);
- we envisage a continuum with greater and lesser amounts of this trait, giving different locations along the unidimensional continuum, based on different quantities of the trait;
- we can find reliable ways of identifying the different locations along the continuum – that is, we can identify the indicators that will provide empirical representation of those locations; then we can assign numbers to these locations to calibrate the continuum;
- we believe that the trait shows observable regularities, and that it is reasonably stable over time – or, if it varies, it varies in a systematic instead of a random way. To put it another way, we do not think the trait we want to measure is in a constant and unpredictable state of change.

If these ideas apply, we have a situation where we can construct a measure of the trait. Given situations where we *can* measure, when in research *should* we measure, and when not? The approach taken in this book is that we need to assess each research situation and make a considered decision, case by case. Four general points can help in doing that.

First, making comparisons is fundamental in research, and measurement is a very effective way of making comparisons systematically, formalising and standardising these comparisons. We can therefore consider measuring whenever we want to make systematic comparisons, and whenever the conditions shown above apply. Recognising that this can occur very often in research, including in qualitative research, enables measuring instruments to be employed alongside qualitative data in appropriate situations. On the other hand, however, the advantages we might gain through measurement need to be weighed against possible disadvantages. For example, there may be paradigm objections to measurement, in a particular piece of research, whereby the researcher may reject the assumptions on which measurement is based – and especially the assumption that the reality to be studied can be conceptualised as variables and measured. This is a complicated matter, and full discussion of it is beyond the scope of this book.

Second, measurement involves the disentangling and some simplification of concepts. To see complex phenomena as unidimensional variables is to disentangle and simplify. There are some research situations where we would not want to do this – where, on the contrary, we want a more holistic approach to the phenomenon. The implication of this is that we often cannot get the full picture about something just by measuring it. However, we can get part of the picture, and often a very valuable part, by measuring aspects of it. In these situations, measurement should not be the only way of collecting data. What is suggested again is the complementarity of quantitative and qualitative data, combining the measurement data with more holistic qualitative data.

Third, the nature of the reality being studied, and the approach being taken to it, may not make it appropriate to measure. This may be particularly true of some aspects of the social-psychological reality we often study in social science research. It was mentioned above that the reality being measured needs to be seen as stable, rather than in a constant state of 'becoming'. However, seeing social reality as in a constant state of becoming (and never of 'being') is exactly the view that is central to some qualitative perspectives. These perspectives stress the social construction of reality and its constantly negotiated and renegotiated meanings (for example, Berger and Luckman, 1967). If the researcher wants to focus on these aspects, measurement is not a good way. Measurement constitutes a snapshot, usually taken at one point in time. This does not fit well if process and constant change is the focus in the research. However, here again complementary approaches may be valuable. The one-point-in-time still photograph can provide a good background against which to look at the situation's more dynamic and processual aspects. And in some situations, repeated measurements may be possible, to study change over time.

Fourth, measurement necessarily involves imposing a numerical structure on the data. To measure is to use researcher-imposed constructs, rather than constructs that might emerge from the people being studied. The extent to which this is a problem depends on the purposes of the research, but here again, combining approaches might make sense. As a first step, people's own constructs can be elicited. Then measurements for them can be constructed, to take advantage of the comparisons that measurement permits.

These are some of the points that arise when considering the use of measurement in research. We should also note the distinction between established measuring instruments, on the one hand, and shorter, ad hoc, researcher-constructed measures (rating scales – Andrich, 1997) on the other. There is a role for both. The former would normally only be used in a highly-quantitative context, and most likely when relatively complex variables are seen as the main focus of the research. These established instruments are discussed in Sections 11.5 and 11.7. The latter (the rating scales) might well have a role in any research situation, including a qualitative one. They are discussed in the section on survey questionnaire construction, later in this chapter. In some projects, full-scale measurement might not be appropriate, but the use of rating scales might well be.

Latent traits

11.3 In social, psychological and educational measurement, the characteristic or trait that we want to measure is usually not directly observable. It is hidden or latent. We can only measure something that cannot be observed by inference from what can be observed.

The basic idea of latent trait theory is that, while the trait itself is not directly observable, its interaction with the environment produces surface-level, observable indicators (which can be shaped into 'items') which can be used to infer the presence or absence of the trait – or, more accurately, to infer the level or degree of the trait which is present. A measuring instrument can therefore be constructed using these items as the basis for making an inference about the unobservable trait. There is, theoretically, an infinite set of these observable indicators. In order to provide a stable inference, the measuring instrument needs to have a reasonable sample of them. To put it more formally, the measuring instrument samples from among this theoretically infinite set of observable indicators to produce a set of items from which a reliable inference can be made to the unobservable trait beneath. This is the essential idea of latent trait measurement, and it is shown in Figure 11.1. It explains why there are many items, instead of just one, on a typical social science measuring instrument. Clearly one item is not enough to provide a stable inference. In fact, the more items the better, within reason. Latent trait theory is central to item response theory, which has become the new theoretical basis for testing and measurement (Embretson and Yang, 2006).

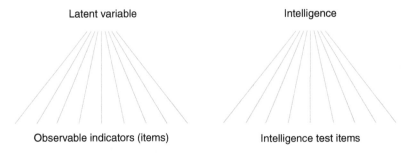

Latent variable   Intelligence

Observable indicators (items)   Intelligence test items

FIGURE 11.1   Latent trait measurement

We should note three things about latent trait measurement. First, it requires that we define the trait, and specify the indicators from which we will make the inference, showing the relationship of these indicators to the trait. This points again to the question of measurement validity, to be discussed in Section 11.8. Second, we will use multiple indicators or items, on the grounds that the more indicators we have the better the inference we can make. We will then need somehow to aggregate the responses to these multiple items. In practical terms, we will need to add up the responses. This raises the issue of adding like with like, making sure that the items whose responses we add up are measuring aspects of the same thing. This issue is revisited in Section 11.9.1. Third, the different items are interchangeable, in the sense of being equally good indicators of the trait. In Chapter 9 we saw the similarity between these ideas and grounded theory analysis in qualitative research.

Measuring techniques

11.4   We can look at some basic ideas involved in measuring techniques by using attitude measurement as an example. Measuring attitudes emerged as an important research area in the 1920s and 1930s, and has continued to attract attention in social science research. The sheer size and volume of this research effort means that attempts have been made to measure almost any variable one can think of. That does not mean that all attempts have been equally successful, and each has to be reviewed critically before being adopted in research. But it does mean that we should keep this point in mind when we are planning research. We return to this point in Section 11.7.

Three of the main names in the history of attitude scaling are Thurstone, Guttman and Likert. They took different approaches to the scaling of attitudes, but their central ideas can be briefly summarised (a detailed description of their work is given in Edwards, 1957).

Thurstone's technique was called the 'equal appearing interval scale'. Recognising that different attitude items fall at different points along a unidimensional attitude continuum, he devised a method of calculating the scale value of each attitude item, and then used those scale values to scale people with respect to the attitude. *Guttman* similarly saw the different attitude content of different items, but used this information in a different way. He proposed a form of scaling whereby the ordering of items according to their attitude content could be used, in conjunction with a dichotomous response format, to determine the location of people along the attitude continuum. This method came to be called 'cumulative scaling'. Some years later, *Likert* proposed a simpler format, whereby a respondent would respond to each item according to a simple response scale, rather than a dichotomy, and responses to the items could be summed. This method is called the 'method of summated ratings' or, more commonly, the 'Likert method'.

Studies comparing these three methods seemed to indicate that they produced similar results (Edwards, 1957). This being so, the simpler procedures of Likert came, over time, to be preferred. As a result, the Likert summated rating procedure is widely used in social science research today, and is the form of scaling most often seen on questionnaires and instruments used in research. However, the gains in ease of construction and administration in moving from Thurstone and Guttman to Likert come at a cost. Thurstone and Guttman recognised that different statements, or items, carry different amounts of the attitude being measured. This is the idea of the scale value of the item. They developed ways to formalise and make use of this property in their measurement procedures. With Likert, the scale value of the item has disappeared. Important recent work has been done on this point, bringing together the methods of attitude scaling, and calibrating both people and items onto the same scale of interest. This is Rasch measurement, a specialised development beyond the scope of this book (Andrich, 1988).

These basic ideas involved in measurement can now be made more concrete by considering the steps to use in constructing a measuring instrument for use in research.

Steps in constructing a measuring instrument_____

11.5   This section outlines a general set of steps by which a measuring instrument can be constructed, based on the description of measurement just given. The question of using an already existing measuring instrument, or constructing one specifically for a project, is discussed in Section 11.6.

For simplicity, let us assume that we are measuring some attitude-type variable, as we often want to do in social science research. If we are constructing a descriptive, fact-gathering questionnaire, we have a simpler task, though it is along these same general lines – Section 11.9 deals with this. We may of course be combining the two – some fact-gathering and some attitude-type scaling. We can describe the construction of a measuring instrument under six main steps:

1. **The first step is a definitional one. We must define clearly what we are setting out to measure. In technical terms, we need to produce a conceptual definition of the variable. The measuring instrument will then become its operational definition.**

2. Next, we select a measuring technique. There are several possibilities here, but most likely some type of Likert response format will be used. The actual words to be used in the scaled item responses will depend on the subject matter we are dealing with, and may require some pilot testing.[3]

3. Items now need to be generated – how many, and where do they come from? Since latent traits are involved, the draft form of the scale will need many items – as many as can be practically administered in a pilot test. When it comes to the final length of the scale, practical considerations will be important, especially the question of how many items respondents can deal with. Within reason, there should be as many items for each dimension as respondents can respond to validly. The items themselves can come from anywhere at all – from analysis of the definition, from discussion and reading, from the literature, or from ideas from other measures.

4. We now have a draft form of the measure. It is a good idea to go through this with a small group of people who are typical of the people we want to measure. We go through the items and the procedures for answering the questionnaire, and have them discuss each item. This enables us to see what meaning they give to each item, and to compare this with the meaning we had in mind when we generated the item. We also want to see to what extent they are easily able to respond to each item. During this stage, we are not so much interested in their actual responses as in their interpretations, and whether they can easily respond to each item. A good item is (among other things) one that people can quickly and easily respond to, with conviction. One characteristic of a poor item is that people have difficulty placing their response on the scale. This step will often produce numerous modifications, and will likely show us things we had not thought of.

5. We pre-test this modified second-draft scale more formally now, with a group of 25 or so typical respondents, and analyse their responses in the light of the criteria in Section 11.8.

6. We then modify and reduce the scale in the light of the results of this analysis, selecting the best items for each dimension. Item analysis gives criteria for selecting the best items for a scale (see Oppenheim, 1992; Friedenberg, 1995).

This sixth step may or may not finalise the scale. If necessary, therefore, we repeat steps 5 and 6, until a satisfactory final version is available. This description shows that considerable detailed work is involved in achieving good measurement. For this reason, the decision whether to construct a measuring instrument or to use an already existing one is important.

To construct an instrument or to use an existing instrument?

11.6 This is a common question in research: Should we use an already existing research instrument, or should we construct our own? No blanket rules apply, and we have to assess each case, but we can make some general comments. Of course, we will assume that the measure we have located is a good one, in terms of the criteria to be discussed in Section 11.8.

First, as noted, good measurement is achievable, but considerable development work is involved. If the variable is complex and multidimensional, the amount of work is increased. The more complex the variable, the more work, time and resources are required to achieve good measurement. This is an argument for using what already exists. A second argument for using what already exists is that the more an instrument is used in research, the more we learn about its properties. If the variable involved is a central variable in an area, this is an important consideration. A third argument is that research results from different studies are more easily compared, and integrated and synthesised, if the same measuring instrument for a central variable has been used.

However, as a fourth point, we need to think about the construct validity (see Section 11.8.2) of the instrument, in relation to the study we are proposing. Any measuring instrument represents one operational definition of a variable, and operational definitions differ, just as measuring instruments do. In any particular study, it may be that the operational version in the existing instrument does not fit well enough with the conceptual definition preferred. In such a case, it might be preferable to develop a new measure. This of course must be set against the effort and resources involved in developing a new measure.

On balance, therefore, we would need good reason for passing over an already existing instrument, particularly if the variable is a central variable in a research area. For this type of variable, I would not recommend developing a new measure, especially if a reasonable instrument is already available. I would modify this conclusion, however, for the common research situation where ad hoc quantitative data can be obtained with rating scales – attitudes towards specific issues are a good example. If the procedures described in Section 11.5 are followed, perhaps in truncated form, effective data can be produced which will add to the precision and value of the research. That is, there is an important role for short rating scales, tailor-made to the purposes and context of a particular project. They can be used in a variety of research situations, including qualitative ones, and for a variety of research purposes. They have great flexibility, and they can assist in making the comparisons we want.

Locating existing measuring instruments

11.7 As mentioned, literally hundreds of measuring instruments have been developed by social science researchers over many years. The first problem is to locate them, and the second is to assess their quality and value in a particular research situation. Help in locating them comes from collections of research instruments which have been compiled, numerous examples of which are shown in the further reading suggestions at the end of this chapter.

The Mental Measurements Yearbook series is produced by the Buros Institute of Mental Measurements at the University of Nebraska. This is a particularly distinguished series, which includes not only collections of research instruments, but expert critical reviews of them and their psychometric characteristics. It is therefore helpful in both locating and assessing instruments. The volume *Tests in Print* includes a comprehensive index to the *Mental Measurements Yearbooks*. The publication, edited by Goldman and Mitchell (1996), concentrates on tests that are not commercially available.

Older collections of instruments also exist (e.g. Shaw and Wright, 1967). Some of these cover attitudes in general, and others, such as those from the Institute of Social Research at the University of Michigan, concentrate on particular attitudes, such as political attitudes or occupational attitudes (Robinson et al., 1969; Robinson and Shaver, 1973). Though older, they may still be useful to the researcher reviewing measurement attempts in an area, or looking for ideas for items when constructing an instrument (see pp. 254–5, for collections of measuring instruments).

It is worthwhile to spend some time browsing these collections, especially the *Mental Measurements Yearbooks*. They give an idea of the vast amount of work that has been done in developing measuring instruments, and they are also a good starting point in the search for instruments. Despite these collections, however, the search may need to go further, because current research may use and report new scales well before they appear in these collections. 'Going further' means reading research journals and dissertations. It is unusual for a journal to publish a new scale, because of space limitations, even though it may report research using the scale. In such a case, the author(s) can be contacted directly, using information provided in the journal. Dissertations are harder to keep up with, because they are not published. Regular reading of *Dissertation Abstracts International* and national dissertation indexes can help here. Again, while a scale will not be published in an abstract, contact details for the author are normally provided.

Reliability and validity

11.8 If we find a measuring instrument in the literature, how do we assess its quality for use in research? Similarly, if we are developing our own measuring instrument, what qualities should we try to build into it? For both questions, the two main technical criteria are reliability and validity. These are sometimes called the psychometric characteristics of an instrument.

11.8.1 Reliability

Reliability is a central concept in measurement. It basically means consistency. There are two main aspects to this consistency – consistency over time (or stability) and internal consistency. We will deal with each briefly.

First, *consistency over time, or stability*. This means the stability of measurement over time, and is usually expressed in the question: If the same instrument were given to the same people, under the same circumstances, but at a different time, to what extent would they get the same scores? To the extent that they would, the measuring instrument is reliable. To the extent they would not, it is unreliable. Stability over time can be directly assessed, under certain circumstances, by administrations of the same instrument (or by parallel forms of the instrument)[4] at two points in time. This is called test–retest reliability and requires two administrations of the measuring instrument (and the assumption that the trait being measured would not have changed substantially between the two administrations).

Second, *internal consistency*. Internal consistency reliability relates to the concept-indicator idea of measurement described earlier. Since multiple items are used to help us infer the level of the latent trait, the question now concerns the extent to which the items are consistent with each other or all working in the same direction. This is the internal consistency of a measuring instrument. Various ways have been devised to assess the extent to which all items are working in the same direction. The best known are the split-half techniques, the Kuder-Richardson formulas and coefficient alpha (Cronbach, 1951; Anastasi, 1988). Internal consistency reliability estimation requires only one administration of the instrument.

These two different methods (test–retest reliability and coefficient alpha) tap the two different meanings of consistency. Either or both can be used to estimate the reliability of a measuring instrument. Why is reliability important? Intuitively, we would want consistency of measurement, but there are important technical reasons too, which involve a little more classical measurement theory.

In this theory, any actual (or observed) score can be thought of as having two parts: the true score part and the error part. As an example, take the measurement of weight. When we step on the scales, we get an actual (or observed) measurement. We know that any one observed measurement is not perfectly accurate. We know that it contains some error. We also know that the smaller the error the more accurate the measurement, and the larger the error the less accurate the measurement. Intuitively, we control for the error and estimate the true score by taking several readings and averaging them. We regard this average of several readings as a better estimate of the true score, the measure we really want.

These ideas are formalised in the concept of reliability. Observed scores are made up of the true scores, which we want to estimate, and error. The smaller the error, the closer the observed scores are to the true scores. Reliability enables us to estimate error, and reliability and error are related reciprocally – the larger the reliability, the smaller the error and conversely, the smaller the reliability, the larger the error. Measures with high reliability produce observed scores that are close to true scores.

Now we can relate reliability to variance, distinguishing between reliable variance and error variance. A good measuring instrument for research purposes picks up differences between people, producing variance in the scores. We can divide the total variance in a set of scores into reliable variance and error variance. This is the reciprocal relationship between the two – when reliability is high, error variance is low; when reliability is low, error variance is high. The reliability of a measure tells us how much error variance is in the scores. Reliable variance produced by a measuring instrument is true variance. That is, the differences in scores between people produced by a measure with high reliability are real differences. This is important, because what is not true variance is error variance. Error variance is spurious variance, or random variance, or 'noise'; it is variance that proceeds purely from the fact that the measure itself is not 100 per cent reliable; it is not real variance. When a measure has low reliability, some of the differences produced in scores between people are spurious differences, not real differences. Error variance, by definition, cannot be accounted for by relationships with other variables. This is important, because, as discussed earlier, a central strategy in research is the accounting-for-variance-through-relationship-with-other-variables strategy.

We should note that all measures have some unreliability. Even physical measurement does not produce exactly the same measures of the same object at two different points in time. Therefore social science measurement is not unique in having some unreliability or error variance. It is harder to reduce error variance in educational, social and psychological measurement than in (say) physical measurement, but error variance is present wherever measurement is used. Because one of our central strategies in research is accounting for variance in a dependent variable, it is necessary that we have estimates of the reliability of all measures, especially of the dependent variable. We want to know how much of the variance is able to be accounted for, after measurement error is estimated.

11.8.2 Validity

A second central concept in quality of measurement is validity. Validity is a technical term with specific meanings – here, we are focusing on measurement validity. Its meaning is shown in this question: How do we know that this measuring instrument measures what we think it measures? Measurement validity thus means the extent to which an instrument measures what it is claimed to measure – an indicator is valid to the extent that it empirically represents the concept it purports to measure.

Because of the latent nature of the variables we want to study, there is an inference involved, between the indicators we can observe (that is, the items people respond to) and the construct we aim to measure. Validity is about this inference. So the validity question is: How reasonable is the inference we make from indicators (items) to concept? The measuring instrument or procedure itself is not valid or invalid. The validity question strictly only applies to the inference we make from what we observe. Among the various approaches to the validation of instruments, the three main ones are content validity, criterion-related validity (which includes concurrent validity and predictive validity) and construct validity.

Content validity focuses on whether the full content of a conceptual definition is represented in the measure. A conceptual definition is a space, holding ideas and concepts, and the indicators in a measure should sample all ideas in the definition (Neuman, 1994). Thus the two steps involved in content validation are to specify the content of a definition, and to develop indicators that sample from all areas of content in the definition.

In *criterion-related validity*, an indicator is compared with another measure of the same construct in which the researcher has confidence. There are two types of criterion validity. *Concurrent validity* is where the criterion variable exists in the present – for example, a researcher might wish to study the awareness of students about their performance in school during the past year. In this situation, each student could be asked the question: 'What was your grade point average last year?' This response could then be concurrent-criterion-validated by correlating it with the grade point average obtained from the school's records office. *Predictive validity* is where the criterion variable will not exist until later – the researcher might wish to have students anticipate their performance in school during the next year, asking each student the question: 'What do you think your grade point average will be next year?' This response could then be predictive-criterion-validated by correlating it with the grade point average obtained from the school's records office after a year (Zeller, 1996).

Construct validity focuses on how well a measure conforms to theoretical expectations. Any measure exists in some theoretical context, and should therefore show relationships with other constructs which can be predicted and interpreted within this context. An example would be validating a measure of alienation by showing its relationships with social class (de Vaus, 2013). Zeller (1996) gives a detailed description of the six steps involved in establishing construct validity.

There is no foolproof procedure to establish validity, and the validation methods used should depend on the situation. Because all methods have limitations, Zeller believes that inferences about validity cannot be made solely on the basis of quantitative or statistical procedures. He advocates a validation strategy that combines quantitative and qualitative methods. 'A valid inference occurs when there is no conflict between messages received as a result of the use of a variety of different methodological procedures' (Zeller, 1996: 829). We saw in Chapter 9 that this same issue of validation runs through approaches to the way qualitative data are analysed.

Reliability and validity are two important psychometric characteristics of measuring instruments. One other psychometric characteristic is mentioned here – sensitivity – because it fits in with the research strategy outlined in Chapter 10. *Sensitivity* here means the ability of a measuring instrument to pick up differences between people – to discriminate between them and produce variance. Other things being equal, the best measuring instruments for research purposes (and the best items) are those which spread people out and produce the greatest variance. But it must be true or reliable variance in the sense discussed above.[5]

This criterion can be used in assessing and selecting individual items and subscales in developing a measuring instrument. It is also consistent with the overall research strategy based on variance and accounting for variance. This strategy will not work if there is no variance (or little variance). A measuring instrument that does not differentiate between people produces little or no variance.[6] We can use this idea to develop a three-part research strategy, based around a central variable in an area. The first part requires developing a measure of the variable which produces substantial reliable variance. The second part involves accounting for this variance, investigating the factors which produce or influence this variance, using the question: What accounts for these differences? This is about identifying independent variables that relate to the dependent variable. The third part asks about the effects of this variance, or the outcomes that follow from it, using the questions: What difference does it make that people differ on this variable? What are the results or consequences of this variance? In the second part, the variable we are considering is the dependent variable, and independent variables are related to it. In the third part, it is the independent variable and it is related to dependent variables. This general strategy is useful when we are organising research in a new area. We understand a variable through understanding how it varies and the antecedents and consequences of this variance, and this strategy formalises that.

Developing a survey questionnaire

11.9 In Chapter 10 we focused on the correlational survey as a major quantitative design. Its centrepiece is the survey questionnaire. The correlational survey is not a simple descriptive survey, but rather a multivariable survey, seeking a wide range of information, and with some conceptual framework of independent, control and dependent variables. It is likely, therefore, that the questionnaire will seek factual information (background and biographical information, knowledge and behavioural information) and will also include measures of such variables as attitudes, values, opinions or beliefs. One useful framework for developing such questionnaires distinguishes between cognitive, affective and behavioural information; another divides it up into knowledge, attitudes and behaviours (Punch, 2003: 53). Any of these areas may use, in whole or in part, already existing measures, or may develop them specifically for this research.

The development of the survey questionnaire can proceed along the lines suggested in Section 11.5. In this case, definitional questions are perhaps even more important. Because a wide range of information is usually sought in a correlational survey questionnaire, a clear conceptual map of the questionnaire is the first step in its development, and this is often best done in diagram form. The map should work from the general to the specific, first showing the general type of variable and then translating this down to specific variables, with the dimensions and subscales as appropriate. Then specific questions and items can be developed.

Development of its specific parts then depends on the types of measurements involved. In some respects, developing the factual questions will be easier, but here again we should aim to build on previous work, in two ways. First, extensive consideration has been given to the whole topic of asking factual questions for research purposes. Of course, there are many ways to ask even a simple factual question, and some ways are better than others. We do not have space to go into this topic here, but a number of books deal with it (for example, Moser and Kalton, 1979; Sudman and Bradburn, 1982; Lewins, 1992; Oppenheim, 1992). Second, many excellent survey questionnaires have been developed and can be useful in various ways. Help in locating them comes from Converse and Presser (1986), who list nine sources of survey questions they have found useful. In addition, survey questionnaires are often included in the published reports of large surveys; Jaeger (1988) reviews a number of important social and educational surveys in the United States, and Thomas (1996) indicates ten major surveys that are carried out regularly in the UK.

11.9.1 Subscales with multiple items

As indicated earlier, when latent trait theory is used to create a variable using multiple items, special considerations are involved. This is because an overall or aggregate score for the variable is to be obtained by adding responses to the individual items. This means we have to be sure that we are adding 'like with like'. We have to be sure that each item really is an indicator of the variable we wish to measure. In other words, we have to be sure that the scale itself is internally consistent. We try to ensure this in scale construction, using content validity (Black, 1999: 231–2) to check that each item is an indicator of the variable. In the analysis of responses, we need to demonstrate empirically the internal consistency of a multiple-item scale. A useful technique for doing this is based on the correlations of the scale items with each other, and the correlation between each item and the total score. In fact, the degree of inter-item correlation is summarised by coefficient alpha, mentioned earlier. This is one reason that coefficient alpha is probably the most widely used measure of the internal consistency of a multiple-item scale (Black, 1999: 279).

Collecting the data: administering the measuring instrument

11.10   This section is about procedures for data collection, since these too affect the quality of the data. Empirical research is only as good as the data on which it is based, so the check mark responses to questionnaire items (which become the quantitative researcher's data) and the frame of mind and conscientiousness of the respondent when they were made, are all-important. It is worth taking every precaution possible to ensure that the data be as good as they can be, whatever the mode of administration of the instruments. The main modes of administration are individual or group administration face to face, by telephone, by mail (Jaeger, 1988) or by Internet (Dillman, 2006). Two general points to keep in mind are:

1. Ensure that respondents have been approached professionally, and, within limits, fully informed about the purpose and context of the research, about confidentiality and anonymity, and about what use will be made of, and who will make use of, the information they provide. It also helps to point out that this sort of research is not possible without their cooperation, and they should know clearly what they are being asked to do. Experience shows that when this is done properly and professionally, people will usually cooperate, and the quality of the data is improved.

2. As far as possible, the researcher should stay in control of the data collection procedure, rather than leave it to others or to chance. Thus, if face-to-face administration (single or group) is possible instead of a mailed questionnaire, it is to be preferred, despite the additional work. Again, if it is a choice between the researcher administering the questionnaire, and somebody else administering it on the researcher's behalf, the former is better. If others have to do it, they need training in the procedures to follow.

These things may involve trade-offs, especially with sample size, but it is better to have a smaller data set of good quality, than a larger one of lower quality. It is unfortunate in research when an excellent job has been done of developing a data collection instrument, but the same thought and effort have not been put into the data collection procedures. Both are important in determining the quality of the data. One particular aspect of this, and a hurdle for all survey research, is the issue of response rates. Very low response rates are both disappointing and troublesome, since they carry the possibility of biased results. If response rates are given due importance in the data collection planning stage, there are often procedures that can be used to maximise them. It is important, therefore, to include the issue of response rates in the planning for the research, ahead of the data collection, rather than have it occur as an afterthought following the administration of the questionnaire.

Sampling

11.11 Sampling has been an important topic in the quantitative research methodology literature, with well-developed and mathematically sophisticated sampling plans (see, for example, Cochran, 1977; Jaeger, 1984). This does not seem so true today, probably because of three trends – the growth of interest in qualitative methods, a swing away from large samples in quantitative studies and, as social science research has proliferated, the growing practical problem of obtaining access to the large and neatly configured samples required by sophisticated sampling plans. Very often indeed the researcher must take whatever sample is available, and the incidence of convenience samples (where the researcher takes advantage of an accessible situation that happens to fit the research context and purposes) is increasing.

Despite this, the basic ideas involved in sampling remain important. In some quantitative research situations we may still need to use sophisticated sampling plans. Also, sampling models are the basis of statistical inference, and statistical inference remains a key decision-making tool in quantitative research. Finally, these ideas give us a useful model to keep in mind when planning actual sample selection in a study. Therefore we need to look at the basic ideas involved in sampling. This section should be read in conjunction with Section 12.7, on the logic of statistical inference.

All research (including qualitative research) involves sampling. This is because no study, whether quantitative, qualitative or both, can include everything. As noted

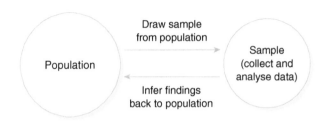

FIGURE 11.2   Populations and samples

earlier, 'you cannot study everyone everywhere doing everything' (Miles and Huberman, 1994: 27). Sampling in quantitative research usually means 'people sampling'. The key concepts therefore are the population (the total target group who would, in the ideal world, be the subject of the research, and about whom the researcher is trying to say something) and the sample (the actual group who are included in the study, and from whom the data are collected).[7]

The logic of people sampling is that the researcher analyses data collected from the sample, but wishes in the end to make statements about the whole target population, from which the sample is drawn. This logic is shown in Figure 11.2. The data are collected from the sample, and analysed to produce the study's findings. But these findings are still only about the sample, so the next step is concerned with generalising the findings from the sample to the population. This involves a sample-to-population inference, the central question in which is: How representative is this sample of the population? Representativeness is a key concept, though, as noted below, it is more applicable to some studies than to others. Sampling to achieve representativeness is usually called probability sampling, and while different strategies have been designed to achieve it, the main one is some form of random selection. This is a quite different meaning of random from that used in experimental design in Chapter 10. There, the idea was random allocation to treatment groups, and this was done to ensure control of extraneous variables. Here, the idea is random selection of a sample, which is done to ensure representativeness. In random selection, each element in a population has an equal chance or equal probability of being chosen. Stratifying the population along different dimensions before random selection produces stratified random samples.

A sampling plan is not independent of the other elements in a research project, particularly its research purposes and questions. This is another instance of the fit between a project's parts, as discussed in Chapter 2. The sampling plan should have a logic that fits in with the logic of the research questions. Thus, if the research questions require representativeness, some form of representative sampling should be used. On the other hand, if the research questions highlight relationships between variables, or comparisons between groups, some sort of deliberate or purposive sampling may well be more appropriate, since it makes sense to select the sample in such a way that there is maximum chance for any relationship to be observed. Similarly, if the design is experimental or quasi-experimental, the sample should be selected to make comparisons as clear-cut as possible. Deliberate or purposive sampling resembles theoretical sampling as used in qualitative research, and as discussed in Chapter 8. We saw there that sampling strategies are equally important in qualitative research.

Whatever sampling strategy is used, the research proposal (and report) need to address three questions:

- How big will the sample be, and why?
- How will it be chosen, and why?
- What claims will be made for its representativeness?

The first two questions tie the sampling strategy and plan to the overall logic of the study. The third question becomes especially important in those cases where convenience samples are used in the research. There is nothing wrong with this, and valuable knowledge can be gained by studying these samples, but the researcher needs to assess the extent to which the sample is typical of some larger population.

Secondary analysis

11.12 Secondary analysis is the term used for the re-analysis of previously collected and analysed data. It is important in quantitative work (especially in surveys), and is growing in importance in qualitative research as well. There are some clear advantages to working with an existing body of data, including cost (for many survey researchers, there is little chance of obtaining funding to carry out large-scale data collection), time (the researcher can begin analysis soon, rather than investing large amounts of time in data collection), quality (an existing data bank is likely to have higher quality data than the lone, inexperienced researcher can hope to obtain), and making difficult populations accessible (Procter, 1996). It is increasingly important also for students to be aware of the possibilities of secondary analysis and the data banks that support it (see Chapter 8, Section 8.6), and it has special attractions given the cost and time limits involved in student project work (including dissertations).

However, these attractions do not mean that secondary analysis is always straightforward. There can be both methodological difficulties and difficulties of interpretation of the raw data (Reeve and Walberg, 1997), and the possibility always exists that the original questions and data are not relevant to the present problem: 'The real challenge in secondary analysis lies in finding ways of forcing the data, collected by someone else, quite often with entirely different theoretical and analytical orientations, to answer your questions' (Procter, 1996: 262). While important and appealing, therefore, it is necessary that a proposed secondary analysis be accompanied by careful planning and consideration of the data in the light of the proposed research. Procter's advice (1996: 257) is valuable – by all means to explore the possibility of secondary analysis, but not to commit oneself to it without discussing its pitfalls with an experienced adviser. Useful references on secondary analysis are Hakim (1982), Stewart (1984), Kiecolt and Nathan (1985), Dale et al. (1988) and Procter (1996).

Chapter summary

- The distinction between categorical and continuous variables is important, and has significance for measuring techniques and for the analysis of data.
- The process of measurement uses numbers to link concepts with their empirical indicators, when the trait of interest is seen as a continuum.
- An understanding of the process of measurement, and analysis of research situations and purposes, can help in deciding when measurement is appropriate in a research project.
- Much social measurement uses latent trait theory, because the traits to be measured are usually hidden from view (or latent).
- Different measuring techniques have been developed by researchers; the most commonly used today is the Likert summated rating technique.
- A set of straightforward steps can be used to develop a measuring instrument, but often previous work will have developed relevant instruments.
- Various collections of measuring instruments exist, the most important of which is the Mental Measurements Yearbook series.
- Reliability and validity are two of the most important psychometric characteristics for assessing the quality of a measuring instrument; reliability concerns stability, and allows us to estimate error variance; validity is concerned with whether an instrument in fact measures what it is claimed to measure; there are several different types of validity, and validation.
- Survey questionnaires can be developed on the basis of conceptual/definitional work, backed up by careful item development and pre-testing; multiple-item scales require special consideration.
- The procedures used in administering measuring instruments can strongly affect the quality of data, including response rates in surveys.
- Sampling in quantitative research is often probabilistic (directed at representativeness), but can also be deliberate (purposive); the sampling strategy used should fit in with the overall research strategy.
- Secondary analysis becomes increasingly important, as more and more social science research data is collected and archived.

KEY TERMS

Categorical variable: a variable which varies in kind, rather than degree

Continuous variable: a variable which varies in degree, rather than in kind

Measurement: the process of using numbers to link concepts to indicators, when a continuum is involved

Latent trait: the trait we want to measure is hidden; we measure it by inference from its observable indicators

Likert summated rating technique: the most common measuring technique used in social science research today

Reliability: a key psychometric characteristic concerned with the consistency or stability of a measuring instrument, in two senses – consistency over time, and internal consistency when there are multiple items

Validity: another key psychometric characteristic concerned with whether a measuring instrument measures what it is claimed to measure; different aspects are content validity, criterion-related validity and construct validity

Population: a target group, usually large, about whom we want to develop knowledge, but which we cannot study directly; therefore we sample from the population

Sample: a smaller group that is actually studied, drawn from some larger population; data are collected and analysed from the sample, and inferences are then made back to the population

Probability sampling: a sampling strategy where each unit of the population has an equal chance of being selected in the sample; directed at representativeness and generalisation, it is sometimes called representative sampling

Purposive sampling: a sampling strategy where the sample is drawn from the population in a deliberate or targeted way, according to the logic of the research; also called deliberate sampling

Secondary analysis: the re-analysis of previously collected and analysed data

Exercises and study questions

1. Define and give examples of (a) categorical variables; (b) continuous variables.
2. Of these two survey questions, which form of question is generally better in research, and why?

    – Do you like doing research? (Answer yes or no)
    – To what extent do you like doing research? (Answer: a great deal, quite a lot, not very much, not at all)

3. Measurement was controversial during the paradigm war debates about research. In your opinion, what is the role of measurement in research? For what topics and questions is measurement (a) well suited; (b) not well suited?
4. In your own words, describe the latent trait theory of measurement.
5. What are the advantages and disadvantages of (a) using an existing instrument; (b) developing your own?
6. If you choose to develop a measuring instrument, what steps can you go through?
7. Spend some time in the library browsing the latest *Mental Measurements Yearbook*. Select a major variable of interest (for example, self-esteem, anxiety, attitudes towards authority or personality) and familiarise yourself with some of the instruments available to measure it.

8. Define (a) reliability; (b) validity. What types of reliability and validity are there? How can they be assessed?
9. To what extent can the ideas of reliability and validity be applied to qualitative data?
10. What can you do, in administering a survey questionnaire, to maximise the quality of the data?
11. What are the main methods of questionnaire administration and what are the advantages and disadvantages of each?
12. What do the terms sample and population mean, and what is the relationship between the two? What is probability sampling, and what is deliberate sampling? When is each appropriate?

Further reading

Allen, M.J. and Yen, W.M. (1979) *Introduction to Measurement Theory.* Monterey, CA: Brooks/ Cole.

Carley, M. (1981) *Social Measurement and Social Indicators.* London: Allen and Unwin.

Converse, J.M. and Presser, S. (1986) *Survey Questions: Handcrafting the Standardized Question- naire.* Beverly Hills, CA: SAGE.

Cronbach, L.J. (1990) *Essentials of Psychological Testing.* 5th edn. New York: Harper and Row.

de Vaus, D.A. (2013) *Surveys in Social Research.* 5th edn. London: Routledge.

Edwards, A.L. (1957) *Techniques of Attitude Scale Construction.* New York: Appleton-Century- Crofts.

Fink, A. and Kosecoff, J. (1985) *How to Conduct Surveys: A Step-by-Step Guide.* Beverly Hills, CA: SAGE.

Henry, G.T. (1990) *Practical Sampling.* Newbury Park, CA: SAGE.

Jaeger, R.M. (1988) 'Survey methods in educational research', in R.M. Jaeger (ed.), *Complemen- tary Methods for Research in Education.* Washington, DC: American Educational Research Association. pp. 301–87.

Kalton, G. (1983) *Introduction to Survey Sampling.* Beverly Hills, CA: SAGE.

Moser, C.A. and Kalton, G. (1979) *Survey Methods in Social Investigation.* 2nd edn. Aldershot: Gower.

Oppenheim, A.N. (2000) *Questionnaire Design, Interviewing and Attitude Measurement.* 2nd edn. London: Continuum.

Punch, K.F. (2003) *Survey Research: The Basics.* London: SAGE.

Rossi, P.H., Wright, J.D. and Anderson, A.B. (1983) *The Handbook of Survey Research.* New York: Academic Press.

Collections of measuring instruments

Bearden, W.O. (1999) *Handbook of Marketing Scales.* Chicago IL: American Marketing Association.

Bonjean, C.M., Hill, R.J. and McLemore, S.D. (1967) *Sociological Measurement.* San Francisco, CA: Chandler.

Bowling, A. (1991) *Measuring Health: A Review of Quality of Life Measurement Scales.* Philadel- phia, PA: Open University Press.

Bruner, G.C. and Hansel, P.J. (1992) *Marketing Scales Handbook: A Compilation of Multi-Item Measures.* Chicago, IL: American Marketing Association.

Frank-Stromborg, M. (ed.) (1988) *Instruments for Clinical Nursing Research*. Norwalk, CT: Appleton & Lange.

Geisinger, K.F., Spies, R.A., Carlson, J.F. and Plake, B.S. (2007) *The Seventeenth Mental Measurements Yearbook*. Buros Institute of Mental Measurements, Lincoln, NB: University of Nebraska Press.

Hersen, M. and Bellack, A.S. (eds) (1988) *Measures for Clinical Practice*. New York: The Free Press.

Maddox, T. (ed.) (1997) *Tests: A Comprehensive Reference for Assessments in Psychology, Education and Business*. 4th edn. Austin, TX: Pro Ed.

McDowell, I. and Newell, C. (1987) *Measuring Health: A Guide to Rating Scales and Questionnaires*. Oxford: Oxford University Press.

Miller, D.C. (1991) *Handbook of Research Design and Social Measurement*. 5th edn. Newbury Park, CA: SAGE.

Murphy, L.E., Close, C.J. and Impara, J.C. (1994) *Tests in Print IV: An Index to Tests, Test Reviews, and the Literature on Specific Tests*, Vol. 1. Buros Institute of Mental Measurements, Lincoln, NB: University of Nebraska Press.

Price, J.M. and Mueller, C.W. (1986) *Handbook of Organizational Measures*. Marshfield, MA: Pitman.

Shaw, M.E. and Wright, J.W. (1967) *Scales for the Measurement of Attitudes*. New York: McGraw-Hill.

Stewart, A.L. and Ware, J.E. (eds) (1992) *Measuring Functioning and Well-Being*. Durham, NC: Duke University Press.

Straus, M.A. and Brown, B.W. (1978) *Family Measurement Techniques: Abstracts of Published Instruments, 1935–1974* (revised edn). Minneapolis, MN: University of Minnesota Press.

Streiner, D.R. and Norman, G. (1995) *Health Measurement Scales: A Practical Guide to Their Development and Use*. Oxford: Oxford University Press.

Sweetland, R.C. and Keyser, D.J. (1986) *Tests: A Comprehensive Reference for Assessments in Psychology, Education, and Business*. 2nd edn. Kansas City, MO: Test Corporation of America.

Notes

1. This point has implications for constructing data collection questions in a survey. For example, many questions are asked with a dichotomous yes/no or true/false response, when a scaled response to the same question would be better, and would produce more information.

2. This is a slight modification of Zeller's (1996) definition. He uses, as an 'adequate' definition, the process of linking concepts to indicators. He describes the earlier well-known definition of Stevens (1951) – 'the assignment of numbers to objects or events according to rules' – as 'inadequate', and gives reasons.

3. Probably the most common form of words is 'strongly agree, agree, disagree, strongly disagree', but other forms are possible (see Punch, 2003: 59).

4. Parallel forms are different forms of the instrument constructed to be equivalent. This indicates a third (more technical) form of consistency – consistency of the instrument over item content sampling.

5. In other contexts than research, it may not be important for a measuring instrument to spread people out, and to produce variance. An example would be testing for mastery learning in education.

6. To put it in different terms: We are studying relationships between variables. Relationships means correlation. Conceptually, correlation is the same as covariation. If there is no variation, there can be no covariation. One of the factors influencing the size of the correlation is the amount of variance in the scores of each variable. The relationship between variables may be underestimated if measures produce little variance.

7. The terms 'sample' and 'population' are therefore technical terms which should be used accurately. In particular, the confused term 'sample population' should be avoided.

twelve

ANALYSING
QUANTITATIVE DATA

Contents

After studying this chapter you should be able to:

- Name and describe three of the main tools used in summarising quantitative data
- Explain how a cross-tabulation can be used to study the relationship between two variables
- Describe the basic logic of analysis of variance (ANOVA) and covariance (ANCOVA)
- Explain what is meant by interaction
- Explain the basic logic of simple correlation
- Show how simple correlation extends to multiple correlation and regression
- Show how multiple linear regression (MLR) fits with an accounting-for-variance research strategy
- Explain the basic logic of factor analysis
- Explain the basic logic of statistical inference

Quantitative data are analysed using statistics. There are scores of books written for the field of statistics, and there is no point in producing another. This chapter therefore takes a different approach. This is not a book about statistics, but about doing research, and its intention is to show the logic behind each stage of empirical research. This point applies particularly to statistics. Statistics is one of the many tools the researcher needs. Like other tools, it can be used very effectively without the user necessarily having a full technical knowledge of how it works. What is needed, however, is an understanding of the logic behind the statistical tools, and an appreciation of how and when to use them in actual research situations. Thus I stress here the logic of quantitative data analysis, but there are very few equations or formulae. These are dealt with in the statistical literature, to which directions are given later.

In Chapter 10, the two main strands of quantitative research design were identified. These strands continue into this chapter. One strand sits in the tradition of the experiment, and is based on the idea of comparison groups. Its main statistical expression is the analysis of variance (which includes the t-test), univariate and multivariate. As we saw in Chapter 10, this strand looks from the top down, from independent variables to the dependent variable, guided by the question: What are the effects of this cause? The other is the correlational survey strand, and is based more on the idea of relationships between variables in the non-experimental setting. Its main statistical expression is correlation and regression. This strand looks from the bottom up, from the dependent variable back to the independent variable, guided by the question: What are the causes of these effects?

These two strands are related, but they also represent different ways of thinking, and different emphases. The logic of statistical data analysis in both strands is described in this chapter, but the strand emphasised most is the correlation–regression strand. This is because it is easy to interpret, because it is widely applicable across many research areas, and because it connects directly with the accounting-for-variance research strategy of Chapter 10. In that chapter, multiple linear regression (MLR) was proposed as a general research design strategy. In this chapter, MLR is proposed as a general data analysis strategy.

Two other points should be stressed. First, in any project, the way the data are analysed is governed by the research questions. Thus, while this chapter describes the logic of quantitative data analysis, the actual techniques and the way they are used in a project follow from the research questions. Second, the level of measurement of the variables influences the way we do some of the quantitative analysis. The most important distinction is between nominal and interval-level measurement, or between discrete and continuous variables. The quantitative researcher needs to keep this distinction constantly in mind. When a variable is continuous, we can add and average scores. When it is categorical, we cannot. More generally, parametric statstics are appropriate for interval-level data, and non-parametric statistics for nominal and ordinal-level data (Kerlinger, 1973; Siegel, 1988).

Summarising quantitative data

12.1 Quantitative research involves measurements, usually of a number of variables, across a sample. Therefore, for each variable, we have measurements (or scores) for each member of the sample. We call this a distribution and we need ways of summarising it. The two main concepts we use to do this are central tendency and variation. This is modelled on what we do in everyday life. If you ask someone what London weather is like in summer, you might hear 'the temperature averages about 25 degrees [central tendency], but it changes a lot [variation]'.

12.1.1 Central tendency: the mean

There are three common measures of central tendency – the mean, the mode and the median. While there are technical issues in deciding which is the most appropriate, the mode and the median are much less used in research than the mean. Therefore we will deal with the mean here. It is familiar to everyone, and to obtain it we simply add up the scores and divide by the number of scores, averaging them. The more common term is the average; the more technical term, used here, is the mean.

Two features of the mean should be mentioned. The first is technical – it is the point in a distribution about which the sum of the squared deviations is at a minimum. This makes it important for estimating variance, and for least squares analysis, one of the foundations of statistics. The second feature is that the mean is an effective statistic where scores within a distribution do not vary too much, but it is not so effective when there is great variance (when variance is large, the median is a better measure of central tendency). Therefore it is important to know how much spread or variability there is in a set of scores, in order to interpret the mean correctly.

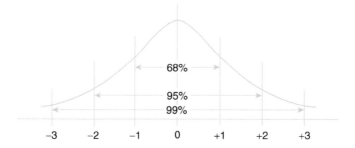

FIGURE 12.1   The normal distribution curve

Source: Jaeger, 1990: 55

12.1.2 Variation: the standard deviation and the variance

Like central tendency, statisticians have developed several ways to measure the variance in a set of measurements. For example, one simple but useful concept is the range – the highest score in the sample minus the lowest score. But the most common measure of variability is the standard deviation. It goes with the mean, because the deviations involved are deviations of individual measurements from the mean of the distribution. These deviations are calculated and standardised, to give us the standard deviation. In one number, it summarises the variability in a set of data. The more spread out the scores, the larger the standard deviation.

From the standard deviation, we can easily obtain the variance. The variance is the square of the standard deviation – or, the standard deviation is the square root of the variance. Like the standard deviation, the variance gives us a numerical estimate of the amount of spread in the data. While the standard deviation is commonly used in descriptive statistics, the variance is more commonly used in statistical inference (see Section 12.7). But we can always obtain one from the other.

Interpreting the standard deviation together with the mean tells us something about how much spread there is in the scores in a distribution, and important properties of the distribution relate to how far away from the mean we move, in terms of standard deviations. In particular, if the distribution is normal or bell-shaped, we know that, as shown in Figure 12.1, approximately:

- 68% of all cases fall within one standard deviation either side of the mean
- 95% of all cases fall within two standard deviations either side of the mean
- 99% of all cases fall within three standard deviations either side of the mean.

The figures will not vary too much from these, even when the distribution is not bell-shaped.

Thus, knowing the mean and the standard deviation tells us a great deal about the distribution of a set of scores. Both the standard deviation and the variance give us numerical estimates of the variability in the distribution. While the standard deviation is helpful in interpreting this variability, variance is the more general concept, and is central both to the analysis of quantitative data and in the overall quantitative research strategy. As shown in Chapter 10, much of our thinking is based on accounting for variance – on finding out how much people (or things) differ, and then accounting for those differences using relationships with other variables. We will return to this theme in Section 12.4.

12.1.3 Frequency distributions

In addition to the mean, standard deviation and variance, simple frequency distributions are a useful way to summarise and understand data. Their calculation is straightforward. The individual scores in the distribution are tabulated, according to how many respondents achieved each score, or gave each response, or fell into each category. Absolute numbers and/or percentages may be used. Depending on the overall score range, it will sometimes be useful to group scores in ranges, so that we can see more easily the distribution of the frequencies. We can show results as frequency distribution tables, or as graphs. Histograms and frequency polygons are the most common, but other graph forms, such as pie charts or horizontal bar charts, are possible.

Frequency distributions of responses can tell us, at a glance, something about the shape of the distribution, and this can be important in determining subsequent steps in the analysis. They also help the researcher to stay close to the data, especially in the initial stages of the analysis. There is great benefit to getting a 'hands-on feel' of the data, especially when the availability of computerised programs makes it so easy for the researcher to be removed from the data.

Relationships between variables: cross-tabulations and contingency tables

12.2

Quantitative research is based on relationships between variables, and many different ways have been developed to study these relationships. Different ways are needed because of variables at different levels of measurement, and the distinction between discrete and continuous variables is especially important. In this section, we will deal with basic cross-tabulations, and show how the logic of chi-square can be combined with them. Because they are so flexible, these methods cover many of the situations encountered in quantitative research. They can also be used for variables at any level of measurement. The important case of relationships between two continuous variables is not considered in this section, but is described in Section 12.4.

The basic cross-tabulation or contingency table[1] is easy to construct and read, applicable to a wide range of situations, and the foundation for more advanced analyses. An excellent treatment of the topic is given by Rosenberg (1968) in *The Logic of Survey Analysis*. He shows how sophisticated analysis of quantitative survey data is possible with nothing more than simple contingency tables. The sociological

TABLE 12.1   Age and listening to religious programmes

Listen to religious programmes	Young listeners	Old listeners
Yes	17%	26%
No	83%	74%
Total	100%	100%

Source: Rosenberg, 1968: 25

example given in Table 12.1 comes from this book. The table contains data about two variables. In its simplest form, each variable has two categories, and the 2x2 table has four cells. But other forms are possible, and each variable can have any number of categories. As Rosenberg's example shows, percentages are a convenient way to show the data, but actual numbers can be used as well.

The contingency table is used in Rosenberg's work basically as a descriptive tool. It can easily be extended to hypothesis testing and inference with chi-square. We can usually learn a lot about the relationship between the cross-tabulated variables just by inspection of the contingency table. If there is a pattern in the table (that is, if the two variables are related) this will be visible in the distributions shown in the cross-tabulation. But often we will also want a more formal test of this relationship. We can use chi-square to do this, and we will now look briefly at its logic.

To use chi-square to see if the two variables are related, we begin with the actual cross-tabulations. These are called the observed frequencies in each cell. Then we calculate what the cross-tabulations would look like if there were no relationship between the variables. This gives a second set of entries in each cell, called the expected frequencies. Now we compare the observed and expected frequencies in each cell of the cross-tabulation. Some simple calculations allow us to summarise this comparison into the statistic called chi-square. We can then use the chi-square statistical inference table to decide on the importance of the difference between observed and expected distributions, and to decide whether the variables are related. Of course, the observed distribution will always differ to some extent from the expected one; they are very unlikely to be identical. The question, here as elsewhere in statistical analysis, is: How much of a difference makes a difference? Or, in statistical terms: Is the difference significant? This is a matter for statistical inference, which we will deal with in Section 12.7.

Comparisons between groups: the analysis of variance

12.3.1 Analysis of variance

12.3 The basic idea here is that we want to compare groups on some dependent variable of interest, which has been measured for each person in each group. The groups may be formed in the design of the study, as in an experiment, or they may be naturally occurring and formed by partitioning of the sample in data analysis (for example, males vs. females, old people vs. young people, born in the UK vs. not born in the UK, etc.). The simplest form of comparison between groups is when there is only one way of classifying the people, only one way of forming the groups. This is one-way analysis of variance, or one-way 'ANOVA'. While there may be any number of groups, the simplest form of ANOVA is when there are only two groups. In this case, ANOVA becomes equivalent to the *t*-test. Since the *t*-test is a special case of one-way analysis of variance, we will deal with the more general case. The logic is the same.

One-way ANOVA

In one-way ANOVA, we are comparing groups on some dependent variable. Imagine three comparison groups, with all people in them measured on some dependent variable of interest. The question is: Do the groups differ on their scores? We have to be careful with this question. People will of course not all have exactly the same score on the variable – not even all the people in one group will have the same score. So the question really is: On average, taken overall, do the three groups score differently? There are two possible sources of variance in our scores. There is variance of scores within the groups, and variance of scores between the groups. Our problem is to decide whether the variance between the groups is larger than the variance within the groups. If it is, we can conclude that the groups differ; if not, we can conclude that the groups do not differ.

This is the basic logic of analysis of variance. We partition the total variance in a set of scores into that part due to individuals' membership in the different groups (called treatment variance, or systematic variance or between-groups variance) and that part due to variation within the groups (called error variance[2] or within-groups variance). This is done by first finding the mean score for each group, then finding out how much individual scores within groups vary around the group means, then finding the overall mean for the whole sample irrespective of groups (the grand mean), then finding out how much group means vary around the overall mean. This enables us to calculate two quantities – the between-groups variance and the within-groups variance. We then form a ratio, called F, to compare the two, such that:

F = between-groups variance/within-groups variance.

When F is large, between-groups variance is much greater than within-groups variance, and there are 'significant' differences between the groups. When F is small, between-groups variance is not much bigger than within-groups variance, and group differences are 'not significant'.

What do we mean by saying that F is large or small? This is a recurrent question in quantitative data analysis. As with chi-square, statistical inference helps here, by providing a decision-making rule. The F-ratio summarises information about the two sorts of variances, the variance between groups and the variance within groups, into one value. This calculated value can then be referred to a statistical table to decide whether it is large or small. Technically, the calculated F-ratio is compared to a critical value, stored in a statistical table, to determine the likelihood that it

	Boys	Girls
High SES	Average score for boys, high SES	Average score for girls, high SES
Medium SES	Average score for boys, medium SES	Averaga score for girls, medium SES
Low SES	Average score for boys, low SES	Average score for girls, low SES

could have come about by chance. The logic of statistical inference, for this and other cases, is explained further in Section 12.7.

Two-way ANOVA

When the people can simultaneously be classified in two ways to form comparison groups, we move from one-way ANOVA to two-way ANOVA. The basic logic is the same, in that we compare between-group variance with within-group variance, but now we have a more complicated situation. In the example shown in Table 12.2, the dependent variable is educational achievement, and students are jointly classified by gender and by socio-economic background (abbreviated to SES – socio-economic status). We cannot now simply ask about differences between groups, unless we specify which groups we mean. There are possible differences between gender groups (the 'main effect' due to gender) and possible differences between SES groups (the 'main effect' due to SES). But there is another possibility also, called interaction between the two classifications. While interaction is a very commonly-used term (often loosely) the meaning of it in this context is precise, technical and important.

12.3.2 Interaction

Interaction is, apparently, ubiquitous in our world, including the world we research. It is one of the reasons for some of the complications of quantitative research design. The essential idea is that the effect of one independent variable on the dependent variable interacts with (or is influenced by or depends on) another independent variable. This is shown in Figure 12.2, which plots the achievement scores of boys and girls from different socio-economic backgrounds.

Do boys score higher than girls in the results shown in this diagram? The answer is that it depends on what level of SES we are talking about – yes for high SES, no for low SES. Similarly, do students from high SES backgrounds perform better than those from middle-class SES backgrounds? Again, it depends on whether we are talking about boys or girls – yes for boys, no for girls. The key phrase is 'it depends on . . .'. Whenever we use this phrase, we have interaction. Given how often we need to use this phrase, it is not surprising that interaction is described as 'ubiquitous'.

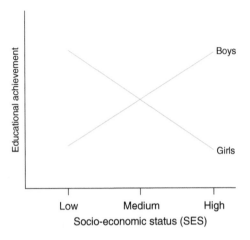

FIGURE 12.2   Interaction between variables

An important consequence of interaction is that its presence invalidates our attempts to make simple and sweeping generalisations. With the results as above, we cannot generalise about gender differences in achievement. That is, we cannot say that boys achieve better than girls, or vice versa. Nor can we generalise about social class differences.

Thus, in two-way ANOVA, we have three different questions we need to ask. Using the above example, the three questions are:

- Is there interaction between gender and SES with respect to achievement? If not,
- Do girls and boys score differently? (that is, is there a main effect due to gender?), and
- Do students from different SES levels score differently? (that is, is there a main effect due to SES?)

We would not normally investigate the main effects of gender and social class until we have investigated interaction effects. It is logical that we first find whether there is interaction between the independent variables. Only if there is no interaction do we proceed to talk about main effects. The situation of no interaction is shown in Figure 12.3.

Education research has a very well-known example of interaction. It is the treatment-by-aptitude interaction, whereby the effectiveness of a method of instruction (the treatment) interacts with and depends upon the level of ability of the student (the aptitude). We can easily imagine that a teaching method that works very well with highly-able students might not work so well with less-able students. Which teaching method works best depends on the ability level of the student. There is interaction between the two.

12.3.3 Analysis of covariance

Analysis of variance (ANOVA) and analysis of covariance (ANCOVA) are closely related and use the same set of ideas. In Chapter 10, ANCOVA was described as the

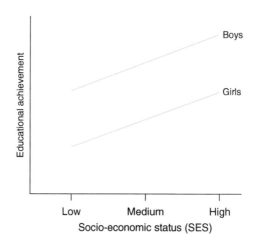

FIGURE 12.3   No interaction between variables

most general of the three ways of controlling a variable in the analysis. To control in this sense means to 'remove the influence of'. We can now briefly describe the logic of analysis of covariance, to see how this is done. For simplicity, we assume there is only one covariate. Because we want to remove the effects of the covariate before we do the comparison between the groups, we first measure the covariate, then use the relationship between the covariate and the dependent variable to adjust the dependent variable scores. This is equivalent to removing its effects from the dependent variable. Then we perform the standard analysis of variance, as described above, on the adjusted dependent variable scores. If between-group differences on the adjusted scores are significantly larger than within-group differences, we know that the independent variable is related to the dependent variable after controlling the effects of the covariate. Thus analysis of covariance is really analysis of variance performed on the adjusted dependent variable scores. The adjustment has been to remove the effects of the covariate, and we can co-vary out more than one variable at one time. We will see in Section 12.4.7 that we can also do ANCOVA using the regression analysis framework.

12.3.4 From univariate to multivariate

An important development in quantitative research methods in the past 40 years or so has been the trend from univariate studies to multivariate studies. Again, these terms have technical meanings:

- Univariate means only one dependent variable
- Multivariate means more than one dependent variable

This trend developed because we want to know about several possible differences between our comparison groups, not just one difference. Or, in experimental situations, we want to know about several effects of some treatment variable, not just one effect. When there is more than one dependent variable, univariate analysis of variance (ANOVA) becomes multivariate analysis of variance (MANOVA). If we are using covariates as well, univariate analysis of covariance (ANCOVA) becomes multivariate analysis of covariance (MANCOVA). These analyses required the development of multivariate statistical techniques.

Why is there a problem here which required new techniques? Why could the several dependent variables not just be treated sequentially, one at a time, requiring simply several ANOVAs? The answer is because the dependent variables are likely to be related to each other. The problem, in other words, is correlated dependent variables. This means that errors of inference in the statistical testing are likely to be compounded if the correlations between the dependent variables are not taken into account. Therefore, if we are planning between-group comparisons on more than one variable, either within or outside an experimental design framework, and if these variables are related to each other, we will need multivariate techniques for the analysis of the data. ANOVA will have to become MANOVA, and ANCOVA will have to become MANCOVA.

Relationships between variables: correlation and regression

12.4

We move now to the relationships-between-variables strand of data analysis, and we begin with the case of simple correlation between two continuous variables which have been measured. This is Pearson product–moment correlation, the most important (but not the only) type of correlation analysis. It tells us the direction and strength of relationships between variables – both how the variables are related, and how much they are related.

12.4.1 Simple correlation

In this situation, we are concerned with the relationship between two continuous variables. The basic idea can be illustrated with a simple example. If a sample of students (say 100) has been measured on two continuous variables, we can plot their scores on a two-dimensional graph. Each of the 100 points is plotted in the two-dimensional space formed by the X and Y axes, and together these points make up a scatter diagram. We can tell a great deal about the relationship between these two variables from the shape of this scatter diagram. Figure 12.4 shows the three main possibilities.

In the left-hand diagram (a), the shape of the scatter is oval or ellipse, and points upwards to the right. We can see that higher scores on X tend to go with higher scores on Y, and lower scores on X tend to go with lower scores on Y. These variables are said to be *positively correlated* (or directly correlated). The two varia-bles go up or down together. We can also see that a reasonably good prediction is possible, from X to Y or vice versa. If we know a student's score on X, we can

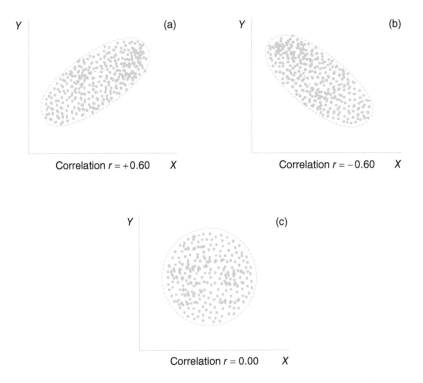

FIGURE 12.4   Scatter diagrams associated with Pearson product–moment correlation coefficients of various magnitudes

Source: Jaeger, 1990: 65

estimate with reasonable precision (that is, with not too much scatter) that student's score on *Y.*

In the right-hand diagram (b), the exact reverse is true. The scatter is still oval or ellipse in shape, but now it points downwards to the right. Higher scores on *X* tend to go with lower scores on *Y,* and lower scores on *X* tend to go with higher scores on *Y.* These variables are said to be *negatively correlated* (or inversely or indirectly correlated). The two variables go up and down in opposition to each other. A reasonably good prediction is still possible, from *X* to *Y* or vice versa. As before, if we know a student's score on *X,* we can estimate with reasonable precision that student's score on *Y.*

In the middle diagram (c), the scatter has a very circular shape. A high score on *X* might be associated with any level of score on *Y,* and vice versa. In this case, the variables are *uncorrelated* – there is no relationship between them. Clearly, prediction here is not possible.

In the left- and right-hand cases, we can summarise and simplify things by placing a 'line of best fit' through the points, sloping as the scatter diagram slopes. This is done by finding the mean of each interval and connecting the means across the different intervals. This line of best fit can then be smoothed into a prediction line between the two variables. The tighter the points in the scatter diagram cluster around such a line, the stronger the relationship and the better the prediction. This line of best fit is also called the regression line of *Y* on *X.*[3]

We have just described simple correlation and regression geometrically. It can also be done algebraically. The algebraic formalisation of these ideas is known as the Pearson product–moment correlation coefficient, symbolised by r, the most widely used measure of correlation. The computation formula ensures that r varies between 0 and 1, positive or negative as the case may be. That is, it can range from -1.00 to $+1.00$. The closer numerically the coefficient is to 1.00 (positive or negative), the stronger the relationship. This is very convenient, for it means that the correlation coefficient can tell us at a glance both the direction and strength of the relationship. A number close to zero tells us that the variables are not substantially related – it describes the middle diagram in Figure 12.4.

Conceptually, correlation is the same as covariation – indeed, correlation can be defined as standardised covariation. When two variables are related, positively or negatively, they vary together. This means they share common variance or co-vary. This points to an important property of the correlation coefficient. If we square it, we get a numerical estimate of the proportion of the variance in one variable which is held in common with, or accounted for by, the other. Thus, a correlation of $+0.50$ between two variables tells us that approximately 25% of the variance is held in common between them. Similarly, if $r = -0.70$, $r^2 = 0.5$ (approximately), and this tells us that some 50% (0.49%) of the variance in one variable can be accounted for by the other. This concept is important as we move from simple to multiple correlation, and fits in very well with our accounting-for-variance strategy.

12.4.2 Multiple correlation and regression

Simple correlation and regression has one independent and one dependent variable. Multiple correlation and regression has more than one independent variable, and one dependent variable. Reflecting the multiple causation concept discussed in Chapter 5, a common situation in research is where we have several independent variables and one dependent variable. We want to study factors affecting the dependent variable; and we want to account for variance in it, by studying its relationship with the independent variables.

The logic and the algebra of simple correlation generalise to multiple correlation, but multiple correlation now involves solving simultaneous equations. Assume we have four independent variables, and one dependent variable measured across a sample of people. (An example of this conceptual framework was shown in Figure 10.4, p. 221). Our input is now five sets of actual scores, one for each independent variable and one for the dependent variable, for each person. We use these actual scores to see how much the variables are related. Specifically, we use them to see how well the independent variables are able to predict the dependent variable. We first estimate the relationship between the independent variables and the dependent variable, using the logic described in simple correlation above. Then we use that knowledge to predict people's scores on the dependent variable, and we compare the predicted dependent variable scores with the actual dependent variable scores. We summarise this comparison with the correlation coefficient already described.

That is, the simple correlation coefficient between the predicted dependent variable scores and the actual dependent variable scores is in fact the multiple correlation between the four independent variables and the dependent variable. The multiple correlation coefficient is written R. When we square it, R^2 tells us how much of the variance in the dependent variable is accounted for.

This is the logic of multiple correlation analysis, and the output from the analysis is of two kinds:

First, the squared multiple correlation coefficient, R^2, is estimated. This gives a direct estimate of the amount of variation in the dependent variable which is explained or accounted for by the independent variables.

Second, the weights (called regression weights) attaching to each independent variable are estimated, telling us how important each independent variable is in predicting the dependent variable.

12.4.3 The squared multiple correlation coefficient (R^2)

The squared multiple correlation coefficient is a particularly important statistic, especially in the accounting-for-variance strategy outlined in Chapter 10. It tells us how much of the variance in the dependent variable is accounted for by this group of independent variables. Thus it provides a direct answer to the central question in the accounting for variance research strategy. Like the simple correlation coefficient (r), R is normalised to vary between 0 and 1, so that R^2 also varies between 0 and 1. The closer it is to 1.00 (or 100%), the more of the variance in the dependent variable can be accounted for. The squared multiple correlation coefficient R^2 also tells us how good our prediction of the dependent variable is, with this set of independent variables. These two ideas are linked. The more variance we can account for, the more accurate the prediction we can make. Conversely, the less variance we can account for, the less accurate is our prediction. This means that the squared multiple correlation coefficient measures for us the predictive efficiency or accuracy of any particular regression model.

12.4.4 The regression weights

It is important to know how good our prediction is, by knowing how much of the variance we can account for. But we also want to know how important each independent variable is in accounting for this variance. This is the concept of the relative importance of predictor variables. The regression weights in our regression equations give a direct estimate of this. The computations produce two types of weights – raw weights, suitable for use with the raw scores as input to the analysis, and standardised weights, for use with standardised scores. We mainly use the latter, since, unlike the former, they can be directly compared with each other. Their full name is standardised partial regression coefficients, usually abbreviated in the literature to beta (β) weights. Their technical interpretation is important. The β weight for (say) independent variable X_1 tells us how much of a change we would make in the dependent variable by making a one unit change in the variable X_1, while keeping all other variables constant.

12.4.5 Step-wise regression

Step-wise regression means dropping out variables from the regression equation, usually one at a time, or step-wise, to see what difference it makes to how much variance we can account for in the dependent variable.[4] It is another way we can assess how important an independent variable is. The basic idea is this. First, we use all the independent variables in our regression equation, to see how much of the dependent variable variance we can account for. This is measured by R^2, which tells us the predictive efficiency of this particular regression equation. Then we drop out an independent variable, re-compute the regression equation, and see what change there has been in how much variance we can account for. This gives us a second R^2. Comparing the two R^2s tells us how important the variable was that we dropped out, in accounting for variance in the dependent variable.

Step-wise regression is very useful and a widely used technique. In fact, it is a special case of a more general procedure we can use, to test the predictive efficiency of regression models. We can think of each regression equation as a regression (or prediction) model. Each model produces a squared multiple correlation coefficient, which tells us how well that model predicts the dependent variable (or how much of the variance in the dependent variable we can account for). Therefore we can compare the predictive efficiency of different models by comparing their squared multiple correlation coefficients. In this way, MLR can be used to investigate many different questions about the effects of different independent variables on the dependent variable, and about how these effects come about. Step-wise regression analysis looks at one particular question – does dropping this particular independent variable reduce the predictive efficiency of our model, or not? But there are many other types of questions we can investigate, using the logical framework of MLR, and comparing squared multiple correlation coefficients (see Punch, 2003: 100–10).

12.4.6 Review: MLR as a general data analysis system

We have covered a lot of material on a logical basis in this section, so it is appropriate that we pause for review. We first covered simple correlation and extended this to multiple correlation. We linked this to the accounting-for-variance strategy directly through the squared multiple correlation coefficient. We then linked correlation to regression, through prediction. This gives us prediction equations, or regression models. We then considered regression weights in those equations, and the logic of step-wise regression. Finally, we generalised this to the comparison of different regression models, through their predictive efficiency.

As presented here, MLR falls within the relationship-between-variables strand of quantitative design and data analysis, and focuses mainly on continuous variables. It provides us with a way of dealing with all types of such continuous variable relationships, from simple to complex. The investigation of all of these can be done within the one regression analysis framework.

However, the technique of MLR also has the flexibility to deal with the comparison-between-groups strand of design and data analysis. That is, the same logical framework of MLR can be used to deal with t-tests, analysis of variance (including interaction) and analysis of covariance. This is because these analyses depend on group membership, and variables to express group membership can be formulated and used in regression equations. In other words, MLR can deal with categorical variables as well as continuous variables. Categorical variables to express group membership are called 'binary' or 'dummy' variables in regression analysis (Hardy, 1993).

With straightforward dummy variables, we can do t-tests, and one-way and two-way analysis of variance using these regression techniques. This also includes interaction questions in two-way ANOVA. And because categorical and continuous variables can be included in the same regression models, we can do analysis of covariance this way as well, as shown below. In short, this one approach can cover all of the main data analysis ideas we have dealt with in this chapter. Table 12.3 summarises the two main strands, showing how they come together using the general linear model.

Thus MLR provides one analytic framework and one set of steps which can be used to investigate a very wide range of data analysis questions, from both main strands identified in this chapter. Because the one analytic framework can handle both categorical and continuous variables, MLR is a tool of great power and flexibility, with application to a wide range of situations. My experience is that students also find it easy enough to understand and apply. Since the same steps can be used to investigate such a wide range of questions, it means that researchers can build their own statistical models for the analysis of data, guided by the specific questions they want to investigate, instead of being limited only to the conventional models routinely described in statistics books. Building these models requires the researcher to make an exact statement of the research questions.

12.4.7 Analysis of covariance using MLR

In Section 12.3.3, we saw the logic of ANCOVA, in the analysis of variance framework. We can now use the same logic here. In the example used earlier, we want to know whether the independent variable affects the dependent variable after removing the effects of the covariate. When done by MLR, this requires the comparison of two regression models. The first uses the covariate only to predict the dependent variable, and produces its R^2. The second uses the independent variable (in the between-groups comparison assumed here, the independent variable is a set of

TABLE 12.3   Quantitative research design and statistics

Comparing groups	Relating variables

Designs

Experimental and quasi-experimental designs	Correlational surveys (non-experiments)

Logic

What are the 'effects' of this 'cause'?	What are the 'causes' of this 'effect'?

Conceptual frameworks

Independent variable   Independent variables   Dependent variable

Comparison groups

X_1
X_2
X_3 ⟶ Y
X_4

Dependent variable

Statistics

t-test (two groups)	simple correlation and regression
ANOVA (more than two groups)	multiple correlation
ANCOVA	multiple regression (MLR)
MANOVA	
MANCOVA	

The two different strands of statistics can be brought
together using the general linear model

binary vectors representing group membership) together with the covariate to pre-dict the dependent variable. Its R^2 is compared with the first model's R^2 to see if its predictive efficiency is better. If it is, group membership adds to knowledge of the dependent variable over and above the covariate. That means there are between-group differences after controlling the covariate. If not, group membership adds nothing to prediction of the dependent variable, over and above the covariate. That means that between-group differences are not significant, over and above the effects of the covariate.

The analysis of survey data

12.5 The correlational survey is the central strategy in the relationships-between-variables strand of quantitative research, so there are likely to be many variables involved, some categorical and some continuous, and many different questions of interest. To simplify what can become a complicated analysis, we can look at it in three main stages (simple descriptive analysis, two-variable relationships, joint and multivariable relationships), which together provide a useful analytic framework. Of course, these stages need to be used in conjunction with the research questions guiding the study.

1. *Descriptive analysis*: With complex survey data sets, an initial descriptive analysis of the data is useful. This would be done on a variable-by-variable basis, and would use the techniques described in Section 12.1 in this chapter – means, standard deviations (or variances) and frequency distributions. If there are scales involved, there might also be some item analysis, and, whether or not there are scales, there might also be some data reduction (see Section 12.6). One benefit to an initial descriptive analysis is keeping the researcher close to the data; another is understanding the distribution of each variable across the survey respondents.

2. *Two-variable relationships*: As a next step, some two-variable relationships in the survey might be singled out for special analysis, guided again by the research questions. Any of the techniques of association might be used, but two approaches are strongly recommended. First, as noted earlier, the approach detailed by Rosenberg (1968) provides a useful framework for working through this stage, stressing the logic of the analysis. A feature of his approach is his clarification of the meaning of relationships between variables (1968: 3–22), and then of the conceptual status of variables in a relationship, systematically extending two variable relationships into three and four variable relationships (1968: 22–158).[5] Second, multiple linear regression analysis can be used to investigate all questions of two-variable relationships and group comparisons, as we have just seen. The same logic lies behind these two approaches.

3. *Joint and multivariable relationships*:[6] Here the value of the MLR approach becomes apparent, since it can easily be extended past two-variable relationships. It is difficult to extend the cross-tabulation approach of Rosenberg to analysis that simultaneously involves many variables, but MLR, on the other hand, extends easily to situations involving many variables. Most of the joint and multivariable questions of interest can be answered using this approach, including detailed questions about relationships between variables, and questions involving comparisons between groups. It requires specification of the conceptual status of variables in the survey (some as independent, some as control variables or covariates, and some as dependent), in accordance with the research questions. Many other questions, including interaction, and non-linear and polynomial relationships, can also be investigated using the MLR approach. As noted, a benefit of this approach is that it forces the researcher to be specific in formulating research questions, and in translating them into data analysis operations.

Data reduction: factor analysis

12.6 Quantitative social science research, especially non-experimental research, is characterised by multivariable studies. Having many variables often makes it difficult to fully understand the data. This difficulty has led to the development of techniques to reduce the number of variables, but without losing the information the original variables provide. Factor analysis is the name given to a group of related techniques developed for this purpose. The idea behind factor analysis is based on the correlation between variables, as shown in Figure 12.5. When two variables are correlated, we can propose the existence of a common factor, which

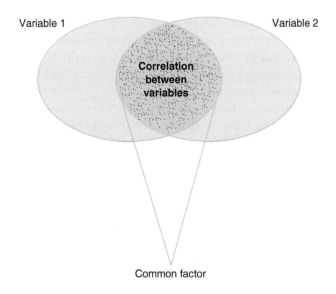

FIGURE 12.5 Factor analysis diagram

both variables share to some extent, and which therefore explains the correlation between them. This idea generalises to any number of variables.

In factor analysis, therefore, we aim to reduce the number of variables by finding the common factors among them. We begin the analysis with the original observed variables we have measured. We then find the correlations between them, and factor-analyse these correlations. We want to end the analysis with a smaller number of derived or unobserved variables called factors.

Consider the example of six educational tests – one in each of arithmetic, algebra and geometry, and one in each of English, French and history. We can easily imagine that, if we measured a sample of students with these six tests, we would find two clusters of correlations among the tests. The first cluster would show the overlap between arithmetic, algebra and geometry, while the second would show the overlap between English, French and history. If this were the case, factor analysis of the correlations among the six tests would produce two main factors, one corresponding to the mathematical variables ('mathematical ability'), and one to the language variables ('language ability'). Based on this factor analysis, we can therefore reduce the number of variables we have to deal with, from six to two. The six were the original measured variables; the two are the extracted or derived factors. These two factors effectively summarise the information contained in the original six tests, so that we have reduced the number of variables without major loss of information. As a result, it is now easier for us to talk about just two factors instead of six variables. We can next calculate scores on the two derived factors for each student, for use in subsequent analysis. These are called factor scores, and we can use them to simplify the subsequent analysis.

Thus the input into a factor analysis is the set of correlations between the original variables. Once the computer has performed the mathematical calculations, the solution will show the derived factors, and the relationship of each factor to the original variables. It shows this through factor loadings – the loading of each original variable on each derived factor. The researcher interprets the meaning of each extracted factor by means of those loadings, usually after *rotation*.

Geometrically speaking, factor analysis can be thought of as placing axes through the space described by the original variables. The objective of *rotation* is to place those axes in the best possible place for interpretation of the factors. The 'best possible place' can be defined mathematically, and set up as a criterion to guide the analysis. The first factor analysis solution from the computer is arbitrary, in terms of the placement of the axes. Therefore the axes can be rotated until this criterion is realised. The original axes are at right-angles to each other in this space. This is called orthogonal factor analysis. If this property is preserved, the factor scores that are calculated will be uncorrelated with each other. However, this property can also be relaxed in rotation, if a non-orthogonal or oblique solution seems preferable. Correlated factor scores would then result.

We should note one other aspect of factor analysis that came up in the analysis of qualitative data (see Section 9.4). It concerns levels of abstraction. In factor analysis, we begin with observed variables, and we end with unobserved or extracted factors. The variables are at a lower level of abstraction or generality than the factors. Thus algebraic ability, for example, is more specific than mathematical ability. Mathematical ability is a more general concept, at a higher level of abstraction.

Actually, this is the second time we have raised the level of abstraction in the analysis of quantitative data. The first time was from items to variables. This second time is from variables to factors. This is shown in the levels of abstraction diagram. It is useful to see clearly these levels of abstraction, and especially to see factor analysis this way. When we discussed the analysis of qualitative data in Chapter 9, we saw that a very similar process of raising the level of abstraction is involved, as indicated in Figure 12.6.

Statistical inference

12.7 Until now in this chapter we have been looking at the logic behind different techniques in the analysis of quantitative data. We have actually been doing *descriptive statistics*,[7] which is concerned with summarising and describing data. The topic of statistical inference, or *inferential statistics*, is different. It is not concerned with summarising and describing data. Rather, it is a tool to assist in making decisions based on the analysis of data using the descriptive statistical techniques already discussed. Statistical inference is one of the many tools needed in research. This section considers the logic behind statistical inference and how it is applied, and should be read in conjunction with Section 11.11 on sampling.

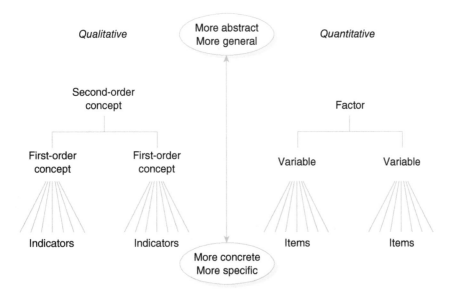

FIGURE 12.6   Levels of abstraction in data analysis

First, what is the problem that gives rise to statistical inference? In our research, we typically select a sample from a population, and we collect data only from this sample. We do this because we normally cannot study whole populations. But after the research is done on the sample, we wish to make statements about the larger population from which the sample was drawn. In other words, we are faced with an inference, from the sample back to the population. There is a symmetry here, as we saw in Figure 11.2 (Section 11.11). We draw a sample from the population, and we study the sample. But then, after studying the sample, we wish to infer back to the population. The inference question therefore is: How likely is it that what I found to be true in my sample is also true in my population?

In order to answer this question, we rephrase it in probabilistic terms. It becomes: How likely am I to be wrong if I infer that what I found to be true of my sample is also true of my population? Since the question is phrased in terms of the likelihood of being wrong, the answer will also be in terms of the likelihood of being wrong, expressed as 'times per hundred' or as 'times per thousand'. This leads to statements such as: 'I will be wrong less than 5 times in 100 if I make that inference' (or less than 5 times in 1000, or whatever). These are the familiar confidence levels, or statistical significance levels or probability levels. They are usually shown in research reports as $p < 0.05$, $p < 0.001$, and so on.[8] p is used to indicate the probability of being wrong.

How do we work out this likelihood of being wrong? We calculate some statistic(s) from our sample data and then we use statistical inference tables to determine this likelihood. These tables are in most statistics books, and now in computers. In the analysis of our sample data, we calculate a statistic, which summarises some aspect of the data we are interested in – it might be chi-square, comparing observed and expected distributions, or r showing the level of association between two variables, or F comparing the predictive efficiency of two regression models. We then refer this statistic to its distribution as shown in statistical inference tables, in order to see how likely it is that a value of this size would be obtained for this statistic, by chance. Thus the analysis of quantitative data uses both descriptive and inferential statistics.

This gives us another perspective on how statistical inference works. We are really asking: How likely is it that my calculated statistic (which of course is based on data obtained from the sample) came about by chance, as an 'accident' of the particular sample I happened to study? As before, the answer is in terms of a probability level. It takes the form: 'A value of this size, for this statistic, would come about by chance (say) 5 times in 100 ($p = 0.05$) with a sample of the size used in this research.' Now, if this value would come about by chance only 5 times in 100, it would be a non-chance occurrence 95 times in 100. In other words, if I am likely to be wrong less than 5 times in 100, in making the inference that what I found to be true in my sample is also true in my population, then I am likely to be right more than 95 times in 100. These seem like good odds. It seems that it is not a chance result, and not an accident of this particular sample. It seems real, and we call it *statistically significant*. The term 'significance' therefore has a special meaning in quantitative analysis.

The above example used 5 times in 100 as the cut-off point. This is the so-called 5% confidence level or 5% significance level. By convention, this is a widely accepted cut-off level in social science research. But if a particular research result had a probability of (say) 7% of occurring by chance ($p = 0.07$), we should not dismiss it as unimportant just on the grounds that it does not actually reach statistical significance ($p = 0.05$). Statistical significance levels are useful in guiding our decisions about when results are 'real' or not. But we should use them intelligently, based on the understanding of what they mean.

This question of inference arises whenever we wish to generalise from a sample to some larger population, whatever descriptive statistics we are using. The question does not arise if we do not wish to generalise, or if we have somehow studied the whole population we are interested in. Sample size is important in determining the outcome of a statistical significance test. The bigger the sample size, the smaller the numerical value of the statistic required in order to reach significance. Conversely, the smaller the sample size, the bigger the numerical value of the statistic required in order to reach significance.

Computer software for the analysis of quantitative data

12.8 Among the many computer packages that have been developed for the analysis of quantitative data, the most widely used in social science research is IBM SPSS Statistics (SPSS). Now in its 21st release, SPSS is an extremely comprehensive package which can perform highly complex data manipulation and analysis with simple instructions. SPSS has a vast number of statistical and mathematical functions, scores of statistical procedures and a very flexible data handling capability.

SPSS can read data in almost any format (e.g. numeric, alphanumeric, binary, dollar, date, time formats) and can read files created using spreadsheet or database software. Thus the statistical analysis power of SPSS can be combined with the flexibility, and other advantages, of spreadsheets (such as Excel).

On the companion website for this book (www.sagepub.co.uk/punch3e), you will find the full text of Chapters 1 and 2 from George Argyrous's book, *Statistics for Research with a Guide to SPSS*. These two chapters introduce you to the SPSS environment, teach you how to set up an SPSS data file and will help you with the first steps of your data analysis. For further detailed coverage of using SPSS, take a look at Andy Field's bestselling SPSS book, *Discovering Statistics with SPSS* (a link to the book can be found on the companion website). In addition to these two titles, a range of other books are also available and links to other options are provided on the companion website.

In addition to books on using SPSS, there are also a wealth of video and text-based SPSS tutorials available online which can help you with the first steps. On the companion website, you will find links to these videos, most of which are free to access.

Alternatives to SPSS

Increasingly popular with researchers is the free statistical environment, R (http://www.r-project.org/). The benefits of R in comparison with SPSS are that it can be downloaded for free, offers a wider range of packages with more functionality than SPSS and is especially strong on graphical techniques. However, it does require learning the R syntax and getting to grips with basic programming, which SPSS does not. Andy Field's new book, *Discovering Statistics with R*, is an accessible guide to using R for social science data analysis for those looking to make the switch. Links to the book and its companion website can be found on the companion website for this book (www.sagepub.co.uk/punch3e).

Other software packages for quantitative analysis you may encounter include:
SAS – http://www.sas.com
STATA – http://www.stata.com/
Minitab – http://www.minitab.com/

Chapter summary

- Two important concepts for summarising quantitative data are central tendency (most often measured by the mean, but sometimes also by the mode or the median) and variation (most often measured by the standard deviation, or the variance); frequency distributions are also useful in summarising data.

- Cross-tabulation – or contingency table analysis – is a very useful and widely applicable way of studying the relationship between variables, whatever level of measurement is involved; chi-square can be used as a formal test of cross-tabulated relationships.
- Analysis of variance (ANOVA) enables us to compare groups on some dependent variable of interest; the t-test is a special case of ANOVA, when there are only two groups. In one-way ANOVA, people are classified on one dimension only; in two-way ANOVA, people are simultaneously classified on two dimensions, and the important concept of interaction is now involved.
- Analysis of covariance (ANCOVA) enables a covariate to be controlled; dependent variable scores are adjusted for the relationship with the covariate (or control variable), and analysis of variance is performed on the adjusted scores.
- Univariate analysis involves one dependent variable; if there are several dependent variables which are correlated, multivariate analysis is required.
- The Pearson product–moment correlation (r) is a widely used statistic for summarising the relationship between two continuous variables; it shows both the direction and strength of the relationship; squaring r estimates how much of the variance in the dependent variable is accounted for by the independent variable.
- Multiple correlation and regression (MLR) applies the same logic to the very common research situation of several independent variables and one dependent variable; the squared multiple correlation coefficient (R^2) estimates how much of the dependent variable variance is accounted for by these independent variables.
- MLR can be seen as a general data analysis system, using binary variables to enable t-tests, analysis of variance and analysis of covariance to be performed.
- The analysis of complex correlational survey data can be divided into three general stages – descriptive analysis, two-variable relationships, and joint and multi-variable relationships.
- Factor analysis is the name given to a group of related techniques whose aim is to reduce the number of variables without significant loss of information, working from the correlation between the variables.
- Statistical inference is a tool for assessing the inference from sample to population; it estimates the likelihood of being wrong in attributing what is found to be true in a sample to a population.

KEY TERMS

Mean: the most common measure of central tendency; also called the average

Standard deviation: the most common way to measure variability in a distribution; squaring the standard deviation gives the variance

Frequency distribution: scores in a distribution are tabulated, according to how many people achieved each score, or gave each response, or fell into each category

Cross-tabulation: two variables are cross-tabulated against each other

Contingency table: uses cross-tabulation to see if the distribution of one variable is related to (or contingent upon) the other

Chi-square: a statistical technique with many uses; commonly used to assess relationships in cross-tabulated data

Analysis of variance (ANOVA): a statistical technique for investigating differences between groups on some dependent variable

Interaction: two (or more) independent variables may jointly affect an independent variable; they interact with each other in their effect on the dependent variable

Analysis of covariance (ANCOVA): a statistical technique for investigating the difference between groups on a dependent variable, after controlling for one or more covariates

Correlation: a statistical technique for showing the strength and direction of the relationship between variables; with two continuous variables (simple correlation), the Pearson product–moment correlation r is commonly used; this generalises to multiple correlation with more than two variables

Multiple linear regression (MLR): a quantitative data analysis strategy with several independent variables and one dependent variable; aims to account for variance in the dependent variable

Factor analysis: a family of statistical techniques for reducing the number of variables without significant loss of information

Statistical inference: a set of decision-making rules to assess the accuracy of an inference made from sample to population

Exercises and study questions_____

1. What is meant by central tendency and variation in summarising the distribution of a set of scores. What is the most common measure of each?
2. Study these three cross-tabulations of pass–fail test results for a sample of 200 students (100 boys, 100 girls):

(a)

	Boys	Girls
Pass	25	70
Fail	75	30
	100	100

(b)

	Boys	Girls
Pass	53	48
Fail	47	52
	100	100

(c)

	Boys	Girls
Pass	80	30
Fail	20	70
	100	100

What relationship is indicated by each of (a), (b) and (c)? Logically, how can we decide whether (b) shows a 'real' relationship? (Hint: how much of a difference makes a difference? Re-read Section 12.2.)

3. What is one-way ANOVA? Explain its logic by comparing test scores between three classes.
4. What is two-way ANOVA? What is interaction and why is it important?
5. What is ANCOVA and when would we want to use it?
6. Redraw the scatter diagram in Figure 12.4(a) showing a stronger positive relationship; redraw the diagram in Figure 12.4(c) showing a weaker negative relationship.

7. What is the relationship between Pearson *r* and accounting for variance?
8. How does simple correlation become multiple correlation? When MLR is used to study the joint relationship between (say) five independent variables and one dependent variable, what does R^2 tell us? What does β for each variable tell us?
9. What is the aim of factor analysis and what logic is behind the technique?
10. What is the inference in 'statistical inference'?
11. In your own words, explain the basic logic of statistical inference, and relate it to 'the probability of being wrong'.
12. What is meant by statistical significance? Illustrate with $p < 0.05$.

Further reading

Comfrey, A.L. and Lee, H.B. (1992) *A First Course in Factor Analysis.* 2nd edn. Hillsdale, NJ: Lawrence Erlbaum.

Glass, G.V. and Stanley, J.C. (1970) *Statistical Methods in Education and Psychology.* Englewood Cliffs, NJ: Prentice-Hall.

Jaeger, R.M. (1990) *Statistics as a Spectator Sport.* 2nd edn. Beverly Hills, CA: SAGE.

Kerlinger, F.N. and Pedhazur, E.J. (1973) *Multiple Regression in Behavioral Research.* New York: Holt, Rinehart and Winston.

Kish, L.D. (1987) *Statistical Design for Research.* New York: John Wiley.

Lipsey, M. (1990) *Design Sensitivity: Statistical Power for Experimental Research.* Newbury Park, CA: SAGE.

Rosenberg, M. (1968) *The Logic of Survey Analysis.* New York: Basic Books.

Sirkin, R.M. (2005) *Statistics for the Social Sciences.* 3rd edn. London: SAGE.

Tatsuoka, M.M. (1988) *Multivariate Analysis: Techniques for Educational and Psychological Research.* 2nd edn. New York: Macmillan.

Vogt, W.P. (2005) *Dictionary of Statistics and Methodology.* 3rd edn. London: SAGE.

Notes

1. Cross-tabulation means that two variables will be cross-tabulated against each other. Contingency table means that the purpose of the cross-tabulation is to see if the distribution on one of the variables is related to, or contingent on, the other.
2. This use of the term 'error variance' is different from its use in connection with the reliability of measurements in Chapter 11.
3. There is also the regression line of X on Y.
4. Step-wise can also mean adding in variables, rather than dropping them out. The 'steps' can be done forwards or backwards. We will talk here about dropping variables out, sometimes called 'backward stepping regression analysis'. But the whole idea also works the other way around.
5. Rosenberg's book *The Logic of Survey Analysis* (1968) is strongly recommended for building a foundation in quantitative data analysis – it is clearly written, and it stresses the logic of the analysis.

6. As noted, the term 'multivariate' is a technical term meaning more than one dependent variable. 'Multivariable' is a more general term, simply meaning many variables.
7. With the exception of chi-square, and comparing the predictive efficiency of regression models.
8. $p < 0.05$ actually means that I will be wrong less than 5 times in 100, if I conclude that what was true of my sample is also true of my population. Similarly, $p < 0.001$ would mean being wrong less than one time in 1000, and so on.

thirteen
THE INTERNET AND RESEARCH
WAYNE MCGOWAN

Contents

After studying this chapter you should be able to:

- Understand that the Internet can be seen both as a location for social research, and as a tool for conducting social research
- Describe ways in which the Internet can assist in finding and accessing relevant literature and information
- Explain how the Internet can be used for locating and surveying samples and populations, and identify the issues which arise
- Describe how the Internet can be used for interviewing and observing, and for documentary data, and identify the issues which arise

Introduction

13.1   The use of technology in social science research is not new. For example, since the 1930s, advances in sound recording have seen interview data shift from anecdotal accounts based on recollections and field notes to verbatim transcriptions of naturally occurring talk that can be listened to time and time again. Similarly, developments in communication and recording technologies have made the task of capturing and preserving interview data easier (Murthy, 2008). The telephone has provided quick convenient access to research participants. Today, technological advances such as reliable mobile forms of electronic sound, image and video devices continue to attract the social scientist. In particular, the Internet itself is attracting a lot of interest.

The 'Internet' is a computer-based global information and communication system linked in standardised ways to enable user connectivity (DiMaggio, Hargittai, Neuman and Robinson, 2001). It is understood as a 'network of networks' connecting computer-based websites to form the World Wide Web (Gaiser and Schreiner, 2009). The Internet can be seen as both a location and a tool for research (Buchanan and Zimmer, 2012). As a location, the Internet offers a new space for social inquiry. The Internet as a social medium can be studied like any other place where people gather and interact. For example, Gaiser and Schreiner (2009) point out how online communication environments such as listserv discussion lists, chat rooms, game rooms and Secondlife offer research opportunities to observe social interaction on the Internet. But the Internet is also a research tool. For example, it facilitates data collection by making contact and interaction with informants quicker, cheaper and easier. In this section, we concentrate on the Internet as a research tool, or what Hewson and Laurent (2008) describe as *Internet-mediated research* for research in virtual or actual locations.

As a research tool, the Internet offers many ways for people to interact, communicate and share information. As at 30 June, 2012, the number of Internet users worldwide was estimated at over seven billion (Internet World Stats, n.d.). What these people are doing and how they are doing it on the Internet cannot be described as consistent, homogenous or uniform, and the number of people communicating at any one time can vary significantly. Communicating information over the Internet by email, for example, often happens on a one-to-one basis, whereas information communicated through discussion forums and blogs can involve not only a many-to-many or one-to-many relationship but also one-way or two-way interaction. The timing of people's communications and interactions also varies. Chat rooms, for example, provide synchronous communication whereas email is asynchronous, while online virtual worlds like Secondlife and gaming occur in real time. How people access the Internet also differs. Webpages can be viewed by any interested party at any time or be restricted by a login requiring a valid username and password. The capacity to observe so many, doing so much and in so many different ways makes the Internet an extremely attractive yet challenging research tool for social researchers.

Social scientists are drawn to the richness of interactions on the Internet. In addition, they are also attracted to its promise to make research faster, cheaper and easier (Lee, Fielding and Blank, 2008). Madge and O'Connor (2002: 100), however, warn: '. . . the potential of on-line research should not be exaggerated: many of the issues and problems of conventional research methods still apply in the virtual venue.' Internet research has to contend with issues facing conventional social research design (Wakeford, Orton-Johnson and Jungnickel, 2006). It still needs to be located within a relevant body of literature, focused on clear research questions, and based on appropriate methods. Like any research project, good design is essential. As Hewson and Laurent (2008: 59) comment:

> . . . given the widespread perception of Internet-based procedures as being able to quickly and cost-effectively generate large pools of data, and their particular appeal when time and cost constraints are high, there is a danger that researchers may be tempted to implement poorly designed studies.

Against this background, this section examines four broad areas with respect to the Internet as a research tool. The first area – the literature – explores how the Internet helps in finding and accessing information relevant to a research project. The second area – quantitative data collection – discusses the Internet as a tool for locating and surveying a targeted population. The third area – qualitative data collection – looks at the Internet as a tool for interviewing and for observing, and as a source of documentary data. The fourth area concludes the section with a discussion of some ethical issues which emerge when using the Internet as a research tool.

The literature

13.2 Social science research does not take place in a vacuum but is related to, and builds upon, existing knowledge. The social science researcher needs to locate an inquiry within an associated body of knowledge. This involves searching for and accessing published material relevant to the topic under investigation (Ridley, 2008). The volume of literature, however, makes the task of manually locating and accessing material extremely time-consuming. While the Internet as an electronic tool offers a quicker approach to the demands of this task, it does, in other ways, make it more complicated. The amount of information and the number of ways it can be sourced through the Internet provides a new challenge to locating research literature.

The search tools for finding and accessing research literature through the Internet can be divided into five categories (Ridley, 2008):

- Traditional library catalogues available as electronic databases, where catalogued resources are held in a single location or by a single organisation. They offer a brief description of the materials within the database using keywords, subject headings, author and title.
- Bibliographic databases, which are electronic databases of published literature, including journals, conference proceedings, government and legal publications, books, and so on. Unlike the traditional library catalogue online, they focus primarily on journal articles and conference papers rather than books and monographs and offer richer description of materials such as abstracts and pdf files of complete articles. Examples of this type of database are: British Humanities Index (BHI), Social Sciences Citation Index using WoK (Web of Knowledge), MEDLINE for biomedical literature, ProQuest for literature on Education, Index to Theses (for UK theses) and Dissertation Abstracts (for US and European dissertations and theses).
- Open access databases, which are electronic databases freely available to anyone with access to the Internet. Unlike the previous databases, permission in the form of membership or subscription is not required to gain full access to materials.
- Internet subject gateways, which are databases manually created by subject specialists who select and organise existing subject-specific websites into directories according to a hierarchy of subject categories.
- Internet search engines, mechanical programs which create databases by matching keywords to content stored on the Internet and then organise and display the results in a readily accessible way.

The Internet search engine, like the Internet subject gateway, is a database. The key difference distinguishing Internet subject gateways from Internet search engines is the means by which databases are created. While subject specialists manually create Internet subject gateways, search engines are databases created by machines. In this sense, the computer electronically trawls countless websites and compiles a database of relevant information by matching keywords entered by a user with words found in web documentation. Researchers are advised to treat the resources compiled by this automated process with caution (Ridley, 2008). Different search engines search and collect information in different ways. 'Search engines do not index the entire Internet, and their ordering of results depends on proprietary algorithms. Using ready-to-hand tools such as search engines can therefore lead to a biased portrayal of whatever actually is out there on the Internet' (Hine, 2011: 3). Hence, the same keywords entered into different search engines will render different results.

In response, Ridley recommends taking a proactive approach to managing the outcome of a search. This requires researchers to exercise greater control over the retrieval process by familiarising themselves with how a search engine compiles web documentation and how to use advanced search options. Nevertheless, a database compiled in this way does not guarantee retrieval of reliable academic sources. Before making use of resources gathered in this way, Ridley (2008) stresses the need for researchers to trace who produced the material and why.

The Internet offers new approaches and new challenges to the conventional research practice of locating existing knowledge. The new approaches make the conventional practice of locating relevant literature faster and more convenient. However, they also make it more complex. More and more, researchers need to know about the capacity and functions of an ever-expanding range of online services dedicated to finding and retrieving information. The complexity of the relationship between the literature and the Internet is underlined by the need to learn how to use new tools to find and access data in the form of material and documentation published online.

Collecting quantitative data

13.3 The survey as a means of collecting quantitative data using a standard-ised questionnaire is a very prominent method for empirical research in the social sciences (Vehovar and Manfreda, 2008). During the twentieth century, the survey proved adaptable in taking advantage of advances in technology such as the telephone. Advances in computer technology over the past decade mean the survey is no longer dependent on interviewer administration or the posting out of a paper-based questionnaire. It is possible for anyone these days to set up a self-administered survey by making a questionnaire electronically available on the Internet.

Broadly speaking, there are two types of Internet surveys – those which collect data using '. . . surveys executed on a respondent's machine (client-side) . . .' or those which '. . . execute on the survey organization's Web server (server-side) . . .' (Couper, 2008: 2). The use of email to send a survey questionnaire to the machine of potential respondents over the Internet is a prime example of the *client-side approach*. This involves introducing the purpose of the study and inviting completion of a question-naire that is either embedded in the body of an email message or attached to the email as a downloadable document (Couper, 2008; Gaiser and Schreiner, 2009). It is more likely for researchers using email to attach the questionnaire as a document for down-load in an effort to avoid the problems that arise when the plain text of the email message fails to preserve and reproduce accurately the formatting necessary to ensure survey questions correspond to the right choices for all respondents. The use of email offers a cheaper and faster delivery and return of the self-administered questionnaire than the conventional postal service. However, the completing and transmitting of the survey done in this way is not completely seamless.

Recipients of a survey questionnaire through email are required to do more than simply respond to a series of questions. There is also the expectation that they will have the necessary skills as well as software on their computer to enable them to download the questionnaire, input their responses, save them and return them as an email reply (Gaiser and Schreiner, 2009). Beyond the speed and cost savings associated with delivery and reply, the advantages of using the Internet to email a self-administered questionnaire to potential respondents over a paper-based approach using the postal service are negligible. The client-side approach does little to reduce the demands on researchers to read replies and transcribe data. While those with the technical expertise may be able to write programming scripts to automate this process, most researchers receiving email responses, like those receiving posted questionnaires, will need to enter data manually.

One way to automate this process is to make the Internet survey executable on a Web-server rather than respondents' machines. The Web survey is a prime example of the *server-side approach* (Couper, 2008). As Gaiser and Schreiner (2009: 47) explain: 'The alternative to emailing the survey and reading the reply is to put the survey up on a web site and use email to send a URL link to the web site and request the recipient to visit the web site.' Unlike the email survey, the Web survey takes advantage of the software on the web-server to manage data entry automatically.

Andrews, Nonneck and Preece (2003) distinguish between a client-side and a server-side approach in terms of a 'push' or 'pull' strategy. While the email (client-side) survey pushes by urging potential respondents to participate through direct communication, the web-based (server-side) survey pulls by being designed to attract respondents. The ease and appeal of a user-friendly interface of the web-based survey that automatically verifies and stores responses offers a pull factor aimed at attracting a high response rate. The use of a web-survey as a pull strategy is evident in Madge and O'Connor's (2002) study of *Babyworld*. They undertook a web-survey rather than an email approach because it would reach a wide audience quickly and cheaply, receive responses around the clock and automatically load responses into an analytical package. Additionally, web-based surveys provide a far superior questionnaire interface making them more user-friendly and attractive than email surveys. The web-based survey can also be hosted on a dedicated website, which can be used as a platform to provide more information about the project, the researchers and the affiliated institution. As Vehovar and Manfreda (2008: 178–9) write:

> . . . computerized questionnaires using the graphical interface of the World Wide Web (WWW) offer advanced designing features, like question skips and filters, randomization of answers, control of answer validity, inclusion of multimedia elements, and many others.

Despite these advantages in design and distribution, there are a number of sampling issues facing the Internet survey (Couper, 2008; Tourangeau, 2004).

The objective in much survey sampling is to find information, and reach conclusions, representative of some larger population. While some argue that the census is the only truly reliable way of achieving this outcome, surveying an entire population is an extremely resource-intensive exercise (Andrews, Nonneck and Preece, 2003), and usually well beyond the capacity of the average researcher. To avoid the high costs and slow data collection associated with conducting a census, surveys can quickly and cheaply estimate aspects of a whole population by collecting data from a representative sample drawn from the population. Probability sampling methods, generally based on the idea that every individual in a population has an equal chance of being selected in the sample, offer a way of generating unbiased descriptions about an entire population. As an ideal, however, probability sampling methods face the inherent biases of Internet user populations.

The bias of access and self-selection renders the Internet problematic as a means of generating a representative sample. While recent studies point to a shrinking 'digital divide', access to the Internet remains stratified by class, race and gender (Murthy, 2008). In a study of social stratification and the digital divide in the United States, for example, Wilson, Wallin and Reiser (2003) reported that African American respondents were less likely to have a computer and to be connected to the Internet than white respondents. In Brazil, Soong (2004) reported socio-economic level as a factor strongly influencing Internet access. He argues that while the digital divide may be shrinking in advanced Internet countries like the USA due to lower costs and higher educational opportunities, the extent to which Internet penetration will be the same across the entire population in Brazil is far more problematic. In a study of gender and cultural differences on the Internet, Li and Kirkup (2007) found gender in both China and the UK to be a significant factor in computer usage. They reported that male students in both countries were more likely to have positive attitudes towards the Internet, spend more time on the Internet and use the Internet more extensively (Li and Kirkup, 2007: 313). At present, says Couper (2001: 467), '. . . coverage error presents the biggest threat to representativeness of sample surveys conducted via the Internet'.

To some extent, sampling bias might be overcome by clearly identifying the Internet population being studied. For example, Hewson and Laurent (2008) establish a sampling frame by identifying and listing all the email addresses of a population from which a random or cluster sample could be drawn. Nevertheless, they note how problems of representation can still arise even when the target population is operationally defined in this way. For example, the transient nature of the Internet can see one Internet user with multiple email accounts. Moreover, software – installed on some computers but not others – that automatically filters incoming emails with the aim of redirecting unsolicited bulk messages away from a user's inbox makes for an inconsistent delivery system. Such conditions make it impossible to know if the sample emerging from the frame of listed email addresses is comprehensive or accurate. 'At present', say Hewson and Laurent (2008: 66), 'probability sampling on the Internet is not very feasible'. Until the virtual environment can be managed to ensure all email invitations are received and checked, giving every member within a sampling frame an equal chance of participation, true probability sampling on the Internet remains difficult to achieve.

The most common sampling technique for quantitative surveys on the Internet is not representative. Nonprobability samples such as the 'volunteer opportunity sample' can be created when an invitation to participate is posted '. . . to newsgroups, mailing lists or on webpages' (Hewson and Laurent, 2008: 66). In this situation, the sample selected may or may not be representative of the target population, making any attempt at generalisation difficult, and in need of qualification. Couper (2001) identifies entertainment, self-selection and volunteer surveys as three types of survey commonly used on the Internet that make use of nonprobability – or volunteer opportunity – sampling.

Entertainment surveys are not true social science research, being, in most cases, merely opinion polls conducted by media outlets. Fortunately, they claim to reveal no more than the views of those who participate. Unlike the entertainment survey, however, some designers of self-selected web surveys claim findings to be representative of a target population. Couper (2001: 482) argues that it is hard to support such claims in the absence of restrictions on survey access and the possibility of multiple completions. In contrast to the entertainment and self-selected survey, voluntary panels do restrict survey access. The call for volunteers posted on popular websites creates, in the first instance, a self-selected sample as a group of potential respondents. Demographic information provided by volunteers can then be matched against predetermined criteria for the purpose of selecting an online survey panel. Despite greater control over access and selection, however, members of a voluntary panel, like respondents to the entertainment and self-selected survey, come from an unknown source. This means that trawling for research participants by posting invitations to newsgroups, mailing lists or advertising on webpages produces a sample whose relationship to some larger population is unknown, making generalisation problematic. In addition, response rates and response bias cannot be measured.

Sampling offline may overcome this problem. In doing so, however, Hewson and Laurent (2008) note that many of the benefits of Internet research such as speed and access to geographically diverse populations may be lost. Thus the decision as to whether or not to use the Internet as a tool for the collection of quantitative data needs to be made after weighing the advantages (for example, saving time and money and the potential to access geographically and socially diverse groups) against the disadvantages (for example, the drawbacks associated with sampling and the need for greater computing skills and more equipment) in the light of the aims of the study.

Collecting qualitative data

13.4 The Internet can be used for collecting qualitative data. For example, one-on-one interviewing and focus group interviewing are important methods of qualitative data collection that can be undertaken synchronously or asynchronously, using the communication capabilities of the Internet such as chat rooms, email (and email services such as group mail and listserver), MOOs (multi-user domains oriented) or MUDs (multi-user domains). Email, for example, provides a cheap, fast and modern form of asynchronous communication (Gaiser and Schreiner, 2009). It is 'one of the most widely used Internet-mediated methodologies to date' (O'Connor, Madge, Shaw and Wellens, 2008).

The asynchronous nature of email offers room for reflection. Prior to submitting a posting, a participant has ample time to reflect and, if necessary, reconsider or consult. This extended timescale can result in more thoughtful and detailed responses. Respondents living in different time zones can read and respond to questions at times convenient to them. Those with less proficient keyboard skills and those with physical or psychological impairments can have more time to think and type outside the pressure and stress of real-time interaction. An asynchronous approach, however, runs the risk of data loss when too much time curtails the flow and spontaneity of the exchange. It can lose 'the impulse response' or 'Freudian slips' capable of generating useful insights (Gaiser and Schreiner, 2009: 51). While the in-depth nature of a thoughtful detailed posting may compensate for this loss, it does not make up for the possible loss of participants. The asynchronous nature of email postings makes it easier for a participant simply to stop responding. To reduce this possibility of withdrawal, Gaiser and Schreiner (2009) advise researchers to manage expectations. In doing so, researchers need to scope interviews and focus group sessions in such a way that time commitments and the number of topics to be covered are made explicit to potential participants at the outset.

The online experience of a synchronous approach to interviewing and focus group sessions removes the delays of the asynchronous exchange, making it more like the traditional face-to-face interaction. The immediacy of synchronous exchanges offers other advantages. It allows focus group members to interact with one another directly in real time. Participants have less time to 'doctor' responses in an effort to make them more socially desirable or acceptable, allowing for more candid, honest and authentic comments to emerge. On the other hand, however, the fast pace of an exchange can make responses disjointed. Comments and questions can be posted before a reply to a previous message is received, making the final transcript difficult to interpret. The pressure to contribute in real time can make for reponses which are both less serious and less detailed (Hewson and Laurent, 2008). In addition, the online synchronous interview or focus group session is more complicated to set up. It can involve either the use of conferencing software or chatroom access. For conferencing, researchers may have to arrange access to the appropriate software for participants to download and install on their computer.

Other challenges face both asynchronous and synchronous approaches to collecting qualitative data. For example, participants may choose to leave an online interview or focus group session should the purpose of the research become lost, blurred or less salient. A wandering discussion is likely to generate suspicion rather than trust in the purpose of the study, leaving participants uneasy and more likely to withdraw. This can arise using either an asynchronous or a synchronous approach, especially if the researcher sees the technology as facilitating a self-functioning process. While good management and facilitation help to retain research participants, and generate a large volume of data, the lack of a personal presence in individual and focus group interview sessions presents a significant challenge to collecting qualitative data using the Internet.

The Internet removes a personal presence from interviewing by reducing communications to text only. The absence of facial expressions, head nodding, eye contact, body language, pauses, pitch, 'umms and arhhs', 'uh-huhs', prompts and so on can reduce data gathering to an emotionally sterile exchange. In an emotionally barren environment, what participants truly think and feel about a topic may become harder to pin down. Critical expressions that create meaning are lost to the qualitative researcher. To compensate, Hewson and Laurent (2008) suggest creating a richer communication environment by using audio/visual software. For example, *Skype* allows participants to hear and see one another. Taking this approach, however, researchers can run into technical problems. The quality of the data collected can be reduced due to low bandwidth or heavy Internet traffic. Alternatively, Gaiser and Schreiner (2009) advise researchers to make use of online visual and verbal cues by the insertion of encouraging mood texts [sigh, brilliant, annoyed], emoticons [J] and punctuation [??, !!!, **WHAT**] to indicate excitement, pleasure, disappointment, and so on. Building rapport in the absence of a personal presence, however, calls for different strategies. Although little is known about building rapport online, Hewson and Laurant (2008) point to some evidence that suggests the use of self-disclosure and ice-breaker exercises as introductory 'get-to-know-you' techniques can be helpful. However, building rapport in this way may reduce participants' perception of anonymity and privacy, making them less willing to be forthright and outspoken about themselves and their views (Hewson and Laurent, 2008).

Observation has also been a prominent social science data collection method. Like individual and group interviews, observing human behaviour by means of the Internet makes use of forums and social networking sites, but in a different way (Hewson and Laurent, 2008). While the interviewer uses the Internet to interact, the observer seeks to be less obtrusive. The Internet is a good tool for social researchers interested in collecting qualitative data in this non-reactive way. A rich and abundant display of ephemeral minutiae of daily life online can be made easily amenable to research by logging and storing it so that it can be searched and analysed at a later date (Hewson and Laurent, 2008). Since the advent of Web 2.0, observing any aspect of social life existing somewhere online becomes feasible.

The term 'Web 2.0' is best thought of as a changing relationship rather than any significant change in technology. Since the turn of the century there has been a clear change in the way we think about and use the Internet. Before this time, the Internet was seen primarily as a source of information. It was treated like a library for the storage and retrieval of electronic information. The ordinary Internet user was mostly a passive browser, consuming content. Metaphorically, the relationship was a business one with the Internet user as customer and the software developer as supplier. The term 'Web 2.0' signalled the emergence of a more interactive phase. At this point, the role of Internet users changed from passive consumers to active creators of content. Internet users were now able to interact and collaborate with other users to create their own content. Common Web 2.0 applications today such as Wikis, blogs, MySpace, Facebook, twitter and so on allow everyday people to work, play and talk with lots of other people online. For example, two years after its public launch in September 2006, Facebook alone had grown to more than 7.5 million members (Murthy, 2008). These days, Internet users are doing more and more things online:

> More people, and a more diverse range of people, are now online, doing a wider array of things, including participating in discussion forums and building web sites as they were in 2000, but also using social networking sites, uploading their photographs and videos, leaving their opinions via tagging, commenting and reviewing and leaving electronic traces of their actions in logs of server activity, search engine usage and the like. (Hine, 2011: 1–2)

According to Hine (2011), researchers interested in the unobtrusive nature of observation as a non-reactive approach to data collection are starting to make more and more use of the growing amount of online activity. She points to recent studies by a range of researchers collecting data from an online health forum, email messages sent to a health site, MySpace home pages, twitter messages and the headings of messages exchanged by Facebook users. Essentially, observations can be undertaken in any number of online spaces from simple text-based environments to 3D graphic representations such as MUDs (Multi-user Dungeons), MOOs (Multi-user Object Oriented) and MMORPGs (Massive multi-player online role-playing games). The sheer 'scope for unobtrusive observation . . . in a way not previously possible, so effectively using offline methods' is a key advantage attracting greater interest in online observation (Hewson and Laurent, 2008: 70). Prior to taking advantage of these types of observation opportunities, the online observer needs to weigh up the advantages and disadvantages of different observation strategies.

Similar to synchronous or asynchronous interviews, online observations can be conducted in real or non-real time. The extent to which observing in real time rather than non-real time is beneficial will depend on the aims of the research. The greater the demand for contextual information, the more likely the presence of an observer taking field notes in real time will prove beneficial. Computer logs of online activity, for example, can lose or confuse the temporal context. Despite advantages such as availability and easy access, Hewson and Laurent (2008) point out that gaps can occur in archived material. In addition to a lack of demographic information, computer logs can go missing, become corrupt or go out of sequence in whole or in part. Moreover, sorting out problems, if this is possible, can require a high degree of technical expertise. The following exchange on stackoverflow (2009, online) illustrates this issue:

I've got an apache web server, and when a certain user accesses a certain page I get a log line who's timestamp is out of sync.

Sample output:

```
IP1 - - [22/Jun/2009:12:20:40 +0000] "GET URL1" 200 3490 "REFERRING_URL1" "Mozilla/4.0 (co

IP2 - - [22/Jun/2009:12:11:47 +0000] "GET URL2" 200 17453 "-" "Mozilla/5.0 (Macintosh; U;

IP1 - - [22/Jun/2009:12:20:41 +0000] "GET URL3" 200 889 "REFERRING_URL2" "Mozilla/4.0 (com
```

(I've anonymised requesting Ips – Ip1, Ip2 and Ip3, requested URLs – URL2 and URL3, and the two referrer URLs)

As can be seen the three lines (which appeared in the log in this order), are out of sync. This only happens when IP2 requests URL2 – all other logs seem normal.

Any ideas?

The logs are written when the request is completed, so early long requests may be written after late short ones. Add the %D to tour logFormat definition to see the time taken to serve the request, in microseconds.

Maybe you're doing some kind of COMET requests?

My first thought is that the log only records the time at which the request finished? So may be IP1's request took a while to complete but arrived before IP2's. Only requests I know that behave that way are AJAXey comet requests.
Probably not the correct answer, but maybe a clue.

Edit:http://www.linuxquestions.org/questions/linux-networking-3/apache-log-entries-order-516354/ confirms that the time in the log includes the time required to transfer the content to the browser.

In conventional ethnographic work, the presence of a researcher taking field notes in real time makes the task of maintaining covert observations more difficult. The physical presence of the observer means there is always the possibility that those being observed may approach and ask, 'What are you doing?' The absence of a physical presence, however, now means that conducting unobtrusive surveillance in cyberspace is no longer a matter of chance, but one of choice in research design.

Ethnographers have often valued the benefits of a covert approach to research (Murthy, 2008), on the grounds that covert participation holds the promise of producing data that is more candid and honest. Thus Seale, Charteris-Black, MacFarlane and McPherson (2010) note how the feeling of an observer-free zone makes participants unusually frank and less concerned about meeting the perceived expectations of a researcher. However 'covert' for ethnographic observation is not synonymous with 'absent'. Ethnographic observation has typically involved participation in the situation being studied. Conventionally, ethnographically describing and interpreting cultural behaviour requires fieldwork. 'Ethnography unites both process and product, *fieldwork* and written text', says Schwandt (2001: 80, emphasis in the original). 'Fieldwork, undertaken as participant observation, is the process by which the ethnographer comes to know a culture; the ethnographic text is how culture is portrayed.' According to this definition, the lack of immersion in the cultural life of an online community through active participation means that activities such as simply reading emails or other archived material would not qualify as ethnographic observation. Traditionally, simply viewing how a culture portrays itself is not enough. On the contrary, discovering the meaning of cultural artefacts and symbolic behaviour requires the ethnographer to become actively engaged in cultural life. There are others, however, who argue that ethnographers need to rethink this conventional view of what constitutes the research setting and appropriate methods of data collection if they are to keep up with the rapid growth of online technologies such as instant messaging, tweets and blogs as cultural artefacts (Garcia, Standlee, Bechkoff and Cui, 2009). This move towards a text-based approach makes ethnographic observation as a form of online qualitative data collection look more and more like document analysis.

Online data for document analysis can be either readily available or solicited. The sheer volume of readily available material such as policy statements, news articles, blogs, wikis, online diaries, Youtube clips, photographs, and so on, is staggering. Accessing readily available material resembles the covert online observation discussed above. In contrast, soliciting material requires researchers to take an overt approach. For example, researchers can ask research participants to keep electronic diaries over a period of time before making them available for analysis. However, observation and documentary analysis represent different ways this material can be of interest. The online ethnographer sees this information as a proxy for the lived experience of those who produced it, whereas the document analyst treats the same material not as a window to a culture beyond but as a performance in its own right. Whether for observation or document analysis however, the quick and easy access to this large volume of material does not make its availability for research axiomatic (Hine, 2011). In cases where information and interactions are private in nature, access is available only on the basis of informed consent. This raises the question of ethical issues in research use of the Internet.

Ethical issues

13.5 A comprehensive treatment of ethical issues in research use of the Internet is beyond the scope of this section. Rather than trying to cover all aspects, therefore, the section concentrates on the important issues of autonomy, beneficence and fairness towards people participating in research conducted over the Internet. The legal issues associated with intellectual property, ownership and authorship are not addressed. For those interested in legal questions such as intellectual property rights and the Internet, see Charlesworth (2008). Against this background, the differences between ethics for Internet and conventional research, and what this means for online research design, are addressed.

The ethical issues facing the engagement of human participants in Internet research are not dissimilar to those confronting conventional research (Elgesem, 2002). The need to prevent harm and ensure fairness through practices of confidentiality and informed consent are as important to online researchers as they are to offline researchers. We cannot simply assume, however, that traditional approaches to gaining informed consent and protecting research participants' privacy will prove effective in an online setting (Gaiser and Schreiner, 2009). For example, Buchanan and Zimmer (2012, online) emphasise the number of ethical challenges for Internet research with the following list of questions:

> What ethical obligations do researchers have to protect the privacy of subjects engaging in activities in 'public' Internet spaces? How is confidentiality or anonymity assured online? How is and should informed consent be obtained online? How should research on minors be conducted, and how do you prove a subject is not a minor? Is deception (pretending to be someone you are not, withholding identifiable information, etc.) online a norm or a harm? How is 'harm' possible to someone existing in an online space?

Specific professional and research association guidelines addressing these types of questions for online research are rare. However, the growing body of literature on Internet research (Gaiser and Schreiner, 2009) provides helpful advice when considering such ethical questions.

While Internet research should be no more harmful to research participants than face-to-face methods (Eynon et al., 2008), the nature of the Internet makes assessing the potential for harm more complicated. Unlike a face-to-face experience, a researcher conducting a survey or interview over the Internet cannot call on the immediacy of visual cues to determine the impact of questions or processes on participants. For example, the extent to which a comment by a focus group participant intimidates, or compromises the dignity of, other participants can be harder to judge. To address this problem, Eynon et al. (2008: 27) recommend incorporating into the research design such strategies as 'building good rapport with participants, establishing "netiquette" in group discussions (Mann and Stewart, 2000), and providing participants with an easy way to leave the study' (Hewson et al., 2003; Nosek et al., 2002). Nevertheless, the absence of immediate visual feedback can make these strategies difficult to implement. This means that the complicated nature of ethical obligations for Internet research requires more effort by the researcher.

Adding to the challenge of a virtual environment is the way the Internet renders permeable the conventional division between public and private. In cyberspace, the conventional understanding that 'what is available to everyone' is public becomes extremely porous. On the surface, the ethical position here appears straightforward. As an open space, everything online is publicly available, and therefore no privacy issues requiring ethical consideration arise. This conventional position, however, fails to appreciate the perception of privacy created by different types of Internet activities.

The Internet is not a single purpose device but a forum for multiple activities and interactions. It provides space for discussion about any topic at an individual, community or global level. It is also a space in which to play games, meet others, form relationships, do business, publish and store ideas, information, photographs, and so on. The Internet caters for an extremely diverse range of information, and of user expectations. Within this range, information stored and transmitted by means of the Internet can be of a private nature. Email correspondence, for example, can transmit sensitive information about personal or business matters. In general, email users would expect their correspondence to remain private – that is, not to be accessed and used by a third party without their express permission. Similarly, those posting on sites with access limitations such as an Internet dating service would expect use of their personal details to be limited according to guidelines agreed to when signing up for log-on rights.

Another clear example of the ethical challenges presented by the Internet is provided by chat rooms. Anyone interested in a discussion topic can go online and join the conversation. The topic and what participants have to say about it clearly resides within the public domain. However, the researcher, invisible to other Internet users, can 'lurk' outside chat rooms, 'eavesdropping' on conversations. Terms such as 'lurk' and 'eavesdrop' clearly indicate the questionable ethical nature of behaviours within these forums not directed towards furthering the interests and intentions of those posting information. The metaphors of voyeur and parasite loom large in this construction as researchers collect material of interest by feeding off an unwitting Internet host. While using a public space, however, not all Internet users see themselves as being on public display or making public statements for the consumption of others with a different agenda.

While public information can be disclosed, social science researchers are not at liberty to expose an individual's private details. The researcher must clearly distinguish between what constitutes public and private information in order to protect the privacy of research participants. However, the Internet allows the individual to post personal thoughts as part of the social experience, even though it is virtual in nature. Thus the blurred line separating public and private on the Internet makes the ethics of protecting privacy less clear.

A major ethical question for the researcher concerns the risk of harm to participants should online behaviours, postings, emails, and so on be used in ways for which they were not intended. The notion of 'informed consent' is a common feature of conventional social science research design, aimed at addressing this risk by respecting the autonomy of potential participants. The autonomy of potential participants means that choice is a fundamental principle of the consent process. By specifying aims and risks in a way that makes explicit the voluntary nature of the agreement to participate and the ability to withdraw at any time, potential participants are free to choose whether or not to take part in the study. The process of gaining true, actual 'informed consent', however, poses a challenge when it comes to the question of a participant's understanding and vulnerability in Internet research.

The virtual and ephemeral nature of the Internet complicates the process of gaining informed consent. In contrast to face-to-face research, the Internet makes it harder to judge a participant's understanding in terms of the extent to which the consent gained is truly informed. It is also difficult to determine vulnerability due to doubts surrounding the identity of who is, in reality, consenting. The interpersonal nature of the offline experience provides for the visual cues and verbal interplay of asking questions and seeking further clarification that enables the researcher to gauge the level of understanding of potential participants. As Eynon et al. (2008: 29) explain, 'the researcher can discuss the research with the participant, assess whether the individual fully understands the implications of the research and evaluate whether they are freely entering into the study'. Online research, however, calls for other strategies to determine the extent to which an individual appreciates the demands of participation.

Eynon et al. (2008) point to three online approaches researchers can use to help ensure that participants understand the demands of a proposed study. The first aims to increase the readability of consent forms. They suggest that this can be done by using headings and subheadings, highlighting key points with colour, bolding and underlining, limiting the amount of text and avoiding the use of technical terms and jargon. In the second, awareness of expectations and clarification of concerns can be increased through email exchanges. An electronic discussion of this nature, however, would call for extensive email exchanges which might test the good will and patience of potential participants, thereby increasing the chance of drop-out. Rather than generating a long and protracted email discussion, and as a third approach, researchers can develop a quiz to check participants' understanding. Like the email discussion, however, this strategy places an additional demand on potential participants, increasing the likelihood of early withdrawal. Despite the risk of premature departure, online efforts to gain informed consent are seen as less coercive. When the social pressure of personal contact is missing, participants tend to feel less compelled to agree and more at ease should they decide to pull out of the study. While informed consent demands every necessary precaution be taken to ensure participants are fully aware of what is expected of them, the Internet researcher also faces the problem of identity.

The online environment makes it difficult to verify the identity of potential participants. The question as to who is giving consent to participate in the research is harder to determine. The openness of the Internet means research samples will not be limited to those who are legally, psychologically or culturally capable of giving consent. The possibility that an online sample will contain vulnerable groups such as children, people with mental disorders and the aged is very real (Eynon et al., 2008). In studies where the potential risk to vulnerable groups is extremely low, the need to verify identities is not critical. When the risk is high, however, efforts to verify identities need to be an essential part of the recruitment process. Drawing on the work of Pittenger (2003), Nosek et al. (2002) and Kraut et al. (2004), Eynon et al. (2008: 29) point to the following strategies to help reduce the likelihood of exposing vulnerable groups to harm:

- send specific invitations to known adult participants to access a password-controlled site;
- design advertising material unlikely to attract or interest young people; and
- ask for information that only adults would have such as credit card information.

After gaining informed consent, researchers have the ethical obligation of ensuring confidentiality is not breached through the misuse of the data collected.

The level of responsibility for ensuring confidentiality depends on the sensitivity of the data. More sensitive topics require greater effort to protect the data from any unauthorised access during transmission and storage. Banal topics, of course, involving the collection of readily available information of a non-personal nature, do not require the same level of security. The blurred line between public and private, however, can make the distinction between sensitive and banal data difficult to determine. Regardless of how pedestrian the research topic, the nature of the Internet remains the same. The feeling of privacy conjured by the solitude of certain Internet exchanges can incite participants to proffer details of a sensitive or personal quality. In response, researchers need to respect participants' perceptions of privacy by ensuring the confidentiality of the data collected.

The promise of confidentiality requires the researcher to ensure the security of data transmission and storage. To secure data during transmission, Eynon et al. (2008) suggest encryption, labelling and separation. The security of communications by encryption is possible by using the cryptographic protocols of Secure Sockets Layer (SSL) and the more recent Transport Layer Security (TLS). A less technical approach is to apply unique codes as labels to render data meaningless to others. A third strategy suggests separating data during transmission, making it impossible for others to link private information to the identities of particular individuals. For data stored on servers connected to the Internet, the use of strong passwords is advisable for minimising the risk of a security breach (Gaiser and Schreiner, 2009). Secure storage, however, should not be limited to the use of passwords. In addition, it is advisable to store data offline on a separate localised data server, portable computer and external disk or on storage devices such as a USB drive or CD.

Chapter summary

- The Internet can be seen as both a location and a tool for research. This chapter concentrates on the Internet as a research tool, and considers its use in the areas of finding and accessing relevant literature, collecting quantitative data and collecting qualitative data. It also discusses ethical issues that emerge when using the Internet as a research tool.
- Search tools for finding and accessing research literature through the Internet can be divided into five categories – traditional library catalogue, bibliographic databases, electronic databases, open access databases, Internet subject gateways and search engines.
- In collecting quantitative data, there are two broad types of Internet surveys – client-side surveys, where the survey is executed on a respondent's machine, and server-side surveys, where the survey is executed on the survey organisation's Web server. The two approaches have different strengths and weaknesses, which need analysis by the researcher. Sampling issues arise when using the Internet for survey sampling, and true probability sampling may not yet be possible.
- In collecting qualitative data, both one-to-one interviewing and focus group interviewing are possible on the Internet. Similarly, observation is possible, both in a simple text-based environment and in a graphic 3D environment, and its unobtrusive nature appeals, especially for ethnographically oriented studies. But careful analysis of all of these methods of collecting data using the Internet is needed, in order to understand fully the nature of the data collected in this way.
- The ethical issues involved in Internet-based research are not dissimilar to those faced in traditional research, but traditional approaches may not prove effective in an online setting. The complicated nature of ethical obligations for Internet research typically requires more effort by the researcher.
- Examples of complications with ethical consequences in the online setting are the lack of clarity in the distinction between the private and public domains, the gaining of informed consent, and the questions of identity and the storage of data. The literature is beginning to provide strategies for dealing with such complications.

KEY TERMS

Internet: a network connecting computer-based websites in standardised ways to form the World Wide Web.

World-wide-web: a system of interlinked websites on the Internet commonly known as 'the web'.

Internet research: the use of the Internet as a tool for conducting research in virtual or actual locations.

Cyberspace: a space created by the Internet in which digital objects exist.

Email: a system of communication involving the composing, sending, storing and receiving of messages using the Internet.

Web 2.0: a relationship in which Internet users take an active role by interacting and collaborating with other users through applications such as Wikis, blogs, MySpace, Facebook, twitter and so on to create online content.

Listservers: software applications that allow a mail service provider to control who can read and post to an email list.

Synchronous: communications using the Internet that appear directly on a recipient's computer.

Asynchronous: communications using the Internet that are subject to delays in transmission.

Search engine: a mechanical program that creates a database by matching keywords to content stored on the Internet and then organises and displays the results in a readily accessible way.

Subject gateway: a database containing web resources that have been manually selected, evaluated and checked for quality by subject experts.

Virtual environments: three systems on the Internet that allow users to interact using text or three-dimensional graphics. The original system, MUDs (Multi-User Dungeons), is a simple text-based environment that allows players to interact one at a time. The next generation, MOOs (Multi-user Object Oriented), is a text-based environment which allows more than one player to talk at one time as well as display emotions and manipulate objects. The latest generation, MMORPGs (Massive multi-player online RPG), is a graphics-based environment in which multiple players can interact using text and personally designed three-dimensional images.

Chat rooms: any form of technology allowing participants to chat individually (instant messaging) or in groups (online forums and virtual environments) in real time.

Exercises and study questions

1. Select a topic that you are interested in researching. Locate an online computer database and search for the literature on this topic. Continue to explore different databases until you identify an article that closely resembles your chosen topic.
2. Consider one of the following ethical dilemmas you might face when conducting research using the Internet. Describe how you would address the situation.

   - A participant in an online focus group session, conducted using asynchronous email exchanges, posts a comment in the form of a racist joke that clearly offends another group member. What do you do? What could you do prior to conducting the focus group session in an effort to prevent this type of situation arising?
   - You collect data for a project from several postings listed on an Internet dating site. A number of the postings by one participant detail her personal hopes and desires to form a long and lasting relationship with a suitable respondent. Although the postings clearly reflect your research focus and need to be included in the final written report of your project, you have not gained informed consent from the person who posted this information. What do you do?

3. In contrast to research conducted offline, the virtual nature of the Internet complicates the process of gaining informed consent. Discuss three approaches a researcher can undertake when interacting with potential participants online in an effort to ensure they fully understand the demands of a proposed study.

4. Locate an Internet research project reported in an academic journal (consider using the results of exercise 1 above). Review the online approach and list any issues that were identified.

5. Couper (2008) explains how surveys can be executed in two ways over the Internet – client-side when the survey is executed on the respondent's machine, and server-side when it is executed on the organisation's or researcher's Web server. Discuss the advantages and disadvantages of these approaches to collecting survey data.

6. The objective in most survey sampling is to find information, and reach conclusions, representative of some larger population. Discuss the difficulties associated with generating a probability sample when conducting research using the Internet and how these might be resolved.

7. List the different ways, together with their advantages and disadvantages, of conducting an interview over the Internet.

8. Discuss the advantages and disadvantages of using email as an asynchronous approach for collecting interview data online.

Further reading

Andrews, D., Nonneck, B. and Preece, J. (2003) 'Conducting research on the Internet: Online survey design, development and implementation guidelines', *International Journal of Human-Computer Interaction*, 16(2), 185–210.

Couper, M. (2008) 'Technology trends in survey data collection', *Social Science Computer Review*, 23(4), 486–501. Retrieved from SAGE Journals Online.

Eynon, R., Fry, J. and Schroeder, R. (2008) 'The ethics of Internet research', in N. Fielding, R. Lee and G. Blank (eds), *The Sage handbook of online research methods* (pp. 42–57). London: SAGE.

Lee, R., Fielding, N. and Blank, G. (2008) *The Sage handbook of online research methods*. London: SAGE.

Gaiser, T. and Schreiner, A. (2009) *A guide to conducting online research*. London: SAGE.

Garcia, A., Standlee, A., Bechkoff, J. and Cui, Y. (2009) 'Ethnographic approaches to the Internet and computer-mediated communication', *Journal of Contemporary Ethnography*, 38(1), 52–84. Retrieved from SAGE Journals Online.

Hewson, C. and Laurent, D. (2008) 'Research design and tools for Internet research', in N. Fielding, R. Lee and G. Blank (eds), *The Sage handbook of online research methods* (pp. 58–78). London: SAGE.

Hine, C. (2011) 'Internet research and unobtrusive methods', *Social Research Update*, 16, pp. 1–4. Retrieved from http://sru.soc.surrey.ac.uk/SRU61.pdf

Mann, C. and Stewart, F. (2000) *Internet communication and qualitative research*. London: SAGE.

Murthy, D. (2008) 'Digital ethnography: An examination of the use of new technologies for social research', *Sociology*, 42(5), 837–855. Retrieved from SAGE Journals Online.

O'Connor, H., Madge, C., Shaw, R. and Wellens, J. (2008) 'Internet-based interviewing', in N. Fielding, R. Lee and G. Blank (eds), *The Sage handbook of online research methods* (pp. 42–57). London: SAGE.

Ridley, D. (2008) *The literature review: A step by step guide for students.* London: SAGE.

Vehovar, V. and Manfreda, K. (2008) 'Overview: Online surveys', in N. Fielding, R. Lee and G. Blank (eds), *The Sage handbook of online research methods* (pp. 177–194). London: SAGE.

fourteen
MIXED METHODS AND EVALUATION

After studying this chapter you should be able to:

- Define mixed methods research and describe its development
- State the fundamental principle of mixed methods research
- State the basic idea of pragmatism and show its significance for mixed methods research
- Discuss the main strengths and weaknesses of qualitative and quantitative research
- Describe the three dimensions involved in combining qualitative and quantitative approaches
- Describe briefly the four main mixed methods designs (triangulation, embedded, explanatory, exploratory)
- Describe and explain what is meant by disciplined inquiry
- Explain why the critical evaluation of research is necessary and important
- List and explain important questions for evaluating a piece of research

In this book we have used the distinction between qualitative and quantitative research as a way of organising and presenting the methodological foundation for empirical research. I believe it is important for the social science researcher today to have an understanding of both, and especially of the common logic that drives the two approaches. As a way of stressing similarities in the underlying logic, we have dealt with qualitative and quantitative research under the same main headings of design, data collection and data analysis. I believe it is also important for the researcher today to understand the growing popularity of combining the two approaches, whether in a single study or a series of studies. Therefore the first part of this chapter gives an overview of the development of mixed methods, and of the main designs for use in mixed methods research. The second part presents general evaluative criteria for assessing any type of empirical research.

Mixed methods research is empirical research that involves the collection and analysis of both qualitative and quantitative data. In mixed methods research, qualitative and quantitative methods and data are mixed, or combined in some way. A single study that combines qualitative and quantitative data is mixed methods, but the term can also refer to a programme of several studies combining both types of data.

This definition is straightforward, and it is useful in simplifying and clarifying terminology on this topic, which has sometimes been confusing in the research methodology literature. In the development of mixed methods research, the language used to describe this design has not always been precise and consistent. As Tashakkori and Teddlie (2003a: 212) and Creswell and Plano Clark (2007: 5–6) note, such terms as 'multimethod', 'integrated', 'blended' and 'combined' have been used, along with 'multitrait-multimethod research', 'methodological triangulation', 'multimethodological research' and 'mixed model research'. The publication of *The Handbook of Mixed Methods in Social and Behavioral Research* (Tashakkori and Teddlie, 2003a) increased greatly the precision, visibility and recognition of the term 'mixed methods', urging the use of 'mixed' as an umbrella term to cover the multifaceted procedures of combining, integrating and linking the different types of methods and data. Going further, Creswell and Plano Clark (2007: 6) argue that the consistent and systematic use of the term 'mixed methods' to describe research that combines qualitative and quantitative approaches, methods and data will encourage the research community to see mixed methods research as distinct, and increasingly used by researchers.

History of mixed methods

14.1 As noted in earlier chapters, the historical dominance of quantitative methods in social science research was followed in the 30 or so years after about 1970 by the emergence of qualitative methods into the mainstream, and by their increased acceptance. This did not happen smoothly, producing the paradigm wars, which were characterised by a strong 'either/or' approach to matters of method. During this period, very many researchers were either quantitative or qualitative, and the idea of combining or mixing the two types of methods and data was not popular. In the 1990s, however, researchers began to see past the either/or thinking of the paradigm wars, and began to develop the groundwork for mixed methods designs. Since the turn of the century, there has been a growth of interest in mixed methods research, including the advocacy of mixed methods research as a separate design in its own right. There are now numerous indicators of the current interest in mixed methods research. Examples are the publication of an increasing number of journal articles reporting mixed methods research, the launching in 2005 of the *Journal of Mixed Methods Research*, and the promotion of international meetings devoted to mixed methods research (Creswell and Plano Clark, 2007: 16–18).

This methodological history of social science research is conveniently summarised by describing:

- the dominance of quantitative methods as wave 1;
- the emergence of qualitative methods as wave 2;
- the growth of mixed methods as wave 3.

Rationale for mixed methods

14.2 The fundamental rationale behind mixed methods research is that we can often learn more about our research topic if we can combine the strengths of qualitative research with the strengths of quantitative research while compensating at the same time for the weaknesses of each method. This has been called the *fundamental principle of mixed methods research* (Johnson and Onwuegbuzie, 2004: 18):

Combine the methods in a way that achieves complementary strengths and non-overlapping weaknesses.

Once it is recognised that both quantitative and qualitative methods have their strengths and their weaknesses, it becomes easy to see the logic of this principle. These different strengths and weaknesses have been indicated in numerous places throughout this book. Thus, for example, quantitative research brings the strengths of conceptualising variables, profiling dimensions, tracing trends and relationships, formalising comparisons and using large and perhaps representative samples. On the other hand, qualitative research brings the strengths of sensitivity to meaning and to context, local groundedness, the in-depth study of smaller samples, and great methodological flexibility which enhances the ability to study process and change. Considerations such as these imply that qualitative methods can be strong in those areas where quantitative methods are weak, and similarly that quantitative methods can be strong in those areas where qualitative methods are weak. Combining the two methods therefore offers the possibility of combining these two sets of strengths, and compensating for the weaknesses. The Miles and Huberman comparison between variables and cases, shown later in this chapter, illustrates the same principle.

There is a strong logic to this underlying rationale. However, for mixed methods to develop and grow in popularity in research required the field of research methods to move past the either/or methodological thinking of the paradigm wars period. In addition to acknowledgement and appreciation of the strengths and weaknesses of the two approaches, this development and growth also required:

- moving away from a preoccupation with apparently irreconcilable paradigms, and a willingness to embrace multiple paradigms;
- the subsequent emergence of pragmatism as the underlying philosophical approach, with stress on the idea that the methods used in research should be determined by the questions asked;
- appreciation of important similarities in the underlying logic of the qualitative and quantitative approaches, as different but potentially complementary forms of empirical inquiry.

Pragmatism is not the only philosophy or paradigm associated with mixed methods research, but it is the main one (Tashakkori and Teddlie, 2003b: 20–4; 2003c: 677–80). Pragmatism is a philosophical position with a substantial history (see, for example, Maxcy, 2003), and American philosophers such as Peirce, James, Dewey and George Herbert Mead were important in its early development. As such, it has many important features (Maxcy, 2003). But for present purposes, the essential idea of pragmatism is to reject the either/or choices and the metaphysical concepts associated with the paradigm wars, and to focus instead on 'what works' in getting research questions answered (Tashakkori and Teddlie, 2003b: 20–1; 2003c: 713). Two implications of this stand out.

The *first* is that the research question(s) is more important than, and logically prior to, either the method used or the paradigm underlying the method. *The second* is that specific decisions regarding the use of either qualitative methods, quantitative methods or mixed methods depend on the research question(s) being asked. These two implications are key aspects of the point of view about the logic of empirical research stressed earlier in this book, especially in Chapters 4 and 5. This point of view is summarised by saying that substantive issues come before methodological and paradigmatic issues. Detailed discussions of pragmatism in the context of mixed methods research can be found in Tashakkori and Teddlie (2003b) and in some of the chapters written by other contributors to the *Handbook of Mixed Methods in Social and Behavioral Research* (Tashakkori and Teddlie, 2003a).

With respect to the last of the three points shown above – about the important similarities in the qualitative and quantitative approaches – the first five chapters of this book (and Chapters 4 and 5 in particular) have laid out the logic of empirical research. These chapters have shown how this logic applies to both qualitative and quantitative research, and in so doing they have pointed to numerous similarities in the two approaches. Thus, the same basic model underlies both approaches, and the same main headings of design, data collection and data analysis apply to both. The similar way both approaches move across differing levels of abstraction has also been noted in Chapters 9 and 12. And there are still other similarities and overlaps to those already noted. For example, quantitative research is sometimes thought to be more concerned with the deductive testing of hypotheses and theories, whereas qualitative research is more concerned with exploring a topic, and with inductively generating hypotheses and theories. However, while this is often true, these stereotypes can be overdone. There is, overall, a correlation between the research approach (quantitative or qualitative) and the research purpose (for example, theory testing or theory generating), but this correlation is neither perfect nor necessary. While quantitative research may be mostly used for testing theory, it can also be used for exploring an area and for generating hypotheses and theory. Similarly, qualitative research can certainly be used for testing hypotheses and theories, even though it is the most favoured approach for theory generation. As Miles and Huberman (1994: 42) say: 'Both types of data can be productive for descriptive, reconnoitring, exploratory, inductive, opening up purposes. And both can be productive for explanatory, confirmatory, hypothesis-testing purposes.' We do not need to be restricted to stereotypes in our thinking about the purposes of the two approaches. Each approach can be used for various purposes.

Taking this point further, stereotyped distinctions between the two approaches can also be overdone. Hammersley (1992), in particular, argued some years ago that seven dichotomies typically used to differentiate qualitative and quantitative approaches are overdrawn. Five of the dichotomies he discusses bring together many of the points we have covered in previous chapters, and reflect some of the emphases of this book. They are:

- qualitative versus quantitative data;
- the investigation of natural versus artificial settings;
- a focus on meanings rather than behaviour;
- an inductive versus a deductive approach;
- the identification of cultural patterns as against seeking scientific laws.

For each of these, Hammersley argues that it is more a matter of a range of positions than a simple contrast, that a position on one does not necessarily imply a position on another, and that selection among these positions should depend more on the purposes and circumstances of the research than on philosophical considerations.

Each of these points (the similarity of logic, the overlap of purposes and the weakening of traditional dichotomies) blurs the sharpness of the qualitative–quantitative distinction, making the contrast between the two approaches less stark, and pointing to the possibility of combining them. This possibility is confirmed when we see variables as central in quantitative research and cases as central in qualitative research.

Basic characteristics of the two approaches: variables and cases

14.3 A good way to overview the central characteristics of the qualitative and quantitative approaches is to compare, as Huberman and Miles (1994: 435–6) do, variables and cases. It is also a good way to see the importance of the logic behind mixed methods.

14.3.1 A crucial distinction: variables and cases

Consider a typical study, one trying to predict the decision to attend college, with a sample of 300 adolescents and the following set of predictors: gender, socioeconomic status, parental expectations, school performance, peer support, and decision to attend college.

In a variable-oriented analysis, the six independent (or predictor) variables are intercorrelated and are used to predict – and account for variance in – the key dependent variable, 'decision to attend college'. This might show us that deciding to attend college is mainly influenced by school performance, with additional influences from parents' expectations and SES. We see how the variables as concepts are related, but we do not know the profile of any one individual.

In a case-oriented analysis, we might look more closely into a particular case, say, Case 005, who is female, middle-class, has parents with high expectations, and so on. These are, however, 'thin' measures. To do a genuine case analysis, we need to look at a full history of Case 005: Nynke van der Molen, whose mother trained as a social worker but is bitter over the fact that she never worked outside the home, and whose father wants Nynke to work in the family florist shop. Chronology is also important: two years ago, Nynke's closest friend decided to go to college, just before Nynke began work in a stable and just before Nynke's mother showed her her scrapbook from social work school. Nynke then decided to enrol in veterinary studies.

These and other data can be displayed in matrix form (see Miles, Huberman and Saldana, 2013), where the flow and configuration of events and reactions leading to Nynke's decision would come clear. It would also help to 'incarnate' what the predictors look like singly and how they interact collectively. This, in turn, would bring to the surface recurrent patterns, 'families' or 'clusters' or cases with characteristic configurations.

As Ragin (1987) notes, such a case-oriented approach looks at each entity, then teases out configurations *within* each case and subjects them to comparative analysis. In these comparisons (of a smaller number of cases), underlying similarities and systematic associations are sought out with regard to the main outcome variable. From there, a more explanatory model can be explicated, at least for the cases under study. Variable-oriented analysis in quantitative research is good for finding probabilistic relationships among variables in a large population, but has difficulties with causal complexities, or dealing with subsamples. Case-oriented analysis in qualitative research is good at finding specific, concrete, historically grounded patterns common to small sets of cases, but its findings remain particularistic, although several case writers speciously claim greater generality.

The quantitative approach conceptualises reality in terms of variables, and studies relationships between them. It rests on measurement, and therefore prestructures data, and usually also research questions, conceptual frameworks and design. Samples are typically larger than in qualitative studies, and generalisation through sampling is usually important. It does not see context as central, typically stripping data from their context, and it has well-developed and codified methods for data analysis. Its methods in general are more unidimensional and less variable than qualitative methods. It is therefore more easily replicable.

On the other hand, the qualitative approach deals more with cases. It is sensitive to context and process, to lived experience and to local groundedness, and the researcher tries to get closer to what is being studied. It aims for in-depth and holistic understanding, in order to do justice to the complexity of social life. Samples are usually small, and its sampling is guided by theoretical rather than probabilistic considerations. Prestructuring of design and data is less common, and its methods are less formalised than those in the quantitative approach. They are also more multidimensional, more diverse and less replicable. It therefore has greater flexibility.

Thus there are different strengths in each approach. Quantitative data enable standardised, objective comparisons to be made, and the measurements of quantitative research permit overall descriptions of situations or phenomena in a systematic and comparable way. This means we can sketch the contours or dimensions of these situations or phenomena. That is often what we want to do, either independently of deeper-level qualitative inquiry, or in conjunction with it. Procedures for the analysis of quantitative data, being well-developed and codified, bring objectivity to the research, in the sense that they increase the chances that the results of the analysis do not depend on the researcher doing the analysis. The quantitative approach means that certain types of important questions can be systematically answered, opening the way to the development of useful knowledge.

At the same time, there are important strengths in the qualitative approach. Qualitative methods are flexible, more so than quantitative methods. Therefore they can be used in a wider range of situations and for a wider range of purposes and research questions. They can also be more easily modified as a study progresses. Because of their great flexibility, they are well suited for studying naturally occurring real-life situations. Moreover, they accommodate the local groundedness of the things they study – specific cases embedded in their context. Qualitative methods are the best way we have of getting the insider's perspective, the 'actor's definition of the situation', the meanings people attach to things and events. This means they can be used to study the lived experience of people, including people's meanings and purposes. Qualitative data have a holism and richness, and are well able to deal with the complexity of social phenomena. This is what is meant when qualitative researchers talk about data providing thick descriptions. And qualitative research, especially grounded theory, is well suited to investigating process.[1]

A clear implication of this sort of comparison and analysis of strengths and weaknesses is that we cannot find out everything we might want to know using only one approach, and that we can very often increase the scope, depth and power of our research by combining the two approaches – that is, by mixing the methods.

At this point, however, some complications arise. The key question now is: What does it mean to combine the two approaches, and how will it be done? Creswell and Plano Clark (2007: 79–84) identify three main dimensions in analysing this question:

> *The timing dimension* – what will the timing of qualitative and quantitative methods be? In which order will the researcher collect and use the data? Will it be concurrent (both sets of data are collected at the same time) or sequential (one set is collected before the other)?

> *The weighting dimension* – what will be the relative importance, weight or priority given to qualitative and quantitative methods and data in answering the study's questions? The general possibilities are equal weighting to both approaches, or unequal weighting, with one approach carrying more weight.

> *The mixing dimension* – how will qualitative and quantitative methods be mixed, and especially how will the two data sets be mixed? The possibilities here are that the two data sets can be merged, one can be embedded within the other, or they can be connected in some other way.

The different combinations of answers which are possible to these three questions (timing, weighting, mixing) lead naturally to the topic of mixed methods designs.

Mixed methods designs

14.4 Tashakkori and Teddlie (2003a) show the complexity of this topic by identifying nearly 40 different types of mixed methods designs in the literature, with terminology that varies between different writers adding a further layer of complication. In a major simplification and contribution, Creswell and Plano Clark (2007: 58–88) have devised a four-way classification of the main mixed methods designs. They point out that each main type has variants, and they also analyse the strengths and challenges in using each type of design. Drawing on their work, what follows now is a brief description of the essential nature of each of the four main designs, and examples of each. In four appendices to their book, Creswell and Plano Clark reproduce four articles from research journals, with each article illustrating one of the main mixed methods designs. These articles are briefly summarised here. In addition, a hypothetical example from education research, on the topic of the job satisfaction of teachers, shows how each of the main mixed methods designs might be used.

14.4.1 Triangulation design

The purpose of the triangulation design is to obtain complementary quantitative and qualitative data on the same topic, bringing together the different strengths of the two methods. It is a one-phase design, where the two types of data are collected in the same time frame and are given equal weight. Typically, it involves the concurrent but separate collection and analysis of the two types of data, which are then merged, perhaps through data transformation or perhaps at the interpretation-of-results stage (Creswell and Plano Clark, 2007: 62–4).

The published example of this design (Jenkins, 2001; Creswell and Plano Clark, 2007: 194–203) concerns rural high school students' perceptions of drug resistance difficulties. Jenkins analysed qualitative data collected from focus groups, and quantitative data collected using a semi-structured questionnaire, and merged the two data sets into one overall interpretation.

14.4.2 Embedded design

In the embedded design, one data set plays a supportive secondary role in a study based primarily on the other data type. This design is based on ideas that a single data set is not sufficient, that different questions need to be answered and that different types of questions require different types of data to answer them (Creswell and Plano Clark, 2007: 67–71). The word 'embedded' is used because one type of data is embedded within a design framed by the other type. The two sets of data may be collected at the same time or sequentially – that is, this design may be one-phase or two-phase.

In an example of the embedded design, Rogers et al. (2003; see Creswell and Plano Clark, 2007: 204–15) used qualitative interviews with a group of patients involved in a quantitative experimental study to compare the effectiveness of different interventions in managing anti-psychotic medication.

14.4.3 Explanatory design

This is a two-phase mixed methods design, where the researcher uses qualitative data to help explain, or to build upon, initial quantitative results. The first phase is quantitative, the second phase is qualitative. This design might be used where qualitative data are needed to explain significant (or non-significant) results, outlier results or surprising results (Creswell and Plano Clark, 2007: 71–2). It might also be used where first-phase quantitative results guide the selection of subsamples for follow-up in in-depth qualitative investigation in the second phase. This last type of design in particular is important, with wide potential applicability in social science research.

As a published example, Aldridge, Fraser and Huang (1999; see Creswell and Plano Clark, 2007: 216–38) used a questionnaire assessing perceptions of the classroom learning environment to demonstrate differences between Taiwanese and Australian classroom environments. This provided the starting point for the use of qualitative methods (observations, interviews and narratives) to gain a more in-depth understanding of classroom environments in each country.

14.4.4 Exploratory design

In this two-phase mixed methods design, qualitative data are collected in the first phase, and quantitative data in the second. (With this timing, it is the reverse of the explanatory design.) Its general logic is that quantitative investigation is inappropriate until exploratory qualitative methods have built a better foundation of understanding. Examples would be where the researcher needs to develop a measuring instrument, but needs a deeper understanding of the phenomenon in question; or where it is important to explore some phenomenon in depth before measuring its distribution and prevalence (Creswell and Plano Clark, 2007: 75).

In the published example of this type of design, Myers and Oetzel (2003; see Creswell and Plano Clark, 2007: 239–55) used in-depth qualitative methods with a small sample of newly appointed employees to identify six different dimensions of organisational assimilation. Based on these dimensions, they developed an instrument for use in a quantitative survey of a much larger sample of newcomers.

In addition to these examples, Creswell and Plano Clark (2007: 171–2) give other examples of different types of mixed methods designs reported in articles in research journals across different social science areas. Focusing on education research, and as a further example, consider the planning of a piece of mixed methods research on the general topic of the job satisfaction of teachers:

A *triangulation design* might plan to conduct a survey using a semi-structured questionnaire with one sample of teachers. At the same time, focus groups and individual interviews might be used with another sample of teachers. Both methods would focus on the different aspects of job satisfaction for teachers. The two types of data would then be brought together during the analysis.

An *embedded design* might collect qualitative data (for example, through interviews and narratives) as part of a quantitative correlational study, which aims to trace out relationships between independent variables (gender, qualifications, years of teaching experience, subject teaching area, size of school, etc.) and job satisfaction as the dependent variable. In this case, the qualitative data help to reveal processes or mechanisms by which the independent–dependent variable relationships come about.

An *explanatory design* might first conduct a large-scale quantitative survey focusing on both levels of satisfaction and factors affecting those levels. A second-stage qualitative study might deliberately select subsamples of teachers of differing satisfaction levels for in-depth interviewing, in order to gain a fuller understanding of both the nature of job satisfaction and the way different factors influence it.

An *exploratory design* might aim to develop (or perhaps to refine, extend or improve) an instrument to measure the job satisfaction of teachers. Its first phase would be qualitative – perhaps using both focus groups and individual interviews – to probe fully the nature and dimensions of satisfaction. Its second phase would then be quantitative – developing an instrument based on this work, for use in large-scale quantitative surveys.

Creswell and Plano Clark's four-way classification of the main mixed methods designs gives a very useful framework for thinking about the general possibilities for mixing qualitative and quantitative data. It is based on the three dimensions implicit in the question of how to combine the two approaches – timing, weighting, mixing. At the same time, as the authors stress, each main design has variations.

As in all research, the choice of a design in a mixed methods study should be governed by the inherent logic of the research project, by the way the research problem is framed and set up for research, and especially by the way its research questions are asked and phrased. In mixed methods research, as elsewhere, question–method fit is crucial, and here, as elsewhere, the best way to obtain this fit is to give question development the logical priority, while acknowledging the reciprocal influence of method on question formulation. This means that, in the hypothetical job satisfaction research example shown above, each of the four designs briefly described would need to be preceded by, and closely connected to, carefully developed and appropriate research questions.

Clearly, mixed methods research is a growing field, and this growth can be expected to continue. There are now substantial bodies both of mixed methods methodological literature, and of literature reporting mixed methods studies in the research journals. And special mention should be made again of the *Journal of Mixed Methods Research*, whose policy is to publish both types of literature. Some extracts from this journal's information page are shown in Box 14.1. These bodies of literature should continue to grow with the increasing popularity of mixed methods research.

BOX 14.1

Policy statements from the *Journal of Mixed Methods Research*

Mixed methods research is defined as research in which the investigator collects and analyses data, integrates the findings, and draws inferences using both qualitative and quantitative approaches or methods in a single study or programme of inquiry. The *Journal of Mixed Methods Research* (JMMR) is an innovative, quarterly, international publication that focuses on empirical, methodological and theoretical articles about mixed methods research across the social, behavioural, health and human sciences.

Each issue explores:

- Original mixed methods research that fits the definition of mixed methods research; explicitly integrates the quantitative and qualitative aspects of the study; adds to the literature on mixed methods research; and makes a contribution to a substantive area in the scholar's field of inquiry; and
- Methodological/theoretical topics that advance knowledge about mixed methods research, such as:
  - types of research/evaluation questions;
  - types of designs;
  - sampling and/or measurement procedures;
  - approaches to data analysis;
  - validity;
  - software applications;
  - paradigm stance;
  - writing structures;
  - the value and use of mixed methods research.

Not only does JMMR offer 'the best and brightest' in original mixed methods research and methodological/theoretical discussions, it also includes insightful reflections by the distinguished editor on important issues in mixed methods research and extensive book and software reviews with practical applications.

The *Journal of Mixed Methods Research*'s scope includes:

- Developing and defining a global terminology and nomenclature for mixed methods research
- Delineating where mixed methods research may be used most effectively
- Creating the paradigmatic and philosophical foundations for mixed methods research
- Illuminating design and procedure issues
- Determining the logistics of conducting mixed methods research

The *Journal of Mixed Methods Research* is a premiere outlet for ground-breaking and seminal work in the field of mixed methods research, as well as a primary forum for the growing community of international and multidisciplinary scholars of mixed methods research.

This is not to say that researchers should feel compelled to use mixed methods, however, and it is to be hoped that another unfortunate research methodology fad does not develop around mixed methods. The key, as always, is the logic of the research proposed, and ensuring that methods chosen are appropriate to the questions asked. In developing a mixed methods proposal, this logic begins with how the research topic and problem are introduced, and flows on to how the research questions are phrased. If these things are done successfully, the logic of the proposal leads naturally to mixed methods. In other words, the mixed methods logic runs all the way through the proposal. In this respect, mixed methods research is no different from any other type of empirical research.

Mixed methods research requires specific skills, and it is obviously necessary for the mixed methods researcher to have some background and experience in both quantitative and qualitative research. In addition, the mixed methods researcher needs to have the time and resources to conduct the project successfully. Mixed methods projects are typically more complex in planning and in arranging both data collection and data analysis, although this depends on the specific mixed methods design chosen. And while mixed methods proposals and theses can be more complex to write, they are made easier with a clear and continuous logic, as stressed above.

As an example of this last point, the advice of Creswell and Plano Clark (2007): 86) to write a short paragraph in the research proposal describing a mixed methods study's strategy and design is reproduced here, and is strongly endorsed:

> Because many researchers and reviewers are currently unfamiliar with the different types of mixed methods designs, it is important to include an overview paragraph that introduces the design when writing about a study in proposals or research reports. This overview paragraph generally is placed at the start of the methods discussion and should address four topics. First, identify the type of mixed methods design and variant model, if appropriate. Next, give the defining characteristics of this design, including its timing weighting and mixing decisions. Third, state the overall purpose or rationale for using this design for the study. Finally, include references to the mixed methods literature on this design.

They then provide this actual research example (Ivankova et al., 2006: 5; Creswell and Plano Clark, 2007: 87) to illustrate the points made in the above quotation:

> The mixed methods sequential explanatory design consists of two distinct phases: quantitative followed by qualitative (Creswell, Plano Clark et al., 2007). In this design, a researcher first collects and analyses the quantitative (numeric) data. The qualitative (text) data are collected and analysed second in the sequence and help explain, or elaborate on, the quantitative results obtained in the first phase. The second, qualitative, phase builds on the first, quantitative, phase, and the two phases are connected in the intermediate stage in the study. The rationale for this approach is that the quantitative data and their subsequent analysis provide a general understanding of the research problem. The qualitative data and their analysis refine and explain those statistical results by exploring participants' views in more depth. (Rossman and Wilson, 1985; Tashakkori and Teddlie, 1998; Creswell, 2004)

This is a very good example of the sort of writing that can make a mixed methods research proposal convincing. It is also very good general advice. It is an excellent idea for all proposals – quantitative, qualitative or mixed methods – to include a brief, clear and concise overview paragraph such as this, describing the methodological strategy behind the research, and the reasons for it. This is an example of the point stressed earlier in Chapter 7 (qualitative research design) and Chapter 10 (quantitative research design), that research design is driven by strategy.

It is not my purpose in this book to encourage any particular kind of research approach, whether quantitative, qualitative or mixed methods. Rather, I seek to encourage high quality empirical research, whatever the approach. But now that the heated ideological disputes of the paradigm wars, with their associated either/or thinking, have passed, we can see clearly how many topics require both quantitative and qualitative methods and data if we are to develop a full understanding of them. This point alone should ensure the continued growth of mixed methods. After all, we constantly – and unproblematically – combine quantitative and qualitative data in our personal and professional lives. There seems no reason why the research world should be any different. The caveat is that the mixed methods researcher needs competence in both qualitative and quantitative approaches.

General evaluative criteria

14.5 In this book, we have now overviewed the basic ideas and concepts of qualitative research (Chapters 7, 8 and 9) and quantitative research (Chapters 10, 11 and 12), stressing the logic and the essentials of the two approaches, and using the same broad headings. The first part of this chapter has looked at the similarities and overlap between the two approaches, and their combination in mixed methods. Since there are similarities in the logic of inquiry in both approaches, there is a set of general evaluative principles which can be applied to both. These are equivalent to general evaluative criteria for all empirical research. This part of the chapter now deals with these criteria.

Ever-increasing amounts of research are done and published in today's world, and this can be expected to continue, since the idea of research as the way we answer questions and solve problems is deeply embedded in our culture. This applies as much to social science research as to any other field. As readers of research, we need to know what confidence we can have in its findings and conclusions; we need to be able to judge its quality. What criteria should be used? How do we answer the question: how good is this piece of work?

We first distinguish between general evaluative principles and specific evaluative criteria. We will deal here with the former. Literature listing specific evaluative criteria is mostly written from within either the quantitative or the qualitative approach, rather than to apply across them. Mostly, also, it gets down to technical issues in the form of detailed checklists for evaluating research proposals and reports. In line with the overall approach of this book, we concentrate more here on general criteria, both because the similarities between quantitative and qualitative empirical research are at a general level, and because it is also more helpful. At more specific levels, the technical differences between the two approaches can obscure their similarities.

Before getting to the general evaluative criteria, revisiting two concepts helps to establish a background to this question of evaluation. They are the two concepts of disciplined inquiry, and of the fit between the different parts of research. We deal with the more general of the two (disciplined inquiry) first.

14.5.1 Disciplined inquiry

The term 'disciplined' has been used frequently throughout this book, to indicate that good research is a disciplined form of inquiry. Thus disciplined inquiry provides a convenient way to begin this section, and a background for thinking about general evaluative principles. What follows draws on the work of Shulman (1988), who refers to the earlier work of Cronbach and Suppes (1969), and is quoted here at some length:

> When we speak of research, we speak of a family of methods which share the characteristics of *disciplined inquiry*. Cronbach and Suppes (1969) attempted to define disciplined inquiry a number of years ago . . . Here are some of the definitions of disciplined inquiry they suggest:

> Disciplined inquiry has a quality that distinguishes it from other sources of opinion and belief. The disciplined inquiry is conducted and reported in such a way that the argument can be painstakingly examined. The report does not depend for its appeal on the eloquence of the writer or on any surface plausibility. (p. 15)

Cronbach and Suppes continue:

> Whatever the character of a study, if it is disciplined the investigator has anticipated the traditional questions that are pertinent. He institutes control at each step of information collection and reasoning to avoid the sources of error to which these questions refer. If the errors cannot be eliminated he takes them into account by discussing the margin for error in his conclusions. Thus, the report of a disciplined inquiry has a texture that displays the raw materials entering the argument and the logical processes by which they were compressed and rearranged to make the conclusion credible. (pp. 15–16)

The definition of disciplined inquiry could be misconstrued to imply that the appropriate application of research methods always leads to a sterile, ritualised and narrowly conceived form of investigation. This is not the case. As Cronbach and Suppes observe subsequently:

> Disciplined inquiry does not necessarily follow well established, formal procedures. Some of the most excellent inquiry is free-ranging and speculative in the initial stages, trying

what might seem to be bizarre combinations of ideas and procedures, or restlessly cast-
ing about for ideas. (p. 16)

What is important about disciplined inquiry is that its data, arguments, and reasoning be
capable of withstanding careful scrutiny by another member of the scientific community.

These quotes capture the essence of what it means to conduct disciplined
inquiry, and show the fundamental requirements that need to be met for a piece of
research to be taken seriously. They are also excellent general ideas to keep in mind
when planning and writing a project, and they reappear in more specific form in the
evaluative principles which follow. One thing they stress is the idea of a piece of
research as a structured and coherent argument. This argument is strengthened
when the different parts of a project fit together well.

14.5.2 The fit between the component parts of a research project

The world of social science research today is much more complex and multidimensional than it was 20 or 30 years ago. There are different paradigms, two main different approaches, variations within those two main approaches, different methods
and different combinations of methods. This complexity makes it important that
the various components of a project fit together, and are aligned with each other.

The point of view stressed throughout this book is that in most cases the best
way to do this is to get the research questions clear, and then align the design and
methods with those. We have noted the reciprocal influence between question and
methods, and limitations as to what can be done in terms of design and method
impose limitations on questions that can be asked, but the argument is that this
direction of influence should be minimised. The main influence should be from
questions to methods.

This point about the fit between a study's components is really about the overall
validity of the research. A project whose components do not fit together has questionable validity. This is because we can have little confidence in the answers put
forward to research questions on the basis of a design and methods which do not fit
with each other, or with the questions. In that case, it is not the stated questions, but
some other questions, which have been answered. Under these circumstances, the
argument behind the research falls down. That is what validity in this overall sense
means. When the questions, design and methods fit together, the argument is strong
and the research has validity. When they do not fit together, the argument is weak-
ened and the research lacks validity.

This point is illustrated by the discussion in Chapter 9 about the variety of
approaches in qualitative data analysis. With the numerous analytic alternatives
available, the need for the method of analysis to fit with the research questions
is even stronger, and this generalises to the other components: 'Whatever
research strategy is being followed, research problems, research design, data
collection methods and analytic approaches should all be part of an overall

methodological approach and should all imply one another' (Coffey and Atkinson, 1996: 11).

These concepts of research as disciplined inquiry and the fit between the component parts of a project give two general standards for assessing the quality of a piece of research. Against this background, we can now consider evaluative criteria.

14.5.3 Criteria for evaluation

As noted, evaluative criteria are considered here at a general rather than specific level. They are presented in terms of a finished research project and report. With slight modifications, what is said can be applied to proposals as well as to reports.

The evaluative criteria are presented as general questions for each of five main areas:

- the set-up of the research;
- the empirical procedures used in the research (design, data collection, sample and data analysis);
- the quality of the data;
- the findings and conclusions reached in the research;
- the presentation of the research.

The set-up of the research

There are four general questions about the set-up of the research, and each is briefly discussed:

1. Is it clear what position the research is 'coming from'?
2. Is the topic area clearly identified?
3. Are the research questions appropriate?
4. Is the research appropriately set in context?

Is it clear where the research is coming from?   Social science research today is characterised by multiple approaches, methods and paradigms. A reader of such research has to keep that in mind. But the writer, correspondingly, has to accept the responsibility to make clear what position the research takes. A project may or may not take a particular paradigm position; it may aim at theory verification or theory generation; it may or may not mix methods; it may be a tightly structured design or an emerging design; it may take a particular approach in the analysis of its data, especially if the data are qualitative. Any of these positions is acceptable, and each can be justified, but the writer needs to make clear what position is behind the research. This is part of its setup, and making this clear is the best way of avoiding confusion and mistaken expectations on the part of the reader. A research project normally involves many different decisions, with most of the time no right or wrong criteria applying to those decisions. But they need to be made from some consistent base ('principled choices' – Coffey and Atkinson, 1996). The writer needs to inform the reader about this base.

Whether the planning for the research proceeded deductively from topic area to research questions, or inductively from research questions to topic area, there needs to be a clear identification of the topic area early in the report (or proposal).

In Chapter 4 it was pointed out that good research questions organise a project, and are:

- Clear. They can be easily understood, and are unambiguous.
- Specific. Their concepts are at a specific enough level to connect to data indicators.
- Answerable. We can see what data are required to answer them, and how the data will be obtained.
- Interconnected. They are related to each other in some meaningful way.
- Substantively relevant. They are interesting and worthwhile questions for the investment of research effort.

These characteristics enable us to judge the research questions. In Chapters 4 and 5 we put special emphasis on the empirical criterion (the third point above), which gives a specific principle for judging research questions: is it clear what evidence will be required to answer them? In a finished report, it does not matter whether the questions were fully prespecified or emerged during the study. In a proposal, the position of the research on this matter should be made clear.

This means two things. First, is the relevance of the research either to some theoretical concern, or to some practical or professional concern, made clear? Second, has the connection of this study to the relevant literature been made, and handled appropriately? There are two main ways in which this connection to the literature can be handled. One is for a full literature review to be carried out ahead of this project. If this is the case, it is necessary for the review to be critical, and for this project to be connected to this review. Too often we see the required literature review, but the study itself is not integrated with the review. The other way, as in a grounded theory study, is for consideration of some of the relevant literature to be delayed until a certain stage is reached in the empirical work. The literature is then introduced into the study as further data. There are of course variations on these two main approaches, but whichever way is chosen, the approach needs to be explained.

Empirical procedures

Empirical procedures here means the design of the study, and the tools and techniques it uses for its data collection and data analysis. These matters are the focus of three of the questions in this section. In addition to those three, the first question concerns the level of information given about the procedures, and the fifth question concerns the study sample. The five questions are:

1. Are the design, data collection and data analysis procedures reported in sufficient detail to enable the research to be scrutinised and reconstructed?

2. **Are the strategy and design of the study appropriate for the research questions?**
3. **Are the data collection instruments and procedures adequate and appropriate for the research questions?**
4. **Is the sample appropriate?**
5. **Are the data analysis procedures adequate and appropriate for the research questions?**

Again, brief comments are given for each question.

Are the design, data collection and data analysis procedures reported in sufficient detail to enable the research to be scrutinised and reconstructed? The section on disciplined inquiry stressed that the research needs to be conducted and reported in such a way that all stages of it can be thoroughly examined. Therefore the reader needs to be able to follow the full sequence of steps, and each should be described in sufficient detail to enable the audit trail through the study to be followed.

Are the strategy and design of the study appropriate for the research questions? The function of research design is to connect the research questions to the empirical procedures and to data. The design is based on a strategy, and it situates the researcher in the empirical world. It answers these general questions:

- **Who or what will be studied?**
- **What strategies of inquiry will be used?**
- **What methods will be used for collecting and analysing empirical materials?**

The design gives the overall framework for the empirical procedures, showing what they are and how they fit together. Therefore it is important that the design be reported in detail, and that it fits with the study's research questions.

A major consideration in the design is the overall approach: will the research be quantitative, qualitative or both? If quantitative, is the design experimental, quasi-experimental or survey? Is the focus on relationships between variables or accounting for variance? If qualitative, what cases were studied, and from what perspective? If combined, in what way and with what logic? In both approaches, but especially in qualitative studies, there is often the additional question of a prespecified versus emerging design. Like the research questions, it does not matter in a finished report whether the design was prespecified, emerged or some mixture of the two. In a proposal, this matter needs consideration. If the design is prespecified, the accompanying conceptual framework should also be shown. Whatever the design chosen, it should fit with the research questions. This fit is part of the integrity or overall validity of the research. The design itself is about the internal logic, or internal validity, of the research. Internal validity is discussed later in this chapter.

Are the data collection instruments and procedures adequate and appropriate for the research questions? This leads directly to the question of the quality of data, discussed in the next section. In quantitative studies, measuring instruments are involved. Either they are already existing instruments, or they were developed for this study. If already existing, the criteria given in Chapter 11 apply, especially reliability and validity. If they were developed, the steps in doing this should be shown, along with the consideration of these same criteria. Qualitative research, depending on its orientation, may involve similar instruments – for example, interview schedules. In this case, the technical criteria of reliability, validity and reactivity apply.

Whatever the instruments, data collection procedures are also involved. They were described in some detail in Chapter 8 for qualitative data and Chapter 11 for quantitative data. The issue here is that the procedures are appropriate for the study, tailored to the circumstances to maximise the quality of the data, and reported in appropriate detail. If more than one person was involved in data collection, the way in which data collection procedures were standardised needs to be described.

Is the sample appropriate?   For any empirical study, the logic of the sample selection should be congruent with the overall logic of the study, and of the research questions. The sample needs to be properly described, and the basis for its selection made clear. In a quantitative study, the size and structure of the sample need to be described, along with its logic, its method of selection and the claims made for its representativeness. The last point needs to take account of the response rate, if a survey design is used. In a qualitative study, if purposive or theoretical sampling is used, the logic behind this needs to be made clear, and its connections with the research questions demonstrated.

In addition, it needs to be demonstrated that data were collected across the full range of conditions indicated in the research questions. This is important in both quantitative and qualitative studies, and in both theory testing and theory generating studies. It also influences the generalisability or transferability of the findings.

Are the data analysis procedures adequate and appropriate for the research questions?   Again, this overlaps with the quality of data, discussed in the next section. 'Adequate' here relates to the audit trail through the data analysis itself. It also means transparent. We need to be able to see how the researcher got from the data to the findings and conclusions, in order to know what confidence to have in the findings. This is important in both approaches, though historically it has been easier to demonstrate in quantitative research. With procedures now available for the analysis of qualitative data, it is equally important for qualitative researchers to show how they got from data to conclusions. 'Appropriate' here means consistent with the research questions.

The quality of the data   The findings and conclusions of empirical research are only as good as the data on which they are based. 'Quality control of data' in empirical research is therefore important. It is discussed first in terms of procedures in the collection of the data, and then in terms of three technical aspects of the quality of the data: reliability, validity and reactivity. Each of the latter issues is discussed in both the quantitative and qualitative contexts.

Procedures in the collection of the data   Care, control and thoroughness in the procedures for data collection were stressed in both quantitative and qualitative contexts.

In Chapter 11, we saw what this means both in the development of a measuring instrument, and in the procedures by which it is used. Earlier, in Chapter 8, we looked at the same matters in qualitative data collection. In both cases, the points raised are more common sense than technical and esoteric, but they are important nonetheless. They come down to careful thinking and planning, anticipation and pilot testing (where appropriate), and thorough preparation. They have a major impact on the more technical aspects of the quality of data.

Reliability   In Chapter 11, reliability of measurement was defined in terms of consistency, in the sense of both stability over time and of internal consistency. Procedures for estimating each type of reliability were described, and its interpretation in terms of error variance was given. The reliability of measurement data should be reported. For qualitative data, there is some translation of the concept of reliability, in line with the rethinking associated with newer paradigms. Thus, for example, the term 'dependability' is proposed to parallel reliability in the constructivist paradigm (Lincoln and Guba, 1985). But the basic idea is similar, and the concept of reliability has relevance for qualitative data in two respects. First, the same questions can be asked of qualitative data as of quantitative data: how stable are these data over time? And if multiple data sources are used, are they internally consistent? That is, to what extent do the data converge or diverge? Second, to what extent is there inter-observer agreement when observation data are involved? A related question concerns the early processing and analysis of qualitative data: does the check coding show inter-coder agreement?

Validity   Validity here means the validity of the data. In Chapter 11, the validity of measurement data was discussed. The usual form of the validity question in that context is: how do we know this instrument measures what we think it measures? We discussed there the three main forms of quantitative validation: content, criterion-related and construct validity. A broader version of the validity question makes it directly applicable to all empirical research, quantitative and qualitative. The question 'How valid are the data?' really means, in this broader version: how well do the data represent the phenomena for which they stand?

In measurement, because of latent trait theory, the validity question in the first instance concerns the inference from items to variables, and in the second instance from variables to factors. With qualitative data, the first level of analysis concerns the inference from indicators to first-order concept, and the second level the inference from first-order to second-order concept. Because of the similarity in conceptual structure, the question about the validity of data is virtually identical in the two approaches. The research report needs to consider this question. Quantitative data are validated as above. Qualitative data are validated, in this technical sense, through the use of check coding, and by following the audit trail through the analysis.

Reactivity   Reactivity concerns the extent to which the process of collecting the data changes the data. It is a common issue in research, applying not only in the social sciences. Thus, in quantitative research, reactivity of measurement means the extent to which the act of measuring something changes that thing. Attitude scales, for example, may provoke or influence the attitude in question, changing it in some way.

Reactivity is also a clear possibility in observational research. The same sorts of possibilities exist in collecting qualitative data. A participant observer's presence may change the behaviour of those being observed, or there may be interviewer effects in the data as a result of the presence or style of a particular interviewer.

The evaluative question concerns whether the possibility of reactivity in the data has been considered, reported and taken into account, and what steps have been taken to minimise its effects. In a general sense, reactivity concerns both the reliability and the validity of the data, and the sampling of the data. The question is whether the data obtained in the research are a true sample of the data. Would these be the data if the research were not being done? Has the research process itself, and specifically the collection of data, somehow influenced the data, or even created the data? This question applies in both approaches. Associated questions, which also apply in both approaches, concern respondents' or informers' knowledgeability (Are these people really able to answer these questions, or provide this information?) and the possibilities of deceit (Are they telling me the truth?) and of social desirability (Are they telling me what they think I want to hear, or what they think makes them look good?).

Reliability, validity and reactivity are technical issues about the quality of data in empirical research, and the ideas behind them apply in both approaches. For qualitative data, however, there is one other issue, as noted in Chapter 7. A strength of qualitative data, and often a reason for adopting a qualitative approach, is to see a phenomenon in its context, to study it both holistically and in detail. If the aim of the research is to obtain rich, holistic data, then it needs to be asked, and demonstrated, how well that was done. The central issue is: did the research provide a sufficient description of the context to enable the reader to judge both the validity and the transferability of the study's findings? (see especially Miles and Huberman, 1994: 279, for more specific questions on this issue).

The findings and conclusions reached in the research

Findings can be seen as answers to research questions, and conclusions as what can be said on the basis of those findings. There are three questions here:

1. Have the research questions been answered?
2. How much confidence can we have in the answers put forward?
3. What can be concluded from the research on the basis of what was found?

The first question requires little comment. The first objective of the research is to answer its research questions (or test its hypotheses, if it is a theory verification study). The report should contain answers to these questions (or tests of these hypotheses). These answers are the findings of the research (though of course there may be other findings as well, which have come up during the research, but which were not phrased as research questions).

Answers to the second and third questions above depend in part on the evaluative criteria we have already considered, but they also go further than this. These two questions overlap, and come together in assessing the way evidence has been used to answer questions and draw conclusions, and in assessing the generality and applicability of the findings and conclusions. These two points correspond, respectively, to the technical concepts of internal validity and external validity.

Internal validity   Internal validity refers to the internal logic and consistency of the research. If research is seen as an argument (where questions are asked, and data are systematically collected and analysed to answer these questions) then internal validity is about the logic and internal consistency of this argument. Internal validity is most clearly and narrowly defined in the quantitative context. There it means the extent to which the relationships between the variables are correctly interpreted. It has been well studied in this context, and the reference by Campbell and Stanley (1963) lists the various threats to internal validity which accompany different quantitative designs.

The same idea applies in the qualitative context, but it needs broadening in view of the greater range of purposes and designs in qualitative research. Denzin and Lincoln give a very broad definition: internal validity refers to 'the isomorphism of findings with reality' (1994: 114). This means the extent to which the findings faithfully represent and reflect the reality which has been studied, and it has two aspects. The first is whether the research has internal consistency. This means both whether all the parts of the research fit together, as discussed in Section 14.5.2, and whether the findings themselves have internal consistency and coherence. The second is whether the ways in which propositions have been developed and confirmed are described, including the elimination of rival hypotheses, the consideration of negative evidence, and the cross-validation of findings with other parts of the data. In quantitative research, progressively more complex designs have been developed to counter the various threats to internal validity. This is the same thing as eliminating rival hypotheses. The same idea applies in qualitative studies, especially those whose purpose is explanation. The objective of theoretical sampling in qualitative research, including the systematic study of negative cases, is to incorporate these aspects into the study.

Qualitative designs sometimes incorporate another feature which is not typical in quantitative research, but which is part of internal validity. It is 'member checking'. It means checking back with the people who are being studied, and who gave the data. It is not appropriate in all situations, and its use and limitations need to be assessed. When appropriate, it can be applied first to the data, whereby an interview transcript, for example, is taken back to the interviewee before analysis to check that the record is accurate. Second, it can be applied to the analysis as it develops. Here, it means taking the developing products of the research – its concepts, its propositions, the emerging cognitive map – back to the people being studied, for confirmation, validation and verification. When the purposes of a qualitative study are interpretive, and centred on meanings and symbolic significance as in an ethnographic description, the developing description can be checked by the members at different stages. When the purposes are more abstract, as in conceptualising and explaining, the same thing can be done as the analysis proceeds. Thus member checking is often important in grounded theory studies.

The questions about internal validity are therefore: how internally consistent is this study? What threats are there to its internal validity, and how have those threats been taken into account?

External validity External validity is the question of generalisability. How far are the findings of this study generalisable? For quantitative studies, part of this generalisability is 'people generalisation', based on probability sampling. Bracht and Glass (1968) label this 'population validity', and acknowledge its importance. But they also make clear that this is not the only aspect of quantitative generalisation – there is also the question of 'ecological validity' when generalising from a quantitative study.

With the qualification given in Chapter 7 (that there are some studies where generalisation is not the objective), the question of generalisability can also be asked of findings in a qualitative study. How far can these findings be generalised? Are the conclusions transferable to other settings and contexts? The concept of transferability is often preferred to generalisability in qualitative writing, and in this context we can focus the question on three aspects. First, on the sampling itself: is it theoretically diverse enough, or does it capture enough variation, to encourage transfer of the findings to other situations? Second, on the context: is the context thickly described, so that the reader can judge the transferability of findings to other situations? Third, on the level of abstraction of the concepts in the data analysis: are they at a sufficient level of abstraction to permit their application to other settings?

The questions regarding external validity are therefore: what claims can be made for the generalisability of these findings (if appropriate)? What possible threats are there to their generalisation, and have those threats been taken into account? Does the report suggest how the generalisability of these findings could be assessed in other situations?

Presentation

Finally, there is the written report of the research (or the written proposal). Research writing is discussed in the next chapter.

Chapter summary

- Mixed methods research aims to combine the collection and analysis of both qualitative and quantitative data in a way that achieves complementary strengths and non-overlapping weaknesses.
- The methodological history of social science research shows three main waves – the dominance of quantitative methods, the emergence of qualitative methods and the growth of mixed methods.
- Pragmatism has emerged as the main philosophy or paradigm associated with mixed methods.
- Combining quantitative and qualitative approaches involved the three dimensions of timing, weighting and mixing of the different components.

- A four-way classification of the main mixed methods designs helps to organise the complexity of possible combinations; the designs are labelled triangulation, embedded, explanatory and exploratory.
- Clear strategy statements are useful in describing mixed methods designs, just as with all other designs.
- It is important that empirical research is scrutinised and evaluated, especially with respect to its methods.
- At the most general level, good empirical research shows the characteristics of disciplined inquiry; similarly, a good research project shows internal validity and consistency, with a close fit between all of its component parts.
- More specific criteria for evaluating a research project are suggested for five main areas – the set-up of the research, the empirical procedures used, the quality of the data, the findings and conclusions reached and the presentation.

KEY TERMS

Mixed methods research: empirical research which involves the collection and analysis of both qualitative and quantitative data

Pragmatism: the main philosophical position associated with mixed methods research, focusing on 'what works'

Mixed methods designs: there are many ways qualitative and quantitative data can be combined, leading to many mixed methods designs; four main designs are labelled triangulation, embedded, explanatory and exploratory

Disciplined inquiry: research which has internal validity, and which is conducted and reported in such a way that its data and argument can be scrutinised by the scientific community

Reactivity: the idea that the process of collecting the data changes the data

Internal validity: the internal logic and consistency of the research

External validity: generalisability – how far can these findings be generalised? To what extent are the conclusions transferable to other settings and contexts?

Exercises and study questions

1. Define mixed methods research, and briefly explain why and how it has emerged as a 'third wave' in social science research methodology.
2. What is the fundamental principle of mixed methods research and what is its logical basis?
3. List some of the main strengths and weaknesses of (a) qualitative research and (b) quantitative research.
4. What is the essential idea of pragmatism, and what are its implications for research questions and methods?
5. In combining qualitative and quantitative approaches, what three dimensions need to be considered?

6. Briefly describe each of the four main mixed methods designs – triangulation, embedded, explanatory, exploratory.
7. Sketch the research questions and design for an explanatory mixed methods design with the topic of student alienation from school. (Design Stage 1 as a quantitative survey with a large sample, and Stage 2 as follow-up in-depth interviews with a deliberately selected subsample from Stage 1.)
8. Study the two strategy–design statements reproduced from the book by Creswell and Plano Clark at the end of Section 14.4 (p. 313). Construct such a statement for the study you sketched in Question 7.

Further reading

Brewer, J. and Hunter, A. (2005) *Foundation of Multimethod Research: Synthesising Styles.* 2nd edn. Thousand Oaks, CA: SAGE.

Creswell, J.W. (2008) *Educational Research: Planning, Conducting and Evaluating Quantitative and Qualitative Research.* Upper Saddle River, NJ: Pearson.

Creswell, J.W. and Plano Clark, V. (2007) *Designing and Conducting Mixed Methods Research.* Thousand Oaks, CA: SAGE.

Journal of Mixed Methods Research

Plano Clark, V. and Creswell, J. (2008) *The Mixed Methods Reader.* Thousand Oaks, CA: SAGE.

Tashakkori, A. and Teddlie, C. (2003a) *Handbook of Mixed Methods in Social and Behavioral Research.* Thousand Oaks, CA: SAGE.

Tashakkori, A. and Teddlie, C. (2003b) 'Major issues and controversies in the use of mixed methods in the social and behavioral sciences', in A. Tashakkori and C. Teddlie (eds), *Handbook of Mixed Methods in Social and Behavioral Research.* Thousand Oaks, CA: SAGE. pp. 3–53.

Tashakkori, A. and Teddlie, C. (2003c) 'The past and future of mixed methods research: From data triangulation to mixed model design', in A. Tashakkori and C. Teddlie (eds), *Handbook of Mixed Methods in Social and Behavioral Research.* Thousand Oaks, CA: SAGE. pp. 671–702.

Note

1. A summary of the strengths and weaknesses of the two approaches is given by Bryman (1988: 94). A summary of the criticisms and weaknesses of the quantitative approach (which they call the 'received view') is given in Guba and Lincoln (1994: 106–7). They see five main internal criticisms: context stripping, exclusion of meaning and purpose, grand theories not fitting local contexts, inapplicability of general data to individual cases, and excluding discovery. To these we could add simplification and reductionism. They also see four main external criticisms: the theory-ladenness of facts, the under-determination of theory, the value-ladenness of facts, and the interaction between the researcher and researched.

fifteen
RESEARCH WRITING

Contents

Writing is an important part of research. Getting a project started usually means taking it from ideas to a written proposal. At the other end, a project is not complete until it is shared, through writing. Thus, a written proposal is required for the project to commence, and a written report is required after the project. It follows that the quality of research is judged in part by the quality of the written document (proposal or report).

The first part of this chapter gives some background to the topic of research writing, by looking briefly at writing in the quantitative tradition and at the much greater range of writing choices in qualitative research, and by using the 'analytical mix' as a device for thinking about quantitative and qualitative writing together. The second part then deals in some detail with research proposals and, in less detail, with abstracts and dissertations. Final sections then discuss briefly the distinction between writing to report and writing to learn and some of the choices facing the social science researcher when it comes to writing.

Background

15.1.1 The quantitative tradition

15.1 The conventional format for reporting (or proposing) quantitative research has such headings as these (Miles, Huberman and Saldana, 2013):

- statement of the problem;
- conceptual framework;
- research questions;
- method;
- data analysis;
- conclusions;
- discussion.

A still briefer form used by some journals (for example, journals with a strong behaviourist leaning in psychology and education) has just four headings – introduction and research questions, method, results, discussion. For much quantitative research reporting, this framework of headings is still quite appropriate – Gilbert (2008), for example, describes the conventional (quantitative) sociological paper with similar headings. But many qualitative researchers today would find such headings too constraining. The headings are still relevant to much of what we do, but we often have different and broader expectations, for a qualitative research report especially, than can be met by these headings. Once again this reflects the range of perspectives in qualitative research in contrast with the relative homogeneity of much quantitative research.

15.1.2 Qualitative research writing

Throughout this book I have used the timing-of-structure continuum (Section 2.6) to stress the range of social science research, especially qualitative research. Writing about quantitative research has typically been a relatively straightforward matter, with conventional models and structures such as those in the previous section to guide the writer. Writing for qualitative research, however, like the research itself, is much more varied and diverse, and not at all monolithic (Coffey and Atkinson, 1996). Thus, towards the right-hand end of this continuum, there is a greater range of writing models, strategies and possibilities. Some of the perspectives of contemporary qualitative research (such as feminism and postmodernism, especially in ethnography) broaden the range even further.

The rethinking of research which has accompanied both the paradigm debates and the emergence of new perspectives has included research writing – how the research is to be put into written form and communicated. Especially when seen in a discourse analysis or sociology of knowledge perspective, this rethinking has brought awareness of the choices about writing, identifying the conventional quantitative writing model as just one of the choices. The appreciation of a wider range of choices has meant also the freeing up of some of the restrictions about writing, and the encouraging of experimentation with newer forms of writing.

As a result, there is a proliferation of forms of writing in qualitative research, and older models of reporting are being mixed with other approaches:

> The reporting of qualitative data may be one of the most fertile fields going; there are no fixed formats, and the ways data are being analyzed and interpreted are getting more and more various. As qualitative data analysts, we have few shared canons of how our studies should be reported. Should we have normative agreement on this? Probably not now – or, some would say, ever. (Miles, Huberman and Saldana, 2013)

15.1.3 The analytical mix

In this chapter I discuss research writing for both quantitative and qualitative approaches, keeping in mind but not overemphasising their differences, and keeping in mind also mixed methods studies that combine both approaches. Adapting Miles

TABLE 15.1   Terms in the analytic mix

Quantitative	Qualitative
Variable-oriented	Case-oriented
Categorising	Contextualising
Analytical	Synthetic
Etic	Emic
Variance theory	Process theory

and Huberman's 'analytic mix' (1994: 301–2) is a helpful device in doing this, since it brings key elements of the two approaches together.

One part of this analytic mix was used in Chapter 14 (pp. 292–5), where variable-oriented research (quantitative) was compared with case-oriented research (qualitative). As Table 15.1 shows, other writers have used slightly different terms.

Miles and Huberman write about this mix from within qualitative research, expressing strongly the view that good qualitative research and reporting requires both types of elements from the mix. We can use it as a framework for all research writing.

The framework echoes the two tensions within qualitative research described by Nelson et al. (1992) in discussing cultural studies, and paraphrased by Denzin and Lincoln (2011). On the one hand, qualitative research is drawn to a broad, interpretive, postmodern, feminist and critical sensibility. On the other, it is drawn to more narrowly defined positivist, post-positivist, humanistic and naturalistic conceptions of human experience and its analysis. These latter conceptions correspond more to the left-hand side of Table 15.1, whereas the former conceptions are closer to the right-hand side.

Miles and Huberman note that Vitz (1990) reflects these two views, seeing conventional data analysis, involving propositional thinking, as the fruit of abstract reasoning, leading to formal, theoretical interpretations. Figural genres, such as narratives, entail more concrete, holistic reasoning; they are 'stories' retaining the temporal configurations of the original events.

When it comes to writing, Miles and Huberman recommend a mixture of these two ways of seeing the world. As they see it, the problem is that:

> Stories without variables do not tell us enough about the meaning and larger import of what we are seeing. Variables without stories are ultimately abstract and unconvincing – which may explain certain scrupulous rules for reporting quantitative studies, as well as the familiar comment, 'I couldn't really understand the numbers until I looked at the open-ended data'. (1994: 302)

The challenge therefore is to:

> combine theoretical elegance and credibility appropriately with the many ways social events can be described; to find intersections between the propositional thinking of most

conventional studies and more figurative thinking. Just as good analysis nearly always involves a blend of variable-oriented, categorizing, 'paradigmatic' moves, and case-oriented, contextualizing, narrative ones, so does good reporting. (1994: 299)

These ideas of the range of styles, and of mixing and blending them, are a useful background against which to consider proposals, abstracts and dissertations.

Research documents

15.2 There are two main types of research documents – proposals and reports (which may be dissertations, journal articles or reports for other purposes). Since this book is an introduction to social science research, with much focus on getting the research started, most attention here is on proposals. Much of what is said carries over naturally to dissertations and articles. Abstracts and titles are also briefly considered in this section.

15.2.1 Proposals

This section summarises my views on research proposals. A full description of these views is given in Punch (2006), where all of the points made below are described in detail, and where five exemplary proposals are presented in full.

What is a research proposal? In one sense, the answer is obvious – the proposal describes what the proposed research is about, what it is trying to achieve and how it will go about doing this, and what we will learn from this and why it is worth learning. In another sense, the dividing line between the proposal and the research itself is not so obvious. The proposal describes what will be done, and the research itself is carried out after approval of the proposal. But preparing the proposal itself may also involve considerable research.

The three most basic questions are useful in guiding development of the proposal:

- *What?* What is the purpose of this research? What are we trying to find out?
- *How?* How will the proposed research answer these questions?
- *Why?* Why is this research worth doing (or funding)? Or, what will we learn, and why is it worth knowing?

The first question (what?) is dealt with in Chapters 4 and 5. The second question (how?) is dealt with in Chapters 7, 8 and 9 for qualitative research, and Chapters 10, 11 and 12 for quantitative research. The third question (why?) is discussed later in this section.

Maxwell (2012) stresses that the form and structure of the proposal are tied to its purpose – 'to explain and justify your proposed study to an audience of non-experts on your topic'. *Explain* means that your readers can clearly understand what you want to do. *Justify* means that they not only understand what you plan to do, but why. *Your proposed study* means that the proposal should be mainly about your study, not mainly about the literature, your research topic or research methods in general. *Nonexperts* means that researchers will often have readers reviewing their proposals who are not experts in the specific area.

It is helpful to see the proposal itself as an argument. Seeing it as an argument means stressing its line of reasoning, its internal consistency and the interrelatedness of its different parts. It means making sure that the different parts fit together, and showing how the research will be a piece of disciplined inquiry, as described in Chapter 14. As an argument, it should explain the logic behind the proposed study, rather than simply describing the study. In so doing, it should answer the question of why this design and method is chosen for this study.

What follows now is a suggested set of guidelines for developing a research proposal, shown in Table 15.2. Because no prescription is appropriate, but certain content is expected, and because there are both similarities and differences in quantitative and qualitative proposals, it seems best to present a full checklist of possible sections and headings. Some clearly apply to both quantitative and qualitative research, whereas some are more applicable to one approach. Not all would necessarily be required in any one proposal, and they can be used as appropriate. They are things to think about in proposal preparation and presentation, and they are useful in developing full versions of the proposal – where shorter versions are required, a good strategy is to prepare the full version, then summarise it.

Many of these headings (for example, general and specific research questions) do not now require comment, because of what has already been said in previous chapters. Where this is the case, the reader is referred to appropriate parts of the book. Where new points need to be made, or earlier ones reinforced, or where important distinctions apply between quantitative and qualitative approaches, brief comments are made. I stress that these are suggested guidelines. As with writing a report or dissertation, there is no fixed formula for a proposal. There are different ways to present the material, and different orders the sections can follow.

It is easier in many respects to suggest proposal guidelines for a quantitative study, since there is greater variety in qualitative studies, and many qualitative studies will be unfolding rather than prestructured. An emerging study cannot be as specific in the proposal about its research questions, nor about details of the design. When this is the case, the point needs to be made in the proposal. A discussion of qualitative proposals follows this section (see Section 15.2.2).

Introduction

There are many ways a topic can be introduced, and all topics have a background and a context. These need to be dealt with in the introduction, which sets the stage for the research. A strong introduction is important to a convincing proposal. Its purpose is not to review the literature, but rather to show generally how the proposed study fits into what is already known, and to locate it in relation to present knowledge and practice. In the process of doing this, there should be a clear identification of the research area and topic, and a general statement of purpose. This can

TABLE 15.2 Checklist of possible sections for research proposals

- Title and title page
- Abstract
- Introduction: area and topic
                background and context
                statement of purpose
- Research questions: general and specific
- Conceptual framework, theory, hypotheses (if appropriate)
- The literature
- Methods: strategy and design
              sample and sampling
              data collection – instruments and procedures
              data analysis
- Significance
- Consent, access and human participants' protection
- References
- Appendices (e.g. timetable, budget, instruments, etc.)

then lead into the research questions in the next section. Specific features of the proposed study can also be identified here, as appropriate – for example, if personal knowledge or experience form an important part of the context, or if preliminary or pilot studies have been done, or if the study will involve secondary analysis of existing data (Maxwell, 1996).

For qualitative proposals, two other points may apply here. One is the first general evaluative question given in Chapter 14 – What is the position behind this research? If this question is applicable, it can be answered in general terms, to orient the reader early in the proposal. The other is more specific – Where on the structure continuum is the proposed study? This strongly influences later sections of the proposal. If a tightly structured qualitative study is planned, the proposal can proceed along similar lines to the quantitative proposal. If a more emergent study is planned, where focus and structure will develop as the study proceeds, this point should be made clearly. In the former case, there will be general and specific research questions. In the latter case, there will be only general orienting research questions.

Research questions

These were discussed in detail in Chapters 4 and 5. In the proposal outline suggested, they can follow from the general statement of purpose given in the introduction.

Conceptual framework, theory and hypotheses (if appropriate)

There is wide variation in the applicability of this section. If it applies, it is a matter of judgement whether the conceptual framework goes here, or in the methods section later in the proposal. Theory and hypotheses are included if appropriate, as explained in Chapter 4. If theory is involved, it may be included in the literature review section, rather than here. The role of theory in the research should be made clear here, however.

The literature

The proposal needs to be clear on the position taken with respect to the literature in the proposed study. As discussed in earlier chapters, there are three main possibilities:

- The literature is reviewed comprehensively in advance of the study, and this review is included as part of the proposal.
- The literature will be reviewed comprehensively ahead of the empirical stage of the research, but this review will not be done until the proposal is approved. In this case, the nature and scope of the literature to be reviewed, and familiarity with it, should be indicated.
- The literature will deliberately not be reviewed prior to the empirical work, but will be integrated into the research during the study, as in grounded theory research. In this case too, the nature and scope of the literature should be indicated.

For some qualitative proposals, the literature may be used in sharpening the focus of the study, and to give structure to its questions and design. If so, this should be indicated, along with how it is to be done. In all cases, the researcher needs to connect the proposed study to the literature (see, for example, Marshall and Rossman, 1989; Locke et al., 1993; Maxwell, 1996).

Methods

Strategy and design   In all proposals, whether quantitative, qualitative or mixed methods, it is a good idea to start this section with a short clear paragraph describing the strategy the research will use for answering the research questions (see the example given at the end of Section 14.4.4, p. 313). The basic quantitative designs we have discussed are the experimental, quasi-experimental and correlational survey designs. For these designs or variations of them, the conceptual framework may be shown here, instead of earlier. In qualitative studies, the location of the study along the structure continuum is particularly important for its strategy and design. As noted in Chapter 7, qualitative designs such as case studies (single or multiple, cross-sectional or longitudinal), ethnography or grounded theory may overlap, and elements of these strategies may be used separately or together. This means it will be difficult to compartmentalise the study neatly. This is not a problem, but it should be made clear that the proposed study uses elements of different strategies. Qualitative studies vary greatly on the issue of predeveloped conceptual frameworks, and the position of the proposed study on this matter should be indicated. A fully or partly predeveloped framework should be shown.

Where one will be developed, it needs to be indicated how this will be done. This will interact with data collection and analysis, and may be better dealt with there. Mixed methods studies should identify, describe and justify which mixed methods design is proposed.

Sample   As shown in Chapter 11, the three key sampling issues for quantitative research are the size of the sample, how it is to be selected and why, and what claims are made for its representativeness. The qualitative proposal should deal with the questions of who or what will be studied, and why. The sampling strategy is important for both types of studies, and especially important for both the quantitative and qualitative parts of a mixed methods study, and its logic needs to be clear. Where the sampling strategy itself is emergent, as in theoretical sampling, this needs to be explained.

Data collection   The two matters here are the instruments (if any) that will be used for data collection, and the procedures for administering the instruments. If a quantitative study proposes to use instruments that already exist, and information about their psychometric characteristics is available, it should be included. If the instruments are to be developed, the general steps for developing them should be shown. If a qualitative study proposes to use instruments (for example, observation schedules, structured or semi-structured interviews), the same comments apply. Less structured qualitative data collection techniques should be indicated and discussed, especially in terms of the quality of data issues shown in Section 14.5.3. For quantitative, qualitative and mixed methods studies, the procedures proposed for data collection should also be described, and the description should show why these data collection activities have been chosen. Possible threats to the validity of data, and strategies to minimise or control these threats, can also be indicated here.

Data analysis   Quantitative proposals should indicate the statistical procedures by which the data will be analysed. Similarly, the qualitative proposal needs to show how its data will be analysed, and how the proposed analysis fits with the other components of the study (see Section 9.8, p. 200). A mixed methods proposal needs to cover both types of analysis. If applicable, all types of proposal should indicate what computer use is planned in the analysis of the data.

Significance

The particular topic and its context will determine the study's significance. Other terms for this might be 'justification', 'importance' or 'contribution' of the study – they all address the third earlier overarching question: Why is this study worth doing? There are three general areas for the significance and contribution of the study – to knowledge in the area, to policy considerations and to practitioners (Marshall and Rossman, 1989). The first of these, contribution to knowledge, is closely tied to the literature in the area. One function of the literature review is to indicate gaps in the knowledge in the area, and to show how this study will contribute to filling those gaps. This has to be set against the position taken on the literature, as discussed above.

These are dealt with in Chapter 3 on ethical issues.

This is a list of the references cited in the proposal.

These may include any of the following: a timetable for the research, letters of introduction or permission, consent forms, measuring instruments, questionnaires, interview guides, observation schedules, examples of pilot study or other relevant work already completed (Maxwell, 2012).

15.2.2 Qualitative proposals

Qualitative studies vary greatly, and in many, the design and procedures will evolve. This obviously means that the writer cannot specify exactly what will be done in advance, in contrast with many quantitative proposals. When this is the case, there is a need to explain the flexibility the study requires and why, and how decisions will be made as the study unfolds. Together with this, as much detail as possible should be provided. Review committees have to judge both the quality, feasibility and viability of the proposed project, and the ability of the researcher to carry it out. The proposal itself, through its organisation, coherence and integration, attention to detail and conceptual clarity, can inspire confidence in the researcher's ability to execute the research. In addition, where specialised expertise is involved (for example, advanced statistical analysis, or grounded theory analysis), it helps for the researcher to indicate how this expertise will be acquired.

Marshall and Rossman (1989) stress the need for the qualitative proposal to reassure the reader as to the academic merit and discipline of the proposed research. This need is less pronounced today, when there is very much greater recognition and acceptance of qualitative research. However, there are two main ways the qualitative proposal can provide this reassurance. One is by giving information about the technical issues of the research, under research methods, as is routinely done in quantitative proposals; this means the sampling plan, the data collection and quality of data issues, and the proposed methods of analysis. The other applies to an unfolding qualitative study. Its proposal should indicate that focus will be developed as the study proceeds, and how this focus will be developed during the early empirical work.

Contrasting design and proposals at different ends of the structure continuum in qualitative research, Denzin and Lincoln (1994: 200) write:

> **The positivist, postpositivist, constructionist, and critical paradigms dictate, with varying**
> **degrees of freedom, the design of a qualitative research investigation. This can be looked**

at as a continuum, with rigorous design principles on one end and emergent, less well-structured directives on the other. Positivist research designs place a premium on the early identification and development of a research question and a set of hypotheses, choice of a research site, and establishment of sampling strategies, as well as a specification of the research strategies and methods of analysis that will be employed. A research proposal may be written that lays out the stages and phases of the study. These phases may be conceptualised ... (reflection, planning entry, data collection, withdrawal from the field, analysis, and write-up). This proposal may also include a budget, a review of the relevant literature, a statement concerning protection of human subjects, a copy of consent forms, interview schedules, and a timeline. Positivist designs attempt to anticipate all of the problems that may arise in a qualitative study. Such designs provide rather well defined road maps for the researcher. The scholar working in this tradition hopes to produce a work that finds its place in the literature on the topic being studied.

In contrast, much greater ambiguity is associated with postpositivist and nonpositivist designs – those based, for example, on the constructivist or critical theory paradigms or the ethnic, feminist, or cultural studies perspectives. In studies shaped by these paradigms and perspectives there is less emphasis on formal grant proposals, well-formulated hypotheses, tightly defined sampling frames, structured interview schedules, and predetermined research strategies and methods and forms of analysis. The researcher follows a path of discovery, using as a model qualitative works that have achieved the status of classics in the field.

Thus, for some types of qualitative research especially, we do not want to constrain too much the structure of the proposal, and we need to preserve flexibility. On the other hand, several writers (Coffey and Atkinson, 1996; Silverman, 2011) point out that this should not be taken to mean that 'anything goes'. Eisner (1991: 241–2) writes in the same vein about qualitative research in education:

Qualitative research proposals should have a full description of the topic to be investigated, a presentation and analysis of the research relevant to that topic, and a discussion of the issues within the topic or the shortfalls within the research literature that make the researcher's topic a significant one. They should describe the kinds of information that are able to be secured and the variety of methods or techniques that will be employed to secure such information. The proposals should identify the kinds of theoretical or explanatory resources that might be used in interpreting what has been described, and describe the kinds of places, people, and materials that are likely to be addressed.

The function of proposals is not to provide a watertight blueprint or formula the researcher is to follow, but to develop a cogent case that makes it plain to a knowledgeable reader that the writer has the necessary background to do the study and has thought clearly about the resources that are likely to be used in doing the study, and that the topic, problem, or issue being addressed is educationally significant.

Lest these comments be interpreted by some to mean that no planning is necessary in conducting qualitative research, or that 'anything goes', as they say, I want to make it clear that this is not how my words should be interpreted. Planning is necessary. Nevertheless, it should not and cannot function as a recipe or as a script. Evidence matters. One has a responsibility to support what one says, but support does not require measured evidence. Coherence, plausibility, and utility are quite acceptable in trying to deal with social complexity. My point is not to advocate anarchy or to reduce the study of schools and classrooms to a Rorschach projection, it is to urge that the analysis of a research proposal or a research study should employ criteria appropriate to the genre. Professors who make such assessments should understand, as should graduate students, the nature of the genre, what constitutes appropriate criteria, and why they are appropriate.

15.2.3 Mixed methods proposals

Once both the research questions and the design to answer them are clear in a mixed methods study, a strategy-design statement such as that shown in Section 14.4.4 can be constructed for the proposal. After this (and depending on the design chosen), it is often convenient to split a mixed methods proposal into its quantitative and qualitative parts, and to describe the sampling, data collection and data analysis for each part. However, while this splitting can help in presentation, it is important also to show the connections between the two parts. This is especially true for sampling – for example, when a qualitative in-depth second stage follows a larger sample quantitative first stage. After describing the sampling strategy for the first stage, an important question is: How will the second stage subsample be chosen and why?

15.2.4 Examples of proposals

The literature contains some useful examples of research proposals. In addition to the five shown in Punch (2006), a detailed treatment of proposals of different types is given by Locke et al. (1993). They present four examples of research proposals in full, and they give a detailed critical commentary on the different sections and aspects of each. They have chosen the proposals to illustrate different designs and styles of research, and using topics drawn from different areas. The four proposals are:

1. An experimental study ('The effects of age, modality, complexity of response and practice on reaction time'). This study proposes a two-factor design with repeated measures, to test 14 hypotheses about reaction times.
2. A qualitative study ('Returning women students in the community college'). This study proposes the use of in-depth interviewing to explore the meaning of experiences of older women returning as students to a community college.
3. A quasi-experimental study ('Teaching children to question what they read: An attempt to improve reading comprehension through training in a cognitive learning strategy'). This study proposes a quasi-experimental design to test three hypotheses about the acquisition of reading by children.

4. A funded grant proposal ('A competition strategy for worksite smoking cessation'). This renewal grant proposal also uses a quasi-experimental design, to assess the effectiveness of competition/facilitation on recruiting employees into a self-help smoking cessation programme, and on the outcomes of that programme.

In addition to these examples, Maxwell (2012) presents a qualitative proposal entitled 'How basic science teachers help medical students learn: The students' perspective', and he too gives a detailed commentary on the proposal. The research he describes proposes to use a case study of four exceptional teachers to answer six specific research questions about how teachers help medical students learn. Classroom participant observation and student and teacher interviews are the main sources of data, supplemented by relevant documentary data. Finally, Chenitz (1986) does not include an example of an actual proposal, but writes about the preparation of a proposal for a grounded theory study.

15.2.5 Abstracts and titles

An abstract is a brief summary, whether of a proposal or a finished study. Abstracts play an important role in the research literature, and they are required in proposals (usually), in dissertations and in research articles in refereed journals. Abstracts and titles are at the heart of the hierarchical indexing system for the research literature, which becomes more and more important as the volume of research continues to build. This indexing system enables researchers first to scan a title, to see if they need to go further into a project. If so, they can go to the abstract, which will tell them more, and perhaps enough. If they still need to go further, the last chapter (for example, of a dissertation) will often contain a summary of the study and its findings, in more detail than the abstract. They can then go to the full report if they need still more detail about the research.

Good abstract writing requires the skill of saying as much as possible in as few words as possible. For a proposal, the abstract needs to deal with two main issues – what the study is about and aims to achieve (usually best stated in terms of its research questions), and how it intends to do this. For a report, the abstract would need three main sections – these two, and a third which summarises what was found. The abstract should give an overview not just of the study itself, but also of the argument behind the study, and this should run through these sections. For most of us, abstract writing is a skill that needs to be developed, since we typically use many superfluous words when we speak and write. Together with the title, the abstract is usually written last, since it is difficult to summarise what has not yet been written.

Titles also have importance in the research literature indexing process, as indicated. Therefore a title should not just be an afterthought, nor should it use words or phrases that obscure rather than reveal meaning. Extending the point about abstract writing, the title should convey as much information as possible in as few words as possible. Titles and their role are discussed by Locke et al. (1993).

As noted, much of the focus in this book has been on getting research started, so the emphasis in this chapter is on writing the research proposal. Completed research is reported in several forms, and dissertations are one of the main forms. Because I have emphasised proposals, there is not a detailed description of the dissertation here, nor guidelines for its structure and writing. There is a considerable literature on this topic, and directions into this literature are given in the suggestions for further reading at the end of the chapter. Instead, this section now includes comments about three aspects of a dissertation – about the general content a dissertation should cover, about how a dissertation might be seen, and about the nature of dissertation writing.

Whatever its specific chapter structure, certain basic content is expected in a dissertation, which forms the report of a piece of research. This content includes:

- clear identification of the research area and the topic;
- a statement of purpose(s) and research questions;
- a setting of the study in context, including its relationship to relevant literature;
- a description of methods, including strategy and design, sample and the collection and analysis of data;
- a presentation of the data and of its analysis;
- a clear statement of the findings and a consideration of what can be concluded from those findings.

These headings are general enough to cover quantitative and most qualitative work. They are similar to Miles and Huberman's minimum guidelines for the structure of a qualitative research report (1994: 304):

1. The report should tell us what the study was about or came to be about.
2. It should communicate a clear sense of the social and historical context of the setting(s) where data were collected.
3. It should provide us with what Erickson (1986) calls the 'natural history of the inquiry', so we see clearly what was done, by whom and how. More deeply than in a sheer 'methods' account, we should see how key concepts emerged over time; which variables appeared and disappeared; which codes led into important insights.
4. A good report should provide basic data, preferably in focused form (vignettes, organised narrative, photographs, or data displays) so that the reader can, in parallel with the researcher, draw warranted conclusions. (Conclusions without data are a sort of oxymoron.)
5. Finally researchers should articulate their conclusions, and describe their broader meaning in the worlds of ideas and action they affect.

How the material is divided up into chapters and sections is a matter of judgement for the dissertation writer. In making this judgement, it is useful to remember that a dissertation is essentially the report of a piece of research, and the research itself constitutes a logical argument. Empirical research (quantitative, qualitative or mixed methods) systematically introduces empirical evidence into this argument, as its way of answering questions, testing hypotheses or building understanding. In line with this, one way to look at research, including dissertation research, is as a series of decisions. Especially in planning and designing the project, the researcher faces choices, many of which have been the subject of this book. Therefore the completed project itself is a combination of these choices, and the dissertation is the report of this. It is very often not the case that there is a right and wrong choice in the face of these many decisions. As I have stressed frequently in this book, it is rather a case of assessing each situation in the research, along with its alternative choices and their inevitable strengths and weaknesses, and of making each decision based on this analysis, in the light of the circumstances of the research, and of the need for the parts of the project to fit together.

To reflect this perspective in the writing of the dissertation, the writer can say what the choices were at each point, what choice was made and why. Seeing a dissertation this way makes it clear that there is no one way to do a piece of research, and that any piece of research will have its critics. Recognising this, the objective is to produce a thorough report of a carefully reasoned set of consistent choices, after consideration of the alternatives. In the written report, the writer is, among other things, telling the reader about the decision path taken through the research, and taking the reader down this path. The writing indicates why this path was chosen, the alternatives considered and the decisions taken. Presenting it this way conveys the impression of a thorough and careful project, well planned, well executed and well reported.

Much has been written on the topics of tactics and style in dissertation and academic writing, and both topics are covered in the further reading indicated. The following comments concern the need for clarity, the role of shortening, and the modular and iterative nature of research writing.

Whether proposal or report, research writing needs to communicate clearly and effectively, and striving for clarity is part of the writer's responsibility. Clarity is required in the structure of the document (the sections it will have, the order in which they appear, and how they are connected to each other), and in the words, sentences and paragraphs that make up the sections. Clear guidelines help in these matters in quantitative research, but it is rather more difficult to balance clarity with 'fidelity' in the qualitative context. Quoting Berger and Kellner (1981), Webb and Glesne point out that we have a moral obligation to reflect stories of human meanings as faithfully as possible. Reflecting the style of qualitative analysis emphasised in Chapter 9 of this book, with abstractions from the data to first order and then to second order constructs, they write (1992: 804):

> The second order constructs that social scientists use to make sense of peoples' lives must grow from and refer back to the first order constructs those same people use to define themselves and fill their lives with meaning. Moving gracefully between first and second order constructs in writing is difficult. We have suggested that students have a moral obligation to be clear; otherwise the reader is separated from the lives of the people under study and from the researcher's analysis. We are not suggesting that students should dumb-down their text or simplify what is complex just to make reading easier.

One general strategy to help in being clear is to put oneself (as writer) in the position of reader. What will make most sense to the reader? What will ensure that the reader is easily able to follow the argument and does not 'get lost' in the document? In this way, the writer tries to anticipate reader expectations and reactions. It is useful to remember also that the research document (proposal or report) will, in the end, be a stand-alone document. This means that the writer will not be there to interpret it for the reader, when it is being read.

Shortness is important because it often promotes clarity. There are various pressures today to restrict length – thus research journals restrict article length because of space considerations, and universities place upper limits on the length of dissertations. Ways to achieve shortness include getting straight to the point, cutting out unnecessary padding, not using long words when short ones will do, and keeping sentences short. The problem is that shortening requires reworking, which takes time. Every researcher discovers that lack of time is a problem in making the writing short (and clear). The message is to leave adequate time to do the shortening, if possible.

The organisation and structure of a dissertation (or proposal) usually require that it be segmented into sections. It is useful to see these as modules, to organise these modules into chapters, and to write the dissertation by writing these modules. Breaking it up makes the task less formidable. It is also helpful to write the different sections, or at least to keep full notes and draft the sections, as the stages of the research are being carried out. So many issues and decisions arise during a research project that it is impossible to remember all of them when it comes to 'writing time' without full notes of the various discussions, readings and so on. Wolcott (1990) goes even further with his advice: 'You cannot begin writing early enough.' The strategy of 'writing as you go' helps in making ideas explicit (Miles, Huberman and Saldana, 2013), and it also exploits the value of writing as a part of the learning. Some specific strategies to help in academic writing are given in Punch (2006: 72–4).

Writing to report versus writing to learn: writing as analysis

15.3 In the traditional model of research writing, the write-up does not get done until the research is completed and everything is figured out. 'I've done all the research, now I am writing it up.' Implicit in this is the idea that I don't start the writing until I have 'got it all worked out'. This is *writing to report*.

A different view sees writing as a way of learning, a way of knowing, a form of analysis and inquiry. This is the idea of 'writing in order to work it out'. In this view, I don't delay the writing until I have it all figured out. On the contrary, I use the process of writing itself to help me figure it out, since I learn by writing. Writers interpret, so writing is a way of learning, through discovery and analysis (Richardson, 1994). Thus writing becomes an integral part of the research, and not just an add-on once the 'real' research is completed. This is ***writing to learn.***

Writing to learn is more likely in qualitative research. However, it can also have a role in quantitative studies – for example, when the researcher is interpreting the results from the analysis of complex data sets, as in a multivariable correlational survey. In these cases, building an overall picture of the results, integrating and interpreting them, is similar to describing the emerging picture which accompanies some forms of qualitative data analysis (such as the Miles and Huberman type). At the same time, this model of writing is especially appropriate for some types of qualitative analysis, where the researcher is constructing a map or theoretical picture of the data, which emerges as the analysis proceeds. The process of writing can be a great help in developing this emerging picture. A practical implication of this view is that a useful tactic, when stuck or confused in developing the picture, is to attempt some writing about it.

Qualitative researchers are therefore more likely to stress that writing is analysis, not separated from it. In the 'analytic work of writing' (Coffey and Atkinson, 1996), writing is part of thinking, analysing and interpreting. The 'crisis of representation' (Denzin and Lincoln, 1994) has also brought shifts in conceptions of how to represent the 'reality' with which qualitative research (especially) has to deal, particularly the world of lived real experience. Together, these two points bring a new focus on the form of the written research report:

> The net effect of recent developments is that we cannot approach the task of 'writing up' our research as a straightforward (if demanding) task. We have to approach it as an analytical task, in which the form of our reports and representations is as powerful and significant as their content. (Coffey and Atkinson, 1996: 109)

This view, particularly prominent in recent writing about ethnography (Hammersley, 1995; Coffey and Atkinson, 1996), leads to a realisation of the many choices involved in the production of research documents.

Writing choices

15.4 Webb and Glesne (1992: 803) order the writing choices facing the researcher, especially the qualitative researcher, on three levels. Macro questions are about power, voice and politics in research; middle-range issues concern authorial authority, the marshalling of evidence, and the relationship between the researcher and the researched; micro issues are about whether a piece should be written in the first person, whether its tone changes when the author moves from data to theory, and how the story is told. Miles, Huberman and Saldana (2013) also identify a series of choices about reports and reporting, stressing choices rather than a fixed set of ideas. They include choices about the report's audiences and its hoped-for effects on them, the voice or genre of the report, its writing style, and its structure and format. To go with this array of choices, Denzin and Lincoln add that the process of writing is itself an interpretive, personal and political act (2011).

These writing choices in fact apply across the whole range of research approaches, quantitative, qualitative and mixed methods, though it is the developments in qualitative research in the past 30 years which have demonstrated this most clearly. The further reading indicated below, especially in qualitative research writing, includes discussions and examples of these choices.

Chapter summary

- The quantitative tradition gives us a straightforward set of headings for writing research proposals and reports; by contrast, qualitative research has introduced a much broader range of writing models and structures.
- Research proposals need to address the overarching questions of what, how and why, and a set of headings is presented to show the proposal as an argument, with a good fit between its component parts, while answering these questions.
- Qualitative proposals may require greater flexibility, and in some respects are more difficult to write, especially if an unfolding study is proposed.
- In writing mixed methods proposals, it is often useful to separate the methods section into qualitative and quantitative parts, but an overall description of strategy and design should show how the parts interconnect to answer the research questions.
- Abstracts and titles are important in indexing the research literature, and require the skill of conveying as much information as possible, in as few words as possible.
- Seeing the dissertation as the report of a piece of research leads to a clear view of the content it is expected to contain.
- 'Writing to report' is typical of the quantitative tradition in research; 'writing to learn' is often used in a qualitative context, where writing is seen as part of the analysis and inquiry.

Exercises and study questions

1. What is meant by the quantitative tradition in research reporting? What is the typical structure of a report, in this tradition?
2. How and why has qualitative research broadened writing strategies for proposals and dissertations?
3. What three central questions guide proposal development? Discuss each question, and how each can be dealt with in a proposal.
4. What does it mean to say that a research proposal is an argument?
5. What sections would you expect to find in a research proposal, and what is the function of each?
6. What chapters would you expect to find in a dissertation, and what is the function of each?
7. What is a research abstract, and why is it important?
8. Study a recent edition of a research journal such as the *American Educational Research Journal, The Administrative Science Quarterly*, the *British Journal of Psychology* or *The American Sociological Review*. What do you learn about research writing by studying the titles, abstracts and structure of the articles?

Further reading

Academic writing in general

Broadley, L. (1987) *Academic Writing in Social Practice*. Philadelphia: Temple University Press.

Mullins, C.J. (1977) *A Guide to Writing and Publishing in the Social and Behavioural Sciences.* New York: Wiley.

Strunk, W. Jr and White, E.B. (1979) *The Elements of Style*. 3rd edn. New York: Macmillan.

Zinsser, W. (1976) *On Writing Well*. New York: Harper and Row.

Qualitative writing

Atkinson, P. (1990) *The Ethnographic Imagination: Textual Constructions of Reality*. London: Routledge.

Becker, H.S. (1986) *Writing for Social Scientists: How to Finish Your Thesis, Book, or Article*. Chicago: University of Chicago Press.

Clifford, J. and Marcus, G.E. (1986) *Writing Culture: The Poetics and Politics of Ethnography*. Berkeley, CA: University of California Press.

Geertz, C. (1983) *Works and Lives: The Anthropologist as Author*. Cambridge: Polity Press.

Van Maanen, J. (1988) *Tales of the Field: On Writing Ethnography*. Chicago: University of Chicago Press.

Wolcott, H.F. (1990) *Writing Up Qualitative Research*. Newbury Park, CA: SAGE.

Proposals and dissertations

Glatthorn, A. and Joyner, R. (2005) *Writing the Winning Dissertation: A Step-by-Step Guide*. London: SAGE.

Krathwohl, D.R. (1988) *How to Prepare a Research Proposal*. 3rd edn. Syracuse, NY: Syracuse University Press.

Locke, L.F., Spirduso, W.W. and Silverman, S.J. (1993) *Proposals That Work: A Guide for Planning Dissertations and Grant Proposals*. 3rd edn. Newbury Park, CA: SAGE.

Long, T.J., Convey, J.J. and Chwalek, A.R. (1991) *Completing Dissertations in the Behavioural Sciences and Education*. San Francisco: Jossey-Bass.

Madsen, D. (1992) *Successful Dissertations and Theses*. 2nd edn. San Francisco: Jossey-Bass.

Phillips, M. and Pugh, D.S. (1987) *How to Get a PhD*. Milton Keynes: Open University Press.

Punch, K.F. (2006) *Developing Effective Research Proposals*. 2nd edn. London: SAGE.

Rudestam, K.E. and Newton, R.R. (2000) *Surviving your Dissertation: A Comprehensive Guide to Content and Process*. 2nd edn. Thousand Oaks, CA: SAGE.

Sternberg, D. (1981) *How to Complete and Survive a Doctoral Dissertation*. New York: St Martins.

Thody, A. (2006) *Writing and Presenting Research*. London: SAGE.

Walliman, N. (2004) *Your Undergraduate Dissertation: The Essential Guide to Success*. London: SAGE.

GLOSSARY

Accounting for variance – a central strategy in quantitative research; accounting for the variation in a dependent variable through studying its relationship with independent variables.

Action research – using empirical procedures, in iterative cycles of action and research, to solve practical problems.

Analysis of covariance – a statistical technique for investigating the difference between groups on some dependent variable after controlling for one or more covariates.

Analysis of variance – a statistical technique for investigating differences between groups on some dependent variable.

Asynchronous – communications using the Internet that are subject to delays in transmission.

Audit trail (through the data) – showing how the data were analysed to arrive at conclusions.

Axial coding – discovering connections in the data between abstract concepts; used in grounded theory analysis; produces theoretical codes.

Case study – a research strategy which focuses on the in-depth, holistic and in-context study of one or more cases; will typically use multiple sources of data.

Chat rooms – any form of technology allowing participants to chat individually (instant messaging) or in groups (online forums and virtual environments) in real time.

Chi square – a statistical technique with many uses; a common use is to see whether variables in a cross-tabulation are related to each other.

Coding – placing labels or tags on pieces of qualitative data.

Conceptual framework – a framework showing the central concepts of a piece of research, and their conceptual status with respect to each other; often expressed as a diagram.

Contingency table – uses cross-tabulation to see if the distribution of one variable is related to (or contingent upon) the other variable.

Continuous variable – a variable which varies in degree rather than in kind (e.g. height, level of income, level of achievement); synonym is measured variable.

Control variable – a variable whose effect we want to rule out or control; synonym is covariate.

Correlation – a statistical technique for showing the strength and direction of the relationship between two variables.

Correlational survey – a quantitative survey where the focus is on studying the relationships between variables.

Covariate – see Control variable.

Cross-tabulation – two variables are cross-tabulated against each other.

Cyberspace – a space created by the Internet in which digital objects exist.

Data collection questions – the actual questions asked to collect the data; examples are survey questions in quantitative research, and interview questions in qualitative research; data collection questions follow logically from specific research questions.

Deduction – moving downward in levels of abstraction, from more general and abstract to more specific and concrete; opposite of induction.

Definitions – *conceptual* definition: the definition of a concept (or variable) in terms of other abstract concepts. This brings the need to find observable activities which are indicators of the concept. Those activities constitute the *operational* definition of the concept. Construct validity is enhanced when there are tight logical links between the conceptual and operational definitions.

Deliberate (or purposive) sampling – the sample is drawn from the population in a deliberate or targeted way, according to the logic of the research.

Dependent variable – the variable seen as the 'effect' in a cause–effect relationship. Synonyms are: outcome variable in experimental design; criterion variable in a correlational survey.

Discourse – a system of language which draws on a particular terminology and which encodes specific forms of knowledge; often used to refer to systems of knowledge and their associated practices (Seale, 1998; Tonkiss, 1998).

Discrete variable – a variable which varies in kind, not degree; its variance is in categories (e.g. eye colour, religious affiliation, country of birth); synonyms are categorical variable, discontinuous variable.

Email – a system of communication involving the composing, sending, storing and receiving of messages using the Internet.

Empirical – based on direct experience or observation of the world.

Empirical criterion (for a research question) – is it clear what data are needed to answer this research question? If yes, the research question satisfies the empirical criterion. If no, further development of the research question is necessary.

Empiricism – philosophical term to describe the epistemological theory that sees experience as the foundation or source of knowledge.

Ethical codes – negotiated agreements from professional associations about acceptable practice in particular professional, occupational and institutional contexts; tend to include detailed rules for conducting research.

Ethics – the study of what are good, right or virtuous courses of action; can be approached from different points of view.

Deontological ethics – emphasises acting out of duty, as opposed to pleasure, inclination or interest. What is the right course of action in this situation?

Teleological ethics – emphasises choosing the best course of action, using the 'greatest happiness' or 'utility' principle. What course of action in this situation is likely to result in the greatest good for all concerned?

Aretaic ethics – emphasises the most virtuous ways of being and living. What course of action in this situation accords with the traits or dispositions of the virtuous person?

Situational ethics – emphasises that ethical decisions are contextual, and are never neatly defined or fully resolved.

Ethnography – the preferred research strategy of anthropologists; seeks to understand the symbolic significance of behaviour, in its cultural context, to the participants; aims for a full cultural description of the way of life of some group of people.

Ethnomethodology – examines how people produce orderly social interaction in ordinary everyday situations; exposes the taken-for-granted 'rules' which constitute the infrastructure making everyday social interaction possible.

Experiment – a predominantly quantitative research design where [a] one or more independent variables are manipulated to study their effect on a dependent variable and [b] participants are randomly assigned to treatment or comparison groups.

Factor analysis – a family of statistical techniques for reducing the number of variables without loss of information.

Fact–value gap – the view that statements of fact and statements of value have no *logical* connection between them.

Focus group (interview) – a powerful method of qualitative data collection where a small group (6–8) of people are interviewed as a group.

Frequency distribution – a table or diagram showing the distribution of a set of scores.

Grounded theory – a distinctive strategy for research which aims to generate explanatory theory grounded in data.

Grounded theory analysis – specific procedures in the analysis of data for generating explanatory theory; focuses essentially on raising the conceptual level of (i.e. reconceptualising) the data.

Hierarchy of concepts – a useful tool in planning and organising research; the hierarchy is area-topic-general research questions–specific research questions–data collection questions.

Hypothesis – a predicted answer to a research question; in theory verification research the hypothesis follows from the theory by deduction.

Hypothetico-deductive model – the central strategy of theory verification research which stresses the empirical testing of hypotheses deduced from theory. A *hypothesis* is *deduced* from a *theory* and then tested against data.

Independent variable – the variable seen as the 'cause' in a cause–effect relationship. (Synonyms are: treatment variable in experimental design; predictor variable in a correlational survey.)

Induction – moving upwards in levels of abstraction, from more specific and concrete to more general and abstract; opposite of deduction.

Interaction – a technical term in quantitative research design; two (or more) independent variables may interact in their effect on a dependent variable.

Internet – a network connecting computer-based websites in standardised ways to form the World Wide Web.

Internet research – the use of the Internet as a tool for conducting research in virtual or actual locations.

Latent trait – the trait (or variable) we want to measure is hidden; we measure it by inference from its observable indicators.

Listservers – software applications that allow a mail service provider to control who can read and post to an email list.

Measurement – the operation which turns data into numbers.

Member checking – the qualitative researcher checks the data and the analysis as it develops with the people being studied, who gave the data; typical in grounded theory research.

Memoing – pausing, in qualitative analysis especially, to write down ideas about the data as they occur during coding and analysis.

Mixed-method research – empirical research which brings together quantitative data (and methods) and qualitative data (and methods); there are many models for doing this.

Multiple causation – the idea that a particular 'effect' has multiple causes which are usually interrelated.

Multiple linear regression – a quantitative design and data analysis strategy with several independent variables and one dependent variable; aims to account for variance in the dependent variable.

Multivariate – more than one dependent variable.

Naturalism – the social world is studied in its natural state, rather than contrived for research purposes.

Negative correlation – high scores on one variable go with low scores on the other variable (and vice versa); as one variable goes up, the other variable goes down.

Open coding – concentrates on raising the conceptual level of the data; guided by the question: what is this piece of data an example of? Used in grounded theory analysis; produces substantive codes.

Operationalism – in quantitative research, the idea that the meaning of a concept is given by the set of operations necessary to measure it (see definitions – operational).

Paradigm – a set of assumptions about the social world, and about what constitute proper techniques and topics for inquiring into that world; a set of basic beliefs, a world view, a view of how science should be done (ontology, epistemology, methodology).

Participant observation – the preferred strategy for doing ethnography; the researcher aims to be both observer of and participant in the situation being studied, in order to understand it.

Population – the target group, usually large, about whom we want to develop knowledge, but which we cannot study directly; therefore we sample from that population.

Positive correlation – high scores on one variable go with high scores on the other variable (and vice versa); the two variables go up or down together.

Positivism – in a loose sense, has come to mean an approach to social research that emphasises the discovery of general laws, and separates facts from values; it often involves an empiricist commitment to naturalism and quantitative methods (Seale, 1998: 328).

Principle of Autonomy – the obligation on the part of the investigator to respect each participant as a person capable of making an informed decision regarding participation in the research study.

Principle of Beneficence – the obligation on the part of the investigator to attempt to maximize benefits for the individual participant and/or society, while minimising risk of harm to the individual.

Principle of Trust – the obligation of investigators to safeguard the information entrusted to them by participants in the research; includes the principles of confidentiality, privacy and anonymity.

Purposive (or deliberate sampling) – the sample is drawn from the population in a deliberate or targeted way, according to the logic of the research.

Quasi-experiment – naturally occurring treatment groups permit comparisons between the groups approximating those of true experimental design.

Reactivity – the idea that the data being collected might be somehow changed or influenced by the data collection process itself.

Regression – a statistical technique for predicting scores on one variable from scores on another variable.

Reliability (of data) – in quantitative research, the consistency of measurement: (a) consistency over time – test-retest reliability; (b) consistency within indicators – internal consistency reliability. In qualitative research, the dependability of the data.

Representative sampling – a sampling strategy where each unit of the population has an equal chance of being selected in the sample; directed at generalisation.

Research ethics as situated deliberation – researchers need to interpret ethical codes – which often include abstract principles and standards – in the context of particular research situations.

Research questions – organise the research by showing its purposes. General research questions guide the research by showing the general questions the research aims to answer; too general themselves to be answered directly; need to be made more specific. Specific research questions make the general research questions more specific; connect the general research questions to the data.

Sample – a smaller group which is actually studied, drawn from a larger population; data are collected (and analysed) from the sample, and inferences are then made to the population.

Science as method – an empirical method for building knowledge where the objective is to develop and test theory to explain data.Theory generation research – generating theory from data; theory verification research – testing theory against data.

Search engine – a mechanical program that creates a database by matching keywords to content stored on the Internet and then organises and displays the results in a readily accessible way.

Secondary analysis – the re-analysis of previously collected and analysed data.

Selective coding – used in grounded theory analysis; identifies the core category of a grounded theory, and raises the conceptual level of the analysis a second time.

Semiotics – the science of signs; focuses on the process whereby something comes to stand for something else.

Sensitivity (of measurement) – the ability of a measuring instrument to produce (reliable) variance, to differentiate between the people being measured.

Statistical inference – a set of decision-making rules to assess the accuracy of the inference made from sample to population.

Statistically significant – using inferential statistics to conclude that a particular result is very unlikely to have occurred by chance; such a result is therefore taken as real.

Structured interview – interview questions are pre-established and have pre-set response categories.

Subject gateway – a database containing web resources that have been manually selected, evaluated and checked for quality by subject experts.

Synchronous – communications using the Internet that appear directly on a recipient's computer.

T-test – a statistical technique for investigating differences between two groups on some dependent variable; a special case of analysis of variance.

Theoretical sampling – consecutive cycles of data collection are guided by the theoretical directions emerging from the ongoing analysis; typically used in grounded theory research.

Theoretical saturation – the 'end-stage' of theoretical sampling in grounded theory research, when new data are not showing new theoretical elements, but rather confirming what has already been found.

Theoretical sensitivity – a term used in grounded theory; being alive and sensitive to the theoretical possibilities in the data; the ability to 'see', with theoretical and analytic depth, what is in the data.

Theory – explanatory theory – a set of propositions which explain the data; the concepts in the propositions of the explanatory theory are more abstract than those in the data.

Theory generation research – empirical research where the objective is discovering or constructing theory to explain data; starts with data, ends with theory.

Theory verification research – empirical research where the objective is testing theory against data; starts with theory, uses data to test the theory (see hypothetico-deductive method).

Thick description – the emphasis in qualitative research on capturing and conveying the full picture of behaviour being studied – holistically, comprehensively and in context.

Triangulation – using several kinds of methods or data to study a topic; the most common type is data triangulation, where a study uses a variety of data sources.

Univariate – only one dependent variable.

Unstructured interview – interview questions and response categories are not pre-established; interview questions are deliberately open-ended.

Validity – a complex term with many meanings, both technical and general; three important technical meanings are: the validity of a measuring instrument; the validity of a research design (internal validity); the truth status of a research report.

Validity (of measurement) – the extent to which a measuring instrument measures what it is supposed to measure.

Content (or face) validity: How well does the measuring instrument sample from all areas of content in the conceptual description?

Criterion related validity – How does the measuring instrument compare with another measure of the same construct?

Predictive validity – How well does the measuring instrument predict later behaviour?

Construct validity – How well does the measuring instrument conform with theoretical expectations?

Value judgements – moral or ethical judgements; judgements of what is good or bad, right or wrong, etc.; usually made as terminal values – ends in themselves.

Virtual environments – three systems on the Internet that allow users to interact using text or three-dimensional graphics. The original system, MUDs (Multi-User Dungeons), is a simple text-based environment that allows players to interact one at a time. The next generation, MOOs (Multi-user Object Oriented), is a text-based environment which allows more than one player to talk at one time as well as display emotions and manipulate objects. The latest generation, MMORPGs (Massive multi-player online RPG), is a graphics-based environment in which multiple players can interact using text and personally designed three-dimensional images.

Web 2.0 – a relationship in which Internet users take an active role by interacting and collaborating with other users through applications such as Wikis, blogs, MySpace, Facebook, twitter and so on to create online content.

World Wide Web – a system of interlinked websites on the Internet commonly known as 'the web'.

APPENDIX 1: DRAWING AND VERIFYING CONCLUSIONS IN QUALITATIVE ANALYSIS

This appendix contains the two lists of tactics given by Miles and Huberman (1994), the first for generating meaning in qualitative analysis, and the second for testing or confirming findings. All tactics in both lists are described and discussed in the Miles and Huberman book.

Both sets of tactics fit within the set of six 'fairly classic' analytic moves noted by Miles and Huberman (1994: 8) as common general features of different approaches to qualitative analysis:

- affixing codes to a set of field notes drawn from observations or interviews;
- noting reflections or other remarks in the margins;
- sorting and sifting through these materials to identify similar phrases, relationships between variables, patterns, themes, distinct differences between subgroups, and common sequences;
- isolating these patterns and processes, commonalities and differences, and taking them out to the field in the next wave of data collection;
- gradually elaborating a small set of generalisations that cover the consistencies discerned in the databases;
- confronting those generalisations with a formalised body of knowledge in the form of constructs or theories.

Tactics for generating meaning

A1.1 These tactics are numbered from 1 to 13. They are arranged roughly from the descriptive to the explanatory, and from the concrete to the more conceptual and abstract. They are briefly overviewed and then listed.

Noting patterns, themes (1), seeing plausibility (2), and clustering (3) help the analyst see 'what goes with what'. Making metaphors (4), like the preceding three tactics, is a way to achieve more integration among diverse pieces of data. Counting (5) is also a familiar way to see 'what's there'.

Making contrasts/comparisons (6) is a pervasive tactic that sharpens understanding. Differentiation sometimes is needed, too, as in partitioning variables (7).

We also need tactics for seeing things and their relationships more abstractly. These include subsuming particulars into the general (8); factoring (9) an analogue of a familiar quantitative technique; noting relations between variables (10); and finding intervening variables (11).

Finally, how can we systematically assemble a coherent understanding of data? The tactics discussed are building a logical chain of evidence (12) and making conceptual/theoretical coherence (13).

The 13 tactics are:

1. noting patterns, themes
2. seeing plausibility
3. clustering
4. making metaphors
5. counting
6. making contrasts/comparisons
7. partitioning variables
8. subsuming particulars into the general
9. factoring
10. noting relations between variables
11. finding intervening variables
12. building a logical chain of evidence
13. making conceptual/theoretical coherence (1994: 245–62).

Tactics for testing or confirming findings

A1.2 These tactics are also numbered from 1 to 13, beginning with those aimed at ensuring the basic quality of the data, then moving to those that check findings by examining exceptions to early patterns. They conclude with tactics that take a sceptical, demanding approach to emerging explanations.

Data quality can be assessed through checking for representativeness (1); checking for researcher effects (2) on the case, and vice versa; and triangulating (3) across data sources and methods. These checks also may involve weighting the evidence (4), deciding which kinds of data are most trustable.

Looking at 'unpatterns' can tell us a lot. Checking the meaning of outliers (5), using extreme cases (6), following up surprises (7), and looking for negative evidence (8) are all tactics that test a conclusion about a 'pattern' by saying what it is not like.

How can we really test our explanations? Making if–then tests (9), ruling out spurious relations (10), replicating a finding (11), and checking out rival explanations (12) are all ways of submitting our beautiful theories to the assault of brute facts, or to a race with someone else's beautiful theory.

Finally, a good explanation deserves attention from the very people whose behaviour it is about – informants who supplied the original data. The tactic of getting feedback from informants (13) concludes the list.

The 13 tactics are:

1. checking for representativeness
2. checking for researcher effects
3. triangulating
4. weighting the evidence
5. checking the meaning of outliers
6. using extreme cases
7. following up surprises
8. looking for negative evidence
9. making if-then tests
10. ruling out spurious relations
11. replicating a finding
12. checking out rival explanations
13. getting feedback from informants (Miles and Huberman, 1994: 262–77).

REFERENCES

Abbott, P. and Sapsford, R. (2006) 'Ethics, politics and research', in R. Sapsford and V. Jupp (eds), *Data Collection and Analysis*. London: SAGE. pp. 291–312.

Ackoff, R. (1953) *The Design of Social Research*. Chicago: University of Chicago Press.

Adler, P.A. and Adler, P. (1994) 'Observational techniques', in N.K. Denzin and Y.S. Lincoln (eds), *Handbook of Qualitative Research*. Thousand Oaks, CA: SAGE. pp. 377–92.

Alder, N. (2002) 'Interpretations of the meaning of care: Creating caring relationships in urban middle school classrooms', *Urban Education*, 37(2): 241–66.

Alderson, P. and Morrow, V. (2011) *The Ethics of Research with Children and Young People: A Practical Handbook*. London: SAGE.

Aldridge, J.M., Fraser, B.J. and Huang, T.I. (1999) 'Investigating classroom environments in Taiwan and Australia with multiple research methods', *Journal of Educational Research*, 93(1): 48–62.

Amundsen, C. and Wilson, M. (2012) 'Are we asking the right questions? A conceptual review of educational development in higher education', *Review of Educational Research*, 82(1): 90–126.

Anastasi, A. (1988) *Psychological Testing*. 6th edn. New York: Macmillan.

Andrews, D., Nonneck, B. and Preece, J. (2003) 'Conducting research on the Internet: Online survey design, development and implementation guidelines', *International Journal of Human-Computer Interaction*, 16(2): 185–210.

Andrich, D. (1988) *Rasch Models for Measurement*. Newbury Park, CA: SAGE.

Andrich, D. (1997) 'Rating scale analysis', in J.P. Keeves (ed.), *Educational Research, Methodology, and Measurement: An International Handbook*. 2nd edn. Oxford: Elsevier. pp. 874–80.

Anward, J. (1997) 'Semiotics in educational research', in J.P. Keeves (ed.), *Educational Research, Methodology, and Measurement: An International Handbook*. 2nd edn. Oxford: Elsevier. pp. 106–11.

Apple, M. (1991) 'Introduction', in P. Lather (1994) *Getting Smart: Feminist Research and Pedagogy With/In the Postmodern*. New York: Routledge.

Asch, S.E. (1955) 'Opinions and social pressure', *Scientific American*, 193: 31–5.

Asher, H.B. (1976) *Causal Modeling*. Beverley Hills, CA: SAGE.

Aspin, D.N. (1995) 'Logical empiricism, post-empiricism and education', in P. Higgs (ed.), *Metatheories in Philosophy and Education*. Johannesburg: Heinnemann. pp. 21–49.

Atkinson, J.M. (1978) *Discovering Suicide: Studies in the Social Organization of Sudden Death*. London: Macmillan.

Atkinson, P. (1992) *Understanding Ethnographic Texts*. Newbury Park, CA: SAGE.

Atkinson, P. and Hammersley, M. (1994) 'Ethnography and participant observation', in N.K. Denzin and Y.S. Lincoln (eds), *Handbook of Qualitative Research*. Thousand Oaks, CA: SAGE. pp. 248–61.

Ball, S.J. (1981) *Beachside Comprehensive: A Case Study of Secondary Schooling*. Cambridge: Cambridge University Press.

Barker, R.G. and Gump, P.V. (1964) *Big School, Small School: High School Size and Student Behavior*. Stanford, CA: Stanford University Press.

Bean, J. and Creswell, J.W. (1980) 'Student attrition among women at a liberal arts college', *Journal of College Student Personnel*, 3: 320–7.

Becker, H. (1971) *Sociological Work*. London: Allen Lane.

Behar, R. (1993) *Translated Woman: Crossing the Border with Esperanza's Story*. Boston: Beacon.

Bentham, J. (1823) *An Introduction to the Principles of Morals and Legislation*. London: W. Pickering and W. Wilson.

Berelson, B. (1952) *Content Analysis in Communication Research*. New York: Hafner.

Berger, P.L. and Kellner, H. (1981) *Sociology Reinterpreted: An Essay on Method and Vocation*. Garden City, NY: Anchor/Doubleday.

Berger, P.L. and Luckman, T. (1967) *The Social Construction of Reality*. Harmondsworth, Middlesex: Allen Lane.

Billig, M. (1991) *Ideologies and Opinions*. London: SAGE.

Black, T.R. (1999) *Doing Quantitative Research in the Social Sciences*. London: SAGE.

Blaikie, N. (1993) *Approaches to Social Enquiry*. Cambridge: Polity.

Blau, P.M. and Duncan, O.D. (1967) *The American Occupational Structure*. New York: Wiley.

Blommaert, J. and Bulcaen, C. (2000) 'Critical discourse analysis', *Annual Review of Anthropology*, 29: 447–66.

Bloor, M. (1978) 'On the analysis of observational data: A discussion of the worth and uses of inductive techniques and respondent validation', *Sociology*, 12(3): 545–52.

Blumer, H. (1969) *Symbolic Interactionism: Perspective and Method*. Englewood Cliffs, NJ: Prentice-Hall.

Bohanek, J.F. (2008) 'Family narratives, self and gender in early adolescence', *Journal of Early Adolescence*, 28(1): 153–76.

Bourdieu, P. (1973) 'Cultural reproduction and social reproduction; in R. Brown (ed.), *Knowledge, Education and Cultural Change*. London: Tavistock. pp. 71–112.

Bracht, G.H. and Glass, G.V. (1968) 'The external validity of experiments', *American Educational Research Journal*, 5(4): 437–74.

Brandt, R.M. (1981) *Studying Behavior in Natural Settings*. Washington, DC: University Press of America.

Brewer, J. and Hunter, A. (2005) *Foundations of Multimethod Research: Synthesizing Styles*. 2nd edn. Thousand Oaks, CA: SAGE.

Brodbeck, M. (ed.) (1968) *Readings in the Philosophy of the Social Sciences*. London: Macmillan.

Brody, H. (2002) *Stories of Sickness*. 2nd edn. New York: Oxford University Press.

Broudy, H.S., Ennis, R.H. and Krimerman, L.I. (1973) *Philosophy of Educational Research*. New York: Wiley.

Brown, G. and Yule, G. (1984) *Discourse Analysis*. Cambridge: Cambridge University Press.

Bryant, A. and Charmaz, K. (2007a) 'Grounded theory research: Methods and practices', in A. Bryant and K. Charmaz (eds), *The Sage Handbook of Grounded Theory*. Thousand Oaks, CA: SAGE. pp. 1–28.

Bryant, A. and Charmaz, K. (eds) (2007b) *The Sage Handbook of Grounded Theory*. Thousand Oaks, CA: SAGE.

Bryman, A. (1988) *Quantity and Quality in Social Research*. London: Unwin Hyman.

Bryman, A. (1992) 'Quantitative and qualitative research: Further reflections on their integration', in J. Brannen (ed.), *Mixing Methods: Qualitative and Quantitative Research*. Aldershot: Avebury. pp. 57–78.

Buchanan, E. and Zimmer, M. (2012) 'Internet research ethics', in E. Zalta (ed.) *The Stanford Encyclopedia of Philosophy*. Retrieved from http://plato.stanford.edu/archives/win2012/entries/ethics-internet-research (accessed 18 October 2013).

Burns, R.B. (2000) *Introduction to Research Methods*. 4th edn. London: SAGE.

Burns, A. and Radford, J. (2008) 'Parent-child interaction in Nigerian families: conversation analysis, context and culture', *Child Language Teaching and Therapy*, 24(2): 193–209.

Burton, S. and Steane, P. (2004) *Surviving Your Thesis*. London: Routledge.

Caird, J., Kavanagh, J., Oliver, K., Oliver, S., O'Mara, A., Stansfield, C. and Thomas, J. (2011) *Childhood obesity and educational attainment: A systematic review*. University of London: EPPI centre. Retrieved from eprints.ioe.ac.uk/16316/1/Caird_et_al._2011._Childhood_obesity_and_educational_attainment._a_systematic_review.pdf (accessed 24th September 2013).

Calder, J. and Sapsford, R. (1996) 'Multivariate analysis', in R. Sapsford and V. Jupp (eds), *Data Collection and Analysis*. London: SAGE. pp. 262–381.

Campbell, D.T. and Stanley, J.C. (1963) *Experimental and Quasi-Experimental Designs for Research*. Chicago: Rand McNally. pp. 37–64.

Charlesworth, A. (2008) 'Understanding and managing legal issues in internet research', in N. Fielding, R. Lee and G. Blank (eds), *The Sage Handbook of Online Research Methods*. London: Sage. pp. 42–57.

Charmaz, K. (2006) *Constructing Grounded Theory: A Practical Guide Through Qualitative Analysis*. London: SAGE.

Charters, W.W. Jr (1967) 'The hypothesis in scientific research'. Unpublished paper, University of Oregon, Eugene.

Chenitz, W.C. (1986) 'Getting started: The research proposal for a grounded theory study', in W.C. Chenitz and J.M. Swanson (eds), *From Practice to Grounded Theory: Qualitative Research in Nursing*. Menlo Park, CA: Addison-Wesley.

Clandinin, D.J. and Connelly, F.M. (1994) 'Personal experience methods', in N.K. Denzin and Y.S. Lincoln (eds), *Handbook of Qualitative Research*. Thousand Oaks, CA: SAGE. pp. 413–27.

Cochran, W.G. (1977) *Sampling Techniques*. 3rd edn. New York: Wiley.

Coffey, A. and Atkinson, P. (1996) *Making Sense of Qualitative Data: Complementary Research Strategies*. Thousand Oaks, CA: SAGE.

Coleman, J.S., Campbell, E.Q., Hobson, C.J., McPartland, J., Mood, A.M., Weinfeld, F.D. and York, R.L. (1966) *Equality of Educational Opportunity*. Washington, DC: US Government Printing Office.

Coles, R. (1989) *The Call of Stories*. Boston: Houghton Mifflin.

Coley, S.M. and Scheinberg, C.A. (1990) *Proposal Writing*. Thousand Oaks, CA: SAGE.

Connelly, F.M. and Clandinin, D.J. (1999) *Shaping a Professional Identity: Stories of Educational Practice*. New York: Teachers' College Press.

Converse, J.M. and Presser, S. (1986) *Survey Questions: Handcrafting the Standardized Questionnaire*. Beverly Hills, CA: SAGE.

Corbin, J. (1986) 'Coding, writing memos and diagramming', in W.C. Chenitz and J.M. Swanson (eds), *From Practice to Grounded Theory: Qualitative Research in Nursing*. Menlo Park, CA: Addison-Wesley. pp. 102–20.

Cortazzi, M. (1991) *Primary Teaching: How It Is – A Narrative Account*. London: David Fulton.

Coulthard, M. (1985) *An Introduction to Discourse Analysis*. 2nd edn. London: Longman.

Couper, M. (2008) 'Technology trends in survey data collection', *Social Science Computer Review*, 23(4): 486–501. Retrieved from SAGE Journals Online.

Cressey, D.R. (1950) 'The criminal violation of financial trust', *American Sociological Review*, 15: 738–43.

Cressey, D.R. (1971) *Other People's Money: A Study in the Social Psychology of Embezzlement*. 2nd edn. Belmont, CA: Wadsworth.

Creswell, J.W. (2013) *Research Design: Qualitative, Quantitative and Mixed Method Approaches*. 4th edn. Thousand Oaks, CA: SAGE.

Creswell, J.W. and Plano Clark, V. (2007) *Designing and Conducting Mixed Methods Research*. Thousand Oaks, CA: SAGE.

Cronbach, L.J. (1951) 'Coefficient alpha and the internal structure of tests', *Psychometrika*, 16: 297–334.

Cronbach, L.J. (1957) 'The two disciplines of scientific psychology', *American Psychologist*, 12: 671–84.

Cronbach, L.J. and Suppes, P. (eds) (1969) *Research for Tomorrow's Schools: Disciplined Inquiry for Education*. New York: Macmillan.

Dale, A., Arber, S. and Procter, M. (1988) *Doing Secondary Analysis*. London: Unwin Hyman.

Davis, J.A. (1985) *The Logic of Causal Order*. Beverley Hills, CA: SAGE.

Delamont, S. (1990) *Sex Roles and the School*. 2nd edn. London: Routledge and Kegan Paul.

Delamont, S. (2012) *Sex Roles and the School*. 2nd edn. London: Routledge.

Denzin, N.K. (1983) 'Interpretive interactionism', in G. Morgan (ed.), *Beyond Method: Strategies for Social Research*. Beverly Hills, CA: SAGE. pp. 129–46.

Denzin, N.K. (1989) *The Research Act: A Theoretical Introduction to Sociological Methods*. 3rd edn. New York: McGraw-Hill.

Denzin, N.K. (1997) *Interpretive Ethnography: Ethnographic Practices for the 21st Century*. London: SAGE.

Denzin, N.K. and Lincoln, Y.S. (eds) (1994) *Handbook of Qualitative Research*. Thousand Oaks, CA: SAGE.

Denzin, N.K. and Lincoln, Y.S. (eds) (2011) *The SAGE Handbook of Qualitative Research*. Thousand Oaks, CA: SAGE.

de Vaus, D.A. (2013) *Surveys in Social Research*. 5th edn. London: Routledge.

Dillman, D.A. (2006) *Mail and Internet Surveys: The Tailored Design Method*. 2nd edn. New York: Wiley.

DiMaggio, P., Hargittai, E., Neuman, W.R. and Robinson, J.P. (2001) 'Social implications of the Internet', *Annual Review of Sociology*, 27: 307–36.

Douglas, J.D. (1985) *Creative Interviewing*. Beverly Hills, CA: SAGE.

Durkheim, E. (1951) *Suicide: A Study in Sociology*. Trans. J. Spaulding and G. Sampson. Glencoe, IL: Free Press.

Eco, U. (1976) *A Theory of Semiotics*. Bloomington, IN: Indiana University Press.

Edley, N. (2001) 'Analysing masculinity: interpretive repertoires, ideological dilemmas and subject positions', in M. Wetherell, S. Taylor and S.J. Yates (eds), *Discourse as Data: A Guide for Analysis*. London: SAGE. pp. 189–228.

Edwards, A.L. (1957) *Techniques of Attitude Scale Construction*. New York: Appleton-Century-Crofts.

Edwards, R. and Mauthner, M. (2002) 'Ethics and feminist research: Theory and practice', in M. Mauthner, M. Birch, J. Jessop and T. Miller (eds), *Ethics in Qualitative Research*. London: SAGE.

Eisner, E.W. (1991) *The Enlightened Eye: Qualitative Inquiry and the Enhancement of Educational Practice*. New York: Macmillan.

Elgesem, D. (2002) 'What is special about ethical issues in online research?', *Ethics and Information Technology*, 4(3): 195–203.

Elliott, J. (2005) *Using Narrative in Social Research: Quantitative and Qualitative Approaches*. London: SAGE.

Embretson, S. and Yang, X. (2006) 'Item response theory', in J.L. Green, G. Camilli and P.B. Elmore (eds), *Handbook of Complementary Methods in Education Research*. Mahwah, NJ: Lawrence Erlbaum. pp. 385–409.

Enns, C.Z. and Hackett, G. (1990) 'Comparison of feminist and non-feminist women's reactions to variants of non-sexist and feminist counseling', *Journal of Counseling Psychology*, 37(1): 33–40.

Erickson, F. (1986) 'Qualitative methods in research on teaching', in M.C. Wittrock (ed.), *Handbook of Research on Teaching*. 3rd edn. New York: Macmillan. pp. 119–61.

ESDS (2004) ESDS Qualidata website. *Economic and Social Data Service*. http://www.esds.ac.uk/qualidata/about/introduction.asp

Evans, A.E. (2007) 'Changing faces: Suburban school response to demographic change', *Education and Urban Society*, 39(3): 315–48.

Eynon, R., Fry, J. and Schroeder, R. (2008) 'The ethics of Internet research', in N.G. Fielding, R.M. Lee and G. Blank (eds), *The SAGE Handbook of Online Research Methods*. London: SAGE. pp. 23–57.

Fairclough, N. (2001) *Language and Power*. 2nd edn. London: Longman.

Feldman, M. (1995) *Strategies for Interpreting Qualitative Data*. Thousand Oaks, CA: SAGE.

Festinger, L., Riecken, H.W. and Schachter, S. (1964) *When Prophecy Fails: A Social and Psychological Study of a Modern Group that Predicted the Destruction of the World*. New York: Harper Torchbooks.

Fetterman, D.M. (2010) *Ethnography Step by Step*. 3rd edn. Thousand Oaks, CA: SAGE.

Fielding, N. (1981) *The National Front*. London: Routledge and Kegan Paul.

Fielding, N. (1996a) 'Ethnography', in N. Gilbert (ed.), *Researching Social Life*. London: SAGE. pp. 154–71.

Fielding, N. (1996b) 'Qualitative interviewing', in N. Gilbert (ed.), *Researching Social Life*. London: SAGE. pp. 135–53.

Fielding, N. (2008) 'Qualitative interviewing', in N. Gilbert (ed.), *Researching Social Life*. 3rd edn. London: SAGE. pp. 245–65.

Fink, A. (2005) *Conducting Research Literature Reviews: From the Internet to Paper*. 2nd edn. London: SAGE.

Finn, J.D. and Achilles, C.M. (1990) 'Answers and questions about class size: A statewide experiment', *American Education Research Journal*, 27: 557–77.

Finnegan, R. (2006) 'Using documents', in R. Sapsford and V. Jupp (eds), *Data Collection and Analysis*. 2nd edn. London: SAGE. pp. 138–52.

Firestone, W.A. (1993) 'Alternative arguments for generalizing from data as applied to qualitative research', *Educational Researcher*, 22(4): 16–23.

Foddy, W. (1993) *Constructing Questions for Interviews and Questionnaires: Theory and Practice in Social Research*. Cambridge: Cambridge University Press.

Fonow, M.M. and Cook, J.A. (eds) (1991) *Beyond Methodology: Feminist Scholarship as Lived Research*. Bloomington, IN: Indiana University Press.

Fontana, A. and Frey, J.H. (1994) 'Interviewing: The art of science', in N.K. Denzin and Y.S. Lincoln (eds), *Handbook of Qualitative Research*. Thousand Oaks, CA: SAGE. pp. 361–76.

Foster, P. (1996a) 'Observational research', in R. Sapsford and V. Jupp (eds), *Data Collection and Analysis*. London: SAGE. pp. 57–93.

Foster, P. (1996b) *Observing Schools: A Methodological Guide*. London: Chapman.

Foucault, M. (1980) *Power/Knowledge: Selected Interviews and Other Writings 1972–1977*. Brighton: Harvester.

Frankena, W. (1973) *Ethics*. Englewood Cliffs, NJ: Prentice-Hall.

Frey, J.H. (1993) 'Risk perceptions associated with a high-level nuclear waste repository', *Sociological Spectrum*, 13: 139–51.

Friedenberg, L. (1995) *Psychological Testing: Design, Analysis and Use*. Boston: Allyn and Bacon.

Gaiser, T. and Schreiner, A. (2009) *A Guide to Conducting Online Research*. London: SAGE.

Garcia, A., Standlee, A., Bechkoff, J. and Cui, Y. (2009) 'Ethnographic approaches to the Internet and computer-mediated communication', *Journal of Contemporary Ethnography*, 38(1): 52–84. Retrieved from SAGE Journals Online.

Garfinkel, H. (1967) *Studies in Ethnomethodology*. Englewood Cliffs, NJ: Prentice-Hall.

Gee, J.P., Michaels, S. and O'Connor, M.C. (1992) 'Discourse analysis', in M.D. LeCompte, W.L. Millroy and J. Preissle (eds), *The Handbook of Qualitative Research in Education*. San Diego, CA: Academic. pp. 227–91.

Gerstl-Pepin, C.I. (2006) 'The paradox of poverty narratives: Educators struggling with children left behind', *Educational Policy*, 20(1): 143–62.

Gilbert, G.N. and Mulkay, M.J. (1984) *Opening Pandora's Box: A Sociological Analysis of Scientists' Discourse*. Cambridge: Cambridge University Press.

Gilbert, N. (2008) 'Writing about social research', in N. Gilbert (ed.), *Researching Social Life*. 3rd edn. London: SAGE. pp. 485–503.

Glaser, B. (1978) *Theoretical Sensitivity*. Mill Valley, CA: Sociology Press.

Glaser, B. (1992) *Basics of Grounded Theory Analysis: Emergence vs Forcing*. Mill Valley, CA: Sociology Press.

Glaser, B. (ed.) (1993) *Examples of Grounded Theory: A Reader*. Mill Valley, CA: Sociology Press.

Glaser, B. and Strauss, A. (1965) *Awareness of Dying*. Chicago: Aldine.

Glaser, B. and Strauss, A. (1967) *The Discovery of Grounded Theory: Strategies for Qualitative Research*. Chicago: Aldine.

Glaser, B. and Strauss, A. (1968) *Time for Dying*. Chicago: Aldine.

Glass, G.V. (1976) 'Primary, secondary and meta-analysis of research', *Educational Research*, 5: 3–8.

Glass, G.V. (1988) 'Quasi-experiments: The case of interrupted time series', in R.M. Jaeger (ed.), *Complementary Methods for Research in Education*. Washington, DC: American Educational Research Association. pp. 445–61.

Glass, G.V., McGaw, B. and Smith, M.L.O (1981) *Meta Analysis in Social Research*. Beverly Hills, CA: SAGE.

Gluck, S.B. (1991) 'Advocacy oral history: Palestinian women in resistance', in S.B. Gluck and D. Patai (eds), *Women's Words: The Feminist Practice of Oral History*. London: Routledge. pp. 205–20.

Goffman, E. (1961) *Asylums: Essays on the Social Situation of Mental Patients and Other Inmates*. Harmondsworth, Middlesex: Penguin.

Gold, R.L. (1958) 'Roles in sociological field observations', *Social Forces*, 36: 217–23.

Goldman, B.A. and Mitchell, D.F. (eds) (1996) *Directory of Unpublished Experimental Mental Measures*. Vol.6. Washington, DC: American Psychological Association.

Gomm, R. (2004) 'Research ethics', in R. Gomm, *Social Research Methodology: A Critical Introduction*. Basingstoke: Palgrave Macmillan. pp. 298–322.

Goode, W.J. and Hatt, P.K. (1952) 'The case study', in W.J. Goode and P.K. Hatt (eds), *Methods of Social Research*. New York: McGraw-Hill. pp. 330–40.

Goodson, I. (1992) *Studying Teachers' Lives*. London: Routledge and Kegan Paul.

Gough, D., Oliver, S. and Thomas, J. (2012) *An Introduction to Systematic Reviews*. London: SAGE.

Greenwood, E. (1968) 'The practice of science and the science of practice', in W.G. Bennis, K.D. Benne and R. Chin (eds), *The Planning of Change*. New York: Holt, Rinehart and Winston. pp. 73–82.

Guba, E.G. and Lincoln, Y.S. (1994) 'Competing paradigms in qualitative research', in N.K. Denzin and Y.S. Lincoln (eds), *Handbook of Qualitative Research*. Thousand Oaks, CA: SAGE. pp. 105–17.

Gubrium, J.F. and Holstein, J.A. (2000) 'Analyzing interpretive practice', in N.K. Denzin and Y.S. Lincoln (eds), *Handbook of Qualitative Research*. 2nd edn. Thousand Oaks, CA: SAGE. pp. 487–508.

Haig, B.D. (1997) 'Feminist research methodology', in J.P. Keeves (ed.), *Educational Research, Methodology, and Measurement: An International Handbook*. 2nd edn. Oxford: Elsevier. pp. 180–5.

Hakim, C. (1982) *Secondary Analysis in Social Research*. London: Allen and Unwin.

Hammersley, M. (1992) 'Deconstructing the qualitative–quantitative divide', in J. Brannen (ed.), *Mixing Methods: Qualitative and Quantitative Research*. Aldershot: Avebury. pp. 39–55.

Hammersley, M. (ed.) (1993) *Social Research: Philosophy, Politics and Practice*. London: SAGE.

Hammersley, M. (1995) *The Politics of Social Research*. London: SAGE.

Hammersley, M. and Atkinson, P. (1995) *Ethnography: Principles in Practice*. 2nd edn. London: Routledge.

Hammersley, M. and Atkinson, P. (2007) *Ethnography: Principles in Practice*. 3rd edn. London: Routledge.

Hammersley, M. and Traianou, A. (2012) *Ethics in Qualitative Research*. London: SAGE.

Hardy, M.A. (1993) *Regression with Dummy Variables*. Newbury Park, CA: SAGE.

Hart, C. (2001) *Doing a Literature Search: A Comprehensive Guide for the Social Sciences*. London: SAGE.

Hattie, J. (2008) *Visible Learning: A Synthesis of over 800 Meta-Analyses Relating to Achievement*. London: Routledge.

Haviland, W.A., Walrath, D., McBride, B. and Pins, H.E.L. (2013) *Cultural Anthropology*. 14th edn. Wadsworth: Cengage.

Heath, C. and Luff, P. (1996) 'Explicating face-to-face interaction', in N. Gilbert (ed.), *Researching Social Life*. London: SAGE. pp. 306–26.

Heritage, J. (1984) *Garfinkel and Ethnomethodology*. Cambridge: Polity.

Hesse, E. (1980) *Revolutions and Reconstructions in the Philosophy of Science*. Bloomington, IN: Indiana University Press.

Hewson, C. and Laurent, D. (2008) 'Research design and tools for Internet research', in N. Fielding, R. Lee and G. Blank (eds), *The SAGE Handbook of Online Research Methods*. London: SAGE. pp. 58–78.

Hewson, C., Yule, P., Laurent, D. and Vogel, C. (2003) *Internet Research Methods: A Practical Guide for the Social and Behavioural Sciences*. London: SAGE.

Hine, C. (2011) 'Internet research and unobtrusive methods', *Social Research Update*, 16, pp. 1–4. Retrieved from http://sru.soc.surrey.ac.uk/SRU61.pdf

Holmes, R.M. (1998) *Fieldwork with Children*. London: SAGE.

Homan, R. (1998) *The Ethics of Social Research*. London: Longman.

Homan, R. (2004) 'The principle of assumed consent: The ethics of gatekeeping', in M. McNamee and D. Bridges (eds), *The Ethics of Educational Research*. Oxford: Blackwell.

Howard, M.C. (1997) *Contemporary Cultural Anthropology*. 5th edn. New York: Pearson.

Huberman, A.M. and Miles, M.B. (1994) 'Data management and analysis methods', in N.K. Denzin and Y.S. Lincoln (eds), *Handbook of Qualitative Research*. Thousand Oaks, CA: SAGE. pp. 428–44.

Hughes, E.C. (1958) *Men and Their Work*. Chicago: Free Press.

Hunter, J.E. and Schmidt, F.L. (2004) *Methods of Meta-Analysis: Correcting Error Bias in Research Findings*. 2nd edn. Thousand Oaks, CA: SAGE.

Irwin, D.M. (1980) *Observational Strategies for Child Study*. New York: Holt, Rinehart and Winston.

Ivankova, N.W., Creswell, J.W. and Stick, S. (2006) 'Using mixed methods sequential explanatory design: From theory to practice', *Field Methods*, 18(1): 3–20.

Jaeger, R.M. (1984) *Sampling in Education and the Social Sciences*. New York: Longman.

Jaeger, R.M. (1988) 'Survey methods in educational research', in R.M. Jaeger (ed.), *Complementary Methods for Research in Education*. Washington, DC: American Educational Research Association. pp. 301–87.

Jaeger, R.M. (1990) *Statistics as a Spectator Sport*. 2nd edn. Beverly Hills, CA, SAGE.

Janesick, V.J. (1994) 'The dance of qualitative research design: Metaphor, method-olatry, and meaning', in N.K. Denzin and Y.S. Lincoln (eds), *Handbook of Qualitative Research*. Thousand Oaks, CA: SAGE. pp. 209–19.

Jayaratne, T.E. and Stewart, A.J. (1991) 'Quantitative and qualitative methods in the social sciences: Current feminist issues and practical strategies', in M.M. Fonow and J.A. Cook (eds), *Beyond Methodology: Feminist Scholarship as Lived Research*. Bloomington, IN: Indiana University Press. pp. 85–106.

Jenkins, J.E. (2001) 'Rural adolescent perceptions of alcohol and other drug resist-ance', *Child Study Journal*, 31(4): 211–22.

Johnson, J.C. (1990) *Selecting Ethnographic Informants*. Newbury Park, CA: SAGE.

Johnson, R.B. and Onwuegbuzie, A.J. (2004) 'Mixed methods research: A research paradigm whose time has come', *Educational Research*, 33(7): 14–26.

Jones, C. (2011) *Ethical issues in online research*. British Educational Research Association online resource. www.bera.ac.uk.

Jones, S. (1985) 'Depth interviewing', in R. Walker (ed.), *Applied Qualitative Research*. Aldershot: Gower. pp. 45–55.

Jupp, V. (1996) 'Documents and critical research', in R. Sapsford and V. Jupp (eds), *Data Collection and Analysis*. London: SAGE. pp. 298–316.

Jupp, V. (2006) 'Documents and critical research', in R. Sapsford and V. Jupp (eds), *Data Collection and Analysis*. 2nd edn. London: SAGE. pp. 272–90.

Kant, I. (1964) *Groundwork to the Metaphysics of Morals*. London: Routledge.

Keats, D.M. (1988) *Skilled Interviewing*. Melbourne: Australian Council for Educational Research.

Keesing, R.M. (1976) *Cultural Anthropology: A Contemporary Perspective*. New York: Holt, Rinehart and Winston.

Kelle, U. (ed.) (1995) *Computer-Aided Qualitative Data Analysis: Theory, Methods and Practice*. London: SAGE.

Kemmis, S. and McTaggart, R. (2000) 'Participatory action research', in N.K. Denzin and Y.S. Lincoln (eds), *Handbook of Qualitative Research*. 2nd edn. Thousand Oaks, CA: SAGE. pp. 567–605.

Kerlinger, F.N. (1973) *Foundations of Behavioral Research*. New York: Holt, Rinehart and Winston.

Kerlinger, F.N. (1999) *Foundations of Behavioral Research*. 4th edn. New York: Wadsworth.

Kerlinger, F.N. and Lee, H.B. (2000) *Foundations of Behavioral Research*. New York: Harcourt.

Kiecolt, K.J. and Nathan, L.E. (1985) *Secondary Analysis of Survey Data*. Beverley Hills, CA: SAGE.

Kirk, R.E. (1995) *Experimental Design: Procedures for the Behavioral Sciences*. 3rd edn. Belmont, CA: Brooks/Cole.

Kraut, R., Olson, J., Banaji, M., Bruckmann, A., Cohen, J. and Couper, M. (2004) 'Psychological research online: Report of the board of scientific affairs' advisory group on the conduct of research on the Internet' *American Psychologist*, 59(2): 105–17.

Labov, W. and Waletzky, J. (1997) 'Narrative analysis: Oral versions of personal experience' (Reprinted from 'Essays on the Verbal and Visual Arts. Proceedings of the 1996 annual spring meeting of the American Ethnological Society', pp. 12–44, 1967), *Journal of Narrative and Life History*, 7(1–4): 3–38.

Larreamendy-Joerns, J. and Leinhardt, G. (2006) 'Going the distance with online education', *Review of Educational Research*, 76(4): 567–605.

Lather, P. (1991) *Getting Smart: Feminist Research and Pedagogy With/In the Postmodern*. New York: Routledge.

Lather, P. (1994) *Getting Smart: Feminist Research and Pedagogy With/In the Postmodern*. New York: Routledge.

LeCompte, M.D. and Preissle, J. (1993) *Ethnography and Qualitative Design in Educational Research*. 2nd edn. San Diego, CA: Academic.

Lee, R., Fielding, N. and Blank, G. (2008) *The SAGE Handbook of Online Research Methods*. London: SAGE.

Lewins, F. (1992) *Social Science Methodology*. Melbourne: Macmillan.

Li, N. and Kirkup, G. (2007) 'Gender and cultural differences in internet usage: A study of China and the UK', *Computers & Education*, 48(2): 301–17.

Liebert, R.M. (1995) *Science and Behavior: An Introduction to Methods of Psychological Research*. Englewood Cliffs, NJ: Prentice-Hall.

Lieblich, A., Tuval-Maschiach, R. and Zilber, T. (1998) *Narrative Research: Reading, Analysis and Interpretation*. Thousand Oaks, CA: SAGE.

Lincoln, Y.S. and Guba, E.G. (1985) *Naturalistic Inquiry*. Beverley Hills, CA: SAGE.

Lindesmith, A. (1947) *Opiate Addiction*. Bloomington, IN: Principia.

Lindesmith, A. (1968) *Addiction and Opiates*. Chicago: Aldine.

Little, D. (1991) *Varieties of Social Explanation: An Introduction to the Philosophy of Social Science*. Boulder, CO: Westview.

Locke, L.F., Spirduso, W.W. and Silverman, S.J. (1993) *Proposals That Work*. 3rd edn. Newbury Park, CA: SAGE.

Locke, L.F., Spirduso, W.W. and Silverman, S.J. (2010) *Proposals That Work*. 6th edn. Thousand Oaks, CA: SAGE.

Lofland, J., Snow, D., Anderson, L. and Lofland, L.H. (2004) *Analyzing Social Settings*. 4th edn. Belmont, CA: Wadsworth.

Lonkila, M. (1995) 'Grounded theory as an emerging paradigm for computer-assisted qualitative data analysis', in U. Kelle (ed.), *Computer-Aided Qualitative Data Analysis: Theory, Methods and Practice*. London: SAGE. pp. 41–51.

Lynch, M. (2006) 'Cognitive activities without cognition? Ethnomethodological investigation of selected "cognitive" topics', *Discourse Studies*, 8(1): 95–104.

MacDonald, K. and Tipton, C. (1996) 'Using documents', in N. Gilbert (ed.), *Researching Social Life*. London: SAGE. pp. 187–200.

Madge, C. and O'Connor, H. (2002) 'On-line with e-mums: Exploring the Internet as a medium for research', *Area*, 34(1): 92–102.

Mann, C. and Stewart, F. (2000) *Internet Communication and Qualitative Research*. London: SAGE.

Manning, P.K. and Cullum-Swan, B. (1994) 'Narrative, content, and semiotic analysis', in N.K. Denzin and Y.S. Lincoln (eds), *Handbook of Qualitative Research*. Thousand Oaks, CA: SAGE. pp. 463–83.

Marsh, C. (1982) *The Survey Method: The Contribution of Surveys to Sociological Explanation*. London: Allen and Unwin.

Marshall, C. and Rossman, G.B. (1989) *Designing Qualitative Research*. Newbury Park, CA: SAGE.

Marshall, C. and Rossman, G.B. (2010) *Designing Qualitative Research*. 5th edn. Thousand Oaks, CA: SAGE.

Martin, J. (1990) 'Deconstructing organizational taboos', *Organization Science*, 1(4): 339–59.

Maxcy, S.J. (2003) 'Pragmatic threads in mixed methods research in the social sciences: The search for multiple modes of inquiry and the end of the philosophy of formalism', in A. Tashakkori and C. Teddlie (eds), *Handbook of Mixed Methods in Social and Behavioral Research*. Thousand Oaks, CA: SAGE. pp. 51–90.

Mavers, D. (2007) 'Semiotic resourcefulness: A young child's email exchange as design', *Journal of Early Childhood Literacy*, 7(2): 155–76.

Maxwell, J.A. (1996) *Qualitative Research Design: An Interactive Approach*. Thousand Oaks, CA: SAGE.

Maxwell, J.A. (2012) *Qualitative Research Design: An Interactive Approach*. 3rd edn. Thousand Oaks, CA: SAGE.

Maynard, B.R., McCrea, K.T., Pigott, T.D. and Kelly, M.S. (2012) 'Indicated truancy interventions for chronic truant students: A Campbell systematic review', *Research on Social Work Practice*, 23(1): 5–21.

McCarthy, M. (1991) *Discourse Analysis for Language Teachers*. Cambridge: Cambridge University Press.

McCracken, G. (1988) *The Long Interview*. Beverly Hills, CA: SAGE.

McGrew, K. (2011) 'A review of class-based theories of student resistance in education', *Review of Educational Research*, 81(2): 234–266.

McLaren, P. (1986) *Schooling as a Ritual Performance: Towards a Political Economy of Educational Symbols and Gestures*. London: Routledge and Kegan Paul.

McNamee, M. and Bridges, D. (eds) (2002) *The Ethics of Educational Research*. Oxford: Blackwell.

McRobbie, A. (2000) *Feminism and Youth Culture: From Jackie to Just Seventeen*. 2nd edn. London: Palgrave.

Measor, L. and Woods, P. (1984) *Changing Schools*. Milton Keynes: Open University Press.

Menard, S. (1991) *Longitudinal Research*. Newbury Park, CA: SAGE.

Merton, R.K., Fiske, M. and Kendall, P.L. (1990) *The Focused Interview*. 2nd edn. New York: Simon & Schuster.

Miles, M.B. (1979) 'Qualitative data as an attractive nuisance: the problem of analysis', *Administrative Science Quarterly*, 24: 590–601.

Miles, M.B. and Huberman, A.M. (1994) *Qualitative Data Analysis*. 2nd edn. Thousand Oaks, CA: SAGE.

Miles, M.B., Huberman, A.M. and Saldana, J. (2013) *Qualitative Data Analysis*. 3rd edn. Thousand Oaks, CA: SAGE.

Milgram, S. (1974) *Obedience to Authority*. New York: Harper and Row.

Mill, J.S. (1863) *Utilitarianism*. London: Parket, Son and Bourn.

Miller, D.C. and Salkind, N.J. (2002) *Handbook of Research Design and Social Measurement*. 6th edn. Thousand Oaks, CA: SAGE.

Mills, C.W. (1959) *The Sociological Imagination*. New York: Oxford University Press.

Minichiello, V., Aroni, R., Timewell, E. and Alexander, L. (1990) *In-Depth Interviewing: Researching People*. Melbourne: Longman Cheshire.

Mishler, E. (1986) *Research Interviewing*. Cambridge, MA: Harvard University Press.

Morgan, D.L. (1988) *Focus Groups as Qualitative Research*. Newbury Park, CA: SAGE.

Morgan, D.L. (1997) *Focus Groups as Qualitative Research*. 2nd edn. Thousand Oaks, CA: SAGE.

Morse, J.M. (1994) 'Designing funded qualitative research', in N.K. Denzin and Y.S. Lincoln (eds), *Handbook of Qualitative Research*. Thousand Oaks, CA: SAGE. pp. 220–35.

Moser, C.A. and Kalton, G. (1979) *Survey Methods in Social Investigation*. 2nd edn. Farnborough: Gower.

Murthy, D. (2008) 'Digital ethnography: An examination of the use of new technologies for social research', *Sociology*, 42(5): 837–55. Retrieved from Sage Journals Online.

Myers, K.K. and Oetzel, J.G. (2003) 'Exploring the dimensions of organizational assimilation: Creating and validating a measure', *Communication Quarterly*, 51 (4): 438–57.

Nagel, E. (1979) *The Structure of Science: Problems in the Logic of Scientific Explanation*. 2nd edn. New York: Hackett Publishing.

Nelson, C., Treichler, P.A. and Grossberg, L. (1992) 'Cultural studies', in L. Grossberg, C. Nelson and P.A. Treichler (eds), *Cultural Studies*. New York: Routledge. pp. 1–16.

Neuman, W.L. (1994) *Social Research Methods: Qualitative and Quantitative Approaches*. 2nd edn. Boston: Allyn and Bacon.

Noblit, G. and Hare, R.D. (1988) *Meta-ethnography: Synthesizing Qualitative Studies*. Newbury Park, CA: SAGE.

Nordenbo, S.E., Larsen, M.S., Tiftiçi, N., Wendt, R.E. and Østergaard, S. (2008) *Teacher competences and pupil achievement in pre-school and school: A systematic review*. University of Aarhus: Danish Clearinghouse. Available from www.dpu.dk/fileadmin/www.dpu.dk/en/aboutdpu/danishclearinghouseforeducationalresearch/abouttheclearinghouse/products/udgivelser_clearinghouse_20080908120312_srii-english-senfinal.pdf (accessed 24th september 2013)

Nosek, B., Banaji, M. and Greenwald, A. (2002) 'Harvesting implicit group attitudes and beliefs from a demonstration web site', *Group Dynamics*, 6(1): 101–15.

O'Connor, D.J. (1957) *An Introduction to the Philosophy of Education*. London: Routledge and Kegan Paul.

O'Connor, H., Madge, C., Shaw, R. and Wellens, J. (2008) 'Internet-based interviewing', in N. Fielding, R. Lee and G. Blank (eds), *The SAGE Handbook of Online Research Methods*. London: SAGE. pp. 42–57.

O'Donoghue, T. (2007) *Planning Your Qualitative Research Project: An Introduction to Interpretivist Research in Education*. Abingdon: Routledge.

O'Leary, Z. (2004) *Researching Real World Problems: A Guide to Methods of Inquiry*. London: SAGE.

Oakley, A. (1981) 'Interviewing women: A contradiction in terms', in H. Roberts (ed.), *Doing Feminist Research*. London: Routledge and Kegan Paul. pp. 30–61.

Oppenheim, A.N. (1992) *Questionnaire Design, Interviewing and Attitude Measurement*. London: Pinter.

Patton, M.Q. (2002) *Qualitative Evaluation and Research Methods*. 3rd edn. Thousand Oaks, CA: SAGE.

Peaker, G.F. (1971) *The Plowden Children Four Years Later*. London: National Foundation for Educational Research in England and Wales.

Pendlebury, S. and Enslin, P. (2001) 'Representation, identification and trust: Towards an ethics of educational research', *Journal of Philosophy of Education*, 35(3): 361–70.

Peters, T.J. and Waterman, R.H. Jr (1982) *In Search of Excellence: Lessons from America's Best-Run Companies*. New York: Harper and Row.

Phelps, R., Fisher, K. and Ellis, A. (2007) *Organizing and Managing Your Research*. London: SAGE.

Pittenger, D. (2003) 'Internet research: An opportunity to revisit classic ethical problems in behavioural research', *Ethics and Behaviour*, 13(1): 45–60.

Popper, K. (2002) *The Logic of Scientific Discovery*. 2nd edn. London: Routledge.

Potter, J. and Wetherell, M. (1987) *Discourse and Social Psychology: Beyond Attitudes and Behaviour*. London: SAGE.

Potter, J. and Wetherell, M. (1994) 'Analyzing discourse', in A. Bryman and R.G. Burgess (eds), *Analyzing Qualitative Data*. London: Routledge. pp. 47–66.

Pring, R. (2004) *Philosophy of Educational Research*. 2nd edn. London: Continuum.

Procter, M. (1996) 'Analysing other researchers' data', in N. Gilbert (ed.), *Researching Social Life*. London: SAGE. pp. 255–86.

Punch, K.F. (2003) *Survey Research: The Basics*. London: SAGE.

Punch, K.F. (2006) *Developing Effective Research Proposals*. 2nd edn. London: SAGE.

Punch, M. (1994) 'Politics and ethics in qualitative research', in N.K. Denzin and Y.S. Lincoln (eds), *Handbook of Qualitative Research*. Thousand Oaks, CA: SAGE. pp. 83–97.

Ragin, C.C. (1987) *The Comparative Method: Moving Beyond Qualitative and Quantitative Strategies*. Berkeley, CA: University of California Press.

Ragin, C.C. (1994) *Constructing Social Research*. Thousand Oaks, CA: Pine Forge.

Reason, P. and Bradbury, H. (eds) (2008) *The SAGE Handbook of Action Research*. 2nd edn. London: SAGE.

Reeve, R.A. and Walberg, J.J. (1997) 'Secondary data analysis', in J.P. Keeves (ed.), *Educational Research, Methodology, and Measurement: An International Handbook*. 2nd edn. Oxford: Elsevier. pp. 439–44.

Reinharz, S. (1992) *Feminist Methods in Social Research*. New York: Oxford University Press.

Richards, L. (2005) *Handling Qualitative Data: A Practical Guide*. London: SAGE.

Richardson, L. (1994) 'Writing: A method of inquiry', in N.K. Denzin and Y.S. Lincoln (eds), *Handbook of Qualitative Research*. Thousand Oaks, CA: SAGE. pp. 516–29.

Ridley, D. (2008) *The Literature Review: A Step-by-Step Guide for Students*. London: SAGE.

Riessman, C.J. (1993) *Narrative Analysis*. Newbury Park, CA: SAGE.

Robinson, J.P. and Shaver, P.R. (1973) *Measures of Social Psychological Attitudes*. Ann Arbor, MI: Institute for Social Research.

Robinson, J.P., Athanasiou, R. and Head, K.B. (1969) *Measures of Occupational Attitudes and Occupational Characteristics*. Ann Arbor, MI: Institute for Social Research.

Rogers, A., Day, J., Randall, F. and Bentall, R.P. (2003) 'Patients' understanding and participation in a trial designed to improve the management of anti-psychotic medication: A qualitative study', *Social Psychiatry and Psychiatric Epidemiology*, 38: 720–7.

Rosenberg, M. (1968) *The Logic of Survey Analysis*. New York: Basic Books.

Rosenberg, M. (1979) *Conceiving the Self*. New York: Basic Books.

Rossman, G.B. and Wilson, B.L. (1985) 'Numbers and words: Combining quantitative and qualitative methods in a single large-scale evaluation study', *Evaluation Review*, 9(5): 627–43.

Rudestam, K.E. and Newton, R.R (2000) *Surviving Your Dissertation: A Comprehensive Guide to Content and Process*. 2nd edn. Thousand Oaks, CA: SAGE.

Rutter, M., Maughan, B., Mortimore, P. and Ouston, J. (1979) *Fifteen Thousand Hours: Secondary Schools and their Effects on Children*. London: Open University.

Sapsford, R. and Abbott, P. (1996) 'Ethics, politics and research', in R. Sapsford and V. Jupp (eds), *Data Collection and Analysis*. London: SAGE. pp. 317–42.

Schwandt, T.A. and Halpern, E.S. (1988) *Linking, Auditing and Metaevaluating: Enhancing Quality in Applied Research*. Newbury Park, CA: SAGE.

Schwandt, T. (2001) *Dictionary of Qualitative Inquiry*. 2nd edn. London: SAGE.

Scott, J. (1990) *A Matter of Record: Documentary Sources in Social Research*. Cambridge: Polity.

Seale, C. (1998) *Researching Society and Culture*. London: SAGE.

Seale, C., Charteris-Black, J., MacFarlane, A. and McPherson, A. (2010) 'Interviews and internet formus: A comparison of two sources of qualitative data', *Qualitative Health Research*, 20(5): 595–606.

Seidman, I.E. (2013) *Interviewing as Qualitative Research: A Guide for Researchers in Education and the Social Sciences*. 4th edn. New York: Teachers College Press.

Selznick, P. (1949) *TVA and the Grass Roots: A Study of Politics and Organization*. Berheley, CA: University of California Press.

Shadish, W.R. and Luellen, T.K. (2006) 'Quasi-experimental design', in J.L. Green, G. Camilli and P.B. Elmore (eds), *Handbook of Complementary Methods in Education Research*. Mahwah, NJ: Lawrence Erlbaum. pp. 539–50.

Shamdasani, P.N. and Rook, D. (2006) *Foucs Groups: Theroy and Practice*. London: SAGE.

Shaw, M.E. and Wright, J.M. (1967) *Scales for the Measurement of Attitudes*. New York: McGraw-Hill.

Sherif, M., Harvey, O.J., White, B.J., Hood, W.R. and Sherif, C.W. (1961) *Intergroup Conflict and Cooperation: The Robber's Cave Experiment*. Norman, OK: University of Oklahoma Book Exchange.

Shulman, L.S. (1988) 'Disciplines of inquiry in education: An overview', in R.M. Jaeger (ed.), *Complementary Methods for Research in Education*. Washington, DC: American Educational Research Association. pp. 3–17.

Siegel, S. (1988) *Nonparametric Statistics for the Behavioural Sciences*. 2nd edn. New York: McGraw-Hill.

Silverman, D. (1985) *Qualitative Methodology and Sociology*. Farnborough: Gower.

Silverman, D. (1993) *Interpreting Qualitative Data: Methods for Analyzing Talk, Text and Interaction*. London: SAGE.

Silverman, D. (2011) *Interpreting Qualitative Data: Methods for Analyzing Talk, Text and Interaction*. 4th edn. London: SAGE.

Simons, H. (2009) *Case Study Research in Practice*. London: SAGE.

Simmons, H. and Usher, R. (eds) (2000) *Situated Ethics in Educational Research*. London: RoutledgeFalmer.

Snee, H. (2010) *Using Blog Analysis*. NCRM Realities Toolkit 10. Online at http://eprints.ncrm.ac.uk/1321/2/10-toolkit-blog-analysis.pdf.

Soong, R. (2004) *Stratification of Internet users in Brazil*. Retrieved from http://www.zonalatina.com/Z1data341.htm (accessed 18 October 2013).

Spindler, G. and Spindler, L. (1992) 'Cultural process and ethnography: An anthropological perspective', in M.D. LeCompte, W.L. Millroy and J. Preissle (eds), *The Handbook of Qualitative Research in Education*. San Diego, CA: Academic. pp. 53–92.

Spradley, J.P. (1980) *Participant Observation*. New York: Holt, Rinehart and Winston.

Stake, R.E. (1988) 'Case study methods in educational research: Seeking sweet water', in R.M. Jaeger (ed.), *Complementary Methods for Research in Education*. Washington, DC: American Educational Research Association. pp. 253–300.

Stake, R.E. (1994) 'Case studies', in N.K. Denzin and Y.S. Lincoln (eds), *Handbook of Qualitative Research*. Thousand Oaks, CA: SAGE. pp. 236–47.

Stanfield, J. (1985) *Philanthropy and Jim Crow in American Social Sciences*. Westport, CT: Greenwood.

Stevens, S.S. (1951) 'Mathematics, measurement and psycho-physics', in S.S. Stevens (ed.), *Handbook of Experimental Psychology*. New York: Wiley.

Stewart, D.W. (1984) *Secondary Research: Information, Sources and Methods*. Beverley Hills, CA: SAGE.

Stewart, D.W., Shamdasani, P. and Rook, D. (2006) *Focus Groups: Theory and Practice*. 2nd edn. Thousand Oaks, CA: SAGE.

Strauss, A. (1987) *Qualitative Analysis for Social Scientists*. New York: Cambridge University Press.

Strauss, A. and Corbin, J. (1990) *Basics of Qualitative Research: Grounded Theory Procedures and Techniques*. Newbury Park, CA: SAGE.

Strauss, A. and Corbin, J. (eds) (1997) *Grounded Theory in Practice*. Thousand Oaks, CA: SAGE.

Strauss, A. and Corbin, J. (2008) *Basics of Qualitative Research: Grounded Theory Procedures and Techniques*. 3rd edn. Thousand Oaks, CA: SAGE.

Stringer, E. (2004) *Action Research in Education*. Upper Saddle River, NJ: Pearson.

Sudman, S. and Bradburn, N.M. (1982) *Asking Questions: A Practical Guide to Questionnaire Design*. San Francisco: Jossey-Bass.

Swanson, J.M. (1986) 'Analyzing data for categories and description', in W.C. Chenitz and J.M. Swanson (eds), *From Practice to Grounded Theory: Qualitative Research in Nursing*. Menlo Park, CA: Addison-Wesley. pp. 121–32.

Tamim, R.M., Bernard, R.M., Borokhovski, E., Abrami, P.C. and Schmid, R.F. (2011) 'What forty years of research says about the impact of technology on learning', *Review of Educational Research*, 81(1): 4–28.

Tashakkori, A. and Teddlie, C. (1998) *Mixed Methodology: Combining Qualitative and Quantitative Approaches*. Thousand Oaks, CA: SAGE.

Tashakkori, A. and Teddlie, C. (eds) (2003a) *Handbook of Mixed Methods in Social and Behavioural Research*. Thousand Oaks, CA: SAGE.

Tashakkori, A. and Teddlie, C. (2003b) 'Major issues and controversies in the use of mixed methods in the social and behavioral sciences', in A. Tashakkori and

C. Teddlie (eds), *Handbook of Mixed Methods in Social and Behavioral Research*. Thousand Oaks, CA: SAGE. pp. 3–53.

Tashakkori, A. and Teddlie, C. (2003c) 'The past and future of mixed methods research: From data triangulation to mixed model design', in A. Tashakkori and C. Teddlie (eds), *Handbook of Mixed Methods in Social and Behavioural Research*. Thousand Oaks, CA: SAGE. pp. 671–702.

Taylor, S. (2001) 'Locating and conducting discourse analytic research', in M. Wetherall, S. Taylor and S.J. Yates (eds), *Discourse as Data: A Guide for Analysis*. London: SAGE. pp. 5–48.

Tesch, R. (1990) *Qualitative Research: Analysis Types and Software Tools*. Basingstoke: Falmer.

Theodorson, G.A. and Theodorson, A.G. (1969) *A Modern Dictionary of Sociology*. New York: Crowell.

Thomas, R. (1996) 'Statistical sources and databases', in R. Sapsford and V. Jupp (eds), *Data Collection and Analysis*. London: SAGE. pp. 121–37.

Thomson, P. (ed.) (2008) *Doing Visual Research with Children and Young People*. Abingdon: Routledge.

Tonkiss, F. (1998) 'Analyzing discourse', in C. Seale (ed.), *Researching Society and Culture*. London: SAGE. pp. 245–60.

Tourangeau, R. (2004) 'Survey research and societal change' *Annual Review of Psychology*, 55: 775–801. Retrieved from www. annualreviews.org

Van den Berg, R. (2002) 'Teachers' meanings regarding educational practice', *Review of Educational Research*, 72 (4): 577–625.

Vehovar, V. and Manfreda, K. (2008) 'Overview: Online surveys', in N. Fielding, R. Lee and G. Blank (eds), *The SAGE Handbook of Online Research Methods*. London: SAGE. pp. 177–94.

Vitz, P.C. (1990) 'The use of stories in moral development: New psychological reasons for an old education method', *American Psychologist*, 45(6): 709–20.

Wakeford, N., Oroton-Johnson, K. and Jungnickel, K. (2006) 'Using the internet', in N. Gilbert (ed.) *From Post-graduate to Social Scientist: A Guide to Key Skills.'* London: SAGE. pp. 25–42.

Walford, G. (2005) 'Research ethical guidelines and anonymity', *International Journal of Research and Method in Education*, 28(1): 83–93.

Wallace, M. and Poulson, L. (2003) *Learning to Read Critically in Educational Leadership and Management*. London: SAGE.

Wallen, N.E. and Fraenkel, J.R. (1991) *Educational Research: A Guide to the Process*. New York: McGraw-Hill.

Webb, E.J., Campbell, D.T., Schwartz, R.D. and Sechrest, L. (1966) *Unobtrusive Measures*. Chicago: Rand McNally.

Webb, R.B. and Glesne, C. (1992) 'Teaching qualitative research', in M.D. LeCompte, W.L. Millroy and J. Preissle (eds), *The Handbook of Qualitative Research in Education*. San Diego, CA: Academic Press. pp. 771–814.

Whyte, W.F. (1955) *Street Corner Society: The Social Structure of an Italian Slum*. Chicago: University of Chicago Press.

Wiles, R., Prosser, J., Bagnoli, A., Clark, A., Davies, K., Holland, S., and Renold, E. (2008) *Visual Ethics: Ethical Issues in Visual Research*. ESRC National Centre for

Research Methods Review Paper. Southampton: NCRM. Online at: http://eprints. ncrm.ac.uk/421/1/MethodsReviewPaperNCRM-011.pdf.

Williams, T.M. (ed.) (1986) *The Impact of Television: A Natural Experiment in Three Communities*. Orlando, FI: Academic Press.

Wilson, M. (1996) 'Asking questions', in R. Sapsford and V. Jupp (eds), *Data Collection and Analysis*. London: SAGE. pp. 94–120.

Wolcott, H.F. (1973) *The Man in the Principal's Office: An Ethnography*. Chicago, IL: Waveland.

Wolcott, H.F. (1982) 'Differing styles of on-site research, or, "If it isn't ethnography, what is it?"', *The Review Journal of Philosophy and Social Science*, 7(1–2): 154–69.

Wolcott, H.F. (1988) 'Ethnographic research in education', in R.M. Jaeger (ed.), *Complementary Methods for Research in Education*. Washington, DC: American Educational Research Association. pp. 187–249.

Wolcott, H.F. (1990) *Writing Up Qualitative Research*. Newbury Park, CA: SAGE.

Wolcott, H.F. (1992) 'Posturing in qualitative inquiry', in M.D. LeCompte, W.L. Millroy and J. Preissle (eds), *Handbook of Qualitative Research in Education*. San Diego, CA: Academic Press. pp. 3–52.

Wolf, F.M. (1986) *Meta-Analysis: Quantitative Methods for Research Synthesis*. Beverly Hills, CA: SAGE.

Woods, P.H. (1979) *The Divided School*. London: Routledge and Kegan Paul.

Woods, P.H. (1986) *Inside Schools: Ethnography in Educational Research*. London: Routledge and Kegan Paul.

Woods, P.H. (1992) 'Symbolic interactionism: Theory and method', in M.D. LeCompte, W.L. Millroy and J. Preissle (eds), *The Handbook of Qualitative Research in Education*. San Diego, CA: Academic Press. pp. 337–404.

Wooffitt, R. (1996) 'Analysing accounts', in N. Gilbert (ed.), *Researching Social Life*. London: SAGE. pp. 287–305.

World Medical Association (WMA) (2000) *Declaration of Helsinki*.

Worrall, A. (1990) *Offending Women*. London: Routledge.

Yin, R.K. (2013) *Case Study Research: Design and Methods*. 5th edn. Thousand Oaks, CA: SAGE.

Zeller, R.A. (1996) 'Validity', in J.P. Keeves (ed.), *Educational Research, Methodology, and Measurement: An International Handbook*. 2nd edn. Oxford: Elsevier. pp. 822–9.

Znaniecki, F. (1934) *The Method of Sociology*. New York: Farrar and Rinehart.

INDEX

Abbott, P., 118
abstraction, 177–179, *271*
abstracts, 339
access, 43–44
accountability, 40
Achilles, C.M., 212
Ackoff, R., 114
action research, 135–138
Adler, P., 156
Adler, P.A., 156
Alder, N., 183, 184
Aldridge, J.M., 310
American Educational Research Association, 42
The American Occupational Structure (Blau and Duncan), 217
analysis of covariance (ANCOVA), 215–216, 223, 259–260, 266–267
analysis of variance (ANOVA), 252, 256–258
analytic induction, 170–171
analytic mix, 329–330, **330**
Andrews, D., 284
anonymisation, 48
anonymity, 43, 47
appendices, 336
Apple, M., 117
applied ethics, 36
applied feminist ethics, 40
applied social sciences, 9–10
aretaic ethics, 40
Argyrous, G., 273
Asch, S.E., 212
Atkinson, J.M., 33n5
Atkinson, P.
  on causation, 82
  on coding, 174, 175
  on documentary data, 197
  on ethnography, 125, 126, 127
  on interviews, 157
  on narrative analysis, 188
  on observation, 166n1
  on qualitative data analysis, 169, 170–171, 187
ATLAS.ti, 199
attitude, 233–234
audio recording, 151, 155, 280

audit trail, 169–170
Australian Association for Research in Education, 42
autonomy, 43–46, 293
Awareness of Dying (Glaser and Strauss), 131
axial coding, 180, 183–184

Barker, R.G., 214
basic social sciences, 9–10
Basics of Grounded Theory Analysis (Glaser), 132
Basics of Qualitative Research (Strauss and Corbin), 132
Bazeley, P., 199
Bean, J., 217
Becker, H., 133
Belmont report (1979), 41
beneficence, 49–52
benefits, 50
Berger, P.L., 341
Beyond Methodology (Fonow and Cook), 118
bibliographic databases, 282
Blau, P.M., 217
Bloor, M., 171
body language, 288
Bohanek, J.F., 189
Bradburn, N.M., 150
Bradbury, H., 135, 136, 137
Brewer, J., 29, 78, 121
Brink, P.J., 6
British Educational Research Association, 42
Bryant, A., 132, 186
Bryman, A., 326n1
Buchanan, E., 292
Burgess, R. G., 44
Burns, A., 191
Buros Institute of Mental Measurements (University of Nebraska), 236
Burton, S., 102

Campbell, D.T., 212, 214, 323
CAQDAS (Computer Assisted Qualitative Data Analysis Software), 198, 199